Britain Since 1945

David Childs

Britain Since 1945
A Political History

THIRD EDITION

London

First published in 1979 by Ernest Benn Limited

First published as a University Paperback in 1984 by
Methuen & Co. Ltd

Second edition first published in 1986 by Methuen & Co. Ltd

Third edition first published in 1992 by
Routledge
11 New Fetter Lane, London EC4P 4EE

Reprinted in 1993

© 1979, 1986 and 1992 David Childs

Printed in Great Britain by
J. W. Arrowsmith Ltd, Bristol

British Library Cataloguing in Publication Data
Childs, David
Britain since 1945: a political history.
— 3rd edn.
1. Great Britain — Politics and
government — 1945–
I. Title
941.085   DA588

ISBN 0–415–06024–9

Contents

Acknowledgements   ix
Note and Acknowledgements to the Second Edition   x
Acknowledgements to the Third Edition   xi
Abbreviations   xii

1 Labour's Summer of '45   1

    Churchill's 'Gestapo' speech   1
    Waiting for the results   4
    Reactions to Labour's win   6
    Morrison – Attlee rivalry   8
    The results analysed   10

2 Achievement and Austerity under Attlee, 1945–51   16

    The new Parliament   16
    Clement Attlee   18
    Attlee's Cabinet   21
    The terms of the United States loan   23
    Nationalization measures   25
    The National Health Service   29
    Housing and education   32
    Communists change front   34
    Conservative Party reforms   37

3 Colonial Retreat and Cold War   43

    Relinquishing India   43
    War in Palestine   46
    Colonies: guided progress   53
    Cold War in Europe   56
    Korea and Iran   62
    The Conservatives' 1951 Victory   65

4 From Churchill to Eden, 1951–57   71

    Churchill's team   71
    Stalin's death   77

Eden: rebel with velvet gloves 80
Suez 1956 83
The aftermath of Suez 88

5 Macmillan and the Affluent Society, 1957–59 94

Macmillan takes over 94
Slow economic growth 98
'Most of our people have never had it so good' 105
Russians in space 107
Problems in Africa and Aden 109
Labour in turmoil 115
The New Left 120

6 The Tories in Trouble, 1959–64 126

Iain Macleod 126
The Future of Socialism 127
Labour's EEC debate 131
De Gaulle's veto 135
Macmillan's purge 138
Lord Home becomes Prime Minister 143
Expansion in education 146
Wilson elected Labour's leader 151
Election 1964 154

7 The Wilson Years, 1964–66 159

Wilson's Cabinet 159
The balance of payments deficit 164
Ian Smith's UDI 167
Rethinking nuclear defence 169
Sir Alec goes 172
Wilson's 1966 victory 175

8 The Wilson Years, 1966–70 179

Seamen's strike 179
Economic crisis, 1966 183
Rhodesia 185
Wilson's EEC attempt 190
The cutting of Britain's defence commitments 194
Enoch Powell 196
Eruption in Northern Ireland 203
Industrial relations: *In Place of Strife* 207
Fulton on the Civil Service 209
June election, 1970 215

9 Britain under Heath, 1970–74   219

   Heath's trouble with the press   219
   Cuts in government expenditure   220
   Industrial relations   223
   Northern Ireland's continuing conflict   227
   Immigration and Rhodesia   230
   Battle for Common Market entry   232
   Oil crisis   234
   Heath's February election   237

10 Labour's Minority Governments, 1974–79   243

   Wilson's new Cabinet   243
   October election, 1974   248
   Britain's EEC referendum   252
   Problems with industrial management   255
   Margaret Thatcher   259
   Callaghan becomes Prime Minister   261
   Bullock on industrial representation, and North Sea Oil   265
   Referenda in Scotland and Wales   269
   Northern Ireland peace hope   270
   Crime and police computers   272
   A decade of 'Women's lib'   276
   Labour's incomes policy   281

11 Britain Under Thatcher, 1979–83   287

   Election 1979   287
   Margaret Thatcher's first Cabinet   290
   Thatcher looks abroad   292
   Thatcherism   293
   From Rhodesia to Zimbabwe   299
   Labour in turmoil   301
   Thatcher in trouble   302
   The 'gang of four' and the SDP   305
   War in the Falklands   309

12 Thatcher's Second Term, 1983–7   316

   Victory in June   316
   The miners' strike   319
   Television battles   324
   Security, law and order   326
   Tories in revolt   328
   Confusion on defence   329
   EEC, Gibraltar, Hong Kong   331

Britain in 1985	331
The Anglo-Irish Agreement	336
The Westland Affair	336
Moscow journey	337
Thatcher's hat trick	338

13 The End of Thatcher: and Thatcherism? 340

'Black Monday', 1987	341
Poll tax revolt	343
Prison riots	344
Peter Wright and official secrets	346
Disasters	347
Football hooliganism	348
Continuing terrorism	348
Education reforms	349
NHS 'terminally ill'?	351
Rushdie and race relations	353
Labour win European elections	353
Resignations, sackings and reshuffles	354
Thatcher's fall	355
John Major	356
War in the Gulf	358
'Greed is everything'	359
'What is the lady up to?'	362
Which way for Europe?	363
Major's April victory	365

List of Tables	367
Index	383

Acknowledgements

I want to express my sincere thanks to a number of people who have read and commented on various chapters of this book – Dr David Butler, Nuffield College, Oxford (chapter 1); Col. R. L. Frazier, Department of History, University of Nottingham (chapters 2, 7 and 8); Professor F. S. Northedge, Department of International Relations, London School of Economics and Political Science (chapter 3); the Rt. Hon. Lord Boyle, Vice-Chancellor, University of Leeds (chapters 4, 5 and 6). The writer alone bears responsibility for any errors of fact or judgement contained in the book.

In addition my thanks are due to many busy people who have either agreed to be interviewed or who have taken the trouble to reply to written questions. Among them are Kingsley Amis, the Lady Attlee, the late Lord Avon, Mr A. A. Best, Lord Boothby, Lord Brockway, Lord Butler, Douglas Dodds-Parker MP, Bob Edwards MP, the Rt. Hon. Ernest Fernyhough MP, the late James Griffiths, Arthur Lewis MP, Marcus Lipton MP, Christopher Mayhew, the Rt. Hon. Philip Noel-Baker MP, Maurice Orbach MP, John Parker MP, Baroness Phillips, the Rt. Hon. J. Enoch Powell MP, J. B. Priestley, Lord Ritchie-Calder, the Rt. Hon William Ross MP, Alan Sillitoe, Mrs Margaret Simpson, the Rt. Hon. Michael Stewart MP, Lord Taylor of Mansfield, Woodrow Wyatt, Lord Wigg.

Finally, I should like to thank Mrs Ann Morris and Miss Elaine Dexter for typing substantial parts of the manuscript.

Nottingham
April 1979   D.H.C.

Note and Acknowledgements
to the Second Edition

I was very pleased to be asked, as a result of readers' requests, to write an extended version of *Britain Since 1945*.

I have tried to take the second edition as seriously as the first by attempting to talk to a wide variety of witnesses. It was a pleasant surprise to find so many busy individuals who were prepared to be interviewed or reply to written questions. Unfortunately, one or two MPs felt unable to help. I am therefore all the more grateful to those who did: Joe Ashton, Margaret Beckett, Alan Beith, Mark Carlisle, Kenneth Clarke, Don Concannon, Roy Hattersley, Denis Healey, Jim Lester, Sir Anthony Meyer, Richard Ottaway, David Owen, Cyril Smith and Ray Whitney. I am equally grateful to Beryl Bainbridge, Lynne Reid Banks, Stan Barstow, Melvyn Bragg, Malcolm Bradbury, Maureen Duffy, John H. Gunn, Ken Livingstone, David Lodge, Iris Murdoch, Tom Sharpe, Leslie Thomas, Stuart Thompstone, Fay Weldon and Arnold Wesker. Finally, I want to thank my old friend Karl Sparrow for his continuing interest in my work. With so many different and conflicting points of view represented among those who have helped me I must emphasize very strongly that all the views, ideas, interpretations and descriptions in this book are entirely my own responsibility – as are any errors.

There are obvious pitfalls in writing about events as recent as those between 1979–85 (or even between 1945–79). Some events (the Falklands War?) which seem important at the time will seem less so at greater distance. Other events (like the miners' strike and changes in South Africa and China) could prove to be of very great significance for the future of Britain. I hope the reader will take this into account and also remember the limitations of time, space and resources open to the writer of a book of this kind and not judge the result too harshly.

Nottingham
September 1985

D.H.C.

Acknowledgements
to the Third Edition

Since the second edition, many dramatic changes have occurred in the world such as the demise of Communism and the restoration of German unity, the further development of the 'ever closer union' of the European Community and the Gulf War. At home in Britain, we have witnessed the fall of Margaret Thatcher and the victory of the Conservative Party under John Major. Britain has further declined in international importance and most of its politicians and people seem to accept this as they are more and more influenced by American culture, foreign travel, the economies of Japan, the USA and Germany and by Britain's membership of the EC.

On my many travels since 1986, I have had the opportunity to discuss the changes in Britain and elsewhere with a considerable number of politicians, businessmen, academics and diplomats. I am grateful for these opportunities. I am also grateful to Martin Brandon-Bravo (MP, Nottingham South 1983–92) and to Sir Frank Roberts, GCMG, CGVO, who gave me some of their time to discuss our changing world and their views on it. Professor Vincent Porter gave me the benefit of his experience of the changes in the mass media and I want to take this opportunity to thank him. Finally, I want to thank my old friend, Dr Robert L. Frazier, for reading the new material and making many useful suggestions.

Nottingham   D.H.C.
April 1992

Abbreviations

ACAS	Advisory Conciliation and Arbitration Service
AEI	Associated Electrical Industries
AEU	Amalgamated Engineering Union
AIOC	Anglo-Iranian Oil Company
ANF	Atlantic Nuclear Force
BBC	British Broadcasting Corporation
BMA	British Medical Association
BNOC	British National Oil Corporation
BP	British Petroleum
CAP	Common Agricultural Policy
CBI	Confederation of British Industry
CDS	Campaign for Democratic Socialism
CID	Criminal Investigation Department
CND	Campaign for Nuclear Disarmament
CP	Communist Party
CSE	Certificate of Secondary Education
DEA	Department of Economic Affairs
DGB	Deutscher Gewerkschaftsbund
EEC	European Economic Community
EEPTU	Electrical, Electronic, Telecommunications and Plumbing Trades Union
EFTA	European Free Trade Association
FIS	Family Income Supplement
GCE	General Certificate of Education
GDP	Gross Domestic Product
GEC	General Electric Company
GP	General Practitioner
HMG	Her Majesty's Government
IBA	Independent Broadcasting Authority
ICL	International Computers Limited
ILP	Independent Labour Party
IMF	International Monetary Fund
IRA	Irish Republican Army
IRC	Industrial Reorganisation Corporation
ITA	Independent Television Authority
ITV	Independent Television
JRC	Joint Representation Committee

MLF	Multilateral Nuclear Force
MP	Member of Parliament
MRP	Mouvement républicain populaire
NATO	North Atlantic Treaty Organization
NBPI	National Board for Prices and Incomes
NEC	National Executive Committee of the Labour Party
NEDC	National Economic Development Council
NHS	National Health Service
NI	Northern Ireland
NIRC	National Industrial Relations Court
NOP	National Opinion Poll
NPD	Die Nationaldemokratische Partei Deutschlands
NUM	National Union of Mineworkers
NUS	National Union of Seamen
OEEC	Organization for European Economic Cooperation
OAPEC	Organization of Arab Petroleum Exporting Countries
OPEC	Organization of Petroleum Exporting Countries
PLP	Parliamentary Labour Party
PNC	Police National Computer
PPP	People's Progressive Party
PPS	Parliamentary Private Secretary
RAFVR	Royal Air Force Volunteer Reserve
REP	Regional Payroll Subsidy
RSPCA	Royal Society for the Prevention of Cruelty to Animals
SAS	Special Air Service
SDLP	Social Democratic and Labour Party
SDP	Social Democratic Party
SET	Selective Employment Tax
SNP	Scottish National Party
SAS	Special Air Service
TGWU	Transport and General Workers' Union
TUC	Trades Union Congress
UDI	Unilateral Declaration of Independence
YTS	Youth Training Scheme

1 Labour's Summer of '45

At a meeting of the election sub-committee of the NEC on 25 April 1945 Professor Harold J. Laski was asked to write a memo on 'nationalism in politics in general, and in Great Britain in particular'. The reason for this strange request was Labour's defeat at the Motherwell by-election on 12 April by a Scottish National Party candidate. The writer is not clear whether Laski ever completed the essay, but even if he did, it would have been of only academic interest, for it would have been overtaken by events. The Motherwell by-election was one of the last of the, by then, rotten 1935 Parliament. The seat subsequently returned to Labour at the general election less than three months later.

The loss of Motherwell mirrored the impatience of the ordinary working-class voters with the continuing coalition. It was a warning to the Labour leaders that their rank and file would not wait indefinitely for a radical change.

Strangely, Attlee, Bevin, Tom Williams, and some others in the leadership were prepared to stick with Churchill to the bitter end, till after the victory over the Japanese.[1] Others, like Morrison, Laski, Shinwell, and Bevan, favoured an early break-up of the coalition and a general election. As it turned out, it was Churchill who decided to take the initiative on 18 May by forcing the Labour leaders to decide either for an immediate general election, or for a continuation of the coalition until the end of the Japanese war. The NEC meeting on 20 May had no difficulty reaching its decision. It called for an autumn election with a new electoral register. It agreed the coalition should go on until then. This Churchill refused. Egged on by Beaverbrook[2] he wanted an immediate election. He was confident of success. According to Lyttelton, only Butler doubted the wisdom of this timetable. Robert Boothby is also reported to have expected a Labour landslide.[3]

On Wednesday 23 May, Churchill tendered his resignation to the King and was invited to form a new administration. He then asked for a dissolution of Parliament.

Churchill's team had the advantage that, as the caretaker

1

government, they were more likely to be in the public eye than their erstwhile colleagues. Luckily, the Labour Party annual conference could meet before the election. This provided publicity and was a morale booster for the Party workers. In session at Blackpool, 21–25 May, it finalized Labour's election programme, *Let us Face the Future*. This programme set out the catalogue of nationalization and welfare measures which was to be put into effect during 1945–51. The mood of the delegates at the conference was unmistakably radical. They would have endorsed a more thoroughgoing socialist programme.[4] Their fervour was tempered by their fear of harming the Party just before the election, by openly defying their leaders. One sign of the leftward mood was the fact that the Communist Party's application for affiliation to the Labour Party was rejected by the very narrow margin of 1,219,000 to 1,134,000.

Churchill's 'Gestapo' speech

One would have thought that having worked together in coalition for five years any tendency towards electoral aggression by the former partners would have been weakened. This proved not to be the case. Though many of their followers felt aggressively anti-Tory, the Labour leaders left it to Churchill to put the boot in first. On 4 June the Prime Minister made his first, and most notorious, broadcast in which he alleged that no socialist system could be established without a political police, a Gestapo. Socialist policy was 'abhorrent to British ideas of freedom ... there can be no doubt that Socialism is inseparably interwoven with totalitarianism'. The small saver's nest-egg would 'shrivel before his eyes' under socialism.[5] The following evening it was Attlee's turn. He replied with pained irony. Listening to Churchill, he had immediately realized his object:

He wanted the electors to understand how great was the difference between Winston Churchill the great leader in war of a united nation, and Mr. Churchill the party leader of the Conservatives. He feared lest those who had accepted his leadership in war might be tempted out of gratitude to follow him further. I thank him for having disillusioned them so thoroughly.

Attlee said that Churchill had spoken with the mind of Beaverbrook.[6]

There is no doubt that Churchill's speech unleashed feelings of anger, even hatred, among many in the Labour Party.[7] Others felt it was a damned cheek coming from a man who had once admired Mussolini, inventor of the word totalitarian.

Churchill's Gestapo outburst was significant for the Conservative campaign, for he had set a fashion which was followed throughout the country by Conservative candidates.[8] Apart from this type of attack, the Conservatives relied on Churchill's personality. Actual policy came a very poor third. The Prime Minister gave four of the ten pro-government broadcasts.

Labour's broadcasts were more the product of co-ordinated teamwork and attacks on the Conservatives took second place to explaining Labour's own policies. Like the Conservatives they were allowed ten. Attlee led off on 5 June. He was followed by Thomas Johnston MP, and then fellow MPs A. V. Alexander, Ellen Wilkinson, Philip Noel-Baker, James Griffiths, Stafford Cripps, Ernest Bevin, and George Tomlinson. Herbert Morrison concluded the broadcasts.

The Liberals were allocated four broadcasts and the Communists and Common Wealth one short broadcast each. Thus the opposition parties had some advantage on the BBC. In addition there were the traditional meetings, from the well-prepared rallies with nationally known speakers to the outdoor, street-corner meetings. To some extent the election was covered by the cinema newsreels. Obviously, the press had a big role to play. And it is worth recording that Labour was not as badly represented as is often supposed. They were backed by the *Daily Herald, News Chronicle,* and *Daily Mirror* having a total circulation of about 6 million. The total net sales of the Conservative *Daily Express, Daily Mail,* and *Daily Sketch* were about the same.[9] In addition the Conservatives enjoyed the support of the *Daily Telegraph* and most of the provincial press. The *Manchester Guardian* was rather more anti-Conservative than openly pro-Labour.

It must not be thought that the election was the consuming passion of the media or the electorate throughout June and into July. On the serious side there were amazing disclosures of Nazi atrocities and secret weapons, there was the meeting of the Allied leaders in Potsdam, and there was the very real war still being fought in the Far East. General MacArthur, Allied supremo in that campaign, was estimating that this war would last another year. In Europe, however, the slaughter was over and most people in Britain, as elsewhere, felt a sense of profound relief. The sun shone. The mood was festive. This perhaps explains why it was regarded as a quiet election. Some Labour officials were worried by this. In the circumstances, Churchill's 'Gestapo' broadcast was a godsend. It injected enough venom into the campaign to stir the passions.

One other argument which raised the temperature of the contestants was the so-called 'Laski controversy'. Churchill had invited Attlee to accompany him to the Potsdam conference. Laski, as chairman of the NEC, issued a statement in which he said that Attlee should go as an observer only, playing no part in the deliberations, and being in no way bound by decisions which 'have not been debated either in the Party Executive or at meetings of the Parliamentary Labour Party'.[10] Having been given a valuable weapon the Conservatives did not fail to use it. They pointed to the danger that international agreements entered into by Churchill might be broken by a Labour government, thus damaging the country. They also conjured up the image of Attlee and a Labour government being forced to divulge secrets and bow to the dictates of the NEC. As Churchill put it in his final broadcast, 'Ministers would not be primarily responsible to Crown and Parliament but to an utterly unconstitutional and undemocratic body lying in the background'.[11] Attlee responded in a speech at Peckham in which he called Churchill a badly rattled man who had made a 'vile suggestion'. The Prime Minister had worked with his Labour colleagues for five years and knew that they did not reveal secrets. Attlee seemed to get the better of this argument which dominated the last days of the campaign.

Waiting for the results

Voting day was 5 July – but not for everyone. There had been objections to 5 July as polling-day because it clashed with holiday weeks in some northern towns. To cover this, the Postponement of Polling Day Act, 1945 was rushed through Parliament. It delayed voting for a week in eighteen constituencies and for a fortnight in one.[12]

Once the voting was over, there was the long wait until 26 July before the results were known. This was because of the delayed poll in the nineteen constituencies, and to allow the armed services' vote to be brought back from overseas.

The parties got the reports from the constituency organizations and made their predictions. *The Times* on 10 July reported that the Conservatives felt there was no evidence of a swing either way! The Labour Party expected a 1929-style situation in which they would be the largest party without an overall majority. The Liberals were hopeful of having between 80 to 100 seats, and Communists thought they had gained 4 to 5.

While the party headquarters filled in their time with their calculations, the candidates sweated. One candidate who was not prepared to sweat was Mrs Bessie Braddock. She got an expert from the local greyhound stadium to study the figures and make his estimate. This he did, apparently reassuring her that she was in by over 600 votes. This was one prediction which proved correct, and Mrs Braddock became the first Labour MP to represent the Exchange Division of Liverpool.[13] The Jesuits too are said to have got their figures right, though they were not overjoyed at the prospect of Labour coming to power.[14]

Lord Ritchie-Calder later wrote about his impressions of this period,

I was in Berlin, in the interval between the polling-booth returns and the service vote count. The victory parade went down the Tiergarten. Churchill and Monty were in the first weapons carrier. Attlee and General Alexander, at a deferential distance, came behind. Churchill got dutiful cheers, Attlee got resounding ones. The Guards' band stopped playing and shouted 'Good old Clem'. Churchill couldn't get the message and Attlee didn't: People were ready for much more radical changes than the Party manifesto.[15]

As Britain waited the outcome of this bloodless battle, the battle for the eastern world went on. Japan was under constant bombardment by sea and air. Australian troops were fighting it out in Balikpapan Bay in East Borneo. And the aftermath of the old war was being cleared up. Crown Princess Juliana of the Netherlands prepared to sail home from Ottawa. The Czech air force prepared to leave Britain for home. Little known was the forced repatriation of tens of thousands of former Soviet prisoners. The war and occupation had brought political crisis or worse to Belgium, Greece, Italy, and many other states. France arraigned its most illustrious soldier, Henri Philippe Pétain, and Britain planned its revenge on Nazi radio propagandist William Joyce. In *The Times* on 18 July it was reported that Premier De Valera had announced in the Irish parliament that Eire was a republic in no way dependent on Britain. His speech, though it changed little in practice, was a harbinger of Britain's rapidly changing position in the post-war world, the world in which the Labour Party was to come to maturity.

Just after 10 o'clock in the morning of 26 July the first result was announced. It was a Labour gain in South Salford. This could not have been too disturbing for the Conservatives, for the mystery is how they had ever won this love-on-the-dole constituency in the first place. Within minutes the Conservatives heard they had held Kingston-upon-Thames. Then followed three more Labour gains in Lancashire, and two Labour seats held. The tension was heightened with the news – minutes later – that the first Cabinet minister, Harold Macmillan, was out. By 11 a.m. it was clear that the Conservatives were in deep trouble. Over lunch, Britain could ponder over 100 Labour gains and the fact that even Churchill, who had not been opposed by the other parties, though re-elected, had lost 10,000 votes to an unknown independent. During the early afternoon it became clear that Labour had won a decisive victory. Churchill had failed to repeat the success of Lloyd George after the First World War.

Labour had won 393 seats (166 at the dissolution of the old Parliament). The Conservatives and their allies held 213 (397) and the Liberals 12 (20). In addition, Labour could count on 3 ILP MPs (3) and 1 Common Wealth (3). Finally, there were 2 Communists (1), 2 Irish Nationalists, and 14 Independents. Most of the latter were pro-Conservative, 12 of them in university seats. Though it had opposed them, Labour could count on 2 Independents, D. N. Pritt and Vernon Bartlett.

The Conservatives could take a crumb of comfort from the knowledge that the massive change of seats was based on a less decisive shift of votes. On a 72.7 per cent turn-out Labour had received just under 12 million votes, the Conservatives and their allies just under 10 million. The Liberals gained just under 2.25 million. Over 850,000 votes went to other candidates, including 110,634 to Common Wealth, 102,780 to the Communists, 46,679 to the ILP, 122,820 to independent leftists, and 30,595 to the left-inclining Scottish nationals.[16] The vote almost certainly under-estimated the leftward trend in the country by using the old register (thus preventing some young, new voters from exercising their right), underrepresenting the armed services (see below), allowing university graduates to vote twice (117,647 votes were cast in university seats, mostly for pro-Conservatives), and allowing businessmen to vote twice (there were 48,974 business electors in 1945). The business vote probably gave the Conservatives between 3 to 5 seats and the universities returned 9 pro-Conservatives.[17] A bland statement of the results ignores the emotions which they aroused.

Reactions to Labour's win

'I will always remember 26th July as a sunny day – I don't know whether it was', this is how a Northern Labour activist described the day the results came out. He went on.

My friends and I had not expected to win. We remembered 1935 and had heard of 1931. We thought the Tories were too smart. They would always kid the masses. The young people did not know the 1930's. The old ones would thank Churchill for a good war. My heart was in my mouth with every result. I thought I was dreaming.[18]

Margaret Simpson, then a 15-year-old Labour enthusiast, felt similar emotions:

When the results were announced I was in Rochester. We were glued to the radio – the results were compelling listening. As result followed result we were incredulous. In fact we found it hard to believe even after a few days. In Rochester and Chatham where Arthur Bottomley won the seat for

Labour for the first time ever, there was a jubilant, all-night celebration at the Labour headquarters.[19]

Sir John (later Lord) Reith, former Director of the BBC, former Minister of Information, was as wrong as the Labour activists,

I thought that Churchill might have a small majority, but it was obvious at once that he had suffered a crushing defeat, and there was no question about my jubilation on this score, however much I might dislike the Bevins, Morrisons and such like in office. What was particularly gratifying to me was that most of the thugs like Bracken and Sandys were put out.[20]

The Fellows of the Royal College of Physicians heard the news while taking afternoon tea, 'They were so taken aback they stood there in complete silence'.[21] In a copper factory at Widnes where Jack Ashley, later himself an MP, worked, there was jubiliation. 'The latest figures, chalked in large letters near one of the furnaces were continually changed as more sweeping gains were broadcast'.[22] Lord Hailsham, then Quintin Hogg, one of the successful Conservative candidates, naturally felt otherwise, 'Whilst I did not expect a Conservative victory in 1945, I was wholly taken aback by the extent of the Labour victory'.[23] Many of the still Conservative middle classes were likewise taken aback, and apprehensive as well. Marie Belloc Lowndes, the writer, recorded in her diary,

I have never known the people with whom I am in touch, more amazed than at the result of the election. Those who are well off are trembling with fear, some even are afraid of a capital levy. On the other hand, it seems as if certain people connected with the Government – one ought to say the *late* Government – cannot believe that they are really out. Sir John and Lady Anderson gave a lunch party for ten. Three people came on here afterwards and told me about it. They said that no one there seemed to realise what was going to happen.[24]

A minority of the middle classes did not feel like Marie Belloc Lowndes's friends. A. A. Best, a 53-year-old insurance agent in 1945, recalled being on holiday at Hove on that dramatic day,

We were joined at table by a lady of Jersey descent who had been a school teacher. She indulged in an outburst of astonished incredulity as Labour gains mounted and wondered whatever would become of us all. I said that this was something I had been working for during most of my life and was feeling very excited at the prospects. This led to a good deal of political discussion during the rest of the holiday and I learned that other guests shared my feelings in varying degree.[25]

If there was hope, enthusiasm, and expectancy among Labour's masses, and dazed apprehension among Conservative supporters, some members of the Establishment felt as much relief as disappointment at the results. Montagu Norman, Governor of the Bank of England during 1920–44, commented in a letter, in 1946, that if Churchill had been Prime Minister, 'I daresay we should have had more disturbances and ill-feeling within this country and possibly elsewhere in Europe'.[26] Churchill himself is reported to have remarked on hearing the results, 'I do not feel down at all. I'm not certain the Conservative Party could have dealt with the Labour troubles that are coming'.[27] Thomas Jones, intimate of Baldwin, MacDonald, and other top people, wrote to an American friend on 4 August, 'Many old people are alarmed at what may happen. I cannot develop the faintest feeling of panic'. He also felt the Cabinet, including in it seven miners, represented a 'profound social revolution'.[28] Sir William (later Lord) Beveridge, who as a Liberal candidate had himself been swept aside, felt 'that somewhat surprisingly the Conservatives had got what they deserved'.[29]

Churchill heard the results in the map room of the Cabinet Office. 'The Prime Minister was surrounded by gloomy faces. He watched the results coming in with some detachment and far more cheerfully than any of those around him. He made no complaints'.[30]

Morrison – Attlee rivalry

Less than a mile away from the gloomy tension of Churchill's headquarters, there was tension and drama of another kind. Labour's leaders had congregated in Transport House to hear the results. They too were surprised by their victory. Apparently only Bevan, Morrison, and Shinwell had anticipated the great turn of events in their favour. Yet in their moment of glory they were divided. Morrison still felt he should be leader and cautioned Attlee that he should secure a renewed vote of confidence by the PLP before accepting the King's commission to form a government. Morrison's challenge was backed by Bevan, Cripps, and Ellen Wilkinson, who were not there, and by Laski who was.[31] Bevin strongly supported Attlee. And when the King's invitation came that evening as Attlee was having a late tea with his family at the Great Western Hotel, Paddington, he 'accepted . . . without quibble'.[32] The following day he received a vote of confidence from the PLP.

Later Attlee was to claim that the idea of Morrison being Prime Minister at that time was 'fantastic' and that when asked to form a government by the King, you don't say you can't give an answer for forty-eight hours.[33] Obviously, this is a view very convenient to Attlee himself. In fact, as a result of the MacDonald experience, the PLP had decided in 1933 that there should be an annual leadership election. Attlee had never challenged this view. Such a contest could easily have been carried through with slight damage to the Labour Party's image, but little damage to the country. As for the King, there is no evidence that he thought he had any right to decide who should be Leader of the Labour Party and therefore Prime Minister. As the sitting incumbent who had led the Party to triumph, Attlee might well have succeeded. On the other hand, Morrison was better known in the country and, as the majority of Labour MPs knew neither personally, they might have been more impressed by Morrison's public image and more dynamic style. Why the Left preferred Morrison to Attlee is difficult to see. He was to the right of Attlee. Perhaps some despised Attlee intellectually and were either sentimental about Morrison as a former 'worker', or resented being led by a fellow member of the middle class with no more claim to leadership than themselves. As it was, the question was not put to the PLP, and it is doubtful whether a change of leadership would have altered the course of events very much.

In the offices of the *Daily Worker* no less than in those of the *Daily Telegraph* there was dismay and disbelief. One by one the lost deposits were totted up in the *Worker* offices. The only relief was afforded by Phil Piratin's victory at Mile End and 'the realization that among the Labour men returned were a number of our own Party members who had slipped in almost unnoticed as it were'. As Douglas Hyde, who in 1945 was on the editorial staff of the *Daily Worker*, put it:

My first realisation of this came when I answered the phone and the man at the other end announced himself as the new Labour member for his constituency. He followed it with a loud guffaw and rang off. I had known him as a Communist Party man for years. Then over the tape, among the new Labour MP's came others whose candidatures we had hardly taken seriously ourselves. By the time the list was complete we knew that we had at least eight or nine 'cryptos' in the House of Commons in addition to our two publicly acknowledged MP's.[34]

Britain's image was so essentially conservative that few foreign commentators had expected any surprises from the British electorate. In those countries where Britain was better known, the English-speaking world, there was even greater astonishment. Churchill had become the personification of Britain's determination to survive and in the Dominions and the United States it seemed inconceivable that he should be removed. In South Africa, then still in the Commonwealth, financial circles did not expect the Labour victory to have any serious effect on British policy. There was little concern therefore. In the, for Britain, all-important United States reaction was mixed:

The British elections are still an absorbing topic for American commentators, who have been completely unanimous on one score at least – in their astonishment at the emphatic, unqualified verdict given to the Labour Party by the British electorate. The moderately conservative press had expressed mild friendliness to the new Government, while it has taken great pains to explain the essentially conservative nature of the British Labour Party, stressing the fact that this development in British politics is 'evolutionary, not revolutionary'. Liberal and labour groups quite naturally, are highly optimistic, seeing a new Britain emerging in the role of liberal leader. American Labour will use the British election results as a new springboard for pressure on Congress to produce an adequate reconversion policy.[35]

This cautious, balanced report contained a somewhat menacing note towards the end. It found that American bankers 'who have been rather over-eager to negotiate loans to Britain are reported to be slightly less eager now, although they have had no reason to believe that the Conservative Party would have been more willing than Labour to abandon the empire preference or currency controls to which they have always objected'.

Whatever the doubts of American bankers, there was delight and hope among American trade unionists, German Social Democrats, Indian nationalists, Spanish republicans, French and Italian socialists, Zionists, and many others around the world who thought 'Left could talk to Left'.

The results analysed

Writing seven years after the 1945 election Lord Beveridge commented that Churchill in his Liberal days had described July as the month favoured by Tory organizers because 'democracy is supposed to be under the soothing influence of summer weather, and before villadcm has departed on its holidays'.[36] The Conservatives had chosen July in 1892 and won. They expected to do the same in 1945. A July election meant voting on an old register – thus disqualifying young voters – and a register distorted by wartime movements of populations. 'Villadom had lost its importance', Beveridge concluded, 'but July was still as undemocratic a month as could be found'. This was true. The sun did shine, and on polling-day itself, it was rather dull and warm. Individuals lost their votes. Unexpectedly Mr Churchill was one of them. He found he was not on the register for the Abbey division of Westminster, or any other register. His name had been omitted in error. It is likely though that many more potential Labour voters were excluded from the register than Conservatives. The older generation, especially older women, were less likely to have moved and were thus less likely to have failed to be included. They were the backbone of the Conservative Party. And middle-class voters were more likely to have seen to it that they had been included on one register or another. So the Labour vote perhaps underrepresented its true support. Yet Labour won despite the sunshine and the unrepresentative register. Why did it do so?

One factor which is stressed by Conservatives is the superior organization of the Labour Party. It is claimed that, as Lord Butler has put it, 'Our organization up and down the country was in a parlous condition, much harder hit than that of our opponents by the absence of agents and organizers on war service'.[37] It is difficult to be precise about this, but the evidence is not all one way. Apparently a survey carried out in 1944 by the whips of the two main parties did tend to confirm the view that the Conservatives were in worse shape than Labour.[38] But Labour had also been hit hard by the war, as the slump in individual membership of the Party indicated. In 1938 there were 429,000 individual members claimed. In 1939, at a time of increasing popularity, there were only 409,000. By 1941 the ranks had thinned to 227,000. There was a further slight fall in 1942, but an improvement was recorded in 1943. Even in 1944 individual membership stood at only 266,000. By the time of the pre-election conference in 1945, however, membership had leaped to 487,000. No doubt the figures exaggerated the improvement. No doubt, on the other hand, as the NEC files show, Labour was improving its organization, but the real growth of membership was more likely to be a reflection of the popular tide rather than a result of organizational measures. In any case, traditionally the Conservatives enjoyed considerable advantages in organizational resources over Labour. Once the election was announced, the resources of business and the middle classes poured into the Conservative fight – money, cars, office equipment, organizational and publicity skills. The figures make clear that the Conservative candidates had a financial advantage over all other candidates. Their average expenditure throughout the United Kingdom was £780 as against only £595 for the average Labour candidate. The highest single expenditure was that of the unsuccessful Conservative candidate for Kidderminster, £1,931. The lowest outlay by any successful candidate was that of James Maxton in Bridgeton, Glasgow, £165. He was an old ILP campaigner.[39] Turn-out was generally high, at 73 per cent, suggesting that both parties had adequate organization.

Butler also attacked the style of his party's campaign. He, and others, felt that Churchill's 'Gestapo speech' was 'a strategic blunder'. And he was no doubt correct to suggest that 'It would have been better if affirmation of post-war policies had not taken a poor third place to the concentrated exploitation of Churchill's personality and a negative attack on the Labour Party. But the election would probably have been lost in any case'.[40] Yet, even if the Conservatives had tried to make themselves appear twin brothers of Labour, no one would have believed in them. They lacked credibility.

Another leading Conservative, the Earl of Kilmuir, a veteran of the 1945 campaign, has written about the 'irresponsible' mood of that election, and has lamented the 'raucous, ignorant, and ill-tempered audiences' facing Conservative candidates. He then went on to admit: 'Nevertheless, behind this disagreeable façade presented by many thousands of Labour voters, there was unquestionably a profound and burning determination in the election never to go back to 1939'.[41] At the time, *The Economist* (28 July 1945) believed, 'Beyond any possibility of mistake, the country wants a Labour Government and a Socialist programme'. It also believed that causes of the swing to the Left were not hard to seek:

For years past, the electorate has shown by every means open to it under the political truce that it was tired of the Tories. Their pre-war record has not been forgotten. Moreover, in the ten years since the last election, there have been great changes in the social structure of the country; the great paradox of British politics in the past quarter-century – the faithfulness to the Tories of the property-less lower middle class – is at an end. When such Tory strongholds as Dulwich and Chislehurst, Norfolk and Birmingham can fall, it can only mean one thing – the middle class is voting Labour, and Socialism is now respectable.

The Economist continued its analysis on lines very similar to Butler's: that the Conservatives had neglected a reform programme, and that Churchill had let them down, 'in the election campaign so far from raising the Tory stock, it is now clear that he lowered it'. As *The Economist* had pointed out, by-elections had revealed the failing fortunes of Conservatism, and opinion surveys had exposed the reasons for this anti-Tory trend. Tom Harrison, a pioneer in the field of public-opinion research, had drawn attention to the leftward trend in an article he published in 1944. Harrison found that public-opinion polls exposed the myth of Churchill as an electoral asset. Though he was popular as a war leader, many people interviewed had doubts about his ability to deal with post-war problems, especially working-class problems. Surveys indicated that there was a general belief that 'some sort of socialism was inevitable'. The polls also showed that servicemen were more to the left that the rest. Labour's only difficulty, as revealed in these polls of 1942 and 1943, was the doubt in some people's minds about its determination to carry through structural changes in society.[42]

Lord Butler and others have emphasized the importance of the service vote for Labour and it is necessary therefore to say something about it. There were nearly 3 million service voters out of approximately 33 million. Only 59.4 per cent of them actually cast their votes, or about 1.75 million. Just over 1 million of these were cast direct by servicemen, the rest were used by their proxies – wives, fathers, mothers,[43] etc. The service vote could not, therefore, have been decisive. It has been suggested that left-wing lecturers were able to influence, perhaps decisively, perhaps unfairly, the servicemen in their classes. This would seem to be exaggerated. Who were the great majority of servicemen? Nothing more than workers in uniform. The majority of them took with them into the forces their natural inclination to vote Labour. All the lecturers could do was to help them to make their existing loyalties and concerns more articulate, and more informed. In any case, how many servicemen (and women) were subjected to sustained lecture/discussion programmes? But the writer has looked through the literature put out by the Army Bureau of Current Affairs and has not found it very left-wing. The very nature of life in the services led some middle-class officers to question a system they might otherwise not have questioned by bringing them into contact with working men. Woodrow Wyatt, an ex-public-school boy and Oxford graduate, has commented on this aspect of the wartime armed forces: 'Getting to know the soldiers I was struck by the absurdity of class distinctions. Many were highly intelligent and with better educations would have easily got commissions . . .'.[44] Another young officer talked about the wonderful spirit in the Eighth Army and hoped it would survive the war. His brother recalled him putting the case for Labour as follows:

They stand for a square deal for you and me, with food, a house and a job for all who will do it. They stand for everybody having an equal chance and for more even distribution of the wealth of the world – not cigars at the Ritz and starvation at the Rhondda, not duck at the Berkeley and the dole at Barrow.[45]

Pre-election polls spotlighted the Conservatives' weakness and Labour's strengths. Most voters were concerned about houses and jobs and the Labour Party looked more convincing on these issues.

Finally, there was a widespread feeling that the Conservatives were out-of-date, the 'old gang', who had failed to deal with the inter-war problems, the Colonel Blimps and men of Munich, who were hiding behind the Churchillian façade. They had to rely on one man, Churchill, elevating him into a kind of *Führer* figure. Labour were a tried and trusted team of varied talents, speaking in the varied and authentic accents of the people and responsive to their needs.

Notes

1 See B. Donoughue and G. W. Jones, *Herbert Morrison* (London, 1973), 344. Lord Wigg says that Willie Whiteley, Labour's chief whip, was the 'decisive voice' for an election, *George Wigg* (London, 1972), 120; Kingsley Martin, *Editor: a Volume of Autobiography* (London, 1968) says Laski thought Labour would win p.172.
2 Oliver Lyttelton, *The Memoirs of Lord Chandos* (London, 1962), 327.
3 Compton MacKenzie, *My Life and Times Octave Eight 1939–1946* (London, 1969), 245.
4 R. B. McCallum and Alison Readman, *The British General Election of 1945* (London, 1947), 129.
5 ibid., 142.
6 ibid., 143.
7 Lord Butler, *The Art of the Possible. The Memoirs of Lord Butler* (London, 1971), 128, records that Bevin was 'among those who took most offence'.
8 McCallum and Readman, op. cit., 144.
9 ibid., 181.
10 *The Times,* 15 June 1945.
11 *The Times,* 2 July 1945.
12 D. E. Butler, *The Electoral System in Britain since 1918* (London, 1963), 100.
13 Jack and Bessie Braddock, *The Braddocks* (London, 1963).
14 According to Paul Johnson, 'A Sense of Outrage', in *Conviction*, Norman MacKenzie, ed. (London, 1958), 205.
15 In a letter to the author.
16 These figures are from McCallum and Readman, op. cit., 252, D. Butler and J. Freeman, *British Political Facts 1900–1960* (London, 1963), 143.
17 The effect of the business vote is discussed in D. E. Butler, op. cit., 146–8.
18 In a letter to the author.
19 In a letter to the author.
20 Lord Reith, *Diaries,* ed. Charles Stuart (London, 1975), 351.
21 Lord Moran, *Winston Churchill: the Struggle for Survival 1940–1965* (London, 1966), 286. He was Churchill's doctor.
22 Jack Ashley, *Journey in Silence* (London, 1973), 61.
23 Lord Hailsham, *The Door wherein I went* (London, 1975), 124.
24 Susan Lowndes, ed., *Diaries and Letters of Marie Belloc Lowndes, 1911–1947* (London, 1971), 261.
25 In a letter to the author.
26 Andrew Boyle, *Montagu Norman* (London, 1967), 326.
27 Moran, op. cit., 286
28 Thomas Jones, *A Diary with Letters 1932–1950* (London, 1954), 536.
29 Lord Beveridge, *Power and Influence* (London, 1953), 349.
30 Lyttelton, op. cit., 328.
31 Donoughue and Jones, op. cit., 338–44.
32 Francis Williams, *Nothing so Strange: an Autobiography* (London, 1970), 213.
33 ibid, 213.
34 Douglas Hyde, *I Believed* (London, 1950), 201.

35 *The Economist,* 4 August 1945.
36 Beveridge, op. cit., 344.
37 Lord Butler, op. cit., 127.
38 Henry Pelling, *Winston Churchill*(London, 1974), 561.
39 McCallum and Readman, op. cit., 296–8.
40 Lord Butler, op. cit., 128; Jones, op. cit., also attacked Churchill's speech, 536.
41 *The Memoirs of the Earl of Kilmuir* (London, 1964), 138.
42 Tom Harrison, 'Who'll Win?', *Political Quarterly* (1944).
43 McCallum and Readman, op. cit., 43.
44 Woodrow Wyatt, *Into the Dangerous World* (London, 1952), 56.
45 Anne Wolrige-Gordon, *Peter Howard Life and Letters* (London, 1969), 137–8.

2 Achievement and Austerity under Attlee, 1945–51

The new Parliament

The Parliamentary Labour Party which assembled after the election of July 1945 was nearly double that which had emerged from the election of 1935. Labour had won 393 seats as compared with 154 in 1935. In addition, there were three ILP members and a Common Wealth MP who could be regarded as government supporters.

One big difference between the PLP in 1945 and that in the previous Parliament was the relative decline in the trade-union-sponsored element. There had been 78 MPs sponsored by trade unions in 1935. They represented a larger percentage of the smaller PLP in that Parliament than did the 120 elected in 1945 of the larger PLP. With 34 seats, two more than in 1935, the Miners' Union was the best represented. Next came the Transport and General Workers' Union which had successfully sponsored seventeen candidates, as against only seven in 1935. The Railwaymen were still the third largest group, and the National Union of General and Municipal Workers were fourth (with 12 and 10 MPs respectively). The Railway Clerks were the fifth largest contingent with 9 MPs, but the powerful Amalgamated Engineering Union only increased its membership of the Commons from 3 to 4. The Textile-Workers returned to the parliamentary arena for the first time since the 1929-31 Parliament with 3 MPs, as did the Boot and Shoe Operatives with their 4 Members. The Post Office Workers, with one MP, gained their first success since 1924. The Agricultural Workers and the Electrical Trades Union burst onto the Westminster scene for the first time with only one MP each. Finally, the Shopworkers retained their sixth place on the trade-union Westminster league-table with 8 MPs, the Woodworkers returned 3, and there were 9 other trade-union-sponsored Members of Parliament.

The most dramatic change in the PLP was the fact that it had become the most representative parliamentary party in British history, representative, that is to say, in terms of occupations, educational backgrounds, and so on. It spanned all social classes, and adult age-groups, and was made up of individuals from a wide variety of occupations. There was of course a large influx of educationalists of all kinds, barristers, and journalists. And a number of medical practitioners entered the Commons under the Labour colours. There were also sizeable numbers of Labour MPs from other white-collar professions. Swindon's man was Thomas Reid, 'a retired colonial administrator'. From Bootle came Alderman John Kinley, a hairdresser. Konni Zilliacus arrived with some eighteen years in the League of Nations Secretariat behind him. There were also a number of Labour MPs who could be classed as 'capitalists'. Accrington's choice was Captain W. S. Elliot, who had worked in the cotton trade in India and 'is the laird of Arkleton'. Bolton elected John Lewis, a company director and rubber technologist who had 'invented a process for surfacing airfield runways'. The MP for Loughborough, Mont Follick, was the proprietor of the Regent School of Languages in London. David Logan, a pawnbroker, was once again returned for the Scotland Division of Liverpool, which he had represented since 1929. The Romford seat had been won for Labour by a 'foreign and colonial merchant', Thomas Macpherson. J. H. Alpass, an auctioneer and estate agent, had carried Thornbury in Gloucester. A sand and gravel merchant, S. N. Evans, was Labour's successful candidate at Wednesbury. Maurice Edelman, later to become known as a novelist, was listed as a director of a plywood factory, as well as an author and war correspondent.

As one would expect at the end of a world war, military titles were common at Westminster in 1945. There were over sixty Labour MPs who had a military 'handle' to their names at that time. There were, in addition, a few who had been officers in the First World War. Several Labour MPs had served as 'other ranks'. It could not be said that the PLP was unrepresentative of those who had served in uniform, as well as of those who had served on the home front.

Yet despite the varied social, educational, and occupational backgrounds of Labour MPs in 1945, the PLP was unrepresentative in important respects. Though better represented than ever before, there were still only twenty-four women in the 1945–50 House of Commons. Of these, twenty-one were on the Labour benches. And in an age in which there was to be constant argument about industry, technology, management, and science, there was a dearth of expertise in these fields in the House of Commons.

Inevitably, the great victory of 1945 lumbered the winning party with at least some political flotsam and jetsam. Certainly the convictions of some of those elected under the Labour banner in 1945 were questioned by some of their colleagues. As one Labour

17

MP of that Parliament put it bitterly to the author, 'Some of them were bloody Tories in all but name'. Another wrote in 1976, looking back on nearly thirty-one years in Parliament, 'My feelings on first being elected was [*sic*] then (and now) how many so-called idealists use the political machines for their own personal advancement and for career purposes'.[1]

When the new Labour MPs arrived at Westminster on the first day of the 1945 Parliament, they were in a highly emotional state. Many had not expected to be there, few had anticipated the size of the Labour victory. They felt at the beginning of a great era which they could help to shape.

Herbert Morrison recalled later

they broke the rules by singing the 'Red Flag'. Some did not know the words and some, judging by the rendering, the tune. The brief performance horrified some of the Tories and I must admit it mildly disturbed me. These youngsters still had to absorb the atmosphere of the House.[2]

The Labour MPs had been provoked, admitted A. P. Herbert, elected as Independent Member for Oxford University, by some Conservatives singing 'For he's a jolly good fellow!' in honour of Winston Churchill.[3] Herbert accused the Labour intake of arrogance and called the new Parliament, the 'Rude Parliament'. In his memoirs he painted an interesting picture of Westminster at the time. Not only the new Labour MPs, but their friends and relatives were

swarming in too – eager for tea, for seats in the Gallery, for a conducted tour round the People's Parliament – *their* Parliament now. The Central Hall, for a month or two, was like Hammersmith Broadway. I was delighted at least to see the long queues for the Gallery stretching into the open street, for I had lectured so often about the virtues of Parliament and chided thousands for calling it the 'talking-shop', the 'gas-works', and so on.[4]

Clement Attlee

Unlike the previous Labour administrations under Ramsay Mac-Donald, the Attlee governments enjoyed the great advantage that most of the top ministers were well-known public figures experienced in office.

Clement Attlee had held a number of posts in the Churchill coalition between 1940 and 1945. He had been deputy Prime Minister from February 1942 onwards. In addition to Attlee, Bevin, Greenwood, and Morrison had served in the War Cabinet, and Cripps and Dalton had held important posts under Churchill. Of the top echelon of Labour, only Bevan lacked such experience.

Of course, this wartime experience was not without its

drawbacks. The senior members of Attlee's Cabinet had served by 1945 as long as most politicians expect to serve at one stretch. Of the inter-war Prime Ministers, perhaps ironically, only MacDonald served continuously in office as long as Attlee was to do.[5] Clearly, the health of Attlee's team must have taken a severe pounding by the time they took office in 1945. At sixty-two, Attlee was a little younger than Chamberlain and Churchill when they became Prime Minister.

Another possible drawback to having held office under Churchill was that perhaps Attlee's team's method of working was too much determined by the example of their Conservative colleagues. As Morrison is quoted as having told George VI, the Labour leaders 'had learnt a good deal from the Conservatives in how to govern'.[6]

One might think that having worked together both in and out of government for some years, and being pledged to a high ideal, Attlee and his colleagues would have collaborated without great difficulty. This was not so. As Shinwell recalls, 'The brotherly love advocated by the movement was conspicuous by its absence'.[7] Personal rivalries were intense and there was also a natural antipathy between those who had served in the wartime coalition and those, like Shinwell and Bevan, who had often criticized them from the backbenches. Attlee must have had as tough a time as any Prime Minister in holding his team together, made up, as it was, of such 'strong and disparate personalities'[8] and committed to a heavy legislative programme. For these reasons, and as Labour's first majority Prime Minister, he deserves closer attention.

Clement Richard Attlee (1883–1967) was the son of a well-to-do London solicitor. After public school and Oxford, he took his Bar exams in 1906. He was converted to socialism largely by doing social work in the East End of London. He volunteered for service in the First World War, was wounded, and reached the rank of major. Attlee became the Labour mayor of Stepney in 1919, and was elected to the Commons in 1922. He held minor appointments in MacDonald's two minority governments. He was fortunate that his working-class constituency gave him virtual security of tenure at Westminster. His middle-class education helped him immensely at a time when there was a shortage of trained minds on the Labour side. He beat Morrison and Greenwood in 1935 in the fight for the Labour leadership. Perhaps the Labour Party chose him because he was the very opposite in character to their lost leader Ramsay MacDonald. 'In every respect', wrote Josiah C. Wedgwood, who had served in the first Labour administration, 'he is the exact antithesis of MacDonald'. He found him the best-read man in the House 'in my time – save perhaps Baldwin or Sir John Simon', a man devoid of selfishness and ambition.[9] Attlee was widely regarded as a 'cold fish', remote from his colleagues. His friend and press secretary, Francis Williams, believed, 'His own nature in any event inclined him to a solitary role'.[10] The writer has found as many witnesses who believed Attlee was arrogant as those who thought him modest, shy, and retiring. What of his qualities as a politician? Never a brilliant orator, he did improve as he went on. As Kingsley Martin observed,

I have never known anyone with Attlee's deceptive capacity for not being noticed – which no doubt explains why Churchill thought him in 1940 'a decent, modest little man, who of course has a great deal to be modest about'. He had learnt better when Attlee was Premier after the war and scored over a disgruntled Churchill.[11]

Harold Macmillan found Attlee 'unexpectedly effective' against Churchill. 'Beneath his curiously matter-of-fact and pedestrian replies, the whole great Churchillian fabric began to waver and collapse'.[12] Macmillan had been a colleague of Attlee in the wartime coalition and remembered him as 'one of the best Chairmen I have ever sat under . . . he was cool and unexcitable and never lost his head'. Attlee was also a 'good butcher', 'a quality said to be essential for a good Prime Minister'.[13] This impression of Attlee the able chairman, the firm but unobtrusive leader has not gone unchallenged. Hugh Dalton wrote in his diary on 7 January 1944 about attending a Cabinet Committee with 'poor little C.R.A. hardly visible or audible in the Chair'. On 11 February he recorded, 'C.R.A. is very slow in the Chair and doesn't bring things to a point'.

Attlee was a conservative-minded person in a way which might have appeared to be at variance with his proclaimed socialist principles. This was not necessarily the case. If he had a vision of socialism, it was not of the breaking-down of all classes and the forging of a new classless society with a new culture, socialism for him meant a process of 'levelling up', of helping as many pro-letarians as possible to achieve his middle-class standards. Francis Williams remarked that Attlee 'suffered acutely if the port was circulated the wrong way at his dinner table'.[14] He argued with Bevan because of the Celt's refusal to dress 'correctly' for a royal banquet, recalling MacDonald's row with Lansbury over a similar matter.[15] He was proud of his old public school, Haileybury, and retained an interest in it to his dying day. He not only admired George VI as a hardworking public servant, but he idealized the pageantry of monarchy. This caused G. D. H. Cole, the Oxford Labour historian and lifelong Labour activist, to lament:

I used to have some respect for Mr. Attlee; but he forfeited it all when he became an Earl and a Knight of the Garter. How on earth could he wish to be degraded in these ways? . . . he has brought discredit on the Socialist cause.[16]

Perhaps Violet Attlee strengthened her husband's tendency in this direction. She knew little about politics[17] and told the writer in 1963 she 'hated' politics. She had sacrificed much for politics. A thoroughly middle-class soul, perhaps she felt she deserved a little of the colour and pageantry of royal occasions.

As a man Clement Attlee remains an enigma, as a political leader he must be regarded as one of the most remarkable Prime Ministers of the twentieth century.

Attlee's Cabinet

Unlike Ramsay MacDonald, Attlee had no shortage of experienced or talented personalities with which to fill his Cabinet posts. His problem was to find enough senior positions for all the top people he had to include. He had to make sure he did not leave out any potential rebels or neglect any important sectional interests.

Ernest Bevin (1881–1951), the man who had built up the mighty Transport and General Workers' Union, was closest to Attlee and became Foreign Secretary. Bevin has always been regarded as a tough and ruthless individual,[18] but did his toughness enable him to take effective control of foreign affairs? He often consulted Attlee and Attlee was directly involved on key occasions, as at Potsdam, and on his trips to see President Truman. Many in the Labour Party have continued to believe he was a weak minister, the prisoner of his officials at the Foreign Office.[19] Bevin was popular with the King,[20] the crowds in Downing Street,[21] at the Foreign Office,[22] and with the Conservatives.[23] Some in his own party saw him as a megalomaniac, or at least an egoist. From the left Michael Foot has written, 'The egotism was gargantuan, yet oddly inoffensive, almost endearing. Partly it was an expression of his working-class arrogance, his confidence that his own class had the right and capacity to rule'.[24]

The disappointed contender for the Foreign Office, Hugh Dalton, got the Exchequer. Dalton stands out as a booming, affable figure, an intriguer, intellectual snob, a great patriot, a man of many moods, and very human. Though a pre-war academic at the London School of Economics, his close friend Nicholas Davenport, himself a City financial expert, found Dalton 'ill-equipped to handle the complicated details of currency and banking of which he had no practical experience'.[25]

Attlee appointed his rival, Herbert Morrison (1885–1965), deputy Prime Minister. As Lord President of the Council, this son of a London policeman, former Leader of the London County Council, and wartime Minister for Home Security, was responsible for the legislative timetable of the government. Unhappy in his private life, Morrison 'lived politics, ate politics, dreamt politics'.[26] If anything, his vision of the New Jerusalem was even more restricted than Attlee's.

Of the other Cabinet ministers Stafford Cripps (1889–1952) and Aneurin Bevan (1897–1960) were the two most important and the two most outstanding personalities. A science graduate of London University, Cripps was a wealthy barrister, and the son of a wealthy barrister who had left the Conservatives for MacDonald's Labour Party. Stafford Cripps himself briefly served as Solicitor-General in MacDonald's second Labour administration. He became popular in Labour working-class circles for his successful defence of trade unionists in the courts. Expelled from the Party in 1939 for advocating a 'popular front' with the Communists, he had nevertheless been given office by Churchill. He was restored to the PLP in February 1945. Attlee gave him the Board of Trade in 1945, appointed him Minister for Economic Affairs in 1947, and, later in the same year, gave him the Treasury on Dalton's resignation. Those who had dealings with him regarded him as a man of courage, integrity, idealism, and brilliance.[27] He was a high-minded Christian, vegetarian, and teetotaller. He is often regarded as a man of poor political and personal judgment, and lacking a sense of humour.[28]

The personality of Aneurin Bevan could not have been more different from his old comrade-in-arms, Stafford Cripps. A former Welsh miner, he too, by all accounts, was a man of great natural brilliance and courage. Macmillan believed that he was 'in many ways much the most exciting of the Labour team'. He also paid him the highest compliment, 'He was human' and 'free of cant and hypocrisy'.[29] Another political opponent of his, who saw much of him, found he had many pleasing characteristics:

In some ways Bevan was what I expected – rhetorical, argumentative, and lively. What I did not expect was his wit, his gaiety, his range of knowledge – or his cackle; for that is what his laugh really was.[30]

That was the view of Lord Hill (then Dr Charles Hill) who led the BMA team negotiating the setting-up of the National Health Service. Attlee had offered Bevan the Ministry of Health, a key post which could either make him or break him. Bevan took up the challenge.

The only woman in the Cabinet was Miss Ellen Wilkinson, the previous year's Chairman of the Labour Party. She had been PPS to Morrison and had organized the anti-Attlee lobbying in the PLP. She 'admired Morrison to the point of love'.[31] She was regarded as a leftist. Her life ended with an overdose of pills in February 1947.

Attlee's first Cabinet of twenty was a fair balance of Right and Left, the trade union sponsored MPs and their middle-class colleagues, the Prime Minister's friends and his enemies; MacDonald's first Cabinet of twenty in 1924 included nine former officials of working-class organizations, Attlee's included ten. MacDonald's Cabinet included more members of aristocratic or upper-class background than Attlee's, seven against four. Of the Cabinet ministers in Attlee's first government, ten were university educated, five of them at Oxbridge. Five were ex-public-school boys, two of these from Eton. Only two members of the 1945 Labour Cabinet had not previously held government office. It was clearly a very experienced and talented government. One can willingly agree with Harold Macmillan's assessment, 'These fine men constituted a body of Ministers as talented as any in the history of Parliament'.[32]

The terms of the United States loan

Attlee had lost no time in assembling his forces at Westminster. Parliament met on 1 August. Much needed to be done at home, and the Japanese war still had to be brought to a successful conclusion. Unaware of the A-Bomb, most commentators expected that war to go on for months, or even years. The abrupt ending of that campaign later in the same month brought the government its first major crisis. As A.J.P. Taylor has reminded us, 'By the beginning of 1941 British financial resources were almost exhausted . . . Thanks to lend-lease Great Britain kept up a misleading appearance as a Great Power until almost the end of the war'.[33] One could go further and say that in the hour of victory there were very few who could understand the extent of Britain's financial nudity. Attlee and his colleagues had realized that lend-lease would come to an end, but had reckoned with a transitional period, lasting months, as the war with Japan was gradually wound up.[34] Ordinary people could not understand that a winning power, at the head of a great empire, apparently second only to the United States in influence, could be destitute. Faced with the immediate suspension of lend-lease at the end of hostilities, and with prospects 'very grim, grimmer even than the worst nightmares of most experts',[35] Attlee initiated negotiations with the United States for fresh financial help. Misled by the optimism of Lord Keynes, who was the chief British economic negotiator,[36] the Labour leaders were expecting a gift from the Americans in recognition of Britain's war effort. In fact, only after months of negotiations, which nearly broke down, were they able to secure a loan, with interest and other strings attached. Britain had started the war with debts of £496 million and ended it with debts of £3,500 million.[37] But whereas in 1939 it had had vast reserves in gold, dollars, and overseas investments, it had by 1945

23

been stripped of most of these. Run-down as they were, Britain's industries were less able to export, traditional markets had been disrupted, many necessities could only be bought from the United States, and invisible earnings were not as easy to come by as they had been. Moreover, Britain had new international responsibilities which represented a heavy drain on its financial resources. Few could disagree with Dalton that, 'This great load of debt . . . is, indeed, a strange reward for all we, in this land, did and suffered for the common cause . . . It is a strange and ironical reward . . .'[38] To deal with the situation the government was willing to accept an American package which Robert Boothby, Conservative MP for Aberdeen, called 'our economic Munich',[39] and which both he and the Labour Member for Nottingham South, Norman Smith, believed, treated Britain as a defeated nation.[40] Superficially, the American proposals appeared reasonable. A credit of up to $3,750 million was offered at a modest 2 per cent interest. Repayments would be spread over fifty years from 1951. The 'strings' which caused most of the controversy required the abandonment of British Empire preferences and full convertibility for sterling without any reciprocation by the Americans. In 1939 Britain had £117 million-worth of goods from the United States, 13 per cent of total imports of goods, and exported only £28 million-worth, 7 per cent of exports of goods. Earnings on 'invisibles' – shipping, insurance, banking, and tourism – had helped to offset this massive imbalance. Through war losses this was no longer possible.[41] In addition, the Americans required the United Kingdom to settle with its sterling creditors before 1951, freeing them, should they so desire, to shop in the dollar market. To the United States credit was added a Canadian loan of $1,250 million.[42] The opponents of the United States loan argued that American exporters needed Britain as much as Britain needed them, and that the terms should therefore be rejected. They were not impressed by Ernest Bevin's appeal to the spirit of 1940. With many Conservatives abstaining, the government secured acceptance by 345 to 98. Among the Labour 'Noes' were James Callaghan, Barbara Castle, Maurice Edelman, Jennie Lee, and Michael Foot. In all some 21 Labour MPs voted against the government. Interestingly, the two Communist MPs and the fellow-traveller group all voted with the government. The Cold War had not yet reached the House of Commons.

A large body of independent experts believed the conditions of the loan were impossible to fulfil;[43] their view was proved correct when in August 1947 the government was forced to suspend the dollar convertibility of sterling. This was after barely one month of convertibility. Though the government was an easy target for right-wing propaganda that it was squandering the loan, a similar dollar crisis struck western Europe in the same year. Marshall Aid was introduced by the Americans in the following year because by that time the prosperity of western Europe was seen as crucial to American defence. Britain took its share of Aid, but again faced difficulty in 1949. A recession in the United States had made dollar exports more difficult, while strong demand at home placed a new strain on the precarious balance of payments. Cripps, by that time Chancellor, attempted to solve the crisis with a massive devaluation of sterling, from $4.03 to $2.80.

Whatever the rights and wrongs of particular decisions the Attlee administrations can only be judged against the background of constant worries over a balance of payments situation which was largely the result of the war.

Nationalization measures

For very many Socialists and Conservatives alike the core of Labour's programme, the essence of its socialism, was its commitment to widespread nationalization policies. Its constitution pledged it to 'common ownership', and in the inter-war period Attlee and his colleagues had paid homage to the principle both collectively and individually. In 1937 the leader had called for land nationalization, and he had written that 'All the major industries will be owned and controlled by the community, but there may well exist for a long time many smaller enterprises which are left to be carried on individually'.[44] Common ownership had come to mean nationalized public corporations, thanks to the success of Herbert Morrison's London Passenger Transport Board and the Soviet experiment. Labour's programme of 1934 had called for the 'public ownership and control of the primary industries and services as a foundation step, including the banking system, transport, coal and power, water supply, iron and steel, and other key industries'. Arms manufacture and sale of land were also on the 'shopping list'.[45] The *Immediate Programme* of 1937 was more moderate.

Socialists advocated public ownership to prevent unemployment, redistribute wealth, rationalize production and create better relations within industry. The war years saw an increase in interest in public ownership because of the successful role played by the government in the economy at the time, and, not least, because of the successes of the Red Army, which were thought to be based on a highly successful economic system created by the state from nothing. As ministers in the coalition from 1940 on, the Labour leaders had to be circumspect in their statements on the issue. However, by 1943 even Churchill was explaining to the public,

If we can make state enterprise and free enterprise both serve national interests and pull the national wagon side by side, then there is no need for us to run into that horrible devastating slump or into that squalid epoch of bickering and confusion which mocked and squandered the hard-won victory which we gained a quarter of a century ago.

Three sub-committees of Labour's NEC (out of thirteen) were concerned with public-ownership problems. In June 1943, the NEC reported that detailed plans for the future structure of the coal and power industries had been worked out. Later on though, George Wigg was to claim there had been little detailed work done on mining, 'The archives were ransacked and revealed two copies of a paper written by Jim Griffiths, one of them a translation into Welsh!'[46] Having swung to the left on the issue at its conference in 1944, Labour became a little less radical again in 1945.

Committed to a clear programme of public ownership, and having been returned with one of the most convincing majorities in British history, the new regime lost no time in implementing it. The Bill nationalizing the Bank of England received the Royal Assent in February 1946. The Royal Assent was given to the nationalization of coalmining, cable and wireless, and the reorganization of civil aviation in the same year. In the following year it was the turn of transport – railways, canals, and road haulage – and electricity. Gas undertakings were nationalized in 1948 and the Royal Assent was given to iron and steel nationalization in November 1949. The pace set was tough for all concerned considering the complexity of the legislation and the many other important matters competing for time on the parliamentary calendar.

Speaking in the debate on the Second Reading of the Coal Bill, Clement Davies, the Liberal leader, said, 'I am perfectly sure that, given a fair chance, this Bill will not only work but will be one of the most epoch-making Acts of Parliament in our history'.[47] Davies voted for nationalization. Morgan Phillips, Secretary of the Labour Party, wrote about steel nationalization, 'The battle for steel [is] the supreme test of political democracy – a test which the whole world will be watching'.[48] Yet many years later, Emanuel Shinwell, who was responsible for piloting the Coal Bill through the Commons, wrote that, although Labour had carried through a 'bloodless revolution' between 1945 and 1951, most of the nationalization measures were 'little more than a technicality'.[49] What is the truth? Were the nationalization Acts merely a continuation of policies initiated by previous governments? Or, did they constitute a fundamental shift in the power structure of British society, demonstrating the possibility of peaceful change?

Of course, to a considerable extent the nationalization programme *was* a continuation of previous policies. Explaining his party's attitude to public ownership in 1947, Quintin Hogg was happy to remind his readers, 'Disraeli encouraged the purchase by the Government of a minority shareholding in a private profit-making concern, the Suez Canal Company. The British Government became under Conservative auspices perhaps the principal shareholders in the Anglo-Persian Oil Company'.[50] Rail nationalization had first been advocated in the nineteenth century by non-socialists such as William Galt and Edwin Chadwick on the grounds that British railways were less efficient than those on the Continent,[51] and, though nationalization was resisted, successive governments increasingly regulated the railways. In the inter-war period Conservative governments carried out selective nationalization policies. A Conservative government set up the BBC and the Central Electricity Board in 1926. The legislation setting up the London Transport Board, which put public transport in the capital under one authority, was passed by a Conservative-dominated Commons in 1933. The Conservatives were responsible for the nationalization of mining royalties and tithes in 1938 because they had 'become a nuisance in private hands – the former because they interfered with the technical layout of coal mines, the latter because they no longer formed an equitable or even equal impost on property'.[52] Finally, the Chamberlain administration brought Imperial Airways Ltd and British Airways Ltd into public ownership in 1939.

The case for claiming that Labour's nationalization measures represented a continuation of the policies of previous governments is strengthened by noting the comments of Conservatives about such measures. Though the Conservatives formally opposed them all, their attitudes varied from case to case. Quintin Hogg once again: 'Conservatives say that the system of nationalisation is an evil one – and over a long period will be disastrous to the public interest'.[53] But he also wrote at the same time, 'Conservatives felt no particularly violent objection to the nationalisation of the Bank of England or of Cable and Wireless Ltd . . .'[54] And Conservatives heard Winston Churchill tell the Commons in 1946, 'I am not going to pretend I see anything immoral in the nationalisation of the railways provided fair compensation is paid to the present owners. I profess myself . . . in favour of this policy in 1919 . . .'[55] Only over steel did tempers seem to reach boiling-point on the Conservative side. Perhaps this was the reason why some Labour ministers, especially Morrison, would have been prepared to compromise on the issue. But Attlee, relying on his own political instinct, decided to go ahead anyway.

Attlee knew that for many Labour MPs steel nationalization was a crucial test, a crusade even, either to establish a socialist economy, or, more likely, to show the employing class that the old days were gone, their power broken. They warmed to the words of David Mort, a man with thirty years experience of the steel industry, when he said, 'I can remember the time when I represented the men and I was not allowed to sit down in the presence of the manager. I have headed deputations and we have stood talking to the manager for an hour. He was the only man in the room who sat down'.[56] Others who did not have this gut reaction against the employers, remembered the pre-war unemployment in the constituencies and believed public ownership would reduce the likelihood of that happening again.

If the nationalization of the steel industry caused the greatest concern, anger, and alarm on the Conservative side, the nationalization of the mines produced the deepest emotions and satisfaction on the Labour benches. C. F. Grey, not a Marxist, but a Methodist lay preacher newly elected to the Commons, 'hewing in a Durham colliery as recently as June last year', voiced the emotions of the miners he represented.

Low wages, long hours, miserable compensation, bad conditions, wretched death benefits, and virtual slavery were the lot of the miner. For years, the miner stood this, until it got to breaking point. Now we have a younger miner who is determined that he is not going to be a beast of burden.[57]

Time and again during the debates on the nationalization of the mines, bitterness, sarcasm, anger, and cold, devastating fact were flung out from the Labour benches:

Mining accidents kill two men every day, and in 1943, 713 men lost their lives in the industry. One miner in four draws compensation every year for either disease or injury and more than 100,000 workers in the pits today are over 55 years of age. Death, injury and sickness have taken 44,000 men from the pits in 1944, and only 10,000 men have been recruited in the same period. So utterly evil are the conditions which exist in the mines that the Government had to resort to State conscription.[58]

There was anger too on the Labour side about compensation. Grey frankly admitted, 'I think in terms of confiscation, and the less the owners get the better I shall like it'.[59] And George Brown spoke for many other Labour MPs when he commented:

It may be that there would be a willing buyer for certain pits, but not for the whole lot, taking the good with the bad – there is too much bad. I hope that we shall not pay – if I may mix a metaphor – a going price for a white elephant. Even if it is a white elephant, we must have it, but let us pay a white elephant price for it.[60]

The thoughts and the feelings, the anger and the elation, expressed by Labour MPs as the Coal Bill progressed through Parliament, reached out into the mining villages up and down the country, and culminated in the jubilation of Vesting Day, 1 January 1947. There were dances, marches, socials, and bonfires. At Mansfield, Notts, a free social and dance was held in the Drill Hall for miners and their families. Some 200 people attended a dance at the Co-op Hall at Hucknall, and 600 children celebrated with a visit to the pictures, tea and a huge bonfire at Clipstone, also in Nottinghamshire. The Coal Board flag was hoisted at Eastwood (Notts) by an office boy, and at Ilkeston (Derbyshire) by the oldest employee, Mr W. Williamson (74), who had worked at the Manners Colliery 62 years. Gedling Colliery (Notts) turned the highest tonnage of any New Year's Day for five years.[61] About 150 miles away in Murton, Durham, the Minister of Fuel and Power, Emanuel Shinwell, had returned to celebrate with his constituents:

Orators skilled in their art had sent fiery words over the assembled gathering. The platform sustained the imposing authority of the Cabinet, of big business, of smaller business, of the powerful unions and of Civic bodies in the district. The band was smart and vigorous.
But without question, the show belonged to one man – an aged miner in a spotted muffler and a cloth cap. They helped him to the platform. 'I'm ninety-one years old and I've waited all my life for this moment', said Jim Hawkins. 'There's little time left. Let's cut the cackle and get on with it'.
Aided by willing hands, the old man made his way to a flagpole, clutched the cord and ran up a blue flag on which was written in white the letters 'N.C.B.' By his act, Jim Hawkins had translated nationalization into an accomplished fact.[62]

Though many miners realized that, in the words of one Nottinghamshire miner, 'We cannot expect Utopia',[63] there was a feeling of new dignity, of real freedom, after Vesting Day. For the miners and their representatives the Coal Act alone justified the Labour government, it was the acid test of the potentialities of parliamentary politics.

The National Health Service

Though the implementation of the public-ownership pledges was a crucial test for the miners and the committed socialists in the Labour Party, the 'masses' have gained immensely more from the welfare legislation passed in 1946. This legislation included the National Insurance Act, the Industrial Injuries Act, and the National Health Act. In 1948 the work was completed with the establishment of the National Assistance Board. Another piece of relevant legislation, that covering family allowances, had been enacted in 1945, by Churchill's caretaker administration.

Under the National Insurance Act the whole population was brought, for the first time, into a comprehensive system covering unemployment, sickness, maternity, guardianship, retirement, and death. A Ministry of National Insurance was set up and a National Insurance Fund with an initial capital of £100 million. Annual grants from the Exchequer were forseen, but both employers and employees were to make weekly contributions. The latter was something that many in the Labour Party were unhappy about. Some Labour MPs, Sydney Silverman and Barbara Castle among them, rejected the idea that there should be a time limit on the payment of benefits. Under the Act, an unemployed person became eligible, after the first three days of unemployment, to receive a weekly payment for 180 days; an insured person who then got a job and lost it again after not less than thirteen weeks qualified for another period on benefit.

Sickness benefit was provided after three days of enforced absence from work, or for the whole period of the incapacity if it lasted longer than three days. It could be drawn indefinitely up to retirement age when it was replaced by a pension.

The maternity grant consisted of a single payment to the mother on the birth of her baby, and working mothers received an allowance for 13 weeks to compensate for absence from employment.

The death grant was a lump sum to help cover the cost of the funeral. Widows were taken care of under the Act. For the first 16 weeks, a widow under retirement age was paid an allowance. There were allowances for her children up to the age of sixteen (if they remained at school to that age). Widows between fifty and sixty (retirement age for women) could also be eligible for a continuing allowance. Finally, if a widow reached forty while her children were still at school, she could also receive an allowance. To be eligible for these benefits, the widow had to have been married for ten years. One other provision made for death was that an orphaned child's guardian could claim an allowance provided one of its parents had been insured under the Act.

Retirement pensions were granted under the Act to men at sixty-five and women at sixty. Those eligible could continue working for a further five years with a slight reduction of pension. As with all the benefits listed, pensions did not rise automatically with the rise in the cost of living, nor were they related to previous earnings.

Family allowances were given to mothers for the second child and subsequent ones up to the age of fifteen, or sixteen if they remained in full-time education. The allowance was fixed at 5 shillings (25 pence) per week, what Barbara Castle called a 'paltry sum'.[64] In fact it was just about enough to buy 1 lb of Brooke Bond Dividend Tea, a tube of Colgate toothpaste, and a Mars bar.[65]

Despite the wartime agreement on the need for a National Health Service, it was this part of the post-war welfare legislation which was most actively contested. In theory the Conservatives agreed with the principle, but they voiced varying degrees of opposition to the Labour government's proposals. Greater than the opposition of the Conservatives was that of the spokesmen of the British Medical Association, the professional body in which the great majority of medical practitioners were organized.

The National Health Service Act nationalized the nation's hospitals, about half of which had belonged to the local authorities. They were placed under regional boards. The teaching hospitals obtained a special status giving them a large measure of autonomy. The aim was to provide adequate hospitals throughout the country replacing a system based on local initiative and charity, which had resulted in widely differing local and regional standards. The local authorities retained important health functions such as maternity and child welfare, the ambulance service, health visiting, and so on. Aneurin Bevan, the minister responsible, wanted a service which would encompass all the nation's citizens, and provide them all, irrespective of their financial circumstances, with completely free and comprehensive medical care. Broadly speaking, he achieved this, but not without considerable compromises. The buying and selling of practices, which was thought to have led to an imbalance in the distribution of general practitioners, ceased. But doctors did not become salaried employees of the state. Secondly, he agreed to having private beds in the hospitals in order to encourage specialists to join the new scheme. The patient remained free to choose his or her own GP. The Act was a personal triumph for Bevan, and was described by Dr H. B. Morgan, MP, medical adviser to the TUC, as 'as fine a piece of compromise health work as is possible in this country at the present time'.[66]

In judging the effectiveness of the Labour government one can again ask the question: were Attlee, Bevan, and Griffiths merely extending the work of social welfare inaugurated by previous administrations, or were they introducing something more fundamental?

Of course the legislation was based on Sir William Beveridge's report on *Social Insurance and Allied Services* of November 1942 which recommended public protection for all 'from the cradle to the grave'. Churchill, whose coalition had commissioned the report, had not been prepared to implement any legislation incorporating any of the report's proposals during the war.[67] Public opinion polls

31

indicated that the majority of people in the country were disappointed with the government on this issue, feeling that vested interests had won once again. In February 1943 virtually the whole of the Labour backbench voted against the government, and their own leaders, on the issue of the immediate implementation of the Beveridge proposals which they demanded. They were defeated by 338 votes to 121. The backbench rebels included 97 Labour, 3 ILP, one Communist, 9 Liberals, and 11 Independents. Even allowing that had the Conservatives won in 1945, the Tory reformers would have been better represented in the Commons,[68] it seems likely that the Conservatives would have been less ready to realize Beveridge's proposals than were Labour. As it was, their performance over the National Health Service Bill was not very reassuring.

Poor leadership and the absence of a coherent alternative policy allowed the party to drift into a reactionary posture and become the mouthpiece for the vested interests lined up in opposition to the bill . . . the Conservative Party placed itself in the position of seeming to oppose the principle of the National Health Service – a position which they spent the next four years denying.[69]

If Labour built on the foundations laid by others, to many working people the post-war measures appeared revolutionary. Pre-war unemployment relief had still excluded significant sections of the employment population. Once benefit ran out, the unemployed faced the hated 'means test' which enquired into the financial situation of his entire household. And even during the 1930s there was the possibility of being committed to the equally hated workhouse.[70] Sickness insurance was far from comprehensive. It did not cover an insured person's dependents and discriminated against those with a record of poor health. Hospitals charged patients according to means. Children's allowances, maternity and death benefits, did not exist in pre-war Britain, and many were still not included in the old-age pension scheme. The writer cannot but agree with Alan Sillitoe, the author, who in 1945 was working as a capstan-lathe operator in Nottingham:

the Health Service was a sort of enormous sigh of relief – no more Panel – it made the most incredible difference to the mentality of the less well off – probably the greatest single factor in this century in creating a new pride in the English working class.[71]

Attlee told the author he believed it to be his government's biggest single achievement in home affairs.

Housing and education

If unemployment, public ownership, and social security had been key domestic issues for the pre-war Labour movement, housing and education had never been far behind them. Yet in these last two areas Attlee and his colleagues seemed to have less that was new to offer. In both cases lack of time and resources played their part.

Labour inherited a poor housing situation. During the war as many as 4 million houses, perhaps one-third of the total, had been destroyed or damaged by enemy action.[72] In all, 458,000 homes were lost in the war. But one often heard in working-class circles at the time the opinion voiced that it was a pity Hitler's bombing had not been more successful, providing the occupants could have been got out in time, so great was the anger over the slums.

Bevan was also responsible for housing, and throughout his period of office he was under constant pressure both from the Conservatives, and the Left, over the housing situation. On one occasion Major Tufton Beamish, a Conservative MP well-known for his right-wing views, attempted to tease the minister over a Radio Moscow report in which 'it was claimed that hundreds of thousands of low-priced modern houses for collective farmers, to be paid for by the owners in easy instalments . . . have been built in the Ukraine since the war in spite of transport and production difficulties'. Would the minister 'take immediate steps to send a delegation to the USSR to study the methods by which this programme has been achieved'.[73] The writer is not aware that any delegation went to Russia, but, had it done so, it would have come back, as Miss Alice Bacon put it, full of praise for the superior progress made in Britain. Under Attlee's governments over a million homes were built, which was not bad, all things considered. Shortages of men and materials caused constant headaches, as did the anguish of the homeless squatters, who soon after the war made their appearance, and the exasperation of those who had some money but still could not get a home of their own. Factory-made 'pre-fabs' were tried for a time, roughly 124,000 of them being erected by local councils. Yet in spite of their relatively good design and comfortable interiors, most people rejected them as not being quite the real thing. Wartime rent controls were retained and even extended in an effort to prevent profiteering and help steady the cost of living. The Town and Country Planning Act of 1947 obliged local (planning) authorities to survey their areas and present plans for their development. Previously their powers had been merely discretionary. The planning authorities were given extended powers and grants from central government, but many local Labour politicians were disappointed that their authorities did not get greater powers to deal with the complex problems of urban renewal.

As Professor Marwick reminds us, the Labour administration's 'hands were tied', in education, 'by the fact that a major Education

Act had just been put on the statute book, so that it was scarcely feasible to bring in still another one'. And he rightly points out,

Yet if ever there was a good psychological moment for dealing with the snobbism built into the system, it was in the aftermath of the 1945 election victory. The major public schools were then at low ebb, and certainly expected little mercy at the hands of a Labour government.[74]

Given Attlee's own view of socialism as a process of levelling-up, and his own pride in his own school, it is surprising that no attempt was made to integrate the public schools into the state system. One would not have expected nationalization – rather state scholarships for 75 or 80 per cent of the places. This would have been in keeping with wartime discussions and would probably have won the support of Liberal and Conservative reformers.

Labour did implement the pledge to raise the school-leaving age to fifteen in 1947. They also implemented the tripartite system of secondary education embodied in the 1944 Education Act without apparently considering its divisive features.

Communists change front

Apart from its welfare and nationalization measures the Labour government put on the statute book several other measures over which its committed supporters could enthuse. Among them was an Act reducing the delaying power of the Lords from two years to one. This was introduced with Lords opposition to steel nationalization in mind, but in fact the upper chamber had agreed to nationalization after persuading the government to postpone the date of its operation until after the 1950 general election. Secondly, the Representation of the People Act, 1948, abolished the business premises qualification to vote and the university seats. In future no one could enjoy more than one vote. Thirdly, and perhaps more important from the point of view of the Labour movement, in 1946 the Trades Disputes Act of 1927 was repealed. 'Contracting-in' was, once again, replaced by 'contracting-out' for trade unionists paying the political levy to the Labour Party. In other words, if a member of a trade union affiliated to the Labour Party did not wish to pay his contribution, or levy, to the Party, he now had to seek out his branch secretary and sign an appropriate form. Under the Act the onus was on the socialist activist to take the initiative to pay the levy. The importance of this move for the Labour Party is shown by reference to the Amalgamated Engineering Union (AEU). During the war the union tried hard to get its members to pay the levy. By the end of 1943 only 11 per cent did so, double the pre-war figure.[75] By 1945 it was 24.66 per cent. In the first full year after the Act had been repealed, 1947, it was 82.21 per cent.[76] The repeal of the Act also made it possible once again for civil service trade unions to affiliate to the TUC.

Given the economic situation of the country the government needed the trade unions more than ever before. In 1945 it knew it could count on the complete support of the union leaders and most of their members. Later, the government became worried, unduly so, as it turned out, about the Communist influence.

The war had brought impressive gains for the Communists in the unions. They had consolidated their positions in the National Union of Mineworkers in Scotland and Wales. They had a strong following in the AEU, and among the London dockers. They had gained some influence among the Draughtsmen, the Scientific Workers, the Clerical and Administrative Workers, and the lower grades of the non-manual civil service. A Communist had been elected General Secretary of the Fire Brigades Union in 1939, another was elected National Secretary of the Foundry Workers. In the Electrical Trades Union, their men had clawed their way into the posts of President and Secretary. Even in the Transport and General Workers Union, Bert Papworth, the Communist busmen's leader, had been elected in 1944 as one of its two representatives on the TUC General Council. The Communists had warmly welcomed the Labour government in 1945. And even after a year of Attlee in Downing Street they remained enthusiastic.[77] Yet with the coming of the Cold War the Communist line changed. In December 1947 CP Secretary Harry Pollitt laid down the new edict in a special report to the Executive Committee. He declared that the world was clearly divided into two camps, an imperialist and an anti-imperialist, 'with a Labour Government as active partner in the imperialist camp'. In this situation 'important changes in the policy of the Communist Party . . . should be made'. There could be little room for doubt, the Communists were going over to the offensive against the Labour government.

In its all-out campaign against the Attlee government the Communist Party found any amount of combustible material. There were immediate issues which the Communists could take up, not as matters of ideological dispute, but as practical, bread and butter, issues. The White Paper on Wages and Personal Incomes published in February 1948 was the principal one. It was the first of many attempts by post-war governments at an incomes policy. It related personal incomes to increases in the volume of productivity, emphasizing the need to export for Britain to pay its way in the world. It was accepted by the General Council of the TUC and by the bulk of the PLP. Phil Piratin the Communist MP called it 'an attack on the working class'.[78] Another, literally bread and butter issue, was the government's problem of maintaining the rations. At the end of the war the country had expected a steady expansion of the food supply leading to an early end of rationing. Through no fault of the government, this did not happen. In fact, some rations went down. In November 1948 the bacon ration went down from 2 ounces per week to 2 ounces per fortnight. In 1949 the average consumption of many basic items of food was still lower than it had been in 1939. Both Communists and Conservatives[79] alike attacked this state of affairs. For the Communists, the most effective vehicle for their attack was through the trade union movement.

In the tough economic and international situation, with the Cold War getting colder every day, the Labour leaders decided they must act to neutralize the Communist influence. Any form of co-operation between individual Labour members and Communists was prohibited. A purge of the civil service was carried through and the TUC was asked to expose Communists in its member unions. In the Labour Party itself the leadership expelled several Labour MPs who had pretty consistently supported the Communist line. Many other MPs who had opposed government policies, and continued to do so, were not affected. Further, a whole series of Communist-dominated 'front' organizations were proscribed for Labour Party members.

The move against Communists in the civil service came in March 1948. Premier Attlee announced in the Commons that it had been decided that no one known to be a member of the Communist Party, or associated with it, 'in such a way as to raise legitimate doubts about his or her reliability', would be employed on work 'vital to the security of the State'.[80] To mollify opinion among his own backbenchers he said the same rule was being applied to the fascists. This did not convince 43 Labour MPs who put down a resolution regretting the statement. But other MPs rallied to the Prime Minister's defence and 31 Labour MPs put their names to a resolution congratulating Attlee. The Co-operative Party and the TUC later approved the government's action.

Distasteful though many in the Labour Party thought the purge was, they also felt it was necessary. It came within a month of the Communist *coup* in Prague which destroyed democracy in Czechoslovakia. Consciences were eased a little in 1950 when it was announced that the atomic scientist Klaus Fuchs had confessed to having supplied atomic secrets to the Russians. The case of the two defecting diplomats, Burgess and Maclean, in 1951, further strengthened the case for the purge.

The trade unions were far more difficult to police than the civil service. Many members who did not agree with communism felt that once a purge started, it would not stop at Communists but would be directed against anyone considered militant or even just a nuisance to the leadership. It was also felt by many that Communists should be dealt with by the normal democratic machinery, defeated at elections and disciplined if they sought to extend their influence by breaking the unions' rules. On the other hand, some officials saw how the Communists, usually very small minorities, by concerted and untiring action, got their resolutions passed, their nominees elected, and their policies adopted. Such officials, who perhaps had spent all their adult lives building up their unions, felt angry when they observed how the apathy of the majority enabled unrepresentative minorities to push through unrepresentative policies. One such official, Arthur Deakin, General Secretary of the Transport and General Workers Union, in an ill-advised statement urged that Communists be banned.[81] If anything, such statements merely increased sympathy for the Communists as the victims of illiberal trade union bosses. But men like Deakin saw how occasionally, having got control of a union, the Communists would stop at nothing to keep control. Such was the case in the Electrical Trades Union.

The outbreak of the Korean War in 1950, discussed in the next chapter, increased the fear of Communists in the unions, who, it was thought, might seek to interfere with defence supplies or even resort to sabotage. G. A. Isaacs, himself a former printing union leader, warned the Commons about this possible threat. In fact, the fears were greatly exaggerated. Most of the ordinary Communist trade unionists were basically law-abiding citizens who would never have got involved in sabotage. In any case, their influence was very limited. At a time when the Communists were either hostile to strike action, during the war, or still officially reluctant to endorse it, just after the war up to 1948, there were many more workers on strike than later, when the Communists were dedicated to militancy. The incidence of strikes would seem to have nothing to do with Communist influence:[82]

Workers directly involved in strikes in all industries and services

1944	716,000	1949	313,000
1945	447,000	1950	269,000
1946	405,000	1951	336,000
1947	489,000	1952	303,000
1948	324,000	1953	1,329,000

Conservative Party reforms

The Conservative Party responded to its defeat in 1945 with a mixture of arrogance and courage. The arrogance came naturally to a party that considered only it was fit to rule, a party which had suffered its last major defeat in 1906. Having been so heavily defeated at a time when the Left was surging forward throughout Europe, it needed some courage to believe there was any major role for the Party in the future. Not surprisingly there was thought given to the idea of changing the Party's name and broadening it out into an alliance of non-socialists.

The Conservative Party did not succeed in becoming a broad coalition of non-socialists, but it did succeed in attracting some popular figures who had not been closely associated with Conservatism. Most important of them was Lord Woolton, who had shown his skills as Minister of Food during the war. Macmillan called him 'not only a great organiser, but . . . the best salesman that I have ever known'.[83] Churchill made him party chairman with the job of modernizing the Party's organization. Another popular figure was Dr Charles Hill, who had become well known through his broadcasts as the 'radio doctor'. Hill and some of the younger recruits could have been at home in the Labour Party. Certainly Enoch Powell, who joined the Research Department at this time, was not one of these, but one cannot be so sure about Iain Macleod, Edward Heath, and some others.

Woolton got the Party to agree to put the constituency agency service on a more professional basis with great improvements in the standing and remuneration of agents. Certainly, under Woolton's guidance, the Conservatives were able to build up far better constituency organizations than Labour, an advantage they have retained throughout the post-war period. Woolton also played a major role in the building-up of the Young Conservatives. The YCs, as much a social as a political movement, probably did help to orientate young people towards the Conservatives in the 1950s. Another major initiative of Woolton's was his attempt to make party representation in the Commons more 'democratic'. Until the Woolton reform those able to pay the most towards the upkeep of the constituency they sought to represent were most likely to be selected as candidates, especially for the safe seats. This restricted the choice to about 'half a per cent of the population', Woolton claimed. If the Conservatives continued in this way, they deserved to be beaten.[84] The Party therefore agreed that 'In no circumstances shall the question of annual subscription be mentioned by any constituency selection committee to any candidate before he has been selected'. Candidates could, however, contribute up to £25 per annum to their constituency association, MPs up to £50. Though it was certainly a move in the right direction, it is doubtful whether this change has had quite the impact which was expected at the time.

It is even more doubtful whether it played any part in the Conservative revival. Few of the Conservative candidates who fought the 1950 election were chosen after the recommendations of the Maxwell-Fyfe Report, of which this was a part, came into effect. And, as Professor Hoffman has cautioned us, 'Comparison of the class-occupation backgrounds of successful candidates in 1945, 1950 and 1951, suggests that there was very little change in the type of Conservative candidates chosen to contest seats in which the Conservative Party stood the slightest chance of winning'.[85] There was also a tendency, as Maxwell-Fyfe admitted, to select 'obscure local citizens with obscure local interests, incapable – and indeed downright reluctant – to think on a national or international scale'.[86] Still, 'The effect of throwing all the financial burden upon the constituency was in every way salutary'.[87]

During this period the Conservative Party refurbished its policies, committing itself formally to the mixed economy and the welfare state. The focal point of this revised policy was the *Industrial Charter* announced by R. A. Butler in May 1947. An *Agricultural Charter* followed, as well as policy documents on Wales and Scotland, Imperial policy, and women. Butler, who had been given the task of recasting policy by Churchill, later wrote that his aim was to give the party 'a painless but permanent face-lift'.[88] If he did, it was more an operation to remove a few warts than cranial-facial surgery. Butler has himself admitted the Charter was ' "broad" rather than detailed, vague where it might have been specific', because Churchill did not want to be bound too much in opposition.[89] It was also, he admitted, written with 'flatness of language' and 'blandness of tone'.[90] It is doubtful whether it took the Conservatives very far along the road to electoral victory.

In the election of 1950 Labour seems to have been adversely affected by a number of factors which had nothing to do with the refurbishing of the Conservative Party. If in 1945 the electoral system was biased against the Conservatives, the reverse was true in 1950. Boundary revisions probably lost Labour between 25 and 30 seats.[91] The Conservatives were undoubtedly the main beneficiaries of the new postal-vote facility which probably gained them a further 10 seats.[92] On the other hand, the Conservatives lost several seats due to the abolition of university seats. On a higher poll than in 1945, Labour gained 13.2 million votes, the Conservatives 12.5 million, and the Liberals 2.6 million. Overall Labour was reduced to a majority of 6 seats. Labour had retained, even extended, its working-class support, but there had been a hardening of middle-class opposition to Labour. As one Conservative writer has explained,

If there is one conclusion that does emerge from the electoral statistics of 1950 it is the markedly bigger pro-Tory swing in the suburban areas . . . compared with the rest of the country. It is clear that long before 1950 there had grown up in that class a real detestation of the Labour government . . . these years can be seen in retrospect as a sort of twilight period between the era of cheap servants and the era of cheap washing machines. The effect of the disappearance of servants constituted a revolution in the middle class way of life far more drastic than anything that followed the First World War; and the effects were more acutely felt at this time than later when prosperity returned, labour-saving devices became the norm and people had recognised the need to adjust themselves to a change which, they now saw, would never be reversed. However illogically, this state of affairs greatly conduced to middle class disenchantment with Labour.[93]

Notes

1 In a letter to the author.
2 Lord Morrison, *Herbert Morrison: an Autobiography* (London, 1960), 250–1.
3 A. P. Herbert, *Independent Member* (London, 1950), 309.
4 ibid., 308. See also Vernon Bartlett, *And now Tomorrow* (London, 1960), 99. W. Wyatt, *Into the Dangerous World* (London, 1952), 104.
5 Of course the Labour ministers were briefly out of office in 1945 between the break-up of the coalition and the outcome of the general election.
6 John W. Wheeler-Bennett, *King George VI: his Life and Reign* (London, 1958), 653.
7 Emanuel Shinwell, *I've Lived Through It All* (London, 1973), 181.
8 Francis Williams, *Nothing so Strange: an Autobiography* (London, 1970), 219.
9 Rt. Hon. Josiah C. Wedgwood, *Memoirs of a Fighting Life* (London, 1941), 236.
10 Williams, op. cit., 219.
11 Kingsley Martin, ed., *A Volume of Autobiography* (London, 1968), 10.
12 Harold Macmillan, *Tides of Fortune 1945–1955* (London, 1969), 42.
13 ibid., 50.
14 Williams, op. cit., 222.
15 Michael Foot, *Aneurin Bevan 1945–60* (London, 1975), 26.
16 G. D. H. Cole, *World Socialism Restated* (London, 1956).
17 Williams, op. cit., 216.
18 Lord George-Brown, *In My Way* (London, 1971), 58. Williams, op. cit., 214
19 See Lord Wigg, *George Wigg* (London, 1972), 144. This view has been put to the author by several MPs who were in the 1945–51 Parliaments.
20 Wheeler-Bennett, op. cit., 652.
21 *Illustrated,* 23 August 1947: 'Private Life of No. 10'.
22 Harold Nicolson, *Diaries and Letters 1945–62,* ed. Nigel Nicolson (London, 1968), 31.
23 Macmillan, op. cit., 56; see also *The Memoirs of the Earl of Kilmuir* (London, 1964), 145.
24 Wigg, op. cit., 145, regarded Bevin as a megalomaniac. Foot, op. cit., 28.
25 Nicholas Davenport, *Memoirs of a City Radical* (London, 1974), 148.
26 Foot, op. cit., 34.
27 Macmillan, op. cit., 60–1. Williams, op. cit., 244. Foot, op. cit., 35.

28 Williams, op. cit., 225 claims he had 'intellectual coldness' and did not understand ordinary people.

29 Macmillan, op. cit., 66.

30 Lord Hill of Luton, *Both Sides of the Hill* (London, 1964), 75. For a less sympathetic Conservative view see Kilmuir, op. cit., 143–4.

31 B. Donoughue and G. W. Jones, *Herbert Morrison* (London, 1973), 392.

32 Macmillan, op. cit., 64, 67.

33 A. J. P. Taylor, *The Second World War: an Illustrated History* (London, 1975), 86.

34 Hugh Dalton, *High Tide and After: Memoirs 1945–1960* (London, 1962), 68. 'We had expected at least some tapering off of Lend-Lease over the first few years of peace. But now we faced, not war any more, only total economic ruin'.

35 ibid., 70.

36 Lord Halifax, the British Ambassador, officially led the negotiations. Apparently Britain was advised by the United States Secretary of State that Congress would be better disposed towards the loan if Britain made reassuring statements, to the Zionists, on Palestine. Cabinet Papers (CAB) 128/6/CM (46).

37 Dalton, Hansard, vol. 417, 425–6.

38 ibid., col. 424.

39 ibid., col. 468.

40 ibid., col. 469. In Cabinet Bevin and most of his colleagues were concerned about the effect on living standards if the loan was not agreed, Bevan was reluctant to accept it. CAB/4/CM(45).

41 Crane Brinton, *The United States and Britain* (Cambridge, Mass., 1948), 171.

42 Sidney Pollard, *The Development of the British Economy 1914–67* (London, 1969), 356–64 discusses the problem.

43 G. D. N. Worswick and P. H. Ady, *The British Economy 1945–50* (London, 1952), 32.

44 Rt. Hon. C. R. Attlee, MP, *The Labour Party in Perspective* (London, 1937), 152–3.

45 E. Eldon Barry, *Nationalisation in British Politics* (London, 1965), 352–6.

46 Wigg, op. cit., 125.

47 Hansard, vol. 418, col. 738.

48 W. Fienburgh and R. Evely, *Steel is Power. The Case for Nationalisation* (London, 1948), foreword by Morgan Phillips.

49 Quoted Sir Norman Chester, *The Nationalisation of British Industry 1945–51* (London, 1975), 39.

50 Quintin Hogg, *The Case for Conservatism* (London, 1947), 113.

51 Barry, op. cit., 85.

52 Hogg, op. cit., 112.

53 ibid., 286.

54 ibid., 111–12.

55 Hansard, vol. 430, col. 30.

56 Hansard, vol. 458, col. 153.

57 ibid., vol. 418, col. 752.

58 ibid., col. 787 (this was C. R. Hobson).

59 ibid., col. 752.

60 ibid., col. 1771.

61 The *Nottingham Journal,* 2 February 1947.

62 *Illustrated,* 25 January 1947.

63 The *Nottingham Journal,* 1 January 1947; the miner was Mr H. Turner of Annesley Pit.

64 Hansard, vol. 430, col. 398.
65 As advertised in *Illustrated,* 23 August 1947.
66 Hansard, vol. 422, col. 130.
67 Angus Calder, *The People's War: Britain 1939–45* (London, 1969), 531.
68 J. D. Hoffman, *The Conservative Party in Opposition 1945–51* (London, 1964), 46.
69 ibid., 235.
70 Arthur Marwick, *Britain in the Century of Total War* (London, 1968), 172.
71 Letter to the author.
72 Worswick and Ady, op. cit., 21.
73 Hansard, vol. 431. col. 479.
74 Marwick, op. cit., 357.
75 James B. Jeffreys, *The Story of the Engineers 1800–1945* (London, n.d.), 251.
76 Irving Richter, *Political Purpose in Trade Unions* (London, 1973), 246.
77 See review by William Gallacher in *Labour Monthly,* August 1946.
78 Hansard, vol. 447, col. 647–8.
79 These figures are actually taken from *All the Answers* (Conservative Research Department, 1949), 39.
80 Hansard, vol. 448, col. 1703.
81 *The Economist,* 23 September 1950, 502.
82 *British Labour Statistics Historical Abstract 1886–1968* (Department of Employment and Productivity, HMSO, 1971), 396, table 197.
83 Macmillan, op. cit., 292.
84 ibid., 294.
85 Hoffman, op. cit., 96–7.
86 Macmillan, op. cit., 296.
87 ibid.
88 Lord Butler, *The Art of the Possible. The Memoirs of Lord Butler* (London, 1971), 145–6.
89 ibid., 135.
90 ibid., 145.
91 H. G. Nicholas, *The British General Election of 1950* (London, 1951), 4.
92 ibid., 9.
93 Robert Blake, *The Conservative Party from Peel to Churchill* (London, 1970), 263–4.

3 Colonial Retreat and Cold War

Relinquishing India

In his chairman's address to Labour's forty-fifth annual conference at Bournemouth in 1946, Harold Laski praised Foreign Secretary Bevin for the 'unresting zeal he has brought to a very complicated task'; yet he went on to express doubts about most aspects of the Labour government's foreign policy. As the conference debate on foreign policy showed, Laski was voicing the unease, in some cases anger, felt by a sizeable group of Labour's rank-and-file over Bevin's handling of external affairs. The pursuit of a 'socialist' foreign and colonial policy was proving far more difficult than most in the Party had anticipated. However, all could agree with Laski that 'the decision to agree to the independence of India is certain to be a noble page in the archives of freedom'.[1]

It is difficult for anyone who has come to maturity since 1945 fully to appreciate what the Indian Empire meant for the great majority of the politically aware in Great Britain. What it meant for the majority of ordinary, not-so-political, people is another matter. They were probably ignorant and indifferent towards the Empire.[2] On the Left there were those who favoured immediate liberation, at least of India, and those who wanted a more gradual, ordered, withdrawal. On the Right, there were those who accepted that eventually self-government should and must come, and the diehards, who believed Britain was in India by the 'legitimate' right of purchase and conquest, and should remain there indefinitely because the Indians were incapable of ruling themselves.[3] Britain's whole defence strategy, up to the first years of this century, had been orientated towards India. And even in the 1930s Britain's military unpreparedness 'perhaps was also due to the old concentration on India and the Route to it'.[4] In the nineteenth century John Stuart Mill had described India as 'a vast system of outdoor relief for Britain's upper classes'.[5] It had provided vast wealth for a few Britons in earlier times, and in the twentieth century it went on providing a good living for the 1,000–2,000 British members of the Indian Civil Service, the 10,000 British officers of the Indian Army,

43

as well as the thousands of police officials, engineers, lawyers, port and rail officials, teachers, missionaries, traders, and so on.[6] Though in theory the British had always expected to relinquish India one day,[7] 'Undoubtedly it appeared to many ordinary English people – ... during the 1920s – that in a temporal as well as in a spatial sense the sun would not set on the British Empire in any conceivable future, for such people then accepted without question that in the nature of things an Englishman was superior to a man of any other race'.[8] But the 1914–18 War had brought changes in India's status and in the expectations of its rising politically conscious middle classes, and even nascent working class. Lord Chelmsford, the Viceroy, had announced in 1915 that if all went well, India's destiny was self-government.[9] The Government of India Act of 1919 was the beginning of a beginning in this direction. It failed, however, to satisfy the powerful Indian National Congress led by Mahatma Gandhi, 'a baffling combination of the saintly ascetic and the astute party leader'.[10] Ten years later, after much turbulence, MacDonald's Labour government called a round-table conference, representatives of both British and Indian opinion, to discuss India's future. So diverse were the opinions on both sides that 'For the next six years India remained a central, perhaps the central, issue in parliamentary life'[11] – and this at a time when so much needed to be done in Britain! Eventually the Government of India Act was passed in 1935, once again no one was satisfied. At Westminster, Labour felt it did not go far enough in speeding the process of Dominion status, while Churchill opposed it for giving up too much. More importantly, in India, it did not really satisfy Congress, the Muslims led by Jinnah, nor the Indian princes, then seen as a powerful political force. The Viceroy's new palace, designed by Sir Edwin Lutyens, and inaugurated in 1931, was perhaps regarded by many Indians as a visible sign that the British had no intention of an early retreat. Certainly disorder increased over the years. The Second World War brought new antagonisms.[12] India was committed to Britain's war without any consultation of Indian opinion. British defeats brought vague efforts to placate the Indian leaders. The first, following closely the fall of France, merely proposed the immediate enlargement of the Viceroy's council so as to include a certain number of representatives of Indian political parties. The next followed in 1942 after British defeats at the hands of the Japanese. Sir Stafford Cripps, a member of the War Cabinet, was sent to offer the Indians Dominion status, but deferred till victory had been won. Cripps failed because 'There was the certainty of delay and, for many, no corresponding assurance about victory'.[13] The Indian Congress then endorsed a 'Quit India' resolution which resulted in rebellion and led to the internment of the principal nationalist leaders for the rest of the war. Gandhi was, however, released as he was not expected to live.

Once in office Attlee lost no time in sending out a new mission to India to try to arrange 'the most complex divorce in history'.[14] Led by Lord Pethick-Lawrence, the Secretary of State for India, it included Cripps and A. V. Alexander, the First Lord of the Admiralty. Lawrence had first visited India in 1897 and had first met Gandhi before 1914. He had a further advantage in dealing with the Indians – he too had been imprisoned, as a conscientious objector in the 1914–18 War.[15] Apart from indicating the British government's willingness to vacate India, and putting Cripps in hospital for several weeks,[16] the mission accomplished little. Jinnah's Muslim League was determined to establish an independent Pakistan which ran counter to both the desires of Congress and the British. As the situation in India gradually worsened, Attlee called in Mountbatten, as Dalton put it, to 'wind up the show'. Admiral Lord Louis Mountbatten, who knew India through his war service, wrestled with Attlee for six weeks to get the precise brief he wanted for his mission.[17] What he got was a *carte blanche*, including a definite date for British withdrawal – not later than June 1948. The idea was, as Dalton recorded, that this was

the best chance of making the various Indians work together, while letting us out of a situation which was rapidly becoming quite untenable. If you are in a place where you are not wanted, and where you have not got the force, or perhaps the will, to squash those who don't want you, the only thing to do is to come out . . . I don't believe that one person in a hundred thousand in this country cares tuppence about it, so long as British people are not being mauled about out there.[18]

No doubt he was right. Mountbatten could not get the Muslim leaders to agree to a federated India with a weak central administration, and partition followed. Anticipating civil war,[19] Mountbatten speeded up the British withdrawal and on 13 February 1948 the last British soldiers left Indian soil, the transfer of power having taken place on 15 August 1947. Both India and the Jinnah-fathered state, Pakistan, joined the Commonwealth.

The significance of the Attlee government's decision to withdraw from India, Pakistan, Ceylon, and Burma – they gained their independence in 1948 – has long been debated at home and abroad. One widely held view, and one hears it not only in the Soviet bloc, is that Britain merely withdrew because the British Establishment knew there was no holding India. At the time, there were of course some who believed Britain could have held on.[20] And other colonial powers did foolishly hold on, as the French in Indo-China. Though too much must not be made of the friendly ties which linked some of the Labour leaders with the Congress leaders,

Attlee's own longstanding conviction that India must be freed no doubt played an important part. Finally, despite hesitations, detours, and hiccups along the way, independence was the culmination of a process which had started over a decade before Attlee took over. As it was,

Nobody before had ever given freedom in peace to four hundred million people, themselves the heirs to one of the world's greatest and most original civilizations. Nobody before had had so great a dependency reach freedom in such friendliness and keeping so many of the institutions the conqueror had brought.

However,

the British public and Government did not stop to consider what had happened to their position in the world. They were dazzled by the glory of India's freedom. They thought that the new Commonwealth would be the old Empire writ large. . . . The foundation of their power had altered, and they did not really notice.[21]

War in Palestine

That close and friendly ties between the Labour Party and an external movement were not necessarily a decisive consideration when Labour gained office was shown in the case of Palestine. Of all the controversies over external affairs Palestine was the one which caused the Attlee government the most bitter recriminations with its own supporters. It is the issue most frequently mentioned by Labour survivors of the period as having been mismanaged by their government. Alas, it remains of great present-day significance. For these reasons a little more space has been allocated to it.

As part of the doomed Turkish empire Palestine fell under British military occupation at the end of the First World War. The bulk of the inhabitants were Arabs. The Jews had lost their pre-eminence there with the final destruction of Jerusalem in A.D. 135. Britain's official interest in Palestine started with the Balfour Declaration of November 1917. It pledged the British government would use its 'best endeavours' to facilitate the establishment of a 'national home for the Jewish people'. It stressed, however, that 'nothing shall be done which may prejudice the civil and religious rights of existing non-Jewish communities in Palestine'. Finally, it stressed that the existing rights enjoyed by Jews in any other country would not be prejudiced by the establishment of a Jewish home in Palestine.[22] By 1923 the League of Nations had approved the Balfour Declaration and the British occupation. Throughout the inter-war period the Zionists[23] sought to realize the promise of the Declaration and eventually create a Jewish state. British policy, between the wars, was never entirely clear. HMG knew from the start that the

Palestinian Arabs opposed Jewish immigration, and they demonstrated that opposition in civil disorders throughout these years.[24] With a full-scale Arab revolt on its hands, and war approaching, the British government decided to impose a solution. This was set out in the White Paper of May 1939. It called for a two-stage, ten-year, transitional period, leading to independence. Jewish immigration would be allowed until the Jews became one-third of the population. After that it could only take place 'if the Arabs are prepared to acquiesce in it'.[25] In short, Palestine was to become a democratic state, with power-sharing between the Arab majority and the Jewish minority, and linked to Britain by treaty. In the Commons the majority of the Labour Party attacked the new policy, Herbert Morrison being joined by Winston Churchill, still out of office, in the onslaught on Malcolm MacDonald, the Secretary of State for the Colonies. MacDonald, the son of Ramsay, paid tribute to the Jewish settlers, 'they have turned the desert into spacious orange groves', but reminded his critics that the Arabs too had rights, they 'had been in undisturbed occupation of the country for countless generations'.[26]

In 1940 the annual conference of the Labour Party passed a resolution favourable to Zionism, but Labour's participation in government circumscribed the debate during the war years to some extent. Yet the NEC was frequently approached by Zionist bodies for help. In 1942, at its annual conference, the Party once again demanded, after the war, that 'international assistance shall be given to promote immigration and settlement in the Jewish National Home in Palestine'.[27] Within the government Churchill, by 1943, was thinking in terms of making the ex-Italian colonies of Eritrea and Tripolitania into Jewish colonies which might be affiliated to a Jewish national home. Dalton, also in the government, who had been given the job of defining Labour's policy on Palestine, shared Churchill's view. Happily, for the peace of the world, Churchill's idea was dropped. A Cabinet sub-committee chaired by Morrison decided the partition of Palestine would be the best solution.[28] Meanwhile Dalton had formulated his own solution. Slightly amended, it became Labour policy as agreed at the annual conference in December 1944. Earlier representations by the Palestine Arab Workers' Society appear to have been completely ignored.[29] As passed by the conference the resolution called for allowing Jews into

this tiny land in such numbers as to become a majority. There was a strong case for this before the war. There is an irresistible case now, after the unspeakable atrocities of the cold and calculated German Nazi plan to kill all the Jews in Europe.... Let the Arabs be encouraged to move out as the Jews move in. Let them be handsomely compensated for their land and let

47

their settlement elsewhere be carefully organised and generously financed. The Arabs have very wide territories of their own; they must not claim to exclude the Jews from this small part of Palestine, less than the size of Wales. Indeed, we should examine also the possibility of extending the boundaries by agreement with Egypt, Syria and Transjordan. Moreover, we should seek to win the full sympathy and support both of the American and Russian Governments for the execution of this Palestine policy.[30]

Thus encouraged, the Zionists looked forward to a Labour victory.

Before Attlee had had a chance to settle in at Downing Street he felt the pressure from Zionism's most powerful friend. At the end of August 1945 President Truman wrote to the Prime Minister asking that 100,000 Jewish displaced persons be immediately admitted to Palestine. Both because of the practical problems involved and because of the likely reaction of the Arabs, Attlee was not very enthusiastic. After discussions with both Zionist and Arab representatives Bevin announced on 13 November that an Anglo-American Commission of Inquiry would consider the Palestine question. Meanwhile in Palestine itself violence had broken out. Already in November 1944, Lord Moyne, British Minister-Resident in Cairo, had been murdered by Zionist extremists, an act condemned by Dr Chaim Weizmann, President of the World Zionist Organization, and most other Jewish leaders. Now the main Jewish fighting forces in Palestine were embarking on a campaign of rail sabotage and attacks on military installations. In the Arab lands demonstrations turned into riots as the fury against Zionism mounted on 2–3 November 1945. Nearer home Bevin faced criticism from the Board of Deputies of British Jews and, remarkably, on 19 November the Jewish Brigade of the British Army of the Rhine went on hunger strike in protest against Bevin's statement.[31]

The Anglo-American Committee published its report in May 1946. Predictably it satisfied neither side. Basically, it called for a continuation of the mandate regime 'until the hostility between Jews and Arabs disappears'. It recommended the admission of 100,000 Jewish victims of persecution, some easing of the restrictions on Jewish land-purchase, and the suppression of violence. It did, however, talk about 'ensuring that the rights and position of other sections of the population were not prejudiced'.[32] While the British government was considering the implications of the report, the British forces were subjected to renewed violence from the Zionists. On 1 July, Attlee announced with regret the arrest of some leading members of the Jewish Agency, the governing body of the Jewish community in Palestine. Attlee claimed that those arrested were connected with *Hagana*, the Jewish underground army, and that this body had been involved in violence, which it had. The Premier stressed that the security operations were not against the Jewish community as a whole. This assurance did not convince some Labour MPs and Sydney Silverman, a Jewish MP from Nelson and Colne, already known for his forthright views, moved the adjournment of the House to discuss 'a matter of urgent public business' – Palestine. Silverman gained the requisite number of forty MPs to support his motion and a debate was therefore granted. Silverman described the government's action as 'plain, naked war upon the Jewish National Home', and said that if the government were to declare publicly that it accepted the report of the Anglo-American Committee, violence would end. He was backed up by Mrs Ayrton Gould, who spoke as a Labour NEC member of sixteen years standing, Barnett Janner, President of the British Zionists, Konni Zilliacus, the ex-League of Nations official and a non-Jew, and Michael Foot, who pointed out that the accused 'are men we know well, men who have come to our Socialist conferences, and who are colleagues of ours'.[33] Richard Crossman, a member of the Committee, also joined in the criticism of the government. Attlee was not without his defenders on the government benches. Morgan Philips-Price, who had supported the 1939 White Paper, argued that

The Government must . . . resist this wave of terrorism and approach the whole problem on a much broader basis, and not force on the Arabs responsibility for taking a large number of immigrants from Central Europe, but to make other countries responsible, this country and America to play their part.[34]

Even in a world used to violence the blowing-up of the King David Hotel on 22 July 1946 caused genuine shock and anger. The hotel, the biggest in Jerusalem, housed the British military HQ, but it still carried on the civilian functions for which it was built as well. The explosion, which was the work of the Jewish terrorist group Irgun Zvi Leumi, claimed about a hundred deaths. A number of leading British officials were among the dead, and there were also a number of Arab and Jewish victims.[35] Once again the deed was widely condemned by the Jewish Palestinian press and by Jewish leaders, but it could do nothing but worsen relations between the Jews and the security forces. Two days later the Colonial Office issued a White Paper containing evidence which led the government to conclude that acts of violence were committed with the knowledge of leading members of the Jewish Agency and that *Hagana* was working under their control. There was of course no evidence about the David explosion. Inevitably with such violence the forces of the Crown were compelled to step up their anti-terrorist campaign. During the next 23 or so months there followed what one Jewish writer called a 'deadly round-dance of terror raids, assassinations and blind reprisals'.[36]

As a way out of the worsening situation the government put forward the 'Morrison plan' on 31 July 1946. This was a federal plan devised by Anglo-U.S. experts for dividing Palestine into two main autonomous provinces, Arab and Jewish, broadly managing their own affairs, including immigration. But, as Dalton put it, 'the Plan was criticized in detail from many sides, and President Truman was slow to declare himself. Here then, unhappily, after twelve months in office, we halted'.[37] Speaking on 1 August 1946 Churchill urged that if the United States was not prepared to share the burden of the Zionist cause with Britain, the United Kingdom should give notice it would return the mandate to the United Nations and evacuate Palestine. On 14 February 1947 Bevin announced that Britain would submit the problem to the United Nations after both parties had rejected a new federal plan under which 96,000 Jewish immigrants would have been admitted over two years, subsequent immigration being controlled by the High Commissioner after consulting both Jews and Arabs.[38] A special U.N. committee of small and medium states then investigated the problem and on 31 August 1947 issued a minority report, which roughly corresponded to the Anglo-U.S. federal plan, and a majority plan, which called for partition. This majority scheme called for Britain to go on administering Palestine for two years. During this period 150,000 Jews were to be admitted. The weakness of the plan, from the Arab point of view, apart from the fundamental question of the setting-up of a Jewish state, was that it put 500,000 Arabs within the Jewish area. It also deprived them of their only port, Jaffa, and they had no prospect of compensation for their losses. Recognition of the two states was to be dependent on their guaranteeing fundamental liberties and signing a treaty of economic union with each other. This would have soon put the Arabs under the economic domination of the Jews. On 26 September 1947 the Colonial Secretary made it clear that Britain would not feel able to implement a policy not acceptable to Jews and Arabs alike. Early British withdrawal must therefore be planned. The general assembly of the United Nations endorsed the partition plan by a vote of 33 to 13 with 10 abstentions on 29 November. The majority included the United States and the Soviet Union. The Islamic states and India, Cuba and Greece, voted against. Britain, China, Mexico, and Yugoslavia were among those abstaining. The vote was, at least in part, the result of pressure by the United States on its clients.[39]

Throughout this period Palestine suffered from mounting violence, except, that is, for the brief interval of the 22nd World Zionist Congress (December/January 1946–47). There were several angry confrontations between Labour backbenchers and their leaders. Harold Lever, Jewish MP for Manchester Exchange and future Cabinet minister, declared on 12 August 1947, in an impassioned speech, that government policy represented 'two years of planless, gutless and witless behaviour'. He described British rule as 'this military dictatorship . . . this police State, this State of the flogging block and the gallows'.[40] This view was challenged by, among others, Tufton Beamish the Conservative, who had served as a regular in pre-war Palestine. In 1938 and 1939 a total of 109 Arabs had, after being sentenced by the British, 'paid the extreme penalty'. In 1939, 5,700 Arabs were in detention. Arab casualties had been as 'high as 4,000' in these years.

But yet the terrorist activities of the Arabs in those years were never on such a large scale as are the Jewish activities today. These figures provide an extraordinary contrast with the total of only seven Jews who have paid the extreme penalty for their terrorist activities during the last 18 months. I feel that we are entitled to know the reason for this contrast.[41]

When the Commons had discussed the bombing of the King David Hotel, the Labour MP for Wednesbury, Stanley Evans, had warned that 'We have to warn those who failed to cooperate in apprehending murderers that events in the King David Hotel have their repercussions at King's Cross'.[42] Happily, that outrage did not lead to any 'reprisals' in King's Cross. But a year later popular indignation at terrorist activities did boil over. The incident which provoked the storm was particularly unpleasant.

As a reprisal for the execution of three Jewish terrorists two British sergeants were kidnapped and then hanged in a eucalyptus grove on 29 July 1947. One of the bodies was booby-trapped. In Britain during the weekend of 1–2 August and on subsequent days, there were outbreaks of unorganized rioting in Liverpool and Manchester. Incidents, mainly the smashing of the windows of shops owned by Jews, occurred in different parts of London and Glasgow, Cardiff, Halifax, Eccles, and some other places.[43] Although very worrying at the time, this tide of spontaneous violence disappeared almost as suddenly as it had come.

The biggest, and final, revolt of Labour MPs against their government's Palestine policy took place in March 1948. This was over the Palestine Bill which sought to tie up the loose ends of the British withdrawal. The debate on the Second Reading gave the government's critics a chance to have a final go on the issue. The government was accused of running away, of not fulfilling its electoral pledges, of frustrating the work of the United Nations and condoning Arab threats of violence. The government refused to allow the importation of arms by the Jews and refused to give any fresh commitments on Palestine which the British public would not tolerate. One Labour loyalist, Tom Reid from Swindon, a member of the earlier Palestine Partition Commission, summed up the situation as follows:

If this decision of the Assembly is accepted by the Security Council, and the United Nations try to enforce it, I predict . . . that we shall then have war which will last 10, 20 or 50 years. The Arabs will not submit so long as their sovereignty is to be taken away from them . . . What I suggest should be done now . . . is to give independence to a Palestinian State. We promised the Jews a national home and that has been set up; we promised the Arabs independence in Palestine and the Mandate envisaged independence after a period of trusteeship. That is the solution which I recommend to the United Nations organisation, and until that solution is accepted and adopted by U.N.O. there is no chance of a settlement.[44]

The House was then divided by the Labour rebels who were defeated by 242 to 32 (including the tellers). Among the rebels were Sydney and Julius Silverman, Harold Lever, Barnett Janner, Maurice Edelman, Ian Mikardo, Benn Levy, and some other Jewish MPs. Other Jewish MPs supported the government. The rebels were joined by some who were becoming well-known for their opposition to government foreign policy – John Platts-Mills, D. N. Pritt, a pro-Communist Labour independent, William Warbey, and the irrepressible Konni Zilliacus. The Jewish Communist MP Phil Piratin also voted with the rebels. The relatively small vote for the rebel motion did not, of course, tell the whole story. It did not reflect how a considerable number of Labour MPs felt. On the government front bench too there were those who had their doubts – Bevan, Creech Jones, Dalton, Shinwell, Strachey, George Strauss, and Tom Williams among them.[45] The vote was the miserable end to a sad episode.

This sad episode had cost the lives of 338 British subjects since 1945 and the taxpayer had been forced to find £100 million to finance it. Over 80,000 British troops, one-tenth of the total at that time, had been used to police the territory.

The Labour leaders had found themselves in a dilemma, torn between the need for British friendship with the Arabs and their own friendship with the Jews. Attlee himself probably had strong reservations about Labour's pro-Zionist stance before 1945, but had sought, by silence, to avoid a clash with such powerful pro-Zionist colleagues as Dalton and Morrison. For many non-Jewish Labour intellectuals the Jews were a special breed who had made a massive contribution to humanity. They were the victims of the hated Tsar and the detested *Führer*. Moreover, the Jews were often comrades. The Labour government, by 'betraying' the Jews, was betraying itself, probably as a result of 'advice' of reactionary Foreign Office officials.[46] It was a process which had started with

Greece in 1944 (see below), about which the leaders had done nothing. As for the Arabs, British socialists of this type regarded them as the hoodwinked dupes of reactionary rulers in a similar position to British working-class Tories. They were the reserve army of reaction and it was no wonder they found supporters on the Opposition benches. The Jews were the apostles of the new, the modern, of 'progress', and, therefore, as Dalton put it, 'we should lean . . . towards the dynamic Jew, less towards the static Arab'.[47]

The weakness of the pro-Zionist position was precisely that it either treated the Arabs with contempt or simply ignored them. The weakness of the pro-Arabs was that they did not recognize that a new nation had grown up in the womb of the mandate territory. And because of its pride and its experience this nation was not prepared to put its security in the hands of its traditionalist neighbours with vastly different standards from its own.

Colonies: guided progress

During the war the Labour Party had promised the colonies that, should Labour take office, they would experience, '. . . a period of unprecedented development and progress under the guidance of the Mother Country . . . If money is needed for these purposes it should be laid out prudently, but in no niggling spirit'.[48] Once in office, the responsible ministers were to find the situation far more complicated than they had anticipated. The financial resources to make this 'unprecedented development' possible were not available. Secondly, difficult choices had to be made. Should limited funds be channelled into the colonies according to the needs of the inhabitants, or should they go into those colonies where they were most likely to bring a return for Britain in terms of higher living standards and dollar exports? As it was, 'Decision-making on colonial economic policy suffered, as always, from constraints imposed by the Treasury, which had to honour commitments to the U.S.A. and to Britain's Commonwealth partners'.[49] This need to stimulate exports from the colonies certainly influenced government thinking on nationalization of Tate and Lyle sugar interests in Jamaica and United Africa Company mining interests in Rhodesia, 'it appeared wiser not to disturb entrepreneurs British or American'.[50] Nevertheless, British money did get to the colonies. The 1945 Colonial Development and Welfare Act provided some of the means – £125 million to be spent over ten years. In addition, two new corporations were established to develop agricultural and other projects: the Colonial Development Corporation with borrowing powers of £100 million and the Overseas Food Corporation with initial borrowing powers of £50 million. Further

Colonial Development Acts were passed in 1949 and 1950 to increase the funds available. Not all of this money was well spent. Over £30 million were wasted on the Tanganyika groundnuts scheme. The scheme, which originated with the United Africa Company, a subsidiary of Unilever, was based on inadequate analysis of soil and rainfall. John Strachey, Minister of Food, who was ultimately responsible, was mercilessly attacked by the press and the Opposition. But as Strachey's biographer, Hugh Thomas, has reminded us, the loss 'of public money on a scheme which attempted to alleviate the world food shortage is admittedly less of a catastrophe than the loss of many more millions on military projects or upon expensive aircraft such as has occurred since that time'.[51]

Labour's colonial experts had put economic development ahead of political progress in their priorities. Economic advance would lead the way to greater political maturity in the future. As it turned out, they underestimated the development of political consciousness among the Africans. Serious disturbances took place in the Gold Coast (Ghana) in 1948. There was discontent among cocoa-farmers over the low price they received for their products, and among ex-servicemen over poor pensions. When the police fired on a peaceful ex-servicemen's demonstration, riots broke out. After two commissions of inquiry a new constitution was introduced in 1950, 'a system well on the way to responsible government'.[52] Elections under the new constitution were won by Kwame Nkrumah's Convention People's Party, Nkrumah graduating from jail to become Prime Minister in 1952.

There was also a good deal of political activity in these years in central Africa – Northern Rhodesia (Zambia), Southern Rhodesia, and Nyasaland (Malawi). The war had brought about the awakening of African political consciousness in these territories as in the Gold Coast and elsewhere. African National Congresses were formed in Nyasaland in 1943 and in Northern Rhodesia in 1948. With the help of British trade unionists the Northern Rhodesian African Mineworkers' Union was set up in the same year. These developments were seen as a threat, as indeed they were, to white supremacy in both Northern and Southern Rhodesia. Most of the white political leaders now sought to retain their supremacy by means of a Central African Federation, a project about which many had had doubts in the past. With the victory of the Afrikaner nationalists in South Africa in 1948, the English-speaking white felt that federation was the only alternative to either eventual domination by the blacks or by the South Africans. To the black Africans, their freedom seemed to depend on maintaining Colonial Office control until they were ready to govern themselves. They saw federation as exchanging control by London for control by the settlers. If the three territories were united, it would be Southern Rhodesia that would play the most influential role. There were nearly two and a half times as many white settlers in Southern Rhodesia as in the other two areas put together. The blacks feared that the racial policies pursued in Southern Rhodesia since it got self-government in 1923, would be extended to the other two territories. Creech Jones believed this too, and during his term of office, to 1950, he played his part in resisting settler pressure.[53]

Another area which caused the Labour government much concern was Malaya. Malaya was important for tin, and, above all, for its rubber, an important dollar-earner. Singapore, at its southern tip, was regarded as a vital naval base. But Malaya had problems. It was a racial melting-pot. Less than half its population were Malay. The Chinese, who dominated the commercial life of the country, actually outnumbered the Malays in 1947. In addition, there were considerable numbers from India and Pakistan, as well as Indonesians and Aborigines.[54] Malaya had been ruled by the British indirectly through the native rulers, the sultans, and this arrangement had seemed to work up to the Japanese invasion of 1942. The occupation which followed greatly influenced Malaya. The native peoples saw the defeat of the British and realized they were not omnipotent. The Japanese military government encouraged, to a limited extent, Malay nationalism, discriminating against the Chinese. The British promoted resistance and the Malayan People's Anti-Japanese Army was established with their help. It was a mainly Chinese, Communist-influenced, force. After the war the British disbanded it, but not before it had settled some old scores against some, mainly Malays, suspected of collaboration with the Japanese. In general there was a feeling that there could be no simple going back to the old scheme of things.[55] The new Labour government recognized this and introduced a constitution designed to reduce the sultans to constitutional figureheads, give Malay citizenship to most inhabitants irrespective of racial origin, and prepare the way for eventual self-government. This radical change met with stiff opposition from influential Malays and their allies in London. Malay nationalism was aroused against the Chinese and Indians, and the British felt forced to back down. The new Federation of Malaya agreement of 1946 restricted citizenship and restored at least some of the privileges of the sultans. At the head of the government system was a British High Commissioner, Sir Edward Gent, responsible to the Colonial Office in London. The reversal of policy provoked unrest among the Chinese and this, and the high price of rice, led to civil disturbances. In 1948 armed struggle replaced civil disturbance as the Malayan Communist Party attempted to exploit genuine grievances. Probably started as part of

Moscow's strategy of militancy introduced world-wide at this time, the guerrilla war which followed tied up considerable numbers of British and native troops and police between 1948 and 1960.[56] Malaya was, of course, ideal guerrilla country, but the rebels lacked a safe cross-border sanctuary so vital in such campaigns. The British found themselves trapped in an 'anti-insurgency' campaign similar, in some respects, to their earlier campaigns in South Africa, Ireland, and Palestine. This involved collective punishments, the forced resettlement of 600,000 Chinese peasants, and abandonment of the normal democratic norms. Both Labour and Conservative governments followed a policy of 'ruthlessness where ruthlessness is necessary' coupled with 'equal firmness and vigour in pressing on with the economic and political development of the country'.[57] In the end, the defeat of the insurgents was probably due more to political developments than to military action. First, the rebellion was largely confined to the Chinese community, a fact which set severe limits on its success.[58] Secondly, most of the fighting was over by 1955. This was a period when both the Soviet and Chinese leaders were seeking *détente*, and had therefore ceased supporting armed insurrection. Thirdly, in Malaya itself constitutional advance had led to the election of the Triple Alliance Party of Tunku Abdul Rahman, a party uniting Malays with Chinese and Indians. A Malay of royal descent, Tunku Abdul Rahman, became Chief Minister, and then Prime Minister of an independent Malaysia in 1957. The Tunku pursued a policy of peace by negotiation, amnesty, and reconciliation towards the rebels. The emergency was formally ended in 1960.

Cold War in Europe

As mentioned above, by June 1946, less than a year after Labour's assumption of office, there was open criticism at the annual conference of Bevin's handling of external affairs. Virtually all the speakers from the floor made some criticism of Bevin. There seemed to be a widespread feeling that Bevin was being blinded by reactionary Foreign Office officials. As William Warbey, MP for Luton, put it,

We have men abroad . . . who are fundamentally anti-Socialist, and who do not disguise it . . . They have to assess political information. They have to form a political judgment . . . If they are drawn from a narrow social circle, a circle that was defeated politically last July, their views must be influenced by that class outlook. Except for very rare exceptions that must be so . . . I am sure that the Foreign Secretary wants to help the growing force of the popular movement in Europe and the world. I know he does. Then let him choose the right tools and get on with the job.[59]

What greatly troubled the Labour delegates, and rightly so, was that British troops had been used to 'restore order' in the European colonies lately under Japanese occupation. This meant suppressing, where necessary, the native resistance movements and restoring Dutch and French colonial administrations. Of course, the situation was far more complicated than Warbey, Zilliacus, and others appeared to think. The French government was a coalition including socialists and communists. And both the French and Dutch governments claimed to be offering a new deal to their colonies, but in the French case this was at best 'enlightened paternalism'.[60] Bevin's 'Conservative' policy in these areas seemed to tie in with his apparent continuation of the previous Conservative policy in Palestine. His failure to stem the growing breach with the Soviet Union, and this caused the delegates the most concern, was believed to result as much from Foreign Office advice, as from any fault on the part of Stalin. Bevin's critics did not understand that Stalin was indifferent to the liberation movements of Asia. In the most important case, China, Stalin had signed a treaty with Chiang Kai-shek in 1945 and did not help the Communists in their struggle with the Nationalists.[61] Though Soviet ideology caused suspicion in the West, the origins of the Cold War were rooted far more in great power rivalry, in an inability to agree on the spoils of the Second World War, than in disputes about Communism or Capitalism. In 1945 the world desperately needed statesmen of vision. What it got was a little-travelled Georgian dictator whose only foreign language was Russian, an American President new to the world stage, and Ernest Bevin, a man already suffering from a terminal illness which forced him from office in 1950. All three thought in terms of their respective 'empires' and their needs. All three were influenced by their countries' experience of pre-war appeasement, and the determination not to be caught off-guard a second time.

In the latter stages of the war the Western powers watched resignedly as Stalin regained most of the outer provinces of the old Tsarist empire, especially in the Baltic states and Poland. Pressure on neutral Turkey in March 1945 to cede the provinces of Kars and Ardahan, taken by Russia in 1878 and retaken by Turkey in 1918, failed, pushing Turkey into the arms of the United States. Pursuit of old Tsarist aims in northern Iran, taken under Soviet military occupation, also helped lead that country into dependence on the United States. Between the end of 1944 and 1947, Britain and the United States fought a weak, diplomatic rearguard action' in Bulgaria, Hungary, and Rumania. They protested as these ex-enemy states were reduced, step by step, to the level of Soviet satellites.[62] They were equally helpless when Poland suffered the same fate. Yugoslavia and Albania too appeared to have allowed themselves to be reduced to the level of Soviet dependencies. Here appearances proved to be deceptive. Apart from certain undercover operations in Albania, only in Greece did Britain, and later America, actively intervene in eastern Europe. The struggle in Greece appears as a turning-point in the Cold War. Greece was a traditional British sphere of interest. Since the end of 1944 Britain had been involved in helping the royalist exile government of Greece prevent the Communist-led, anti-Axis, resistance movement from taking over the country. On 21 February 1947 Britain informed the United States that it was withdrawing financial aid to Greece in five weeks time. It asked the United States to assume the burden of supporting Greece. Truman responded to the British call, introducing the 'Truman Doctrine', involving initially support for Greece and Turkey, and ultimately leading to the Marshall Plan and NATO. If the United States had really been contemplating renewed isolation before February 1947, after that date it became deeply engaged in European affairs once again.[63]

The British withdrawal from Greece was dictated as much by financial as by other considerations, and finance played a major role in shaping British policy in Germany.

Before the surrender of Germany the allies had agreed on the division of the country into four zones of occupation – Russian, American, British, and French – and on the division of Berlin into four sectors. Germany was to be ruled, for the time being, by a four-power Control Council in Berlin. The allies also agreed on the need to eliminate all vestiges of Nazism and militarism, and on the need to give the German people a democratic future. The allies differed to some extent in their views of Germany's frontiers, in their judgement of what Germany should pay in reparations, and in their interpretation of the term democracy. At Potsdam, in July 1945, Britain, the Soviet Union, and the United States, agreed further on treating Germany as an economic whole, that the Germans should have living standards 'not exceeding the average . . . of Europe' (excluding the United Kingdom and the Soviet Union), and that payment of reparations should leave enough resources to enable the Germans to subsist without external assistance. The three powers did not bind themselves to an exact figure on reparations, nor did they reach final agreement on Germany's eastern frontier, which they left for a future peace settlement.

In practice all pursued policies in their respective zones based on their own economic needs, their experience of the Germans, and their own political traditions. The British left many of the old officials, tainted in varying degrees with Nazism, in their posts because, it was thought, their professional experience was vital for the rapid rehabilitation of the administrative machine.[64] At first, the British and Americans, who had co-operated so closely in the war, went their separate ways.[65] Both soon regretted this. Britain had 'gained' an area which was largely industrial and needed foodstuffs from elsewhere. These were not forthcoming and the British people had to tighten their belts just a little more to feed *their* Germans. Clearly this could not go on for long, and Britain welcomed the American proposal, made in July 1946, to merge the economies of the occupation zones. The French and Russians rejected this proposal. By September 1946 it was clear that the United States was taking a much more positive view of how Germany should be treated than hitherto. Secretary of State James F. Byrnes, in a speech at Frankfurt, recognized that European recovery would be that much slower if Germany was 'turned into a poorhouse'. This mirrored the greater realism which was entering into American thinking and the growing belief that Germany could soon be needed as an American ally against the Soviet Union.

Welcome though Anglo-U.S. co-operation was from the standpoint of Britain's precarious finances, it did carry with it one important penalty. In all important respects Britain had to defer to the United States on Germany. One key example of this was the fate of the basic industries in the British zone. In 1946 Ernest Bevin stated the government's position in the Commons:

. . . We have to consider the ownership of the German basic industries. These industries were previously in the hands of magnates who were closely allied to the German military machine, who financed Hitler, and who, in two wars, were part and parcel of Germany's aggressive policy. We have no desire to see those gentlemen or their like return to a position which they abused with such tragic results. As an interim measure, we have taken the possession and the control of the coal and steel industries, and vested them in the C-in-C. We shall shortly take similar action in the case of the heavy chemical industry and the mechanical engineering industry. Our intention is that these industries should be owned and controlled in future by the public.[66]

Bevin's view coincided with that of the German Social Democrats, the left wing of the Christian Democrats, and the Communists. Even though such socialization measures were approved by democratically elected regional parliaments, and by referenda, they were blocked by the United States, because of that country's opposition to socialism.[67]

The Russians in their zone pursued contradictory policies. The excesses of Soviet troops in the early days of the occupation, and Soviet territorial ambitions, greatly weakened the appeal of communism in Germany. Soviet reparations policy had the same effect. Yet at the same time the Russians proclaimed their support for

German anti-Nazis, and talked in terms of a united, democratic Germany deciding its own future.[68] On the whole, the Soviet Union's need for massive reparations determined most of its policies most of the time. Thus it played a decisive part in destroying the Communist movement in Germany, and probably in ending the possibility of any type of socialism in that country. Whether massive U.S. economic assistance for the Soviet Union in 1945–46 could have gained Finnish-style freedom for eastern Europe and the Soviet zone of Germany is open to speculation. Unfortunately American generosity was stirred only by war and cold war. As it was, the Russians took massive reparations from their zone and demanded more from the western zones, including a say in the running of the Ruhr industry. This the British and Americans were not prepared to concede. The conference of the four Foreign Ministers in Moscow in March 1947 ended in failure. Pro-Soviet Communist parties in western Europe implemented a new policy of militancy, at a time when the economies of their countries were facing extreme difficulties resulting from a severe winter and a severe shortage of dollars. It was in these circumstances that the U.S. Secretary of State, George Marshall, made his offer in June 1947 that if the countries of Europe could agree on a combined plan for recovery, the American government would finance it. Britain, France, and the other states of western Europe accepted. The Russians and their clients turned it down. It is doubtful whether the Americans expected them to accept, but the Soviet rejection was a blunder. Their cause would have been better served by subjecting the American proposal to closer scrutiny and perhaps forcing the Americans to reject them. In September 1947 the Russians set up the Communist Information Bureau (Cominform) consisting of the East European Communist Parties together with those of France and Italy. This was probably in part a reaction to growing Western co-operation.[69] A further conference of the British, U.S., French, and Soviet Foreign Ministers held in London in November 1947 ended in deadlock. The French now agreed to allow their zone to be integrated into Bizonia, as the Anglo-U.S. zones were known. The Russians stepped up their control of eastern Europe, the most dramatic event of which was the Communist *coup* in Czechoslovakia in February 1948. Czechoslovakia had been seen as a test case for the ability of Communist and non-Communist, East and West, to live and work together. The West's next move was the signing of the Brussels Pact on 17 March. This united Britain, France, Belgium, the Netherlands, and Luxembourg for defensive purposes. It was designed by Bevin as the forerunner of NATO at a time when West European morale was low, and some responsible politicians even thought 'the Russians would be in Paris by August, an opinion in which the French Chief of Staff concurred'.[70] Allied moves to carry through their West German currency reform in West Berlin led to the Russians withdrawing from the Control Council and blockading the three Western sectors of the city. Cut off from the West by land, West Berlin was, rather miraculously, supplied by air. As part of the Western response to the Berlin crisis two groups of American B29 bombers, with atomic bombs, were dispatched to Britain in July 1948. Czechoslovakia, Berlin, and other Soviet moves[71] made the setting-up of NATO in April 1949 a virtual certainty. Early in May 1949 the Russians called off the blockade, having achieved nothing. In the same year the two German states were called into existence.

As we have seen, Britain took a leading part in the creation of a West European defence community, and in the setting-up of the OEEC, yet it hung back from a future in a united Europe. Attlee was on record, as Leader of the Opposition, in 1939, as saying that Europe must federate or perish. Bevin, Bevan, and other members of the government had expressed similar sentiments. However, post-war Europe appeared less attractive in reality than it had in wartime dreams. Undoubtedly this was due to the fact that the European states, especially Germany, France, and Italy, did not appear to add up to much before the mid-1950s. And Europe's apparent demise enhanced Britain's status and sense of its own importance. The British Empire appeared to have much life in it, and in any case, it could be transformed into a Commonwealth in which Britain would be assured the leading role. In Labour's ranks too there were those who feared that a united western Europe would be capitalist, clerical, and reactionary, especially as Christian Democracy gained the ascendancy in Italy, West Germany, Belgium, and even France. Further, British ministers argued that only 25 per cent of Britain's trade was with Europe, the other 75 per cent was extra-European. Britain helped to found the Council of Europe in May 1949, thus paying lip-service to a united Europe. But Bevin made sure it was harmless with 'splendidly vague' aims 'to achieve a greater unity between its members for the purpose of safeguarding and realising the ideals and principles which are their common heritage, and facilitating their economic and social progress'. Nor did Britain join the European Coal and Steel Community, the forerunner of the EEC, set up on French initiative in 1951. This marked the beginning of the split between Britain and the Six which proved so difficult to heal.

Another reason for Britain's sense of superiority during those years was its application to join the nuclear club. The decision to develop the bomb was taken in 1946 by the Defence Committee of the Cabinet. Attlee had been influenced by the Advisory Committee on Atomic Energy chaired by Sir John Anderson, who had occupied this position under Churchill. Attlee went ahead despite American refusal to provide Britain with the detailed technical know-how. There appears to have been little discussion before the decision was taken, and little questioning of it afterwards. It must be remembered that at the time the United States was not yet committed to European defence, and given Britain's scientific experience of the wartime nuclear project, the temptation to develop the bomb must have been strong. Yet by the time Britain had tested a nuclear device (1952) its defence was based on the nuclear umbrella of the United States. Nor did Britain possess an effective delivery system. Moreover, Britain's bomb was partly designed to wipe out the numerical advantage of Soviet land forces at a time when the Soviet Union did not yet have a nuclear capacity. By 1949, to the surprise of Western experts, the Soviet Union had successfully tested its first bomb. Finally, the cost to Britain must have been tremendous at a time when the nation faced continuing economic difficulties.[72]

Korea and Iran

With the outbreak of the Korean War the Cold War looked as if it were turning into the real thing. Briefly, Japan had controlled the destiny of Korea between 1895 and 1945. Soviet and U.S. troops occupied it in 1945. Both powers set up regimes to their own liking in North and South Korea respectively. In June 1950 North Korean troops crossed the demarcation line into the South. At the time the invasion was seen as part of the Communist global strategy of aggression. Today this interpretation is widely rejected.[73] Dismayed by the Communist takeover in China in 1949, the Americans felt they must act. The United States committed large military forces to the defence of South Korea and got the United Nations to condemn the aggression and authorize counter-action. The war appeared to be almost over as U.S.–U.N. troops rolled back the Communists virtually to Manchuria. The U.N. forces were then taken completely by surprise when Chinese ground units entered the war on 20 October 1950. After initially driving the U.N. forces back, they were held on roughly the original demarcation line along the 38th Parallel. Armistice negotiations began on 10 July 1951. An armistice was signed and a cease-fire came into effect on 27 July 1953. The war involved the loss of 686 British lives, 2,498 British service personnel being wounded. The United States forces lost 33,629 killed and 105,785 wounded.[74]

British support for American action in Korea was 'instantaneous and unqualified'.[75] Early in September British troops were in action there. But despite British support for the Americans, there was also a great deal of anxiety lest General MacArthur, the American

C-in-C, should extend the conflict to China or that America should use the atom bomb on China, provoking a third world war – Mao's China and Stalin's Russia had, by this time, concluded a formal alliance. It was in these circumstances that Attlee flew to Washington in December to seek assurances from President Truman. It appears that Truman had not contemplated using the atom bomb.[76] He did allay Attlee's fears and later relieved MacArthur of his command.

The Korean conflict had important effects on the British economy and on the British political scene. Immediately increased American purchases of Australian wool and Malayan tin and rubber greatly improved the position of the sterling area, leading to suspension of further Marshall Aid to Britain from the end of 1950. Later in 1950 Britain, and other European states, experienced severe balance of payments difficulties as the cost of the raw materials they had to import increased more rapidly than the value of their exports. The massive rearmament programme embarked upon under U.S. pressure[77] greatly handicapped British export industries in competition with those of West Germany, which were not engaged in arms production. Britain was spending a higher percentage of its national income on defence than any of its European NATO allies and as a fraction of national income its defence expenditure was not very much below the U.S. figure.[78] It had doubled its pre-Korea level of defence spending. The government openly admitted that the additional rearmament would lead to a reduction in the standard of living. The increase in the period of conscription from 18 months to two years was also unpopular with many of the government's own supporters. Differences over the pace of rearmament brought about a serious split in the government ranks which made its downfall more inevitable. On 23 April 1951, it was announced that Aneurin Bevan and Harold Wilson, President of the Board of Trade, had resigned from the government. The following day, John Freeman, Parliamentary Secretary to the Minister of Supply, had joined them. A number of Bevan's colleagues have claimed that he resigned because he was a disappointed man. Hugh Gaitskell had replaced Cripps as Chancellor on 17 January, Bevan became Minister of Labour at the same time. On 9 March, Morrison replaced Bevin at the Foreign Office. Bevan felt he had been unjustly passed over. Be that as it may, the fact is that Bevan, whilst in no way rejecting the need for adequate armaments, took a different view of Britain's ability to cope with the actual scale of rearmament proposed. More fundamentally, he took a different view of the Communist challenge. He saw it more as an ideological challenge born of evil social and economic conditions. He feared the Western democracies would weaken themselves to such a point as to provide fertile ground for the growth of communism. He also felt that the Soviet Union was too weak economically to be contemplating military aggression. The decision to introduce National Health charges to help pay for rearmament was just the last straw for Bevan rather than merely a pretext for resignation. What Labour's constituency activists thought of Bevan's action was indicated at the Labour Party conference in October. Bevan topped the list in the election for the constituency section of the NEC. Emanuel Shinwell, identified as an anti-Bevanite, lost his seat after 15 years, and was replaced by Barbara Castle, one of Bevan's supporters.

Before it fell from office the Labour government faced new problems in the Middle East, especially in Egypt and Iran. As the problem with Egypt came to a head after the change of government in Britain, it is best left to the chapter which follows.

Iran decided unilaterally to cancel its 1933 agreement with the Anglo-Iranian Oil Company (AIOC) and nationalize it. Founded in 1909, the company was British owned and operated. In 1914 the British government had obtained a controlling interest. Up to 1933 Iran had received 33 per cent of the profits; from that date it got a better share, but Britain still took the lion's share. Moreover, Britain regarded most of Iran as being in its sphere of influence and treated it accordingly. Reza Shah, dictator throughout the inter-war period, was initially installed by the British. When he showed signs of independence and wished to keep his country out of the war, he was forced to abdicate after an Anglo-Soviet invasion in July 1941. His son succeeded him. In their Tehran Declaration of December 1943, Churchill, Roosevelt, and Stalin recognized Iran's help in the war and promised economic aid after it.[79] It was partly as a result of not receiving U.S. aid that the demands for nationalization grew. A second factor was the Labour government's policy of dividend limitation, which had the unforseen effect of reducing the Iranian government's oil revenue from 1948 onwards. Another important factor was the genuine sense of outrage among Iranians that their only asset was exclusively in foreign hands. Though the British argued they and not the Iranians had developed that asset, the Iranians argued that after over forty years of exploitation, they had more than paid for the development costs. Just as important were the colonial-style relations which existed between the Iranians and the British. As Harold Macmillan has commented, the high AIOC officials 'did not seem to know how to handle so proud and subtle a people' as the Iranians.[80] Few British understood how many Iranians were still angry over the invasion, even though these Iranians were not uncritical of the old Shah. The main weakness of the Iranian position was not the abrogation of the agreement, but the lack of a coherent, stable, national democratic movement. The best-organized component among the anti-British elements was the Moscow-orientated Tudeh Party. Although this party had attracted many intelligent and dedicated sons and daughters of Iran,[81]although it was born of the fearful injustices which existed in that country,[82] its naïve pro-Soviet stance represented a danger not only to British interests but to Iranian as well. Dr Musaddiq, 'an honourable but emotional septuagenarian'[83] and right-wing patriot, who had become Prime Minister, commanded no well-organized movement of his own. At the official level, Britain 'equivocated between gestures of force to protect its Persian oil interests and compliance with United States "representatives" to find a settlement'.[84] At another level, the hysteria of the British popular press, and the pathetic jingoism of some MPs[85] did nothing to help Anglo-Iranian relations or the British public's understanding of the situation. By the time Britain offered a 50-50 share of the profits, and acceptance of the principle of nationalization – already agreed to by the Americans in Saudi Arabia – it was too late. Britain resorted to blockade, effective because Iran had no tanker fleet, independent outlets, or navy.

The Conservatives' 1951 victory

Having been returned with an overall majority of six in 1950, Attlee and his colleagues were hard pressed to retain control of the Commons. MPs were brought from hospital beds in ambulances to Westminster to vote. It was 'an exhausting and undignified process',[86] wrote George Wigg. The government, tired men, nevertheless held out longer than expected from 6 March 1950 to 5 October 1951. Perhaps from Labour's point of view Attlee would have done better to have retired in office, he was already sixty-eight and ill, giving a new leader the chance to establish himself and then fight an election. On the other hand, it was a time of crisis in the world and dissension in the Party. Perhaps he convinced himself that his own personal standing was a great asset to his party, and that it was right to let the country decide as soon as possible for or against the government. The election, when it came, was a relatively quiet one. Labour stood by its record and warned of the dangers of a third world war. It may well be that it warned too much, and like the Conservatives in 1945, it went too far in attributing to its opponents extremist tendencies which were not there, implying that Churchill was not to be trusted with issues like peace or war.

When the election results were in, the Conservatives found they had not done as well as expected. They had a majority over Labour of 26 and 17 over all parties combined. Labour had a net loss of 20 seats. Most of the Conservative gains were probably the result of Liberals turning right, there being only 100 Liberal candidates throughout the country. The Conservatives were better organized and used the postal-vote facilities to greater effect than Labour did. Yet Labour could feel it had scored a moral victory, for it achieved not only a higher vote than the Conservatives, but the highest vote ever recorded for any political party in Britain before or since. Only the peculiarities of the British electoral system had given the Conservatives a majority.

The election of 1945 finally established the Labour Party as a full-sized alternative to the Conservatives. However imperfectly, the working class was represented for the first time at the centre of the political arena. Labour gave hope to the democratic socialists throughout Europe, socialists who sought fundamental change by civilized means. What exactly had Labour achieved, and where had it failed? Abroad it led the way in decolonization in a way which compared favourably with the policies of other colonial powers. It failed to appreciate the opportunities which existed for building a new Europe, though it must be admitted that Europe did not seem to add up to much at that time. It committed Britain to defence expenditure far beyond the means of the country, setting the pattern to be followed by other post-war governments. At home, the Labour government succeeded in shifting the emphasis in the economy from war to peace production remarkably smoothly. It carried through its domestic reform programme in fulfilment of its election promises. This programme seemed more radical at the time than it actually was. For instance, despite the pleas made by Labour educationalists, Attlee's government did nothing to restructure the country's unfair and divisive education system. Its conception of relations within industry was also very limited. It introduced employee participation in industry in the British zone of Germany, but not in British industry. Neither the moderate trade union Right nor the pro-Communist Left thought much of the idea during those years; thus co-determination was not on the agenda. Government is about priorities and power. Politicians in office are harassed individuals with little time to consider anything other than day-to-day issues. When it comes to positive change, they respond only to their perception of the popular mood (as with Beveridge), or strong, organized opinion both inside and outside Parliament (as with coal). Attlee and his colleagues were cautious men who went just about as far as popular consciousness thrust them.

Notes

1 *Report of the Forty-fifth Annual Conference of the Labour Party,* 105.
2 Bernard Porter, *A Short History of British Imperialism 1850–1970* (London, 1975), 312; a poll conducted in 1948 revealed 'three-quarters of the population did not know the difference between a dominion and a colony, and half could not name a single British colony'.
3 See the speech of A. R. Wise, for instance: Hansard (Commons), vol. 260, col. 1360–1, 3 December 1931.
4 Maurice and Taya Zinkin, *Britain and India: Requiem for Empire* (London, 1964), 34.
5 Nicholas Mansergh, *The Commonwealth Experience* (London, 1969), 248.
6 George Woodcock, *Who Killed the British Empire?* (London, 1974), 39, put the Indian Civil Service at usually between 1,000 and 1,200.
7 Larry Collins and Dominique Lapierre, *Freedom At Midnight* (London, 1975), 12: 'As early as 1818, the Marquess of Hastings noted: "A time, not very remote, will arrive when England will, on sound principles of policy, wish to relinquish the domination which she has gradually and unintentionally assumed over this country" '..
8 Woodcock, op. cit., 13.
9 Eric A. Walker, *The British Empire* (London, 1943), 148.
10 ibid., 150.
11 Lord Butler, *The Art of the Possible. The Memoirs of Lord Butler* (London, 1971), 38.
12 Vera Brittain, *Pethick-Lawrence: a Portrait* (London, 1963). Lord Linlithgow, the Viceroy, still found it astonishing (in 1939) that there should be any general impression that public opinion at home or His Majesty's Government, seriously contemplate evacuation in any measurable period of time'.
13 Mansergh, op. cit., 298.
14 Collins and Lapierre, op. cit., 168.
15 Brittain, op. cit., 136.
16 ibid.
17 Collins and Lapierre, op. cit., 53.
18 Hugh Dalton, *High Tide and After* (London, 1962), p. 211.
19 Collins and Lapierre, op. cit., 82.
20 Zinkin, op. cit., 98.
21 ibid.
22 *The Times,* 9 November 1917.
23 Zionists: the followers of Theodor Herzl, who had revived the idea of a Jewish state as a result of anti-Semitic outbreaks in 19th-century Europe. Herzl (1860–1904) lived in Vienna.
24 In 1922, out of a total population of 752,048, there were only 83,177 Jews; in 1941, out of a total population of 1,585,500, there were 474,102 Jews. *Palestine and Transjordan* in *Geographical Handbook Series* (BR 514; Naval Intelligence Division, London, December 1943), 172.
25 Walter Laqueur, *The Israel-Arab Reader: a Documentary History of the Middle East Conflict* (London, 1969), 74.
26 Hansard, vol. 347, col. 1940.
27 *Report of the Forty-second Annual Conference of the Labour Party,* 151.
28 Cohen, 'The British White Paper on Palestine May 1939 Part II: the Testing of a Policy 1942–45', *Historical Journal* (1976), 727–58.
29 International Dept. of Labour Party Box 5 File: Palestine Labour Party Policy 1944–47, letters from Palestine Arab Party (3 May 1944) and Palestine Arab Workers' Society (11 May 1944).

30 Hugh Dalton, *The Fateful Years: Memoirs 1931–1945* (London, 1957), 425–6.
31 *Keesing's Contemporary Archives,* A7563, 17–24 November 1945.
32 George E. Kirk, *A Short History of the Middle East* (London, 1961), 212–13.
33 Hansard, vol. 424, col. 1898.
34 Hansard, vol. 424, col. 1895.
35 *Keesing's Contemporary Archives,* A 8019, 20–27 July 1946.
36 Maxime Rodinson, *Israel and the Arabs* (London, 1968), 37.
37 *High Tide and After,* p. 151.
38 Kirk, op. cit., 218.
39 Walter Millis, ed., *The Forrestal Diaries* (New York, 1951). James Forrestal, U.S. Secretary of Defence, commented on 1 December 1947 that Robert A. Lovett, Under Secretary of State, had said 'he had never in his life been subject to as much pressure as he had been' at that time by Zionists. He mentions pressure on Liberia, 346. See also Margaret Truman, *Harry S Truman* (New York, 1973); the President was 'deeply disturbed by the pressure which some Zionist leaders put on him to browbeat South American countries and other nations where we might have influence into supporting partition'; 384, and 386 on Zionist contributions to Democrats' campaign fund.
40 Hansard, vol. 441, col. 2340–2.
41 Hansard, vol. 441, col. 2354.
42 Hansard, vol. 426, col. 1056.
43 *Keesing's Contemporary Archives,* A 8782, 16–23 August 1947.
44 Hansard, vol. 448, col. 1332–3.
45 The deep emotions felt, not recorded in votes, are shown in the case of John Strachey, who was prepared to use his position in the government to advise the Jewish Agency on whether they should sabotage British installations; 'Strachey gave his approval to Crossman. The Haganah went ahead and blew up all the bridges over the Jordan. No one was killed but the British Army in Palestine were cut off from their lines of supply with Jordan'. For this remarkable incident see Hugh Thomas, *John Strachey* (London, 1973), 228–9.
46 See the comments of Lord Wigg, *George Wigg* (London, 1972), 144. See also the same line in R. H. S. Crossman, *A Nation Reborn* (London, 1960), 67–8. For Dalton's view see *High Tide and After,* p. 147.
47 ibid., 146.
48 Quoted by Partha Sarathi Gupta, *Imperialism and the British Labour Movement 1914–1964* (London, 1975), 282.
49 ibid., 303.
50 ibid., 319.
51 Thomas, op. cit., 254.
52 Sir Andrew Cohen, *British Policy in Changing Africa* (London, 1959), 43.
53 Colin Leys and Cranford Pratt, eds., *A New Deal in Central Africa* (London, 1960), 29–30. Martyn Dyer, *The Unsolved Problem of Southern Africa* (London, 1968), 105.
    As the Cabinet papers indicate, in the Cabinet, Bevan, Dalton, and Creech Jones put the pro-Zionist case. See CAB 128/11/CM(47)4; CAB 129/16/CP(47)32.
54 J. M. Gullick, *Malaya* (London, 1963), 245.
55 ibid., 83.
56 Noel Barber, *The War of the Running Dogs* (New York, 1972), 34 believes there were local causes for the revolt. G. Z. Hanrahan, *The Communist Struggle in Malaya* (New York, 1959), 63 is also quoted by Gullick, op. cit.,

96 as having doubts about the revolt having started as a result of Moscow's orders. Gullick himself believes Moscow was responsible. Barber puts the number of security forces in action in 1952 at 40,000 regular troops (25,000 from Britain), 60,000 full-time police, and 200,000 Home Guards, 156–7. For a critical look at British policy see Victor Purcell, *Malaya: Communist or Free?* (London, 1954).

57 According to Hugh Thomas, op. cit., 264 this was the essence of the policy advocated by Strachey, then Secretary of State for War, to Attlee in December 1950. For another view of Labour policy see James Griffiths (Colonial Secretary, 1950–51), *Pages From Memory* (London, 1969).

58 Gullick, op. cit., 102.

59 *Report of the Forty-fifth Annual Conference,* 162.

60 Jean Blondel and E. Drexel Godfrey Jr, *The Government of France* (London, 1968), 163.

61 George Moseley, *China: Empire to People's Republic* (London, 1968), 88.

62 Elisabeth Barker, *Britain in a Divided Europe 1945–1970* (London, 1971), 44–9.

63 Barker, ibid., 68 and others assume Bevin was having to plot to engage U.S. interest in Greece and other areas in Europe, but U.S. influence in Greece was increasing, though somewhat slowly.
W. N. Medlicott, *British Foreign Policy Since Versailles 1919–1963* (London, 1968), 280 believes Bevin used Greece to get the United States involved in European defence. As it turned out, British troops finally withdrew 1 February 1950 (*The Times,* 6 February 1950).

64 Willy Brandt, *My Road to Berlin* (London, 1960), 154 quotes the example of the police in the British zone. The British liked the old police because they knew their job and obeyed orders promptly! The writer has often heard this grievance voiced by German Social Democrats. Interestingly, Brandt claims Dr Schumacher, the Social Democratic leader, was 'too socialist' for the Americans, 'too aggressive' for the British, and 'too German' for the French (see 152). Ivone Kirkpatrick, *The Inner Circle* (London, 1959), 232 says he was never able to establish relations 'of confidence and friendship' with Schumacher, though he did with some other Social Democrats. Kirkpatrick was High Commissioner in Germany 1950–53.

65 Harold Zink, *The United States in Germany 1944–1955* (Princeton, 1957), 112.

66 B. Ruhm von Oppen, *Documents on Germany Under Occupation 1945–54* (London, 1955), 184.

67 John Gimbel, *The American Occupation of Germany* (Stanford, 1968), 117–20, 228–34.

68 The conflicting Soviet attitudes are brought out in Henry Krisch, *German Politics under Soviet Occupation* (New York, 1974).

69 Barker, op. cit., 77.

70 Kirkpatrick, op. cit., 205.

71 C. J. Bartlett, *The Long Retreat: a Short History of British Defence Policy 1945–70* (London, 1972), 47.

72 For a discussion of this see A. J. R. Groom, *British Thinking about Nuclear Weapons* (London, 1974).

73 Robert G. Wesson, *Soviet Foreign Policy in Perspective* (Homewood, Illinois, 1969): 'There is no clear evidence regarding the Soviet part in starting the war, but in view of the political relations of the parties and the dependence of the North Korean regime on Soviet material, there must have been at least Soviet approval'. Earlier U.S. statements about Korea not being essential to United States defence 'would seem to the Russians practically an

invitation'. See also F. S. Northedge, *Descent from Power: British Foreign Policy 1945–1973* (London, 1974), 196.

74 David Rees, *Korea: the Limited War* (London, 1964), 460–1.
75 Michael Foot, *Aneurin Bevan 1945–60* (London, 1975), 299.
76 See John W. Spanier, *The Truman–MacArthur Controversy and the Korean War* (New York, 1965).
77 Macmillan, *Tides of Fortune 1945–1955* (London, 1969), 334 calls it an 'appeal' from the United States for an increased contribution. Attlee quoted by Foot, op. cit., 310, said in 1959, 'Pressure on rearmament was very heavy from the United States. I think they were inclined to press too hard'.
78 Rees, op. cit., 233. Coral Bell, *Negotiation from Strength* (London, 1962), 56–9 has a good discussion of the economic effects.
79 L. V. Thomas and R. N. Frye, *The United States and Turkey and Iran* (Cambridge, Mass., 1952), Appendix III.
80 Macmillan, op. cit., 343.
81 Sepher Zabith, *The Communist Movement in Iran* (Berkeley and Los Angeles, 1966); this is a detailed history of the party.
82 George Lenczowski, *Russia and the West in Iran* (New York, 1949), supplementary chapter 12, 2.
83 Kirk, op. cit., 274.
84 ibid., 274. For a study of Iran's foreign affairs see R. K. Ramazani, *Iran's Foreign Policy 1941–1973* (Charlottesville, 1975).
85 See, for example, Ray Gunter, 21 June 1951, Hansard, vol. 489, col. 755–9.
86 Wigg, op. cit., p. 151.

4 From Churchill to Eden 1951–57

Churchill's team

At seventy-seven, Churchill was not expected to remain long at the helm. The dismal election result, remarkable though it was considering the defeat of 1945, gave the Conservatives no mandate for great changes. Churchill still felt he had to muster his forces. Apparently he offered a coalition to the Liberals, which they refused.[1] The old chieftain could argue that whatever positive success the Party had achieved was due to his charisma. He felt, therefore, in a strong position to select his Cabinet according to his own preferences, though this inclination was no doubt curbed somewhat by the need to present a broad, moderate image to the electorate. R. A. Butler, who was regarded as a moderate, was assured of high office, and was appointed Chancellor of the Exchequer, an appointment Oliver Stanley would almost certainly have got had he not died in 1950. Oliver Lyttelton, who had 'shadowed' the Chancellor in opposition, was, perhaps, regarded as too close to the City to be suitable. Eden got the Foreign Office, a reward for his ability in foreign affairs, popularity, and, not least, his pre-war anti-appeasement role. Lord Woolton's appointment as Lord President was both a tribute to his services in renovating the party machine, and acknowledgement of his presumed appeal to non-committed middle-class voters. Macmillan, like Woolton and Eden, had served Churchill during the war, and was a moderate on home affairs. He became Minister of Housing and Local Government. The appointment of the Marquess of Salisbury as Lord Privy Seal was a sop to the party traditionalists. Walter Monckton was sent to the highly sensitive Ministry of Labour because of his reputation as a conciliator. Sir David Maxwell-Fyfe was invited to turn his tough legal mind to the problems of the Home Office. Possibly Churchill's view of his colleagues is revealed by the fact that he made himself Minister of Defence, severely restricted his Chancellor's freedom of initiative, and, according to Lord Woolton, ran his Cabinet in a way which was '. . . often reminiscent of bygone times'.[2] Frequently the agenda was ignored, and ministers not in the Cabinet were left waiting outside for long periods.

Few in the Conservative Party or in the ranks of the Opposition believed in 1951 that the Tories were set for thirteen years of office and two more electoral victories. Much of their success, especially in the early years, was due to fortunate domestic and international circumstances beyond their control.

On taking office the Conservatives had to deal with a rapidly deteriorating balance of payments situation. Import cuts were ordered. In his Budget of March 1952 Butler restricted home consumption by making hire purchase more difficult, cut food subsidies, and announced economies in government spending. This was balanced by tax concessions, but also by increases in social service benefits. The Budget does not appear to have been popular. Local elections held in May showed a big swing to Labour. The Scottish local elections in July confirmed the trend. At the Dundee by-election in the same month the trend was still with Labour. It looked as if the Conservative term of office would be a short one. Then in the autumn, the Wycombe by-election was a harbinger of better things to come for the Conservatives. Forces at work in the world economy helped to turn the tide for Britain and the Conservatives. As one Conservative historian has put it.

The terms of trade moved sharply in Britain's favour after the end of the Korean War. The whole economic position eased for the time being. If Labour had hung on a little longer, they might have been the beneficiaries of the rising tide of affluence which would have been to some extent a feature of the 1950s, whichever party had been in office. The years from 1951 to 1955 can be seen in retrospect as a lull in our turbulent post-war history. Churchill's presence at the top masked the decline of Britain's world power status.[3]

Other factors too masked Britain's decline. There was Britain's nuclear bomb in 1952. In the same year the world's first pure jet airliner, the British Comet, went into service with BOAC. In May 1953 Edmund Hillary and Sherpa Tenzing became the first men successfully to climb Mount Everest. Though Hillary was a New Zealander, it was counted as a British success, such was the feeling about the Commonwealth in those days. There was honour too for Winston Churchill; in 1953 he was awarded the Nobel Prize for literature. He was in the company of such literary giants as T. S. Eliot (1948), William Faulkner (1949), Bertrand Russell (1950), François Mauriac (1952), and Ernest Hemingway (1954). In 1954 Roger Bannister thrilled the nation by becoming the first man to run a mile in under four minutes. It seemed there was still a lot of greatness left in Great Britain. One other factor conspiring to give this impression was the coronation. George VI's sudden death in his sleep early in 1952 momentarily helped to unite the nation. A modest man who had overcome considerable personal handicaps to master the job, he had gained wide personal respect over the years. The accession of Elizabeth II and her coronation in June 1953, at a magnificent, feudal, ceremony watched by 25 million people[4] on television, provided the government and much of the press with the opportunity to indulge in some wildly wishful thinking about a 'new Elizabethan age'. It helped to foster illusions about Britain's position in the world at a time when there was an urgent need to understand that it was going to occupy, permanently, a more modest place.

Crashes involving two Comets in 1954 were symbolic of the many reverses to be suffered by Britain's industry. The years which followed were to be littered with the shells of unfinished, abandoned, aviation projects. Britain was attempting to run an unequal race with the Americans, the only other major aviation power, a race Britain could not win. Britain's big mistake was that it tried to do too much. Perhaps the Germans, and even the Japanese, would have tried to do the same had they not been forbidden to do so under the terms of their agreements with the allies. It was the same with arms. Though they had clamoured for more defence spending in opposition, the Conservatives took up a quasi-'Bevanite' position in office. Winston Churchill told the Commons on 30 July 1952 that the original defence programme was utterly beyond the nation's capacity to bear. Cuts followed here too. But Britain continued to suffer a disadvantage in this respect compared with West Germany, Italy, France, and Japan, countries with which it was increasingly competing for world trade.

Mindful of their weak parliamentary position, Churchill and his colleagues sought to appease working-class feeling by an excess profits tax. Macmillan was allowed to get on with the job of providing the 300,000 houses promised at the election. There was caution on denationalization, with only parts of iron and steel and road haulage being sold off. Food rationing was ended during 1953–54. Apart from the modest denationalization measures, the government's own supporters could revel in the 'bonfire of controls' which took place, never mind if Wilson, when he was at the Board of Trade, has been planning much the same.

It was not clear whom the government was appeasing when it introduced legislation providing for the setting-up of commercial television. The BBC pre-war television service had been suspended at the outbreak of war. It was on the air again in June 1946. The BBC expected to keep its monopoly of broadcasting, and had Labour remained in office, it would have undoubtedly done so. The *Report of the Broadcasting Committee 1949* rejected advertising and any breach of the BBC's monopoly. Chaired by Lord Beveridge, the Committee was not, however, unanimous in this view. Selwyn Lloyd, then a Conservative backbencher, favoured a commercial system similar to that in operation in the United States. Churchill never gave a television interview,[5] and was not very interested in it. It appears it was Lord Woolton who sold the idea of commercial television to the Cabinet. Outside Parliament, Norman Collins, author of *London Belongs to Me* and a former BBC executive, was the key figure in promoting the idea. He was backed financially by Sir Robert (later Lord) Renwick, an old Etonian stockbroker, who had been a large contributor to the Conservative election fund and, among others, C. O. Stanley, Chairman of Pye Radio. These, and a small number of determined and powerful business interests, fought the combined opposition of the Churches, including the Archbishop of Canterbury, the universities, and the professional educational bodies, most of the press and cinema industries, the Labour Party and the TUC, and a host of other bodies.[6] The Archbishop of York's view that 'For the sake of our children, we should resist it', was ignored. In addition to the business initiators of this change there were many Conservative backbenchers who were in favour of breaking the BBC's monopoly; why is not entirely clear. Perhaps it was part of the Conservative mood at the time against public ownership, or simply against monopoly. One or two later confessed that, as there were so many other problems on the agenda, the full implications of the move were not thought through. Nevertheless, there was a long debate over the Television Act, which established commercial television under an Independent Television Authority. This became law in July 1954. The new service started to operate in September 1955. The coronation and the election of 1955 showed the potential of television and audiences grew rapidly. Television became a national pastime. In March 1955 4½ million TV licences had been issued: by March 1958 the number had grown to 8 million.[7]

The growth of television and the competition between the BBC and Independent Television (ITV) both reflected changes in society and helped to produce them. The BBC was forced to become more 'popular' in much of its output, with much more emphasis on light entertainment. It was hard pressed to compete with programmes like *Coronation Street* and *Crossroads*. Controversy about television and its allegedly harmful effects on the nation's morals and culture continued and the Pilkington Committee on Broadcasting was appointed to review the situation. Its report was published in June 1962. It showed that the BBC put out more news and current affairs, serious drama, sport, and travelogues. ITV was slightly ahead on light entertainment and religion, but devoted much more of its output to crime, westerns, and comedy series. There was a great deal of concern about violence, sex, and depravity on television. The Committee reported that there was a belief,

deeply felt, that the way television has portrayed human behaviour and treated moral issues had already done something and will in time do much to worsen the moral climate of the country. That this is a time when many of the standards by which people have hitherto lived are often questioned is not itself regrettable. But it is necessary that the questions should be fairly put and fairly answered.

Pilkington also attacked television for being 'trivial'. 'Many mass appeal programmes were vapid and puerile, their content often derivative, repetitious and lacking in real substance'.[8] Other programmes which purported to deal with serious subjects trivialized them. In all of these criticisms the BBC got off lightly compared with ITV. The Committee felt the regions, especially Scotland and Wales, were neglected, as were minority interests and points of view. The report's main recommendation was that power in ITV should be shifted from the programme companies to the government-appointed overseeing body, the Independent Television Authority (ITA). The ITA should plan the programmes and sell advertising time. The companies would then be left to produce the programmes. This proposal was strongly opposed by the companies and rejected by the government. As a result of the Committee's findings, the government did, however, allow only the BBC to go ahead with a second TV channel: BBC-2 began transmitting in April 1964.

There was much substance in the Pilkington Report's criticisms, and they helped to raise television standards. However, the report was not entirely fair to ITV. Granada Television, in particular, had led the way in providing controversial current affairs programmes of a high standard. It also led the way in coverage of election news. In 1959 Granada broke new ground with a series of 'election marathons' in which the candidates from a hundred seats in 'Granadaland', the north-west, debated the issues. This company's documentary producers have continued to set the pace in their handling of controversial and neglected subjects.

The competition between BBC and ITV broadened and raised the level of debate and discussion about all national and international problems. This is not necessarily an argument in favour of commercial television, but it is certainly an argument against any organization having a monopoly in this vital sector of mass communications. (It is convenient to mention here that Edward Heath's Conservative government ended the BBC's monopoly of radio in June 1972 with the passing of the Sound Broadcasting Act. This provided for the setting-up of commercial radio stations. The first such stations went on the air in October 1973. One innovation they forced on the BBC was the phone-in programme, to be widely used in the elections of 1974.)

The development of television hit the cinemas and newspapers alike. There was a massive decline in cinema attendances and more and more of them were converted into bingo halls. Films like *Saturday Night and Sunday Morning* and *The Loneliness of the Long Distance Runner*, adapted from the novels of Alan Sillitoe, and *Look Back in Anger* and *The Entertainer*, based on John Osborne's plays, won critical acclaim as part of the 'new wave' of British films dealing with the problems of present-day society. Yet they could do little to halt the drift away from the cinemas. The very decline of the cinema seemed to make it easier for the independent producers like Tony Richardson or Bryan Forbes. Nevertheless, finance remained a problem despite the existence of the National Film Finance Corporation established after the war by Harold Wilson, then at the Board of Trade, to encourage British film-makers. Most cinemas remained part of two chains, Rank and ABC, which largely determined what the public saw. If neither of these circuits would guarantee to take a film, finance would hardly be forthcoming to make it. The cinemagoing public's diet remained largely American films, British 'Carry On' comedies, and Hammer horror movies. The unanswered question was why could the British not make (cheap) films of the quality of the French *nouvelle vague* or like the Italians, Swedes, or, in the 1970s, the West Germans?

Both cinemas and newspapers were hit by the fall in advertising revenue. According to the Royal (Shawcross) Commission on the Press (1961–62) the percentage of advertising revenue going to the press fell from 55 in 1952 to 47.5 in 1960. It then rose over the 1960s, and according to the next (McGregor) Commission on the Press (1974–77), it reached 70.1 per cent in 1975. By contrast, television's share of advertising rose from 3.4 per cent in 1956 to 17.5 in 1960, and 24.4 in 1975. The percentage of revenue going to the cinemas went one way all the time – down. The Shawcross Commission expressed concern about the continued growth of concentration in the press. In 1948 the top three newspaper groups were responsible for 43 per cent of total daily and Sunday newspaper circulation. By 1961 the top three groups – Daily Mirror group, Associated Newspapers, Beaverbrook Newspapers – controlled 65 per cent of circulation. With costs rising sharply the weaker papers went to the wall. The Liberal *News Chronicle* was closed in 1960. Later the Conservative *Daily Sketch* and the Labour *Daily Herald* died after years of decline. The Shawcross Commission was also concerned about newspaper groups owning substantial shares in television, like the Mirror group's interest in ATV and similar television interests owned by Lord Beaverbrook and Roy (later Lord) Thomson, the two

Canadian newspaper wizards. Thomson owned Scotland's leading paper, the *Scotsman*, and Scottish Television, the leading ITV company in Scotland. He eventually added *The Times* in 1966 to the *Sunday Times* and a string of papers he owned up and down the country and in North America. The *Sunday Times*' main competitor, the *Observer*, was saved from extinction in 1976 by an American concern. Three out of the ten national newspaper companies were by that time controlled from outside the country. The McGregor Commission found that the trends noted in 1961 had continued. These were concentration of ownership, economic difficulties due in part to the massive increase in the cost of newsprint and overmanning, continued dependence on advertising, and a sharp division between the so-called quality papers and the 'popular' press. Left-wing opinion was even more poorly represented than in 1961. The *Sun*, which replaced the *Daily Herald*, owned by the Australian newspaper tycoon Rupert Murdoch, became largely non-political. The Conservatives had an advantage in terms of press support at every election between 1945 and 1979. Neither the Shawcross nor the McGregor Commission could offer any concrete solutions to the unsatisfactory state of the press. Both rejected public subsidies, a system developed in Sweden and a number of other West European countries. McGregor was not satisfied with the working of the Press Council, a body set up in 1953 on the recommendation of the first Royal Commission on the Press (1949). It was meant to oversee all aspects of the press and handle complaints from the public. Neither of the two subsequent Commissions saw it as an effective body. As a result of Shawcross, lay members were introduced with an independent chairman. More outsiders were appointed in 1973, following the Report of the Committee on Privacy. McGregor recommended that the lay members should make up half the total membership. It rejected the Swedish idea of a press ombudsman as inappropriate to British conditions, though it admitted, 'there are still flagrant breaches of acceptable standards'.

Stalin's Death

Luck was on Churchill's side in international affairs as well as at home. The Korean War was effectively over when the Conservatives took office, though the formal armistice was agreed only in 1953. The death of the Soviet dictator Joseph Stalin in March 1953 led to a greatly relaxed international atmosphere. As Eden wrote later, it certainly 'marked the end of an era',[9] but was it more than that? Could the Soviet Union and the West have resolved their major differences at this point? Eden believed quite simply: 'The

77

new Soviet ruling committee, headed by Malenkov, wanted to lower the international temperature, and therefore abandoned much that was uselessly provocative in Stalinist policy; but the "cold war" was their policy and it persisted'.[10] The trouble was that both sides remained suspicious of each other, both believed their own propaganda too much, both were the prisoners of the past, and both suffered from weak or inexperienced leaders. The Soviet leaders, as we later learned, were fighting among themselves. Malenkov was soon to give way to Bulganin and Khrushchev. 'Mr K.' in turn removed his rivals, remaining supreme until he was ousted in 1964. In Britain, Churchill was a 'giant in decay',[11] for long periods seriously incapacitated. Eden too was frequently ill. In 1952 the Leader of the House, Harry Crookshank, was appointed to preside over the Cabinet in the simultaneous absence of Churchill and Eden. A year later, when both were ill, R. A. Butler acted as head of government.[12] In the United States a tired Truman gave way to Dwight D. Eisenhower. 'No president had ever had so little experience of politics and as little first-hand experience of American life', as Eisenhower.[13] He suffered a serious heart attack in September 1955.[14] From January 1947 to June 1954 France had maintained its tradition of frequent changes of government: there had been fifteen Cabinets. Foreign policy, however, had remained in the hands of one party, the Christian Democratic MRP of Georges Bidault and Robert Schuman. In 1953 West Germany, already a factor in European affairs, was led by 76-year-old Konrad Adenauer. Where were the statesmen with the mental and physical stamina, the imagination, and the flexibility of mind needed to grapple effectively with East–West relations?

The defence and foreign policies of Churchill and Eden were a continuation, in large measure, of those of Attlee and Bevin, and perhaps opportunities were missed. Churchill did have the imagination to propose a summit meeting of the four wartime allies just after Stalin's death in May 1953. Nothing came of this. The Americans were sceptical and suggested a Western summit first. This did not come off until December 1953 because of the illness of Churchill and Eden. It took until July 1955 to get the leaders of the four powers together in Geneva, by which time Churchill had resigned in favour of Eden.

The post-Stalin leaders of the Soviet Union had by July 1955 made a number of conciliatory gestures world-wide. In Asia they had added their weight to the achievement of a formal armistice in Korea, which was signed in July 1953. They also used their influence to bring about a cease-fire in Indo-China after the fall of the French garrison at Dien Bien Phu in May 1954. In 1955 they handed over Port Arthur to the Chinese, thus ending their special position in Manchuria. Further west, they had resumed diplomatic relations with Greece and Israel, and dropped their territorial claims against Turkey – without any concessions by that country. They had dropped their hostility to Tito and, in 1955, Khrushchev and Bulganin made a dramatic visit to the Yugoslav leader, apologizing for the past and recognizing Yugoslavia as a socialist state. Quite as unexpectedly, in the same year they agreed to an Austrian state treaty under which Soviet and Western forces vacated their respective zones and Austria became neutral. They also yielded their naval base at Porkalla in Finland, one of the issues in the Soviet–Finnish Winter War of 1939. Finally, the Soviet Union took a more positive line at the United Nations. Such developments led to a good deal of optimism as the Geneva summit approached. Unfortunately, 'Not much more substantial than smiles was exchanged'.[15] The conference was useful in that it gave the leaders a chance to take stock of each other, but no progress was recorded on the key issues of Germany and European security. The U.S. and West German governments had not been prepared to probe Stalin's offer made in 1952 of a united, neutralized Germany with its own defence forces. Instead they had pushed on with plans for German rearmament. In 1955 the Western powers agreed that West Germany should regain its sovereignty, have its own armed forces, and become a member of NATO. The strategy of the Eisenhower–Dulles administration was that by talking, negotiating from strength, they would be able to 'roll back' the Russians from central and eastern Europe. Eden appreciated Soviet fears of a rearmed Germany,[16] but felt obliged to follow the Americans; besides, by 1955, there was little he could have done. From this time on the Russians strove to get the West to recognize the division of Germany, including the East German republic. This the West declined to do. Remarkably though, Adenauer went to the Soviet Union in 1955 and agreed that Moscow and Bonn should exchange ambassadors.

If the British had little choice but to follow the Americans on Germany, they had some choice on defence. Churchill and his colleagues continued the development of nuclear weapons started by Attlee and went in for even bigger bangs. The first British test took place in October 1952; the Russians had already had their bomb over two years by then. Less than a year later the Russians were testing their thermo-nuclear bomb. Britain could not hope to keep up with either the United States or the Soviet Union in this field; why then did the British government decide to keep in the race? Basically, Churchill's idea was that Britain would have more influence with the Americans, and indeed with the rest of the world. The government also believed that nuclear weapons would be cheaper than large conventional armed forces.[17] In fact, Britain increasingly relied on the Americans for its defence; if anything, it lost influence through its decision to make the H-Bomb. And nuclear weapons proved to be anything but cheap.

Eden: rebel with velvet gloves

Anthony Eden took over from Winston Churchill in April 1955. He had been the 'crown prince' since 1942.[18] Educated at Eton and Oxford, Eden (1897–1978) was the personification of the 'English gentleman' of the inter-war period. After service in the trenches in the 'Great War', he entered Parliament in 1923. He was Under Secretary at the Foreign Office in 1931–33, Lord Privy Seal in 1934–35, and Foreign Secretary in 1935–38. When he resigned from Chamberlain's government because he disagreed with appeasement of Hitler, he seemed all set to lead a popular crusade against the government. 'But he ducked the opportunity and the challenge when he could have changed the course of history . . . Having made his gesture of resignation he lacked the courage to continue the fight. He was a rebel with velvet gloves'.[19] On the outbreak of war he rejoined Chamberlain's government as Dominions Secretary. Churchill put him in charge of the army in 1940, transferring him to the Foreign Office in the same year. There he remained until the end of the Churchill administration. Cordell Hull, Roosevelt's Secretary of State, got to know Eden during these war years, and later wrote of him: 'He possessed an agreeable personality and a high order of intelligence. He was always on the alert when any matter pertaining to Great Britain or peace was involved . . . I considered Eden a person of unusual promise in the political field, barring the changes of fortune implicit in politics'.[20] Eden had very little experience of domestic issues when he took over in 1955, he was also a sick man. Some Conservatives thought he should never have taken on the responsibilities of Prime Minister. Later, Reginald Bevins, Macmillan's Postmaster General, was to write:

Eden showed a curious mixture of strength and weakness. In my view . . . Eden ought never to have been Prime Minister. His performance prior to Suez had been feeble. He forever temporised and chopped and changed his mind. He busied himself absurdly with detail. He was no judge of men: no favourite of Eden's ever did any good. While he had a natural charm he was also nervy, jumpy and bad-tempered.[21]

Eden made relatively few changes in the government. Butler continued at the Treasury until replaced by Macmillan in December 1955. He then became Lord Privy Seal and Leader of the House of Commons. Selwyn Lloyd went to the Foreign Office at the same time, as a junior in a senior post under the Prime Minister. He stayed there until July 1960. Lord Kilmuir continued to serve as Lord Chancellor until July 1962. Lord Salisbury remained Lord President and Leader of the Conservative Party in the Lords. Gwilym Lloyd George, son of the Liberal Prime Minister, held on to the Home Office. Alan Lennox-Boyd and Sir David Eccles remained at their respective posts as Colonial Secretary and Minister of Education. Finally, Sir Walter Monckton kept the Ministry of Labour and National Service until December 1955, when he replaced Selwyn Lloyd at the Ministry of Defence.

Eden had no sooner assembled his government before he was placing it before the electorate for approval. On this occasion he had got his timing right. The election took place in May 1955, a very good time for the Conservatives. 'Rab' Butler had cut income tax. There was optimism about the balance of payments, and there was optimism too about the international situation. The Geneva summit was in sight. Some of the old glamour of the 1930s still clung to Eden. He looked younger than he was, and his young wife, the niece of Churchill, helped his image. He presented no easy target for his Labour opponents. Labour, in any case, did not seem to want to win. Attlee fought his last campaign as leader quietly. 'The campaign itself refused to catch fire'.[22] Perhaps Labour feared close scrutiny of the Party would reveal that it was not yet ready to return to office, split as it was both on policies and on personalities. The Bevanite breach had widened since it had gone into opposition. The Parliamentary Labour Party had decided by the small margin of 113 to 104 to support the principle of German rearmament. Bevan had then resigned from the 'shadow cabinet' over the issue. Later in the same year, 1954, the party conference had endorsed this decision, but again only by a very narrow margin, and with allegations that a few small unions' delegates had made it possible by departing from their unions' policy. At the same conference, bitterness had been caused by Hugh Gaitskell's election, with right-wing trade union support, to the treasurership of the Party, against Nye Bevan. In February 1955 the Parliamentary Labour Party revealed its divisions once again, this time over nuclear weapons. The government had announced its intention of manufacturing the hydrogen bomb; Attlee had agreed with this decision. In an able speech[23] Bevan challenged Attlee and called upon his colleagues to abstain on the Opposition amendment to the Defence White Paper. In all, some 62 Labour MPs, Bevanite or pacifist, decided to do so, thus embarrassing the leadership. Bevan faced expulsion from the Parliamentary Labour Party by having the whip withdrawn, a decision endorsed by a majority of 141 of his colleagues to 112. He was not, however, expelled from the Party altogether. [24] With the leadership in such disarray one would expect the Party's supporters to be apathetic. Just how much infighting affected the outcome of the election is impossible to say. Nor is it possible to say whether, or how much, a number of strikes which took place around election time affected the outcome. The London newspaper strike ended on 21 April, after the election was announced. A dock strike, lasting six weeks, broke out three days before polling-day. An economically damaging strike, it was caused by inter-union rivalry. A threatened rail strike because of pay differentials commenced less than 48 hours after the polling-booths closed. The situation could not have been much worse for Labour.

The election results announced on 27 May showed that on a lower poll, the Conservatives had a majority of 58 seats over all other parties – an increase of 41. They had actually lost over 400,000 votes compared with 1951, Labour had lost over 1½ million! The electorate had increased by about 300,000. The Conservative gains were mainly in the south, but they also gained seats in the north of England, in the Midlands, and one in Scotland.[25] Though neither side could be complacent about the results, the Conservatives could be quietly happy. Hostility towards them had lessened. The electors appeared less anxious than before. For the first time in decades the clouds appeared to have lifted from over the British Isles and as a consequence the electorate had become slightly less political.

After the election Labour held its inquest on the results. It found its organization had been defective. The number of full-time agents in the constituencies had fallen from 296 in 1951 to 227 in 1955.[26] Harold Wilson, who was empowered by the Party's NEC to investigate the organization, spoke of Labour's 'penny-farthing' way of organizing elections. Some thought Labour needed younger men at the top, and pressed Attlee to name the day of his departure. Eventually he bowed to the pressure and retired in December 1955, aged seventy-two. Dalton had already stepped down from the 'shadow cabinet'. Morrison, aged sixty-seven, was not prepared to retire and fought hard to succeed Attlee. Who would win the leadership contest was never really in doubt, only the extent of his victory: Gaitskell 157, Bevan 70, Morrison 40. Bevan's defeat as deputy leader by fellow Welshman and fellow ex-miner, James Griffiths, was less painful – 141 to 111.

The new leader, Hugh Gaitskell (1906–63), was only forty-nine at the time of his election and, as we have seen, had served briefly under Attlee as Chancellor of the Exchequer. Like Attlee, he was from an upper-middle-class background; his father was in the Indian Civil Service. After education at Winchester and New College, Oxford, he spent some months as Rockefeller Research

Fellow in Vienna in the exciting and tragic year of 1934. Already a socialist, he came to hate fascism, observing the brief but bloody Austrian civil war. Before taking up a post lecturing in Economics at University College London, he spent a year in Nottingham as an adult education tutor, gaining his first real contact with the working class. During the war Gaitskell worked for Dalton at the Ministry of Economic Warfare, becoming MP for South Leeds in 1945. Gaitskell's public image was that of an austere individual who found it difficult to communicate. Certainly, despite the impression of great sincerity, he often had a somewhat wooden platform manner. He could readily manipulate facts and figures, he was less clever at manipulating words. In private life, his friend John Betjeman remembered the young Gaitskell as 'a gentle and kind person who had no objection to a drop of drink and was very easy company and full of jokes'. [27] One of the most formidable economists in the 1945 Parliament, he stood, according to Dalton, 'high out of the ruck of rivals. During his Ministerial apprenticeship he had displayed, both in public and in inner council, great talent and firm loyalty'.[28] His years as Labour leader were to be years of bitter controversy. Strongly, passionately, convinced of his own intellectual position, perhaps he lacked a certain tact and diplomacy needed in the leader of a mass movement like the Labour Party. Perhaps too, as George Brown believed, he was 'easily cast down and hurt'.[29] This is a luxury no party leader can afford.

Suez 1956

With a thaw in the Cold War and a successful election behind him, all looked well for Eden's new ministry. However, Eden was dogged by back luck, ill health, and his own faulty judgement. At home the economy 'missed a beat. It may have been a mere palpitation, but it was there'.[30] Eden and Butler decided to curb both government and private spending. Housing subsidies were cut, the capital investment programmes of the nationalized industries were curtailed, and further higher-purchase restrictions were introduced. This happened in July. On 27 October, Butler introduced a supplementary Budget which included purchase-tax increases of one-fifth. For the first time even pots and pans were included. As Eden himself later admitted, these measures 'were certainly politically odious and cut across our party's philosophy. It is difficult to advocate a property-owning democracy to the tune of "Your kettles will cost more" '.[31] Increasingly, 'Eden behaved strangely, irritating his colleagues by his alternate high-handedness and irresolution, and especially by his frequent loss of temper. It was all as though the job was too much for him'.[32] Abroad the situation seemed to be growing far more dangerous than at home.

The British were forced to focus their attention on the Middle East once again. In Egypt, as in Iran, the politically conscious younger elements were becoming increasingly dissatisfied with a regime which was corrupt, unwilling to promote a modicum of social and economic progress, and incapable of maintaining national dignity *vis-à-vis* Britain and Israel. In Iran the Americans had intervened covertly in 1953 to restore the crumbling authority of the Shah. In the following year Iran and an international consortium of oil companies, including the AIOC, reached an agreement which fell short of Iranian nationalist demands, but was an improvement on the earlier situation. In that country British influence had been clearly replaced by Americans. In Egypt a similar situation appeared to be developing, but there could be no talk of communist influence there. Nationalist irregulars were carrying on a guerrilla campaign against the British base in the Suez Canal Zone. On 26 July King Farouk, a byword for decadence, was overthrown by a *coup* of younger officers. Major-General Muhammad Neguib was proclaimed President on 18 June 1953, only to be eclipsed by Colonel Gamal Abdel Nasser, the Prime Minister, in February 1954. The new 'strong man' was 'A practising Moslem and a proud Nationalist' who 'had no love for Communism and no wish to be its agent'.[33] In July 1954 Britain agreed to withdraw its troops from the Canal Zone within two years, with the right to return in the event of aggression against an Arab state or Turkey. The installations were to be maintained for seven years by British civilian contractors. Meanwhile, relations between the Arab states and Israel had not improved. Since 1949 a precarious peace had been maintained, but the Arab states had not recognized the new state, and there was constant friction along the armistice line.

Between December 1953 and February 1955 Moshe Sharett was Israeli Premier. He pursued a more flexible policy towards the Arabs, even establishing contacts with Egyptian officers.[34] But he was replaced after the elections of 1955 by the hawkish Ben Gurion. This certainly worried Egypt, which at this time was virtually without an air force and short of munitions.[35] France was supplying weapons to Israel because of the support afforded by Egypt to the Algerian rebels seeking to free their country from French rule. A worried Nasser asked the United States for arms. John Foster Dulles, the U.S. Secretary of State, wanted to use arms as a lever with which to force Egypt into the Baghdad Pact, an alliance of Britain, Iran, Iraq, Turkey, and Pakistan set up in 1955 to keep the Russians out of the Middle East. Nasser rightly believed such adherence would undermine his influence at home and abroad, when he was desperately attempting to woo the Egyptian masses and cut a figure with such Third World leaders as Tito and Nehru.[36] Having failed to get military assistance from the West, he turned to the East. In September 1955 a deal was announced with Czechoslovakia. The Egyptian leader also wanted to obtain a loan from the United States to finance the Aswan Dam project, designed to increase both production of electricity and irrigation on a massive scale. The Americans had agreed, in principle, to fund this together with Britain and the World Bank. Both Egypt and the United States haggled over the terms, the Egyptians fearing new overlordship from America. On the U.S. side, Dulles too was uneasy. Czech arms apart, he was angered when Egypt recognized Communist China in May 1956.[37] After more flirting with the Russians, President Nasser sent his ambassador to Washington to inform Dulles that he had agreed to the loan conditions – too late! Dulles had decided he was not to get it. In any case, the U.S. Senate Appropriations Committee was jibbing at voting the loan. In particular, an alliance of Southern Democrats, who feared increased Egyptian cotton-exports, the Nationalist China lobby, and pro-Israelis, was organized to block the loan in July 1956.[38] According to Lord Butler 'the refusal itself had become the settled policy of the British government several days earlier'.[39] However, Anthony Nutting, who was junior minister at the Foreign Office, has recorded that Eden's fundamental opposition to Nasser started with the dismissal of the British general commanding the Jordanian forces, Glubb Pasha, in March 1956. Eden thought Cairo was behind the dismissal and said, 'Nasser's got to go, it's either me or Nasser'.[40] Seven days after Dulles reneged on the Dam loan the Egyptian reaction came. Nasser nationalized the Suez Canal Company on 26 July.

Britain was the biggest single user of the Canal. No less than 25 per cent of all British exports and imports went through it. Some 75 per cent of Europe's oil originated in the Middle East, and half of this passed through the Canal.[41] It could not be denied that its efficient operation was a matter of serious concern to the United Kingdom and some other states.

Western reaction to the nationalization was not long delayed. Two days after the Egyptian action the Treasury ordered that all Egypt's sterling balances and assets should be frozen. France and the United States took similar action. Britain banned the export of arms and ammunition to Egypt and called up some 20,000 British army reservists. Reinforcements for the three services were despatched to the eastern Mediterranean. Eden sent messages to Eisenhower which seemed to indicate that even at this early stage he wanted to resolve the matter by force.[42] The Prime Minister was urged on by the rulers of Iraq who were on a state visit to Britain at the time.[43] At home the Labour Party did not object to the government's moves. Indeed, on 2 August, Gaitskell compared Nasser to Mussolini and Hitler and even admitted there might be circumstances in which Britain would be compelled to use force. He did, however, link this with reference to the United Nations for that body's approval.[44] Thus far, and superficially, Eden appeared to be in a strong political position. Legally, in international law, his position seemed to be even stronger. The Suez Canal Company was opened in 1869; its shares were largely in British and French hands, the British government having a 44 per cent holding. Freedom of navigation through it was guaranteed under the Constantinople Convention of 1888, signed by Britain and a number of leading powers.[45] Egypt was bound by the Convention, though it was not a signatory. More important was the fact that the new Egyptian regime had agreed to uphold the Convention as recently as 1954. At the same time Nasser's government had recognized the right of the Suez Canal Company to operate the Canal until the expiry of the concession in 1968.

In reality Eden's position was not as strong as it first appeared. The Americans were by no means disposed to use force. Eisenhower sent Dulles to see Eden on 1 August. Dulles agreed with Eden's actions and spoke of a way 'to make Nasser disgorge'. He even admitted the possibility of using force, but only as a last resort.[46] One would have thought Eden would have been well aware of America's reluctance to use force – except as a last resort. The U.S. Presidential elections were under way and 'peace was an essential element of the Republican campaign'.[47] Moreover, the United States was afraid of alienating the Arab–Asian–African world by appearing to side with old-fashioned gunboat diplomacy. Eden's own colleagues were less than united on what should be done. And the Labour Party was by no means prepared to give the government *carte blanche*. Gaitskell was worried about maintaining the Anglo-American alliance; both he and Bevan were concerned about Britain's position at the United Nations, and relations with the Commonwealth and the Third World. Bevan was also very concerned about *détente* with the Soviet Union.[48] Eden was further weakened through his failure to get on with either Dulles or Gaitskell. In addition, although Eden had a sabre to rattle, it was showing signs of rust. Given the state of the British forces, many weeks would be needed before a military solution could be embarked upon. Eden also had other worries. Following Khrushchev's anti-Stalin speech at the 20th Congress of the Soviet Communist Party earlier in the year, the situation in eastern Europe was becoming less stable. In particular both Poland and Hungary were on the boil. Of more direct concern for Eden was the situation in Cyprus. The Greek-speaking majority of this British colony appeared to want union with Greece. As well as normal peaceful agitation to that end a small band of right-wing guerrillas were conducting a relentless campaign of violence against the British. Finally, Eden felt that before he could resort to force against Nasser he would need a pretext; so far, apart from the act of nationalization itself, he did not have one. Nasser 'had not done any injury to British or French lives, nor had he stopped a British or French ship passing through the Canal, despite the refusal of the owners to pay dues to the Egyptian Canal Authority'.[49] He had also promised the shareholders compensation for their shares 'on the basis of their closing price on the Paris Bourse immediately preceding the date on which this law enters into force'.[50]

Throughout August and September, Britain and France tried to mobilize their allies and the users of the Canal into some kind of coherent front. Sir Robert Menzies, the Australian Prime Minister, went to see Nasser with Western proposals, but he was unable to get the Egyptian leader to modify his position. The latter was in no mood to rescind the nationalization measure. Britain and France were not prepared to concede the principle of one state, Egypt, owning and controlling the Canal. All the arguments were put by both sides at the United Nations in late September and early October. By October, Egypt showed signs of being more conciliatory. This was due to the influence of India, the Arab oil states, and pressures on the Egyptian economy.[51] Selwyn Lloyd, the British Foreign Secretary, took up negotiations with Dr Mahmoud Fawzi, Egypt's Foreign Minister, under the chairmanship of Dag Hammarskjöld, the U.N. Secretary-General. They were joined by Christian Pineau, the Foreign Minister of France. According to Anthony Nutting,

Egypt was now willing to negotiate an agreement which gave the maritime powers substantially all that they were asking. The Suez Canal Users' Association, or its equivalent, would now have a real job of work to do as the organised representative of the users and, without prejudice to Egypt's right of ownership, would be able to safeguard the interests of its members with the full agreement of the Egyptian Government. . . . it seemed that agreement had finally been reached that the Suez Canal would be run as a partnership between Egypt and the users.[52]

It was decided that all four would meet again in Geneva on 24 October to finalize the details. What Mr Lloyd did not know was that the French were already so close to the Israelis as to make any agreement virtually impossible. On 14 October, Eden and Nutting conferred with Albert Gazier, the French Minister of Labour, who was acting for his Foreign Secretary, and General Maurice Challe, Deputy Chief of Staff for the air force. The two French representatives offered their hosts what Nutting called an 'invitation to a conspiracy'.[53] Israel would attack Egypt, excusing its actions as a reprisal for raids by Arab irregulars, Britain and France would then give the ultimatums to both sides to withdraw in order to allow Anglo-French forces to occupy the Canal on the grounds of preventing it from being damaged. The Cabinet apparently agreed with this plan at two sessions on 24 and 25 October.[54] The Israelis struck against Egypt as arranged on 29 October. The following day the Anglo-French ultimatum was issued to both sides. The day after that the British and French blocked a U.N. Security Council resolution calling for Israeli withdrawal. On 31 October, Anglo-French air and naval forces attacked Egyptian air and naval bases. Two hundred British and forty French planes operating from aircraft-carriers based on Malta and Cyprus, hit Egyptian positions for the next 48 hours. Operation 'Musketeer' had begun. This operation went on until midnight on 6 November. It involved the dropping of over a thousand British and French paratroops outside Port Said, and much larger numbers of troops invading from the sea. The Egyptians took what action they could. Their pilots were not yet trained in the use of their Soviet jets and attempted, somewhat unsuccessfully, to fly their planes to safe bases. Nasser, perhaps unwisely as it turned out, ordered his troops facing the Israelis to withdraw to defend Cairo. The Egyptians blocked the Canal, and Syrian engineers cut the Iraqi pipeline, a source of oil to Britain. By the end of the operation the British had lost 22 killed, the French 10, the Israelis 200, and the Egyptians probably between 2,650 and 3,000.[55] One American book subsequently described the military operation as 'incompetent', and went on: 'the British force lumbered slowly across the Eastern Mediterranean in the manner of a punitive expedition of the Victorian era'.[56] But despite some hiccups and hitches, from the military point of view, the operations were successful. From the political and economic standpoints they were disastrous.

The Aftermath of Suez

Eden found that he had many critics at home. Most of the press, though previously hostile to Nasser's seizure of the Canal, opposed the military action of Britain and France. The Labour Party found new unity in face of the crisis and, with one or two exceptions like Shinwell and Stanley Evans, was bitterly critical of the government. Typical were the words of James Griffiths in the Commons on 1 November: 'This is for our country a black and tragic week. . . an unjustifiable and wicked war'.[57] Bevan likened the British attack to that of Germany on Norway in 1940.[58] Douglas Jay asked 'do not these operations amount to an act of organised murder by the

British Government?'[59] Eden denied Britain was at war,[60] to which Sydney Silverman retorted, 'What are we at with Egypt then – at peace?'[61] On 4 November the Labour Party organized a very successful mass rally in Trafalgar Square under the slogan 'Law not War'. More disappointing for Eden was opposition from within his own party. Eleven Conservative MPs, among them Walter Elliot, Robert Boothby, Keith Joseph, Peter Kirk, and Nigel Nicolson, signed a letter to Eden 'critically asking about the purpose of the policy of the Government'.[62] Anthony Nutting resigned from the government, as did another Junior Minister, Sir Edward Boyle. William Clark resigned from the government, as Press Officer at 10 Downing Street. Within the Cabinet itself there were doubts, unease, and anxieties. Sir Walter Monckton, Minister of Defence until 18 October and then Paymaster General, spoke out against military action, but remained in the government until the crisis was over.[63] Butler 'had doubts'.[64] As he later wrote about hearing a broadcast by Eden,

My mood was one of deep misgiving and anxiety on hearing this analogy with fascism . . . I thought the Prime Minister had got this part of it wrong . . . Egypt's new revolutionary government was acting contrary to our interests, and probably international law, but it represented a popular movement not an imposed tyranny. [65]

As the situation developed, so the doubts grew. Outside the government Lord Mountbatten, the First Sea Lord, was not happy, 'I carried out my duties but it would be foolish to pretend that I did not have great doubts about the whole thing'.[66] There were many others in this situation.

Worldwide, Britain, France, and Israel were under intense verbal fire, from friends as well as their usual adversaries. Most of the Commonwealth condemned the invasion. Especially severe was India's Premier Nehru, who was normally counted a good friend of Britain, 'I cannot think of a grosser case of naked aggression'.[67] More importantly, in Washington there was anger and dismay. President Eisenhower declared, 'The U.S. was not consulted in any phase of these actions, which can scarcely be reconciled with the principles and purposes of the United Nations'.[68] Dulles, within days of being operated on for cancer, felt 'just sick about the bombings'.[69] And according to Eisenhower, the Secretary of State lamented, 'at this very time, when we are on the point of winning an immense and long-hoped-for victory over Soviet colonialism in Eastern Europe, we should be forced to choose between following in the footsteps of Anglo-French colonialism in Asia and Africa or splitting our course away from their course'.[70] The Americans decided on a temporary split. Already on 30 October the United States had proposed a resolution in the Security Council of the

United Nations ordering Israel to withdraw, and calling on all member states to refrain from force or the threat of force. Britain, backed by France, for the first time used its veto to prevent the resolution from being adopted. The United States proposed another resolution, this time to the General Assembly of the United Nations on 2 November. This called for an immediate cease-fire and the withdrawal of the attacking forces. It was adopted by a large majority. This time the two states said they would agree to cease further military action if a U.N. force would keep the peace until settlements between the Arabs and Israel and satisfactory arrangements for the Canal were established and guaranteed. On 3 November a Canadian resolution was adopted asking the Secretary-General to prepare within 48 hours a plan for a U.N. force. This he was able to do within seven hours. Britain and France then agreed, on 5 November, to cease hostilities at midnight on 6–7 November and to withdraw. Eventually 5,000 men from ten states were deployed. By 22 December the last Anglo-French forces had left Egypt. Israeli forces were eventually withdrawn by 1 March 1957.[71] Worse was to come from the United States. There was speculation against sterling 'mainly in the American market or on American account'.[72] This caused some in the Cabinet to think again about further military action. The Chancellor of the Exchequer, Harold Macmillan, 'switched almost overnight from being the foremost protagonist of intervention to being the leading influence for disengagement—as well he might, for the loss of 279 million dollars in that November represented about 15 per cent of our total gold and dollar reserves'.[73] Further, the U.S. Treasury was opposing the request of Britain to withdraw capital from the International Monetary Fund, in which the United States had a decisive say, to support the pound. Later the Americans agreed to an IMF loan to Britain if it agreed to a cease-fire.[74] Effectively Britain had no choice. It seems this was a more decisive factor than Soviet threats to use rockets against Britain and France if they did not stop their invasion.[75] The Russians were themselves in the dock at the time. World public opinion was heavily against them for their invasion of Hungary, which was attempting to go its own way. This was another reason for the hostility of Britain's friends. They felt the Anglo-French action had helped to make the Soviet invasion possible. Whether that is true or not, Hugh Thomas's comment is appropriate that 'serious was the damage afforded by Suez to the previously growing reputation of Britain as the most progressive and reasonable of the nations of the developed world'.[76]

Remarkably, Eden's popularity in the country did not collapse. The government had been in trouble before the Suez adventure. By-election results, particularly in 'safe' Conservative seats, had been no comfort for the government. In June 1956 the Conservative majority at Tonbridge had dropped from 10,000 to just over a thousand. Opinion polls during November 1956, though they must be treated with some caution, did seem to indicate an increase in the government's popularity. 'A good case might thus be made that Suez briefly helped the Conservatives regain some of their lost popularity'.[77] With the opinion-forming classes, however, Eden's position was much weaker. The Opposition had no confidence in him, not a good thing in a democracy, and in his own party his stock had fallen greatly. On the right, the so-called Suez group had attacked Eden, then Foreign Secretary, for signing the 1954 Agreement with Egypt. They had goaded him on in the summer of 1956, now they were dismayed by his capitulation. In any case, 'After such a colossal defeat for his personal policy in his central area of interest, it is hard to see how the party could have allowed him to stay on'.[78] Britain really needed a new captain on the bridge to convince world public opinion of its renewed sanity. Added to all this, Eden was a very sick man. After a holiday in Jamaica, he resigned on 9 January 1957. At the end, in the Cabinet, he had broken down in tears and cried, ' "You are all deserting me, deserting me." He was in total collapse, weeping unashamedly. Then he went upstairs to compose himself. For such is the agony of power when it denies you'.[79] Eden's tragedy was that 'He was obviously a victim of history, caught between the old Imperial might of the Empire and its total eclipse as a world power'.

Notes

1 Lord Butler, ed., *The Conservatives: a History from their Origins to 1965* (London, 1977), 427.
2 Quoted ibid., 428.
3 Blake, *The Conservative Party from Peel to Churchill* (London, 1970), 269-70.
4 John Montgomery, *The Fifties* (London, 1965), 116.
5 John Whale, *The Politics of the Media* (London, 1977), 22.
6 H. H. Wilson, *Pressure Group* (London, 1961) gives a good account of the campaign for commercial television.
7 Whale, op. cit., 33.
8 Sir Harry Pilkington, *Report of the Committee on Broadcasting 1960* (HMSO, June 1962), Cmnd 1753, 31, 33. Most of the report was written by Professor Richard Hoggart, well-known for his book *The Uses of Literacy*.
9 Lord Avon, *The Memoirs of Sir Anthony Eden: Full Circle* (London, 1960), 50.
10 ibid., 50-1.
11 James Margach, *The Abuse of Power* (London, 1978), 84.
12 Lord Butler, *The Art of the Possible* (London, 1971), 164.

13 Marquis Childs, *Eisenhower: Captive Hero* (London, 1959), 147.
14 Dwight D. Eisenhower, *Mandate for Change 1953-1956* (London, 1963) tells of his heart attack.
15 Robert J. Wesson, *Soviet Foreign Policy in Perspective* (Homewood, Ill., 1969), 225.
16 Avon, op. cit., 302.
17 Andrew J. Pierre, *Nuclear Politics: the British Experience with an Independent Strategic Force 1939-1970* (London, 1972), 86.
18 Avon, op. cit., 266.
19 Margach, op. cit., 102.
20 *The Memoirs of Cordell Hull*, Vol. II (London, 1948), 1474.
21 Reginald Bevins, *The Greasy Pole* (London, 1965), 37.
22 Foot, op. cit., 482.
23 This was Macmillan's view: *Tides of Fortune 1945-1955* (London, 1960), 579.
24 For accounts of this controversy see Foot, op. cit., chapter 12; Henry Pelling, *A Short History of the Labour Party* (London, 1961), 112-13.
25 D. E. Butler, *The British General Election of 1955* (London, 1956).
26 Pelling, op. cit., 114
27 W. T. Rodgers, ed., *Hugh Gaitskell* (London, 1964); contribution by John Betjeman, 'School Days and After', 17.
28 Hugh Dalton, *High Tide and After* (London, 1962), 352.
29 Lord George-Brown, *In My Way* (London, 1971), 242.
30 Gerald Sparrow, *'R.A.B.': Study of a Statesman* (London, 1965), 120.
31 Avon, op. cit., 316.
32 John Ramsden in Butler, ed., *The Conservatives*, 438.
33 Butler, *The Art of the Possible*, 185.
34 Maxime Rodinson, *Israel and the Arabs* (London, 1968), 69.
35 ibid., 71
36 Mohammed Hassanein Heikal, *The Cairo Documents* (New York, 1973), 46.
37 Herman Finer, *Dulles over Suez* (London, 1964), 42.
38 ibid., 45. Childs, op. cit., 205.
39 Butler, *The Art of the Possible*, 186.
40 Alan Thompson, *The Day before Yesterday* (London, 1971), 124.
41 Finer, op. cit., 13.
42 Anthony Nutting, *No End of a Lesson* (London, 1967), 48.
43 ibid., 47–8.
44 Leon D. Epstein, *British Politics in the Suez Crisis* (London, 1964), 66.
45 It is given in full in Nutting, op. cit., Appendix I.
46 ibid., 52.
47 Childs, op. cit., 207.
48 Foot, op. cit., chapter 14.
49 Nutting, op. cit., 55.
50 ibid., Appendix III.
51 ibid., 74.
52 ibid., 77.
53 ibid., chapter 10.
54 ibid., 104.
55 Hugh Thomas, *The Suez Affair* (London, 1966), 151.
56 Roscoe Drummond and Gaston Coblentz, *Duel at the Brink* (London, 1960), 174.
57 Hansard (Commons), vol 558, col. 1631.
58 ibid., col. 1714.
59 ibid., col. 1629.
60 ibid., col. 1640.

61 ibid., col. 1640.
62 Thomas, op. cit., 138.
63 Lord Birkenhead, *Walter Monckton* (London, 1969), 308.
64 Russell Braddon, *Suez: Splitting of a Nation* (London, 1973), 104.
65 Butler, *The Art of the Possible,* 188.
66 Braddon, op. cit., 103.
67 ibid., 99. Unfortunately, as Lord Avon pointed out (op. cit., 545), Nehru did not seem to understand what was happening in Hungary.
68 Braddon, op. cit., 94.
69 ibid., 99.
70 Dwight D. Eisenhower, *The White House Years: Waging Peace 1956-1961* (London, 1966), 83.
71 These details are from H. G. Nicholas, *The United Nations as a Political Institution* (London, 1975), 58-9.
72 Butler, *The Art of the Possible,* 194.
73 ibid., 194; see also Avon, op. cit., 556-7.
74 Thomas, op. cit., 147.
75 ibid., 145. Childs, op. cit., 213 claims the Soviet threat was influential in the British decision. Avon, op. cit., 555-6, plays down the Soviet threat.
76 Thomas, op. cit., 155.
77 Epstein, op. cit., 149.
78 Ramsden, op. cit., 442.
79 Margach, op. cit., 113-14.

5 Macmillan and the 'Affluent Society', 1957-59

Macmillan takes over

When Eden fell in January 1957, the proverbial 'man on the Clapham bus' probably expected that R. A. Butler would become Prime Minister. After all, he had done the job as deputy in the absence of Eden, with apparently as much efficiency as anyone. He was also well qualified in other respects. Only fifty-five, he had served, in a junior capacity, in three ministries before the war. As President of the Board of Education and then Minister of Education, he had been responsible for the 1944 Education Act. He had been in government from 1932 to 1945, and again from 1951 onwards. His term as Chancellor of the Exchequer (1951–55) was regarded as a success. He had followed this as Lord Privy Seal and Leader of the House. In all, he had served under five Prime Ministers. The public remembered him more for his reformism and moderation since 1939 than for his support of appeasement before that date. His trouble was that he was too moderate, too cautious, too statesmanlike for his own party. It could be said he had the qualities of a good Premier rather than the qualities necessary for a successful contender for that office. The widely used term 'Butskellism', used to draw attention to the similarities between his economic policies and those of Gaitskell, did him no good with the Right of Centre in his party. His realism over Suez, coupled with his loyalty to Eden in spite of doubts – and loyalty traditionally was placed high on the list of Tory virtues – should have helped. Quite the reverse was the case. 'Had Rab become Prime Minister it would have been interpreted as the final acknowledgment of guilt by the Suez Group and the Suez Inner Cabinet'.[1] Moreover, with two Suez hardliners, Salisbury and Kilmuir, organizing the consultations, before Salisbury and Churchill advised the Queen on Eden's successor, Butler's fate was sealed.

The new Prime Minister, Harold Macmillan, did not have as much experience as his rival. In the pre-war period he had an honourable record of dissent over the government's failure to deal with unemployment and over appeasement. Not surprisingly, he had first gained office under Churchill during the war, serving as Resident in North Africa. He was a successful Minister of Housing and Local Government (1951–54), then briefly of Defence (1954–55). After a few months at the Foreign Office, he served as Chancellor of the Exchequer (1955–57). Born in 1894, educated at Eton and Balliol, he had gone into his father's publishing business. Like Eden, Macmillan was a survivor of the 'lost generation' of the First World War. A captain in the Grenadier Guards, he was wounded three times, gained a reputation for bravery,[2] went undecorated, and ended the war 'badly wounded'.[3] His military experience became very important for him and he developed a 'certain contempt' for those who had not served in the forces in either of the world wars.[4] This contempt was to influence his judgement of colleagues and opponents.

As MP for Stockton-on-Tees between the wars he had been shocked by the poverty of his working-class constituents and turned left on economic and social questions. It is believed that, had the war not intervened, he would have joined Labour.[5] Macmillan had another life in the inter-war period. In 1920 he married into the influential Cavendish family and soon was related by marriage to sixteen MPs.[6] 'Perhaps most important, the Cavendish connexion increased Macmillan's fascination with the life of the great country-houses – a life which cut across his own austere family background, and his intellectual discipline. He loved the aristocratic style of their politics . . .'[7]

Macmillan was one of those Conservatives who had worked to remove Chamberlain from leadership in 1939, and one of those who voted against him at the end of the decisive debate in 1940. His reward came days later when the new Prime Minister, Churchill, appointed him parliamentary secretary to the Ministry of Supply under Herbert Morrison. In June 1942 he was moved to the Colonial Office with the higher rank of Under Secretary of State, and in November, Churchill asked him to go to North Africa as Minister Resident. This involved the difficult task of co-operation with the Americans and the French. He had the advantage with the Americans that his mother was American, and with the French that he spoke their language. 'He could show his diplomatic skill in a sphere of war where, for the first time, Anglo-American relations were crucial and very difficult'.[8] He impressed many of those he met at this time. Lady Diana Duff Cooper, who had met many men of power, saw in him a future Prime Minister.[9] After a number of other moves in the Mediterranean theatre Macmillan ended his first period of office as Secretary for Air, with a seat in the Cabinet, in Churchill's caretaker government of six weeks duration.

Macmillan first earned the attention and approval of his parliamentary colleagues in the dark days of opposition. Briefly out of Parliament, he was returned at the Bromley by-election in November 1945. As a member of the shadow cabinet he was the Party's expert on industrial policy. He specialized in studied scorn of Labour's proposals, even though, as in the case of coal nationalization, this sometimes involved him in condemning policies he had advocated before the war. He was a member of the committee, chaired by Butler, which drafted the *Industrial Charter*. This period helped to develop his skills as a Commons debater, which were to be of great use after 1951 when the parliamentary technique of many of his colleagues seemed sadly rusty. His 'Edwardian' appearance became fixed at this time.

As Minister of Housing, Macmillan 'brought a special energy and ingenuity to the problem', talking about a housing crusade. Yet his success was not as spectacular as it seemed; he had inherited plans from Dalton for a smaller 'People's House'.[10] His brief period at Defence coincided with the announcement of Britain's intention to build the hydrogen bomb. At the Foreign Office he was largely responsible for the ill-fated Baghdad Pact which helped to push Egypt towards Russia.[11] He also failed to see the significance of the European idea.[12] Though invited, he did not go to the Messina conference in June 1955, the conference which led to the setting-up of the Common Market. As Chancellor he will be remembered, if at all, for his introduction of Premium Bonds. The Bonds 'gave a new glimpse of the more raffish and adventurous Macmillan'.[13] The Suez affair tipped the balance decisively in his favour. Remarkably, considering he was Chancellor, he had been strongly for resolute action against Nasser. He did not appear to consider the possible financial implications. Remarkably too, as one who had worked so closely with Eisenhower, he was obviously wrong in his estimate of American reactions to British intervention. He did, however, have the good sense to advise Eden to accept a cease-fire when he saw the gold and dollar reserves rapidly disappearing. So it was that 'after the Suez debacle the Conservatives chose him in preference to "Rab" Butler in the belief that they were getting a tough-muscled Right-winger'.[14]

Macmillan realized that he needed Butler in the government if further party schisms were to be avoided and he was fortunate that the latter agreed to take over the Home Office, though he wanted the Foreign Office. Selwyn Lloyd was kept on as Foreign Secretary to appease the Suez Group and as an act of defiance to the world. Kilmuir was reappointed Lord Chancellor, and Peter Thorneycroft, another Suez hardliner, became Chancellor of the Exchequer. Alan Lennox-Boyd stayed on at the Colonial Office. Duncan Sandys, a son-in-law of Churchill who had served him during the war, was appointed Minister of Defence with increased powers. It was not surprising that in a Cabinet led by Macmillan the 'Suez Inner Cabinet', those responsible for the planning of the operation, should be well represented. What was surprising, considering the Conservative Party's attempts to present itself as a broad people's party, was the extent to which it was still a highly exclusive body. Of the sixteen members of the Cabinet in January 1957, six had been at Eton, only two had not been at public schools which were members of the Headmasters' Conference. This is a theme we shall return to later. There were no women in Macmillan's Cabinet in 1957. Churchill had thought it necessary to have one and had appointed Miss Florence Horsbrugh Minister of Education in November 1951. She joined the Cabinet in September 1953. In the following year she was succeeded by Sir David Eccles. Eden kept the Cabinet an all-male affair, and at first Macmillan followed Eden's example, even though women, much more than men, were responsible for Conservative electoral victories. Admittedly, Macmillan's choice was limited. There were only ten Tory ladies in the Commons. Labour, even in defeat, had 14 women MPs. One other feature of Macmillan's 1957 government was that the new generation of Conservatives – Heath, Maudling, Powell, Profumo, Soames among them – were starting their rise to prominence. Sir Edward Boyle, who had been with Macmillan at the Treasury, was persuaded to return. He had opposed Suez, but Macmillan 'had a very high regard for his talents as well as for his character'.[15] Boyle served in Education under Lord Hailsham who, like his junior, was an Old Etonian. Hailsham was promoted to the Cabinet in June 1957.

There was another astonishing feature of Macmillan's Cabinets. As Christopher Hollis, himself then a Conservative MP, wrote,

What is even more interesting is the lavishness with which Mr Macmillan had filled his offices with relations by marriage. *John Bull* on January 4, 1958, calculated that of the eighty-five members of his government, thirty-five were related to him by marriage, including seven of the nineteen members of his Cabinet . . . There has been nothing like it in England since the days of the eighteenth-century Duke of Newcastle . . . What is the reason for this extraordinary reversion – particularly at the hands of a man who is, as Conservatives go, more attuned to 'the wind of change' than to traditional policies? Doubtless it simply is that nepotism is one of the strongest of human emotions . . . Mr Macmillan has more cousins and less opposition than any Prime Minister in our history.[16]

Hollis wrote that in 1961. Perhaps some, by no means all, of Macmillan's later difficulties were due to this unusual situation in the government. Certainly it made him an easier target for the Opposition, for his own backbench critics, and for the press. Among his relations were Lord Salisbury, who was married to Elizabeth Cavendish, and three other old Etonians, Sir Reginald Manningham-Buller (later Lord Dilhorne), the Attorney-General, Julian Amery, number two at the War Office, and David Ormsby-Gore (later Lord Harlech), Minister of State at the Foreign Office. Manningham-Buller and Amery were later promoted to the Cabinet. Two further appointments need to be mentioned. Harold Evans (later Sir Harold Evans, Bart) was appointed press spokesman at 10 Downing Street. As the veteran lobby correspondent James Margach has commented,

Macmillan's public panache – the more remarkable since he was shy to the point of sickness before big occasions – is testimony to the value of highly professional public relations behind the scenes. In this crucial sector of power Macmillan avoided the errors committed by so many other Prime Ministers . . . Harold Evans . . . proved the most outstanding No. 10 spokesman in my long experience.[17]

The second appointment was that of John Wyndham (later Lord Egremont) as unpaid private secretary to Macmillan. He had served Macmillan off and on throughout his ministerial career, and he was highly thought of by his boss. Others were perhaps sceptical about his influence: 'Wyndham is rich, high-born and . . . belongs far more to the eighteenth century than to the age of the common man'.[18] Wyndham found his master

always polite, courteous and outwardly calm, and he was very quick in getting through his work . . . because of his seniority both in years and experience, and because despite that gentleness of manner, he was capable of being ruthless – as were his small staff – managed to interfere time and time again with Ministries over the heads of various Ministers. Sometimes this riled other Ministers.[19]

Macmillan annoyed his ministers in another way. As Charles Hill put it, 'now and again the Cabinet was consulted at too late a stage in the evolution of some important line of policy'. Hill did, however, pay tribute to Macmillan's chairmanship of the Cabinet which he dominated by sheer superiority of mind and judgement.[20]

Slow economic growth

The new Prime Minister's first priority was to rebuild the confidence of his colleagues, of the Party at Westminster, and in the country at large. Secondly, he had to reassure the world that Britain was not finished, but was still able to play a considerable role in world affairs. Remarkably, he was able to do both. When he took over, the Conservative Party appeared to be heading for certain defeat. Yet two years later it achieved the peak of its post-war success to date.

Macmillan himself was not at first certain he could achieve these objects and within weeks of his taking over the first crack appeared in his Cabinet. Lord Salisbury resigned on 28 March. The issue was Cyprus. Officially it had been 'leased' from the Turks in 1879 and annexed in 1914. It was seen as a barrier against Russian influence in the Mediterranean. After 1945 the great majority of its people, Greek by language and culture, sought an end to the colonial status and union with Greece. Violence erupted in 1955 after a junior minister at the Colonial Office, Henry Hopkinson, had said on 28 July 1954 that 'there can be no question of any change of sovereignty in Cyprus'. In 1955 Eden had ordered the arrest of Archbishop Makarios, who was the spiritual leader of the Greek Cypriots, and his deportation to the Seychelles. The violence escalated and the incoming Prime Minister realized that the only course was renewed talks with Makarios. To Salisbury and some others in the Conservative Party this appeared another retreat in the face of violence. Hundreds were to die in Cyprus before the Zurich agreement was concluded in 1959. Under this agreement Cyprus became independent within the Commonwealth in 1960. Special safeguards were included to placate the Turkish minority. Britain was able to retain certain bases there. The Americans had thrown their weight behind the ending of the British colonial regime, fearing a conflict between Greece and Turkey, both members of NATO.[21]

Apart from the blow of Salisbury's resignation Macmillan's position started to improve. Much of the débris of Suez had already been cleared up by Butler, acting for Eden, before January 1957. The Canal itself was cleared by 9 April and opened to shipping. Soon oil supplies to Britain had improved so much that petrol-rationing, introduced in December, ended in May 1957. In the same month Britain felt strong enough to ignore protests from Japan, and appeals by the Pope, Dr Albert Schweitzer, and Premier Nehru, and went ahead with exploding its first H-bomb in the Pacific near Christmas Island. Bevan too had made a last-minute appeal against the British H-bomb.[22] For the 'get tough' section of Macmillan's own party, and many of the electorate, the test, and the others which followed, signified Britain's continuing importance. On the other hand, they were worried by the note of 'softness', 'liberalism', or 'realism', depending on one's point of view, which was soon an established theme of Macmillan's ministry. Some regretted the announcement on 4 April that there would be no further call-ups for military service after 1960. In addition to the possible implications of this move for Britain's ability to hold its colonies together, some felt national service had a value as a means of disciplining youth. In March 1957 Ghana gained its independence and Dr Kwame Nkrumah, a man heartily detested by the Right in Britain, and who had been imprisoned by the British (above p. 54), became its President. At the end of August the Federation of Malaya became independent. In Britain itself, the Right could take no comfort from having 'Rab' Butler at the Home Office. Yet the Homicide Act of 1957, which further restricted capital punishment to certain specified types of murder, such as the killing of a policeman or prison officer on duty, was not the work of Butler. He had inherited it from his predecessor.[23] In seeking to modernize the penal system he was to fall foul of the 'hangers and floggers' in his own party in later years and thus weaken his chances of succeeding Macmillan.

Macmillan knew very well, of course, that the electorate was more concerned about economic policy than colonial policy, and it could never be very far from his thoughts. His own analysis of the situation on assuming office was:

as I knew from my year in the Treasury and was to learn for the rest of my active life in politics, to maintain the British economy at the right level, between inflation and deflation, balancing correctly between too much and too little growth, was a delicate exercise. All the clever young economists and journalists and all the armchair experts could not resolve it. There were so many imponderables, and so many uncertainties. It was not a subject to be solved by mathematical formulae, or exact calculation. It was like bicycling along a tightrope.[24]

It is doubtful whether there has been a Prime Minister or a Chancellor since the war who has not thought like that, despite the confident words they have uttered, from time to time, about Britain's economic prospects. Nevertheless, it would be wrong to suggest, as Macmillan seems to be doing, that it is impossible to identify some of the sources of Britain's economic problems during the post-war period, and during his period of office. What experts have differed on is the weighting they have given to particular factors. All agreed that Britain was bound to decline relatively as a world economic power. As other states developed, Britain's share of world trade would inevitably decline. In particular, as pre-war competitors recovered from the ravages of war, this was clearly going to happen. It certainly did under Harold Macmillan:[25]

Share in world trade in percentages

	1938	1950	1951	1959	1962
U.K.	22	25	22	17	15
U.S.A.	20	27	26	21	20
W. Germany	23*	7	10	19	20 *refers to whole of Germany
Japan	7	3	4	7	7

What became controversial was the extent of Britain's decline. Why should West Germany, Italy, Japan, and certain other countries perform consistently better than Britain in the 1950s? One serious answer was that they were starting from such low bases, compared with Britain, that they were likely to find it easier to increase their production of goods and services, at least for a number of years, than the more 'mature' economies. One Conservative Party publication summed it up in 1964 as follows,

For the years up to about 1955, much of the explanation of the rapid growth achieved by European countries lay in catching up wartime arrears. This, however, cannot explain the experience of more recent years. But it is still fair to make the obvious statistical point that if one starts from a low point a percentage increase always tends to look large: the increase from 2 to 4 is 100 per cent, but from 4 to 6 is only 50 per cent.[26]

This did not apply to countries such as Sweden and Denmark, however, which achieved greater increases in their *per capita* gross national product during 1951-62 than did Britain.[27] The movement of relatively cheap labour from agriculture to industry was another factor in some countries – Japan, Italy, France, and later on Spain – which made it easier to increase production compared with highly urbanized Britain. Germany was helped by the refugees from the East. This factor should neither be forgotten nor exaggerated. Andrew Shonfield, in a much praised and much commented-on study, laid bare some of the key causes of Britain's economic weaknesses. One was too much investment abroad and too little at home. 'History', he wrote in 1958,

once again is the greatest impediment to clear thinking on the subject of British investment overseas. The words themselves have a subtly pleasing and adventurous sound. One way or another it has gone pretty deep into the folk myth that British greatness and wealth have depended on pouring out our treasure abroad.[28]

Shonfield found that in most cases, oil being one of the exceptions, it was better to invest in undertakings at home rather than abroad. However, the 1957 Budget encouraged investment abroad at the expense of home investment.[29] A second source of weakness, according to Shonfield and other observers of the British economic scene, was defence expenditure, especially overseas. Aside from the United States, Britain consistently spent more on defence than its NATO allies.[30] With regard to the overseas defence burden, Shonfield urged,

an obvious course for a British government seeking a rapid way of strengthening the country's balance of payments would be to review the whole of this military spending abroad, the subsidies to foreign governments as well as the cost of actual British garrisons, with a determination to make a drastic cut.[31]

He had doubts about Hong Kong, Gibraltar, Malta, and the high cost of British forces in Germany: 'if . . . we had been in the position of Germany and thus prevented from maintaining any troops overseas, then our average balance-of-payments surplus on current account would have been doubled to reach over £300m. This is, in fact, more than the German average for this period'.[32] And an American researcher has established that

The average current-account surplus between 1948 and 1960 is £116 million. Over the same period overseas military deployments have caused outflows which amount to about £150 million a year. The foreign-exchange costs of military deployments abroad thus exceed the average annual surplus earned by the export of British goods and services; it is reasonable to assume that Britain's reserves of gold and hard currency would be much larger had fewer troops been stationed overseas.[33]

The maintenance of the pound as a reserve currency was another factor holding back British industry. As Samuel Brittan put it:

We are often told that growth has had to be halted 'to protect the pound sterling' . . . Yet in the ten years from 1953 to 1963, British prices rose faster than those of every other major European country except France; and our gold and foreign exchange reserves were, at less than £1,000m., hardly any higher at the end of this period than at the beginning . . . Britain now has to maintain the sterling area on a reserve less than half of Germany's and a good deal smaller than that of France. Yet neither country maintains an international currency, and France has a much smaller foreign trade than Britain. Britain has thus done just as badly in the 'sound finance' league of conservative bankers as in the production league of modern-minded economists. We have too often sacrificed rapid growth for the sake of a strong pound and as a result of all our pains frequently ended up with neither.[34]

The trade unions and industrial management were also often criticized for the poor record of the British economy compared to some others. Strikes tended to get a great deal of space in the press and on television. The situation came to be seen as far worse than it was. Gradually, a kind of hysteria built up, which very probably, as to some extent with the balance of payments, made matters worse. British trade unions had, and have, their problems. There were, and are, too many of them. There were well over 180 trade unions affiliated to the TUC in the Macmillan era. In some cases several operated in one industry, leading to inter-union rivalry and demarcation disputes. This contrasted with West Germany's sixteen industrial unions affiliated to the DGB. But whereas Britain's unions had grown up over a long period, West Germany's trade-union structure was based on changes made during the Third Reich which were then taken over by the free trade unions after the war. Britain's trade unionists were criticized for their apathy which led, in some cases, to unrepresentative minorities taking over control. This is a problem common to all voluntary bodies and not just trade unions. Usually, the leadership of the trade unions is more moderate than many of the shop-floor activists who do most of the unpaid, yet necessary, work in trade unions. On this point, a Conservative publication of the day commented,

about 90 per cent of Britain's strikes are 'unofficial', in so far as they are not supported by the executive of a trade union. This may well be evidence of poor communications within some unions, or lack of authority from the top, but it makes nonsense of any implication that our trade unions, as such, are irresponsible or unduly militant.[35]

As mentioned in chapter 2, the only serious case of Communist abuse of power in a British trade union was in the Electrical Trades Union. In that union the Communists used 'fraudulent and unlawful devices' to keep power. This situation was brought to light by Woodrow Wyatt, then a Labour MP, in collaboration with two leading members of the union, Les Cannon and Frank Chapple. Wyatt published the accusations in the *New Statesman* and on BBC television's programme *Panorama*. The union was eventually expelled from the TUC and the Labour Party, but it was six years between the time the allegations were first openly made, in 1956, and the removal of the offenders.[36] The activities of these Communists was a blow against the whole trade union movement. External supervision of trade-union elections and secret ballots on official strike action, had they been introduced, would have helped to assuage public fears, but unfortunately these were not introduced. On the other hand, it must be stressed that the idea that trade-union militancy was to any large extent responsible for Britain's economic problems was false. The Conservatives themselves pointed out in 1964 that

in the past 10 years, Britain has lost fewer days through strikes than any other major industrial country in the free world except Western Germany. And in the 15 years after the Second World War, we lost only one-ninth of the working days which were lost through industrial disputes in the 15 years after the First World War.[37]

Days lost per thousand persons employed in mining, manufacturing, construction and transport 1951–62 (average)[38]

U.S.A.	1,185
Italy	780
Canada	649
Japan	579
Belgium	501
Australia	462
France	391
U.K.	272
West Germany	77
Sweden	53

It is true that the British figures have been subject to criticism at various times as underestimating the amount of industrial unrest in the United Kingdom. The writer is prepared to accept this. He also believes, however, by the same token, that the figures for most other countries underestimate their degree of industrial unrest. Most of the unrest in the 1950s occurred in four industries – shipbuilding, the docks, mining, and motor vehicles – which only employed about 7 per cent of the working population. They were industries with special problems. Certainly in the case of the docks and motor-manufacturing, unrest in them could unduly upset the export trade. Another point which needs to be made in relation to strikes and the economy is that there is not necessarily any relationship between growth and strikes or lack of them. In West Germany there was little labour unrest but much growth. Italy, Japan, and Canada experienced great increases in economic development and industrial relations which were much worse than Britain's. Some other countries came in between on both counts. It is also difficult to prove that radical leadership of trade unions produces more labour unrest in a country. American trade unions were free of Communists, yet they were much more strike-prone than Communist-led French unions. Even in West Germany the biggest trade union, IG Metall, was headed, in the 1950s, by Otto Brenner, a left-wing socialist. If British trade unions were only marginally responsible for the nation's economic problems in the 1950s, what about British management?

Increasingly in the 1950s a feeling developed that somehow British industry was failing to attract enough young people of high calibre to embark upon careers in management. It was also felt that managers were badly trained compared with their rivals abroad, and that there was too little upward mobility from the shop floor.

On the shop floor itself there was not enough technical training, a fact recognized in a White Paper, *Technical Education,* published in 1956. It proposed expansion of technical training opportunities at all levels, including a doubling of workers given 'day-release' by their employers. Higher up the ladder, a committee set up by the Ministry of Labour to investigate on the selection and training of supervisors in industry commented in 1962:

While there has been fair progress since 1954 both in private industry and in the nationalized industries, the provision of systematic training for supervisors is still relatively limited. As against the 1,100 firms in private industry known to have started systematic training, there are in manufacturing industry alone almost 6,000 establishments employing more than 250 workers and a further 8,750 employing more than 100 workers. Moreover, some of the training given is inadequate, superficial and sporadic. The great majority of managements still do not give systematic and well-planned training.[39]

It was not a very reassuring picture of Britain's industrial NCOs.

Higher up still, in the boardroom, an Institute of Directors study early in 1969 revealed that only 18 per cent of their sample of managing directors held a university degree. Most of those who did had been at Cambridge. The majority of managing directors surveyed had had a public-school education. They were mainly from

what might be called the upper and upper-middle class of business owners, executives, and professionals. Seven out of ten managing directors had fathers in this group, while one out of ten had fathers in the last three categories of skilled and unskilled workers and farmers. Overall we can say that potential success in British industry is quite closely linked to parental occupation and family status.[40]

The American management expert Dr David Granick called Britain the home of the amateur. He stressed that professionalism was a serious charge against an individual in British industry.[41] Apparently British managing directors did not think there was any special experience which was useful to a future managing director, though marketing was favoured by some. Foreign experience, legal or technological training, were not considered essentials.[42] Much of this contrasted with top management in the United States, Japan, and West Germany.

'Most of our people have never had it so good'

What is remarkable about the second half of the 1950s, given the discussion above, is that this period came to be regarded as idyllic, the era of the affluent society, a society in which, because of unprecedented prosperity and full employment, Britain was changing fundamentally and for the better. Unemployment had disappeared during the war, had remained minimal under Labour, and stayed that way for the remainder of the 1950s. That in itself was a dramatic change for many in the working class. Better still was the fact that earnings had risen faster than prices. Between October 1951 and October 1963, wage rates rose by about 72 per cent and retail prices by nearly 45 per cent. The increase in earnings had been even greater. On average, earnings of men in industry had risen by 95 per cent since 1951.[43] Further, there had been a reduction in the official working-week. The new degree of affluence was measured in the acquisition of consumer durables: by 1965, 88 per cent of households in Britain had television, 39 per cent were equipped with refrigerators, and 56 per cent with washing machines.[44] The number of TV licences issued had risen from about half a million in

1950 to over 12 million in 1964. In 1951 there had been 2.25 million cars on the roads, in 1964 the figure had increased to over 8 million. This great rise in the ownership of these, and other, consumer goods was the result of the extension of hire purchase, and the lowering of purchase tax, as well as the rise in earnings. In 1951 there had been 100 per cent purchase tax on such items as electric fires, cosmetics, and cars. In 1963 the rate of tax on these goods was down to 25 per cent. Refrigerators, washing machines, vacuum cleaners, radio and TV sets had all been taxed at a rate of 66.33 per cent under Labour. Under Macmillan it was down to 25 per cent. Pots and pans, which had not been subject to tax under Labour, were, as we have seen, taxed by Eden. Under Macmillan there was still a 10 per cent tax on them.[45] Home ownership just about doubled under the Conservatives. Britain was being transformed into a nation of home-owners: over 40 per cent of the population owned their own homes. If there were still too many slum-dwellers, the Conservatives could claim that between 1955 and 1964 over half a million slums had been taken out of the housing stock and over 1.5 million people rehoused from them.[46] Far more people were taking their holidays away from home than ever before – something like three-fifths in 1964, and a significant minority of them were going abroad. In one other area, affecting the standard of living, Macmillan and his colleagues felt proud of their achievements, though this was a more ambiguous achievement than the others. Income tax had been reduced five times during the Conservatives' term of office. The standard rate had fallen from 9s. 6d. (47.5p) to 7s. 9d. (39p) in the pound; cutting income tax is always popular; people seldom ask themselves whether the cuts in government expenditure which must follow are in their, or the country's, long-term interest. Harold Macmillan had commented, rather rashly, some believed, in July 1957, only a few months after becoming Prime Minister:

Indeed, let's be frank about it; most of our people have never had it so good. Go around the country, go to the industrial towns, go to the farms, and you will see a state of prosperity such as we have never had in my lifetime – nor indeed ever in the history of this country.

He went on to admit, 'we cannot forget that some sections of our people have not shared in this general prosperity',[47] and went on to promise them help. The Prime Minister could have said again in 1959, with greater conviction, most people 'have never had it so good', and even more so when he retired from office in 1963. Given Macmillan's own view of the fragile nature of the British economy, one can rightly ask how was it all achieved? The answer was rooted in increased production, improved terms of trade, and some reduction of the burden of armaments. The index of industrial production, which excludes agriculture, trade, transport, and other services, had risen from 85 in 1951 to 115 in 1962.[48] Moreover, the pattern of industrial production was changing. Electronics, computers, synthetic fibres, agricultural machinery, and motor vehicles were making great headway. Britain had developed the largest petro-chemical industry in Europe, and the automobile industry had doubled production since 1951. Great strides had been made in agriculture too. With fewer holdings, less land, and less labour far more was being produced than before the war:[49]

	pre-war average	*1951–52*	*1962–63*
milk (million galls)	1,556	2,014	2,575
eggs (thousand tons)	385	464	768
beef & veal	578	617	891
mutton & lamb	195	147	268
pigmeat	435	477	819

Before the war, Britain had produced, in terms of value, about one-third of its food. By the 1960s it was producing about half. The second source of prosperity was the great improvement in the terms of trade Britain enjoyed in the 1950s. Samuel Brittan estimated that

After the collapse of the Korean boom, food and raw-material prices fell so much that in 1953 we could buy thirteen per cent more imports for the same amount of exports than in 1951. The 1957–8 world recession triggered off another, and a slower slide in commodity prices, which eventually improved our terms of trade by another fourteen per cent, making twenty-nine per cent altogether. These two movements together were worth the best of £1,000m. a year to the British public'.[50]

This happy state of affairs changed in the 1960s. Under the Conservatives defence expenditure declined as a percentage of the gross national product (though it remained higher than that of the other members of NATO excepting the United States). This also made it easier for the government in its efforts to create the affluent society.

Russians in space

[Although British defence expenditure was seen by Macmillan as being at too high a level, it continued to weigh down the economy throughout his period of office.] At the beginning of the 1960s, Britain was still spending £51 every second on armaments; £3,050 a minute, £1,603 million a year. By November 1963 there were still approximately 357,000 regular servicemen and boys in the forces. By comparison, in 1960, £894.6 million was spent in Great Britain on education. Few doubted that Britain needed armed forces, but did it need its own nuclear capacity, and did it need so many troops abroad? Those who did believe Britain required its own 'deterrent' argued, in the words of Harold Macmillan,

The independent contribution . . . gives us a better position in the world, it gives us a better position with respect to the United States. It puts us where we ought to be, in the position of a Great Power. The fact that we have it makes the United States pay a greater regard to our point of view, and that is of great importance.[51]

The arrival of the space age in 1957 indicated, once again, that Britain was, whatever its efforts, no longer in the first division. Contrary to Western expectations, the Russians launched the world's first artificial Earth satellite, Sputnik 1, on 4 October 1957. This successful launching put 83 kg. into space. It remained there until 4 January 1958. On 3 November the Russians followed this up with the equally successful launching of Sputnik 2, containing the dog 'Laika', the first mammal in space. Macmillan records that 'The Americans were not unnaturally alarmed by so striking a proof of Russian scientific and technological progress'. And he wrote in his diary

The Russians have launched another and larger satellite (with a 'little dawg' in it) which has created much alarm and despondency in U.S. The British people, with characteristic frivolity, are much more exercised about the 'little dawg' than about the terrifying nature of these new developments in 'rocketry'. Letters and telegrams were pouring in tonight to No. 10, protesting about the cruelty to the dog.[52]

The first American riposte to the Soviet challenge came only on 31 January 1958, when the United States launched Explorer 1. But the Russians continued their exploits, keeping ahead of the United States for several years. They were the first to 'hit' the moon with an unmanned craft in 1959. In the same year they produced the first photographs of the hidden side of the moon. Their man, Yuri Gagarin, was the first man in space in 1961, and they achieved another first when they put a woman, Valentina Tereshkova, into orbit in June 1963. The Soviet Union had clearly demonstrated its capability of producing intercontinental missiles of the greatest accuracy and of sufficient weight to carry megaton warheads to any town or city of the United States. One would have thought that this would have led to a drastic reappraisal of Britain's independent nuclear deterrent. As Professor Northedge has commented: the Sputniks

had the effect of carrying the two super-Powers still further away from lesser states like Britain which aspired to remain in the nuclear league. This was a moment, if ever there was one, when Britain without any dishonour might have renounced pretensions to remain in the front-rank class of nations and come to terms with the west European states when the shape of the EEC was still in process of moulding. But that opportunity was not taken.[53]

Instead, the pro-British deterrent lobby argued that given the progress of Soviet rocketry, the United States could become increasingly inhibited in using its nuclear retaliatory power to defend western Europe. With the single possible exception of defending West Berlin – and even there the Americans appeared firm when faced with Soviet threats in 1959 – there seemed no likelihood of Eisenhower abandoning his NATO allies. This was equally true of his successors. Nor did there appear to be any conceivable situation in which Britain dare contemplate using its nuclear capacities independently of the United States. Britain relied on the American nuclear umbrella in peace and war. Originally envisaged as the carriers of Britain's deterrent, the V bombers, Vulcans, Valiants, and Victors, were obsolescent when they were first introduced in 1956. The installation in Britain of American 'Thor' Intermediate Range Ballistic missiles in 1957–58, with a two-key system – an American key activated the nuclear warheads and a British key launched the missile – served to emphasize British dependence on American technology and leadership. This was not really changed by Macmillan's success, as a result of meetings with Eisenhower at Bermuda (March 1957) and Washington (October 1957), in getting the Americans to amend the Atomic Energy Act of 1954. Under the amended legislation of 1958 Britain was able to get American nuclear weapons know-how of the kind it had been deprived of since the passing of the McMahon Act in 1946. Britain was able to buy from the United States component parts of nuclear weapons and weapons systems and to make possible the exchange of British plutonium for American enriched uranium. It also made possible the sale to Britain of nuclear propulsion plant for the first British nuclear submarine, the *Dreadnought*. Clearly though, Britain had in no real sense an 'independent' nuclear deterrent.

The other draining and damaging (to Britain's image) aspect of defence was its policeman's role in the Middle East, Africa, and Asia. It is convenient to discuss this in the context of foreign and colonial policy.

Problems in Africa and Aden

As we have seen, British troops had been involved in a shooting war in Malaya and in Cyprus. If Britain's friends had sympathized in the first case, they had been more critical in the second. British forces had been used to suppress the left-wing government of Dr Cheddi Jagan in British Guiana in 1953, and found themselves 'restoring order' there again in 1962 after Jagan's People's Progressive Party had, once again, won the elections. Though there were racial tensions there and the PPP was not above reproach – it looked as though British and American interests were changing the rules of the game – the electoral system was altered, to ensure that a leader enjoying their confidence emerged. British Guiana eventually became independent as Guyana in 1966. The situation in Malta was, to say the least, badly handled. In 1947 Malta had been granted internal self-government and had elected a Labour administration. Britain still regarded the naval and military base there as essential and in 1956 it was agreed that the island should become part of the United Kingdom, sending three MPs to Westminster. Malta had served Britain well for 150 years and had earned itself warm praise for its help during the Second World War. The British government showed itself parsimonious when evaluating Malta's annual grant and the 1956 talks broke down, therefore, on the question of money. At the beginning of 1959 the constitution was suspended and direct rule reimposed. At the elections which followed, Labour was defeated by the (Conservative) National Party backed by the Catholic Church. The new government was also dissatisfied with the financial arrangements and Maltese political opinion turned to thoughts of complete independence. The island, with a population of just over 300,000 and few resources, achieved this in September 1964.

In Africa too hauling down the Union Jack was by no means easy. The difficulty was greater where white-settler interests were involved. This was particularly so in Kenya and Southern Rhodesia. Armed revolt broke out in Kenya in 1952 and continued until 1955, during which time about 11,500 Mau-Mau irregulars were killed, mostly by British troops. The British losses were light, but a considerable number of loyal Africans also died.[54] 'The nationalist wind, which was beginning to sweep across the African continent, went unrecognised by this privileged, anachronistic European society'.[55] Much of the land was in the hands of the 50,000 whites who dominated the 5 million Africans. The situation was further complicated by tribalism, the Kikuyu being the majority, and by the presence of an Asian trading and professional class. Iain Macleod, who became Colonial Secretary in October 1959, recognized the inevitability of majority rule and immediately started to release detained Africans. The London Conference of January 1960 recognized eventual majority rule. In August 1961 Jomo Kenyatta, jailed since 1953 for alleged Mau-Mau activities, was released because his dominance of Kenya African politics was recognized. It was to take two more conferences and two more Colonial Secretaries, Reginald Maudling and Duncan Sandys, to finalize the independence constitution. At midnight on 11 December 1963

Kenya obtained its independence and entered the Commonwealth as the eighteenth sovereign member.

As we saw in chapter 3, the Labour government had resisted the demands of the European settlers for the creation of a Central African Federation. Yet the Federation comprising Southern Rhodesia, Northern Rhodesia (Zambia), and Nyasaland (Malawi) came into being on 1 August 1953. Thus 300,000 white settlers came to dominate 9 million Africans. The scheme had been opposed by the great majority of Africans and, in Britain, by the Labour and Liberal parties, the Archbishop of Canterbury, the Moderators of the Church of Scotland and the Free Church Federal Council. The (non-Communist) International Confederation of Free Trade Unions also opposed the Federation. Opposition from the Africans was never far from the surface, but in early 1959 it boiled over. African organizations held meetings and processions, which were technically illegal. A state of emergency was declared, first in Nyasaland and then in Southern Rhodesia, where deaths occurred when the police attempted to quell protest demonstrations. Many politically organized Africans were arrested including, in Nyasaland, Dr Hastings Banda, widely recognized as that territory's African leader. A British government-appointed commission under Mr Justice Devlin reported adversely on some aspects of the way the disturbances had been handled. Macmillan himself first became convinced that there could be no progress without the release of Banda a year later, on his famous African tour. Macmillan also convinced himself of the increasing African opposition to the Federation, especially in Nyasaland, and to a lesser extent in Northern Rhodesia. It was during this trip in January 1960 that he made the speech in the South African parliament containing the much-quoted passage,

the most striking of all the impressions I have formed since I left London a month ago is of the strength of this African national consciousness. In different places it takes different forms, but it is happening everywhere. The wind of change is blowing through this continent, and, whether we like it or not, this growth of national consciousness is a political fact. We must all accept it as a fact, and our national policies must take account of it.[56]

His hosts refused to bend to this wind of change and left the Commonwealth in 1961. The Macmillan administration recognized the inevitable in Northern Rhodesia and Nyasaland, allowing the development of internal self-government based on African majority rule, with Kenneth Kaunda and Hastings Banda emerging as leaders in the respective territories. Both territories were allowed to secede from the Federation and become independent in 1964.

As the Central African Federation was dying, the British **government was planning other federations. There was the**

Federation of Nigeria, which gained its independence in 1960, a land with a population larger than that of the United Kingdom. Like the Central African Federation, its basic weakness was that it was an attempt to unite separate regions which were different in economic and political development, and whose peoples had different tribal loyalties, different languages, and different religions. In 1966 Nigeria's attempt at a democratic federation ended with a military *coup*. It was then held together by force of arms.

In 1962 the curtain was finally drawn on the West Indies Federation. This had been formally set up in April 1958. But it had been weak from the start. Inter-island communications had been poor in an organization in which Jamaica and Trinidad, the two main components, were a thousand miles apart. The Federation had been run on a shoestring because the central government had had no real power to raise revenue. Jamaica withdrew from the Federation after a referendum, and Trinidad and Tobago after a general election. Both became independent members of the Commonwealth in August 1962. This left the problem of what to do with the smaller islands. However, by 1966 Barbados, with a population of just over 200,000, became independent, Grenada, whose population was 104,000 in 1970, followed in 1974.

Not deterred by such failures, the British government went ahead with the merging of Aden with the Federation of South Arabia. Since the Suez action Egypt had become more, not less, significant in Middle East politics. So had the Soviet Union. Britain and America grew alarmed at every new manifestation of Arab nationalism, wrongly judging it to be a threat to their interests or a device of Soviet imperialism. In July 1958 the pro-British, reactionary, regime of Nuri es-Said was overthrown by a military revolt following the Egyptian model, and Iraq withdrew from the Baghdad Pact. Earlier in the year Syria and Egypt had proclaimed their union in the United Arab Republic. This unhappy experiment was brought to an end by a Syrian military *coup* against the Nasserite officials in Damascus in 1961. It did, however, alarm pro-Western elements in the area at the time. The Lebanese pro-Western President Chamoun requested U.S. help under the Eisenhower Doctrine. He wrongly supposed that Egypt was interfering in the civil war which was developing in Lebanon. American marines were landed, but did not get involved in any fighting, and a compromise resulted. King Hussein of Jordan made a similar request to Britain and paratroops were duly dispatched. These were eventually withdrawn after an all-Arab resolution was agreed in the U.N. General Assembly pledging non-interference between Arab states. British troops were also ordered to Kuwait. Kuwait had been a British 'protected' state since 1899 under a monarchy. It too felt the excitement of Arab nationalism in the 1950s. In 1961 Kuwait, by that time an important producer of oil, became independent. It was immediately under pressure from General Kassim's regime in Iraq and asked for British help. Macmillan complied with the request. He recorded in his diary (8 July 1961)

We worked through some long and anxious nights, especially when we thought Kassem would seize Kuwait city and territory virtually unopposed. Now our worry is the opposite. Since the Iraqi attack has *not* in fact developed, all the pressure will be turned on us. It is going to be difficult, and expensive, to stay; hard to get out. The Opposition in Parliament have behaved pretty well – so far. But this will not last.[57]

British troops did in fact withdraw in September 1961. Kuwait was admitted to the Arab League and the members of this body sent a mixed force, including Egyptians, to ensure its independence from Iraq. Britain also had a problem with the Yemen.

The Yemen was a truly medieval kingdom which laid claim to Aden and the British-protected sheikdoms bordering it. It had been too weak to realize its ambitions, even though from the mid-1950s it had started to receive arms from eastern Europe. In 1962 a revolution broke out and the new rulers orientated the country towards Cairo. Most of the states of western, as well as eastern, Europe recognized the new regime. Foolishly Britain did not. Civil war followed in the Yemen and continued for many years.

Given all this turmoil in the Middle East, Aden did not look like a good prospect as an independent state. With a population smaller than that of Nottingham, and in area only half the size of the Isle of Wight, its inhabitants were dependent largely on a declining entrepôt trade, an oil refinery, and the British base. Seized by the East India Company in 1839, Aden had become a vital refuelling port *en route* to India. In 1937 it became a crown colony. Most of the population of 220,000 in 1963 were Arabs, either born locally or from the British protected states or Yemen. These peoples shared the same language and culture. There was also a minority of Indians and Pakistanis, many of them engaged in trade. The Aden TUC, a body, like the British TUC, affiliated to the International Confederation of Free Trade Unions, had a powerful hold over the Arab workers and was not satisfied with the constitutional progress made in the colony. Even the middle-class moderates in the Aden Association wanted an elected legislature, an elected ministry, Arabic as an official language, and more locals in senior posts. It was 1958 before Arabic was recognized, and fulfilment of the other demands seemed far off.[58] Most of the population were still not eligible to vote. By this time the trade unions, under the leadership of Abdullah al-Asnag, and partly influenced by Nasser's Egypt, had

113

opted for complete independence from Britain. Al-Asnag wanted eventual British withdrawal and some form of association with the surrounding states, but not under their prevailing political regimes. In 1959 there were widespread strikes. The government's answer was to make strikes virtually illegal under the Industrial Relations Ordinance of 1960. Aden was becoming more prominent in British defence planning by the 1960s. It was a familiar pattern. With the liquidation of the Canal Zone base Cyprus had become more important. When Cyprus gained its independence, Kenya was upgraded as a military base. As Kenya had moved towards its freedom, Aden's future was scrutinized more closely. In August 1962 the British government published a White Paper proposing the merger of Aden with the surrounding Arab Emirates to form the Federation of South Arabia. Politically advanced Aden was to be tied to the feudalistic neighbouring sheikdoms which were officially under British protection. Under the proposed constitution Aden would be in a minority position. In the Commons, Denis Healey, for the Labour Party, moved an amendment on 13 November regretting the government's decision. This move, he claimed, meant ranging Britain 'with all that is most backward and anachronistic in the Middle East'.[59] On the same day George Thomson attacked the flogging and imprisonment of several Aden trade unionists who had gone on strike against the proposed merger. They were, he said, the Tolpuddle martyrs of the Middle East.[60] In the same debate Bob Edwards made a prophecy, 'Not merely shall we have to withdraw the British base from Aden in ten years if this proposal goes through. I make this prophecy, that in ten years we shall be swept out of the Middle East, and we shall lose all the oil throughout the whole of the Middle Eastern lands'.[61] In December 1962 Abdullah al-Asnag and some others were jailed for 'conspiring to publish a seditious publication'. More repression followed and the merger took place in spite of local protests on 18 January 1963. It was left to the incoming Labour government to deal with the mounting violence and disorder. In less than ten years the British did leave.

The 'wind of change' also swept through Sierra Leone (1961), Uganda (1962), and Tanganyika and Zanzibar (which joined together to form Tanzania in 1964). All four became independent members of the Commonwealth under the Conservatives.

The one other attempt to set up a federation during this period was in Malaysia. Characteristically, it too failed. In August 1965 Singapore seceded from Malaysia to become an independent republic. Both states, however, remained members of the Commonwealth.

The last military excursion under the Conservatives was happier in its results than most of the others. In January 1964 British troops were sent to Kenya, Uganda, and Tanganyika at the request of their constitutional governments. The British, with speed and efficiency, quelled army mutinies in those countries. The failure of the colonial administrations gradually to lay the foundations of professional officer corps before independence, and the attempt to do so hastily afterwards, together with dissatisfaction over pay, were at the root of the trouble.[62]

Labour in turmoil

The Suez campaign had given the Labour Party the chance to unite over a great national issue. Had the Conservatives been forced into an election in 1957, all would have been well for Labour. Unfortunately for them this did not happen and their unresolved differences soon came to the fore again. They were divided on the issues of public ownership and defence. The first issue was more fundamental than the second and divided the Party longer.

Groups and individuals within the Labour Party started to re-examine Labour's experience of office, and reasons for its two successive electoral defeats. They started to look again at British society and asked themselves whether their policies needed refurbishing in the light of those changes. By 1954 G. D. H. Cole, who as a professor of Politics at Oxford, a writer, and a member of the Labour Party, influenced many who played significant roles in the Labour movement, asked, 'is it towards Socialism we are tending, or towards an anglicized version of the American conception of democracy? Is our goal the classless society, or only the so-called "open" society which is in fact still closed to a majority of the people?'[63] Cole was in no doubt himself what he wanted: 'a society of equals, set free from the twin evils of riches and poverty, mastership and subjection'.[64] He felt Atlee and his colleagues had done little to realize this dream, and the post-Attlee leaders were becoming even more timid.

Democratic Socialism is suffering at present from altogether too many inhibitions. It dare not frighten possible marginal supporters; and it dare not flout that so-called 'public opinion' which is really newspaper opinion put about by the reactionary press. It dare not offend the Americans . . . A Socialism that dares not is bound to fail; for the fighting spirit which created the Socialist movement is no less needed to carry it through to its goal. The use of parliamentary and constitutional methods need not destroy this spirit – though it is all too apt to do so, when constitutional Socialism has become respectable and accepted as part of the national political set-up, and when trade unions no longer have to fight for the right to exist and have become part of the recognised machinery of the capitalist order.[65]

Cole was articulating the doubts, fears, and emotions of thousands of Labour Party members, and a significant minority in the parliamentary party. For these people Labour seemed to be dying from the Establishment embrace. Cole had always consciously rejected Marxism, but he believed that to realize Labour's aims much more public ownership was necessary. But not just public ownership. He had always been for economic democracy, for workers' control of industry, for the participation by those employed in a particular industry in the decision-making about that industry, decisions which affected their lives and livelihoods. He realized the introduction of such a system would not be easy, and he wanted to see many other changes in society as well, but he thought this was the key to the transformation of society. Richard Crossman wrote in a similar vein in his *Socialism and the New Despotism* (1955):

We seek to make economic power responsive both to the community as a whole (the consumer) and to the worker in any particular industry (the producer). Plans for nationalisation which do not satisfy the aspirations to workers' control are the technocrats' perversion of our Socialist ideal. We must frankly admit that, so far, our nationalised industries have been little better than that.[66]

Crossman, who was already a member of the National Executive Committee of the Labour Party, recommended his colleagues to study the experiment of *Mitbestimmung* (codetermination) in German industry. This was something Labour, under the influence of Morrison, had ignored. It was also ignored by more conservative writers who kept referring to West Germany's good industrial relations. Crossman thought Keynsian economics had weakened the economic case for public ownership but not the moral case. He was, however, concerned about all types of irresponsible power – in private industry, in the state, in parties, and in trade unions – in the mass society and the threat to personal freedom. These two influential socialist writers, like many others, were not satisfied with what had developed in the industries nationalized. Though neither sought total socialization of the economy, both felt much more common ownership would be necessary to achieve the socialist ideal. Bevan in his *In Place Of Fear* (1952) concurred with this view.

Other, equally thoughtful, members of the Labour Party, came to rather different conclusions on economic policy. In 1956 the Socialist Union, a group based on the monthly journal *Socialist Commentary*, came out strongly in favour of the mixed economy. They saw a danger in any monopoly in any sector of economic life. They were forcefully impressed by the totalitarian nature of the Soviet economy and the implications of that for the rest of the world.

Where revolutions have overthrown the regimes of the past . . . Private capitalists and landlords have been eliminated, but so have free labour movements. What once were regarded as inherently socialist institutions – public enterprise, a planned economy, even social services – are deliberately employed to reduce every individual to a helpless victim of the state. If communism is to be the result of creating a straight antithesis to the capitalist system, then clearly socialists want to think again.[67]

Cole and the Left would have denied that communism inevitably followed nationalization where there was a free electoral system, free trade unions, and workers' control. But the Socialist Union believed competition was needed for both political and economic reasons. They were not as concerned about expanding the public sector and concluded:

The private sector of a socialist economy is not there merely on sufferance, to be tolerated only on grounds of political expediency, with the Sword of Damocles hanging over it in perpetual threat. On the contrary, it has a legitimate and indeed a necessary function to perform. Within the limits of equality, there must be opportunities for people to spend as they wish, to own, to initiate and experiment; they must be able to form associations to further their economic interests. In all these arenas, the individual must have a chance to act without waiting for the approval of the state.[68]

At greater length, Anthony Crosland argued in the same way in his book *The Future Of Socialism* published in 1956. Hugh Gaitskell, in his contribution to the debate, looked for ways in which his party's aim of a society in which there are no social classes, equal opportunity . . . a high degree of economic equality, full employment, rapidly rising productivity, democracy in industry, and a general spirit of co-operation between its members',[69] could be achieved without nationalization. He felt much more could be done through the growth of social services, severe taxation on high incomes, an increase in the share of national income enjoyed by wage- and salary-earners, and educational reform. He also advocated state shareholdings in mixed enterprises. However, he conceded, while 'there is much to be said for privately owned property being widely spread, it is certainly not along this path alone that we can proceed. The second course, a high proportion of publicly owned property – must also be adopted'.[70] At the same time he stressed,

It is a great deal easier to persuade people that a big change in industrial structure has to be made, when they know there is something seriously wrong with the industry, and they are satisfied that the particular plans for nationalization are based on experience elsewhere, and calculated to ease rather than aggravate the trials of transition.[71]

There seems to be a degree of contradiction here. On the one hand, Gaitskell is admitting that his version of the new Jerusalem cannot be created without 'a high proportion of publicly owned property'. On the other, he is restricting the actual transfer of private to public industries to those clearly not up to the mark, industries about which there has been a great deal of public discussion, as in the case of the easier nationalization of the mining industry.

All the writers, on the left as well as on the right of the Labour Party, were deeply influenced by the new vision of the Soviet Union, a vision strongly coloured by (socialist) George Orwell's *1984*, which was widely discussed in the early 1950s. They were also influenced by the apparent indifference of the majority of the workers to the issue of public ownership. Further, they, and much of the public, had suffered disappointment over the nationalized industries in Britain; though it must be stressed that such disappointment resulted from a naïvely optimistic view of what could be achieved in run-down industries over a short period. Finally, Gaitskell himself, as leader of the Labour Party, more than the others, was concerned about the damage to Labour's 'image' by the close association of the Party with nationalization. At successive elections strongly financed, pro-'Free Enterprise' bodies had launched massive publicity campaigns against further nationalization. For all these reasons, whereas Cole, Bevan, and others still placed a great deal of emphasis on 'common ownership', Gaitskell drastically restricted the role of the public sector. It was the view which prevailed.

At the Labour Party conference at Brighton in 1957 Harold Wilson, for the NEC, introduced *Industry and Society* which set out Labour's view on public ownership. It was basically Gaitskell's conception. It committed the Party to the renationalization of the steel industry and road haulage, but there was no 'shopping-list' of industries to be taken over. Only those industries or large firms which 'failed the nation' would earn the attention of a Labour government looking for candidates for public ownership. According to Wilson, 'failing the nation' included the abuse of monopoly power, bad labour relations, failing to export enough, etc. Different interpretations were possible. The document failed to convince a section of the conference. The National Union of Railwaymen introduced their own resolution which called for the nationalization of all the basic industries, and deplored the present tendency to deviate from accepted socialist principles. It was defeated by 5.3 million votes to 1.4 million. *Industry and Society* was adopted by 5.3 million to 1.4 million. Bevan's wife, Jennie Lee, and, more strangely, Morrison and Shinwell, had supported the railwaymen.[72]

The other big issue which caused the Labour Party so much heart-searching was the H-bomb. As was mentioned above (p. 63),

Bevan and his group had opposed Britain's decision to manufacture the H-bomb. In 1957 Bevan was to change his position dramatically and thus deprive the Left in the Party of its leader, destroying in the process the faith of some of the rank-and-file in all leaders. He announced his new line at the Brighton conference: Britain's bomb could, after all, force the other super-powers to take notice of Britain and could give the United Kingdom a decisive voice in international affairs. In opposing a unilateralist resolution he declared: 'if you carry this resolution . . . you will send a Foreign Secretary, whoever he may be, naked into the conference chamber'. He claimed the bomb could give Britain 'the opportunity of interposing' between the United States and Russia 'modifying, moderating, and mitigating influence'.[73] The offending resolution was then thrown out with the help of the block votes of the big trade unions rather than the rhetoric of Nye Bevan. Most of the delegates from the Labour constituency parties, representing the activists who did most of the menial political work, delegates who had previously supported Bevan, voted the other way.

Some of those dismayed, defeated, and disgusted activists were already working in what was to become a new mass movement to rid Britain of its nuclear weapons – the Campaign for Nuclear Disarmament (CND). CND was officially announced in February 1958, but for some time before this various groups had been set up to oppose the British, and all other, nuclear weapons. As early as 1954 a small group of Labour MPs under the chairmanship of Fenner Brockway formed the Hydrogen Bomb National Campaign Committee. Among its more prominent members were Anthony Wedgwood Benn and Anthony Greenwood. CND itself, a much larger, non-party, non-sectarian movement, resulted from discussions which followed an article of J. B. Priestley in the *New Statesman* (2 November 1957). Priestley wrote,

The British of these times, so frequently hiding their decent, kind faces behind masks of sullen apathy or sour, cheap cynicism, often seem to be waiting for something better than party squabbles and appeals to their narrowest self interest, something great and noble in its intention that would make them feel good again. And this might well be a declaration to the world that after a certain date one power able to engage in nuclear warfare will reject the evil thing for ever.

It was a patriotic appeal to idealism and it impressed many young people who were searching for something more elevating than mere affluence. The new movement was headed by Earl (Bertrand) Russell, the philosopher, its secretary was Canon L. John Collins of St Paul's Cathedral. On the executive committee they were joined by Michael Foot, ex-Labour MP, close friend of Bevan, and editor of the left-wing Labour weekly, *Tribune*; Ritchie Calder, noted as a scientific journalist; J. B. Priestley; James Cameron of the liberal daily *News Chronicle*; Kingsley Martin, editor of the *New Statesman*; Howard Davies of the United Nations Association; and Lord Simon of Wythenshawe.[74] In April 1958 the movement organized a protest march from London to the Atomic Weapons Research Establishment at Aldermaston. Marchers covered the 50 miles between 4 and 7 April. Frank Allaun, Labour MP for Salford East; Dr Donald Soper, the Methodist leader; and Pastor Martin Niemöller, the German pacifist and First World War U-boat commander, led 5,000 marchers on the final day. CND was established 'to demand a British initiative to reduce the nuclear peril and to stop the armaments race, if need be by unilateral action by Great Britain'. Despite the support of a number of Labour MPs, it remained largely a movement of the intelligentsia, the middle classes, and youth. Among the more prominent intellectual supporters of CND were the writers John Braine, John Brunner, Mervyn Jones, Doris Lessing, Sir Compton Mackenzie, Iris Murdoch, Alan Sillitoe, and Arnold Wesker. Others prominent included art critic John Berger, sculptor Henry Moore, historian A. J. P. Taylor, theatre critic Kenneth Tynan, actors Spike Milligan, John Neville, and Vanessa Redgrave, and film directors Anthony Asquith, Basil Wright, and Lindsay Anderson.[75] Such names by no means exhaust the star-studded lists of sponsors and activists.

The New Left

CND drew strength from the anger of a section of the literary class over what was considered to be the complacency which appeared to be smothering post-war Britain. The spokesmen of this section of the community were dubbed by the press the 'angry young men'. One of the most significant of them was John Osborne (born 1929), who became famous overnight with his play *Look Back In Anger*. Put on by the new English Stage Company at the Royal Court Theatre in 1956, it marked a turning-point in the British theatre, with greater interest in social criticism and experimentation. Arnold Wesker (b. 1932) was successful with his portrayals of East End, Jewish working-class life. Alan Sillitoe described the problems, tensions, and hopes of the working class in Nottingham where he himself had been a factory worker. David Storey (b. 1933), the son of a Yorkshire miner, made his name with *This Sporting Life*, about the tough life of Yorkshire Rugby players, which he knew about from first-hand experience. But of all the characters which emerged from the pages of this new genre, the best-known was undoubtedly Joe Lampton, hero of John Braine's *Room At The Top*. Joe 'was brought up on the fringes of poverty and squalor in an ugly North

Country town. He had emerged with one overriding aim: to fight his way up into the bright world of money and influence'.[76] Joe was not particularly political and he, and his creator, subsequently found much of their anger against the system appeased by fame and fortune. These, and some other similar writers, probably did have some marginal political influence, but they were much more important for helping to revitalize the British theatre and cinema. Though that had not been their intention, they also exposed the weakness of the English education system. Only David Storey had managed to get to an institution of higher education. Some of them had not even been to a grammar school.

The angry young writers were not the only young critics of society in the second half of the 1950s. The Suez campaign and the Hungarian revolution had produced what became known as the New Left. Roughly speaking, the New Left was a coming-together of disillusioned Communists, who abandoned the Party as a result of its support for the Soviet suppression of the Hungarian revolution, and disillusioned young members of the Establishment (or potential members), who disapproved of the invasion of Egypt. The core of the New Left was the group of supporters of the *New Left Review*, which was a merger of the *Universities and New Left Review* and the *New Reasoner*. Whether they were ex-Communists or ex-Conservatives, New Lefters were mainly Oxbridge graduates, and virtually all graduates. Ralph Samuel and Stewart Hall were the driving force behind the movement which presided over the establishment of a chain of Left clubs throughout the country. At a time when the political parties were complaining about apathy and the difficulty of finding audiences for prominent politicians, considerable numbers of people in London actually paid to attend New Left meetings where they were entertained, provoked, and challenged by such speakers as Norman MacKenzie of the *New Statesman*; Ralph Miliband of the London School of Economics; Doris Lessing, the Rhodesian novelist; Clive Jenkins, the white-collar trade union leader – all in one evening! They heard Brian Abel-Smith asking, 'Whose welfare state?', and maintaining that the middle classes were doing far better out of it than the working class. Hugh Thomas, ex-Foreign Office, was angry about Suez. Peter Marris, ex-Colonial Service, was angry about Kenya. And Paul Johnson, who admitted to having been a Conservative in 1951, suffered from a sense of outrage. He wanted to see the end of monarchy, the Lords, the corporate bodies which control the public schools and Oxbridge, the regimental system in the army, the Inns of Court system, the honours list, and much else. He warned the Labour Party,

It . . . has the choice of becoming a party of government, concerned primarily with administering a social structure to which it has become reconciled, or attempting to change the structure. I believe it must and will choose the second, even though this involves a retreat into the political wilderness. But if it finally surrenders its sense of outrage, and allows the power-motive to become its political dynamic, it will cease to be a progressive movement, and something else will take its place.[77]

With the CND and the New Left enjoying considerable successes, and the official leadership of the Labour Party appearing to be reasonably united, one can understand how many in the Labour movement thought their day had come once again as the election was called in October 1959. But psephologists were less certain. By-elections had shown substantial swings against the Conservatives in 1957 and 1958. Labour had been heartened by picking up four seats. However, as Parliament drew to a close, Labour's lead vanished. In the summer of 1958 the government's popularity started to rise again. According to David Butler,

Among the factors that may have lain behind this shift in opinion were the lowering of the bank rate, the increase in consumption, the London bus strike, the government's show of force in Jordan, the failure of the Labour Party as an opposition and, last but not least, the success of Mr Macmillan as a television performer and his apparent 'unflappability' in face of adversity.[78]

Conservative opinion would place more emphasis on the London bus strike and the defeat of Frank Cousins, which boosted Conservative supporters' morale. In the April Budget before the election taxes were cut, including the duty on beer. In this writer's view the government was given credit for the general feeling of wellbeing. Most people, most of the time, have only modest ambitions, and most electors did not really think a Labour government would take them much farther along the road to a material utopia. Together with prosperity, peace is the other major concern of the electorate. Macmillan appeared to be doing a great deal to secure it. Earlier in the year he flew to Moscow, Washington, and other important capitals to promote understanding and possible long-term *détente*. It looked as if he was doing his best, what more could one ask? As a 'performer', in what was the first complete TV election, Macmillan had a certain style, a certain authority, a certain eccentric charm. What about Gaitskell? He appeared, by comparison with the Prime Minister, good enough to be a leading politician, but not quite confident enough to lead the nation, intelligent but lacking in imagination, sincere but too sombre; in a word, colourless. Certainly the nation did not want a revolution, but he could only offer his potential clientele better pensions when they needed more compelling reasons for being enthusiastic about his brand of Social Democracy.

The results put the Conservatives back with a net gain of 21 seats. Labour had a net loss of 19 seats. The Liberals stayed as they were with 6 seats. The results were obviously a great boost to the Conservatives and a great blow to the other parties. The Liberals took some comfort from the fact that their share of the vote had increased from 2.5 per cent in 1951, and 2.7 per cent in 1955, to 5.9 per cent in 1959. Both major parties had their share of the poll reduced. Labour by 2.6 per cent to 43.8 per cent, the Conservatives by 0.3 per cent to 49.4 per cent.[79] Labour's only crumb of comfort was that there was still a bias in the electoral system which meant that they needed about 400,000 more votes than the Conservatives to get any given number of seats.[80] Labour had gained slightly among women and lost among men. It had lost any advantage it had had with the young voters, but more older people had voted Labour. Labour had also suffered from abstentions. The swing to the Conservatives tended to be smallest in places where turn-out increased most. Most of the Conservative gains were in the Midlands and outer London. Clydeside and South Lancashire swung more decisively to Labour. The Conservatives now had a hundred-seat majority and an unprecedented three electoral victories in a row. It was all too easy for some commentators to start to write off Labour. As for Macmillan, he wisely restricted his comment to 'It has gone off rather well'.

Notes

1 Gerald Sparrow, *'R.A.B.': Study of a Statesman* (London, 1965), 139.
2 Sir Gerald Nabarro, *NAB 1: Portrait of a Politician* (London, 1969), 32.
3 James Stuart, *Within the Fringe* (London, 1967), 47.
4 Harold Macmillan, *Winds of Change 1914–1939* (London, 1966), 99.
5 James Margach, *The Abuse of Power* (London, 1978), 116–18.
6 Anthony Sampson, *Macmillan: a Study in Ambiguity* (London, 1967), 25.
7 ibid., 25–6.
8 ibid., 64.
9 Diana Cooper, *Trumpets from the Steep* (London, 1960), 174.
10 Sampson, op. cit., 99.
11 ibid., 107.
12 ibid., 109. Reginald Maudling, *Memoirs* (London, 1978), 231 makes the same comment.
13 ibid., 114.
14 Margach, op. cit., 116.
15 Harold Macmillan, *Riding The Storm 1956–1959* (London, 1971), 191.
16 Christopher Hollis, 'The Conservative Party In History', *Political Quarterly*, 3 (July–Sept. 1961), 219–20.
17 Margach, op. cit., 118.
18 Lord Hill, *Both Sides of the Hill* (London, 1964), 237–8.
19 Lord Egremont, *Wyndham and Children First* (London, 1968).
20 Hill, op. cit., 235.
21 F. S. Northedge, *Descent from Power: British Foreign Policy 1945–1973* (London, 1974), 186.

22 Frank Parkin, *Middle Class Radicalism* (Manchester, 1968), 112.
23 Lord Butler, *The Art of the Possible* (London, 1971), 201.
24 Conservative and Unionist Central Office, *The Campaign Guide 1964* (London, 1964), 42; these figures are taken from the *Board of Trade Journal*.
25 ibid., 42.
26 ibid., 11.
27 ibid.
28 Andrew Shonfield, *British Economic Policy since the War* (London, 1958).
29 ibid.
30 See figures in Michael Balfour, *West Germany* (London, 1968), 317; also those in *Stockholm International Peace Research Yearbook 1978*, 144–5.
31 Shonfield, op. cit., 107.
32 ibid., 105–6.
33 William P. Snyder, *The Politics of British Defense Policy 1945–1962* (New York, 1964), 217–18.
34 Samuel Brittan, *The Treasury under the Tories 1951–1964* (Harmondsworth, 1965), 136.
35 *The Campaign Guide 1964*, 153.
36 Henry Pelling, *A History of British Trade Unionism* (London, 1963), 253.
37 *The Campaign Guide 1964*, 153.
38 ibid., 153.
39 Ministry of Labour, *Report of the Committee on the Selection and Training of Supervisors* (HMSO, 1962), 12.
40 'Profile of a M.D.', *Financial Times*, 14 February 1969.
41 ibid.
42 ibid.
43 *The Campaign Guide*, 174.
44 *Observer*, 2 January 1966.
45 *The Campaign Guide*, 31.
46 ibid., 190.
47 ibid., 173.
48 ibid., 9.
49 ibid., 115.
50 Brittan, op. cit., 138–9.
51 Andrew J. Pierre, *Nuclear Politics: The British Experience with an Independent Strategic Force* (London, 1972), 178.
52 Macmillan, *Riding the Storm*, 314.
53 Northedge, op. cit.
54 Frank Kitson, *Bunch of Five* (London, 1977), 11.
55 Nigel Fisher, *Iain Macleod* (London, 1973), 144.
56 Harold Macmillan, *Pointing the Way 1959–1961* (London, 1972), 156.
57 ibid., 385.
58 Gillian King, *Imperial Outpost: Aden its Place in British Strategic Policy* (London, 1964), 48; for an interesting critique of British colonial policy see W. P. Kirkman, *Unscrambling an Empire* (London, 1966).
59 Hansard (Commons), vol. 667, col. 266.
60 Hansard (Commons), vol. 667, col. 309–10.
61 Hansard (Commons), vol. 667, col. 308.
62 W. F. Gutteridge, *The Military in African Politics* (London, 1969), 37.
63 G. D. H. Cole, *Is this Socialism?* (London, 1954), 16.
64 G. D. H. Cole, *World Socialism Restated* (London, 1956), 5.
65 ibid., 47.
66 R. H. S. Crossman, *Socialism and the New Despotism* (London, 1956), 13.

67 Socialist Union, *Twentieth Century Socialism* (London, 1956), 15.
68 ibid., 147.
69 Hugh Gaitskell, *Socialism and Nationalisation* (London, 1957), 5.
70 ibid., 35.
71 ibid., 30.
72 *Keesing's Contemporary Archives 1956–1957*, 15892–3.
73 Michael Foot. *Aneurin Bevan 1945–60* (London, 1975), 575.
74 *Keesing's Contemporary Archives 1956–57*, 16175A.
75 Parkin, op. cit., 104–5.
76 John Braine, *Room at the Top* (Harmondsworth, 1959), inside cover.
77 Norman Mackenzie, ed., *Conviction* (London, 1958), Paul Johnson's 'A Sense of Outrage', 217.
78 D. E. Butler and Richard Rose, *The British General Election of 1959* (London, 1960), 40–1.
79 ibid., 204.
80 ibid., 195.

6 The Tories in Trouble, 1959–64

Iain Macleod

Macmillan did not make too many changes in his Cabinet after the election of 1959. Lloyd remained at the Foreign Office, Butler stayed at the Home Office, and Heathcoat Amory, who had been appointed Chancellor of the Exchequer in January 1958, continued in that capacity until July 1960. One innovation was the appointment of Lord Hailsham to the new post of Minister for Science. The prominence of Hailsham in the Conservative Party indicated that Macmillan regarded this as an important area, but Hailsham's qualifications were not very strong in other respects for this particular post. Macleod was transferred from Labour to the Colonial Office. At forty-six, he was a rising star in the Conservative Party. Though born in Yorkshire, 'Iain came of Highland stock on both sides of the family'.[1] His father, a prosperous medical practitioner, was the son of a crofter, and a Liberal by politics. After Cambridge, international bridge, and wartime service in the army, Macleod joined the Conservative Research Department in 1946. In 1950 he was returned as MP for Enfield West. As Colonial Secretary between October 1959 and October 1961 he earned a reputation as a liberal. Edward Heath took on the, potentially hazardous, Ministry of Labour and National Service, which Macleod relinquished.

His position strengthened by his victory, Macmillan felt 'ready to set out on a new adventure'.[2] He indulged in his undoubted appetite for summitry. In December he was in Paris with de Gaulle, Eisenhower, and West Germany's Konrad Adenauer. The Western leaders invited the Soviet leader, Nikita Khrushchev, to an early meeting to resolve their differences. January found Macmillan in Africa where he took up the 'wind of change' theme. In March he was in the United States discussing nuclear policy with Eisenhower. After the shooting-down of the American reconnaissance plane, U-2, over the Soviet Union, the summit conference collapsed in Paris in May.

Like the world stage, the domestic scene was not entirely

cloudless. From the election to August 1961 the Conservatives led Labour in the polls. In March 1960 they actually won a marginal seat, Brighouse and Spenborough, from Labour. But the Liberals were reviving, the balance of payments was showing cause for concern, and Conservative morale was dented when they failed to clinch local government success, in key areas like Birmingham, early in 1961. However, it looked as if Labour had far more to worry about.

The Future of Socialism

It was inevitable that the third election defeat of the Labour Party would lead to more argument at all levels of the Party about its aims and methods. Crosland, in his *The Future of Socialism*, had argued three years before that 'the much-thumbed guide-books of the past must now be thrown away'.[3] In October 1959 his fellow 'revisionists' took up the cry once again with increasing vigour and even desperation. Immediately after the election they started to prescribe medicine to save Labour from what they diagnosed to be a slow, lingering, but certain, death. Douglas Jay (b. 1907), an able economist who had served as Economic Secretary to the Treasury in the Attlee administration, led the attack in an article published in the Labour weekly *Forward* (16 October). Labour, he wrote, was suffering under 'two fatal handicaps – the class image and the myth of nationalization'. Many of the more prosperous workers, especially the women, no longer classified themselves as working-class. They aspired to something more. They were hostile to more nationalization. Jay therefore proposed Labour should drop nationalization, even the renationalization of steel, and get away from its cloth-cap image. 'What the public wants is a vigorous, radical, reforming, open-minded party'. He thought even the Party's name was a disadvantage in the new, affluent society, but 'It would be unthinkable to give up the name "Labour" which holds the loyalty of millions, but might there be a case for amending it to "Labour and Radical" or "Labour and Reform"?' If Labour did not make the necessary changes, the Tories could be in for forty years. In a subsequent edition of *Forward*, Patrick Gordon Walker (b. 1907), who had served as Secretary of State for Commonwealth Relations (1950–51), argued along similar lines. Gaitskell rightly understood that some of Jay's forthright statements would hurt and outrage wide sections of the movement, and at the annual conference held in November, he expressed himself more cautiously. He had no intention of tampering with the Party's name. He concentrated his attention on the Party's constitution, adopted in 1918, and questioned whether it adequately expressed the full aims and aspirations of the Labour Party. He believed Clause IV, which called for the common ownership of the means of production, distribution, and exchange and the best obtainable system of popular administration and control of each industry or service, gave a false impression of Labour's aims.

It implies that common ownership is an end, whereas in fact, it is a means. It implies that the only precise object we have is nationalisation, whereas in fact we have many other Socialist objectives. It implies that we propose to nationalise everything, but do we? Everything? – the whole of light industry, the whole of agriculture, all the shops – every little pub and garage? Of course not. We have long ago come to accept, we know very well, for the foreseeable future, at least in some form, a mixed economy.[4]

Gaitskell was of course correct that there were very few in the Labour Party who wanted to nationalize, 'all the shops – every pub and garage'. And at the top of the party no one was for such a policy. But he had a much more restrictive view of the role of public enterprise than the 'Bevanites'. He was not quite on the mark when he claimed that common ownership was seen as an end in itself. According to Clause IV the end was 'To secure for the producers by hand and brain the full fruits of their industry'. He was right when he asserted that Labour was not just about common ownership, few wanted to argue with him on that. And he was even more right when he claimed that Labour needed to recast its 'image'. The problem was that the delegates felt bitter and angry about the Party's defeat. They felt it was unfair and had a good deal to do with the Conservatives' slick public relations campaign which had cost far more money than Labour felt it could afford. With talk of changing the Party's constitution and engaging in public relations activities Gaitskell, and those around him, seemed to be indicating a lack of faith in the tenets of Labour, at a time when most party workers wanted a reaffirmation of faith. In other words, his intervention was psychologically ill-timed. It received, therefore, the appropriate rebuff from speaker after speaker.

Gaitskell and his friends did not give up their campaign to change the policy and the image of the Labour Party. An important part of their campaign was to commission a survey of opinion which they felt vindicated their position. Dr Rita Hinden, for ten years secretary of the Fabian Colonial Bureau, and editor of the pro-Gaitskell *Socialist Commentary*, asked,

Why is the tide of opinion set against Labour at the present? The survey suggests three main reasons. The first is that Labour is thought of predominantly as a class party . . . The second reason for Labour's unpopularity is its identification with nationalization . . . The third factor telling against Labour is the impression of weak, divided leadership.[5]

Yet when one looks at the results of the survey, carried out by two skilled investigators of public opinion, Mark Abrams and Richard Rose, the evidence does not support, unequivocally, Hinden's conclusions. It is true that those interviewed, whatever their politics, identified the Labour Party closely with the working class. 89 per cent of Labour supporters felt their party 'Stands mainly for the working class'. Even 61 per cent of non-Labour supporters applied this statement to the Labour Party. But whereas Labour did badly on such statements as 'Out for nation as a whole', and 'Would make the country more prosperous', it did far better than the Conservatives on 'Raise the standard of living of ordinary people'. Far more non-Labour voters believed this of Labour, than Labour supporters applied this to the Conservatives. The survey also indicated that non-Labour working-class voters were more likely to see themselves as belonging to the middle class than were Labour working-class supporters. In other words, Labour's close identification with the working class looked like representing a disadvantage in trying to win over non-Labour workers and their wives. The investigators asked those interviewed whether they thought public ownership of the industries nationalized after the war had been a success, a failure, or had made little difference. The result was

There is no homogeneous, blanket attitude towards public ownership; views on this subject are apparently not the outcome of either blind faith or blind rejection. On some industries – electricity, atomic energy, airlines – those who consider public ownership to be a success outnumber very substantially those who consider it a failure; for gas the votes for success are about 50 per cent higher than for failure; only when people come to judge coal-mining and the railways were they emphatically convinced that public ownership has been a failure.[6]

Even among the Conservative supporters 'favourable attitudes towards public ownership exceed unfavourable views for four out of six listed industries'.[7] Even in the cases of coal and the railways 'there were significant Conservative minorities who felt that public ownership had either been a success or else had made no difference to their performance'.[8] But though a majority recognized the need for government regulation of the economy, there was little enthusiasm for additional nationalization of industries. 'Even among Labour supporters only one in five wanted more public ownership'.[9] Interestingly, the Labour minority in favour of more public ownership 'was made up very largely of the minority of middle-class Labour supporters'.[10] Hinden's conclusion was that the answers to the questions on public ownership 'reveal the empiricism for which British people are renowned. They will judge each case on its merits, and, in so far as Labour appears to be doctrinaire on this subject of ownership, it saddles itself with a liability'.[11] Other conclusions are of course possible. It could be argued that the survey merely revealed the ignorance of the public at large about the problems facing coal and the railways. It is also plausible to conclude that airlines, atomic energy, and electricity benefited from a more modern and exciting image than coal and railways. Much favourable attention had been given to the 'modern' industries by the government. Labour's middle-class minority were likely to be more ideological, but also better informed of the complex histories of the industries concerned than the bulk of Labour's working-class supporters. Further, a great deal of money had been spent on anti-nationalization campaigns; Labour had said little, had been on the defensive on the issue. It could be argued then, from the evidence, that if, and when, the facts were got across to the public about common ownership, attitudes would certainly be much more positive. The Left's mistake was that they were not prepared to admit that hardly anyone in the Party wanted a total state economy. Moreover, the constitution referred to 'common ownership', not nationalization, but they did not think creatively about alternatives to public corporations. Many too had still not digested the negative aspects of Soviet experience. The Right made a mistake with their timing. Some of them were too dogmatic on too little evidence. And, it could be said, were prepared to sacrifice a vital principle for what could be a temporary climate of public opinion. Strangely, few supporters of public ownership in the Labour Party used as evidence the successes of such continental publicly-owned firms as Volkswagen, Renault, and some of the Italian state enterprises.

The survey did show that Labour's image was suffering from its leadership battles, but the Gaitskellites could draw little comfort from the interviewees' comments on their leader. Gaitskell was clearly ahead of Macmillan when the question was put about 'Being in touch with ordinary people'. Macmillan, however, had the advantage when voters were asked about which of the two men was a strong leader or 'Strong enough to make unwelcome decisions', and these were the qualities most sought after in a Prime Minister.[12]

One surprise in the survey was that Labour was seen as the party which was more likely to work to prevent a nuclear war and this was put top of the list of priorities by those interviewed.[13] How best to do this, to work to prevent a nuclear war, was the issue which provoked more controversy than any other in Labour's ranks in the two years which followed.

Labour's EEC debate

The two big events in Labour's history in 1960 were the death of Aneurin Bevan and the defeat of Gaitskell, on the nuclear issue, at the party conference. Despite the fact that the two men did not really see eye to eye over public ownership – Bevan attempted to paper over the cracks on the issue – they stood together in public. James Griffiths had decided, in 1959, not to seek re-election as deputy leader, and Bevan had been unanimously elected in his place by the parliamentary party. Bevan underwent an operation for malignant cancer at the end of 1959, and, apparently unaware of his fatal condition, died in July 1960. Had he lived, it is by no means certain that he could have saved the day for Hugh Gaitskell at the conference. Opinion appeared to be moving in the direction of CND. It was not just that the annual London–Aldermaston marches were growing in popularity. CND's attempts to persuade Britain to give up a defence based on nuclear weapons was gaining ground in the unions. In particular, Frank Cousins, who had led the Transport and General Workers Union (TGWU) since the spring of 1956, had brought his union into line with CND. Cousins, born in Nottingham in 1904, the son of a railwayman, had worked in the pits and then as a truck-driver before becoming a union organizer.[14] He had supported the aims of CND from the start, though had never sought inclusion in its leadership. He had already helped to defeat Gaitskell over the Clause IV issue. Labour's official defence policy was, in any case, under pressure in 1960 quite apart from the activities of Cousins and the CND. There was the Victory for Socialism group which included Ian Mikardo, Michael Foot, Stephen Swingler, Frank Allaun, and some other MPs. It had been revitalized in 1958 and pursued a consistently left-wing line on all aspects of party policy. More important, however, were policy difficulties over nuclear defence. Since 1954 a whole series of missile projects had been cancelled by the government. With the cancellation of Blue Streak in April 1960, after very heavy expenditure, ended all hope of Britain developing an independent delivery system for the British bomb. 'It also caught Gaitskell and the Right off balance as it seemed at first that the defence of British nuclear independence was now academic. Without a delivery system the defence of the British bomb seemed absurd and unrealistic'.[15] Labour's position on the issue became increasingly confused over the next months. George Brown and Harold Wilson seemed to be saying Labour would scrap Britain's existing nuclear forces, the V-bombers; Gaitskell appeared to want to keep them as long as possible. Then when the party conference discussed the issue at Scarborough in October, it was the CND line which carried the day. Frank Cousins, with his union's massive block vote, tipped the balance. He proposed a resolution on behalf of his union calling for 'A Complete rejection of any defence policy based on the threat of the use of strategic or tactical nuclear weapons'.[16] It not only sought the end of the British bomb, it also sought the withdrawal of all American nuclear bases from Britain. It did not, however, call for a withdrawal from NATO and, as Gaitskell was able to point out, left important matters unclear. It was adopted by the slender margin of 3,282,000 to 3,239,000. The leader, despite his passion, oratory, and obvious sincerity, did his cause no good by his comment, 'What sort of people do you think we are? Do you think we can simply accept a decision of this kind? Do you think that we can become overnight the pacifists, unilateralists and fellow-travellers that other people are?'[17] The resolution passed, 'Pandemonium broke out as the left-wing delegates cheered and cheered again. Gaitskell, looking white and weary, slipped off the platform'.[18] Cousins was certainly no fellow-traveller and resented the accusation. The Communists had withheld support from CND until mid-1960 because the movement criticized both the United States and the Soviet Union. Seeing in CND's growing strength a chance to defeat Gaitskell, they changed their tune. Despite their later high visibility on marches, they did not make serious inroads into the movement.

Gaitskell's defeat led to the setting-up of the Campaign for Democratic Socialism (CDS) in November 1960; the brainchild of William Rodgers, General Secretary of the Fabian Society, and Anthony Crosland, its aim was to support Hugh Gaitskell and his policies. Gaitskell, as party leader, was not officially involved with CDS. By March 1961 it could announce that 45 MPs had pledged support; among the more prominent were Crosland, Desmond Donnelly, Geoffrey de Freitas, Douglas Jay, Roy Jenkins, Roy Mason, Christopher Mayhew, Bob Mellish, Fred Mulley, Reg Prentice, and Reginald Paget.[19] None of them were members of the shadow cabinet or the NEC. But several members of the shadow cabinet supported the Campaign, including George Brown, Denis Healey, James Callaghan, and Patrick Gordon Walker. From the House of Lords, Clement Attlee, Hugh Dalton, and Frank Pakenham (Lord Longford) were associated with it. The Campaign also managed to win a number of leading trade unionists such as William Carron, leader of the Amalgamated Engineering Union; Jim Conway, National Organizer of the same union; Sam Watson of the miners; Ron Smith, General Secretary of the Post Office Workers' Union; Anne Godwin, General Secretary of the Clerical and Administrative Workers' Union; and W. J. P. Webber, General Secretary of the Transport Salaried Staffs Association. There were a good many other leading officers of trade unions who sympathized with CDS, but who hesitated to give formal and open support. Just how much support CDS had in the constituency parties is difficult to say, but it does not appear to have been all that impressive. Many local parties did, nevertheless, support a much less unilateralist position on defence than that adopted by the 1960 conference. During the months which preceded the 1961 conference Gaitskell saw his line on defence endorsed by all the leading bodies of the Labour and trade union movement. It seemed inevitable therefore that the conference should support his policy. This in fact happened. By 4.5 million votes to 1.7 million the official policy was endorsed. The main points of *Policy For Peace* were support for NATO, retention of American nuclear bases in Britain, but abandonment of Britain's attempt to be an independent nuclear power; the West should never be the first to use the H-bomb and should work for the creation of a non-nuclear zone of controlled disarmament in Central Europe. Gaitskell's victory was almost negated by two other resolutions passed at the same time. One opposed the establishment of Polaris nuclear submarine bases in Britain, the other condemned the training of West German troops there. The conference also adopted the NEC's home policy document *Signposts for the Sixties*, which was basically Labour's policy for the next general election.

A number of circumstances came together to give Labour a far greater appearance of unity in 1962 than it had possessed in the period since the 1959 election. The concession over Britain's bomb helped; so did the increasing divisions in CND – between Lord Russell's Committee of One Hundred which advocated civil disobedience, and the rest – and the placing of another great issue on the conference's agenda: Britain's proposed entry into the European Economic Community (EEC).

The actual arguments for and against Britain's entry into the EEC are discussed below (pp. 252–5); here we are concerned merely to record Labour's reaction to the issue. Most of the Left were strongly opposed to entry. The Victory for Socialism group issued a statement, published in *Tribune* (19 January 1962), which claimed the Tories were 'selling out' to the EEC 'based on their policy for preserving the old order by keeping Europe and Germany divided, and perpetuating NATO, the arms race and the cold war till the bombs come home'. The Parliamentary Labour Party had by that time tabled a motion (31 July 1961) which read in part 'That this House . . . declares that Britain should enter the EEC only if this House gives its approval and if the conditions negotiated are generally acceptable to a Commonwealth Prime Ministers' conference and accord with our obligations and pledges to other members of EFTA'.[20] The CDS was strongly sympathetic to British entry, but by no means all the 'revisionists' were pro-Marketeers. Douglas Jay parted company with many of his political friends on this issue. Gaitskell was not one of them. At the party conference in October 1962 he announced what amounted to a firm rejection of the Market. On the one hand he did recognize 'the idealism implicit in the desire of European people in Germany and France and Italy and the Low Countries to join together, to get rid of the old enmities . . .'[21] He recognized that this feeling was strong in the Social Democratic parties and that the EEC 'has come to stay'. And he went on: 'the arguments, when you think them through . . . are evenly balanced; and whether or not it is worth going in depends on the conditions of our entry'. But his speech also contained the warning, 'it does mean . . . the end of Britain as an independent European state. I make no apology for repeating it. It means the end of a thousand years of history . . . And it does mean the end of the Commonwealth'.[22] His friend and ally Lord Longford wrote, 'What waves of feeling swept over the Conference as he expounded the anti-Common Market arguments. How tepidly in comparison were the arguments produced in favour'.[23] And Willy Brandt, leader of the German Social Democratic Party and later West German Chancellor, a good European, a good democrat, and a good friend of Britain, has commented on the impression Gaitskell made:

Even as open-minded and widely travelled a man as the then leader of the Labour Party, Hugh Gaitskell, found it quite natural to introduce me to a London gathering in 1962 as 'our friend from overseas'. He had sharply rejected British entry at a Labour Party Conference not long before. My friend Per Haekkerup, the Danish Foreign Minister, who had been a guest at Brighton, told me that he felt throughout Gaitskell's speech as if the doors at the back of the hall might open at any moment and Queen Victoria come striding in.[24]

The Brighton conference agreed a resolution. It opened thus: 'The Labour Party regards the European Community as a great and imaginative conception'. Then it went on to lay down five tough conditions of entry: strong and binding Commonwealth safeguards; freedom to pursue an independent foreign policy; fulfilment of pledges to Britain's partners in the European Free Trade Area; 'The right to plan our own economy'; and guarantees to safeguard the position of British agriculture.[25] It looked like being a moment of triumph for Gaitskell. His speech had certainly endeared him to many constituency activists who had previously regarded him with suspicion. But he was robbed of full and final victory by unexpected illness and death on 18 January 1963.

De Gaulle's veto

All Labour's debates and doubts about the EEC were purely academic; so were the government's negotiations. Britain, it seems, had no chance of entry at that time. At the end of the two-day Commons debate in July 1961 on the government's announcement to seek admission to the EEC, only one Conservative and four Labour MPs[26] had voted against the proposal; 25 Conservative MPs and the official Opposition abstained. Macmillan had already sounded out opinion among influential groups, such as banking and industry, and got a favourable response. Important sections of the press, including the 'quality' papers and the *Daily Mirror,* were positive, and public opinion, to the extent that it existed, did not appear to be hostile. The plan to take Britain into the EEC originated, not in Parliament, press, or public opinion, but in the Treasury, the Foreign Office, and the boardrooms of big business. The EEC, it was argued, would provide British industry with the two things it badly needed: a larger home market, and the stiff competition which would force it to improve. There were those also who were less certain about the future of the Commonwealth and Britain's role in it. Would not Commonwealth states look increasingly to other states than Britain for increased trade and aid? The coming into force of the Commonwealth Immigration Act in July 1962, which greatly restricted the flow of immigrants from the West Indies, India, and Pakistan, represented a turning-away from the older intimacy with the Commonwealth. Implicitly it was part of the reappraisal of Britain's role and direction, but not by the man who carried the responsibility for it, R. A. Butler. He was one of those in the Cabinet who had reservations about the EEC because of the Commonwealth. Macmillan did, however, succeed in convincing his colleagues of the need of this new departure, and the initiative was endorsed by the Conservative Party annual conference. The Prime Minister also got the blessing of President Kennedy in April 1961, and again in April 1962. Kennedy did, nevertheless, warn Macmillan, on the second occasion, 'that Britain must not expect to take care of everyone in its economic wake – either in the Commonwealth or in the European Free Trade Association – at America's expense'.[27] The United States was not prepared to tolerate Commonwealth farm products having a permanently more favourable position in the EEC than its own similar products. The United States wanted Britain in for political, rather than economic, reasons.

If Britain joined the Market, London could offset the eccentricities of policy in Paris and Bonn; moreover, Britain, with its world obligations, could keep the EEC from becoming a high-tariff, inward-looking, white man's club. Above all, with British membership, the Market could become the basis for a true political federation of Europe.[28]

Kennedy had demonstrated how important he thought Britain's membership to be by mobilizing half his Cabinet to impress this on Gaitskell when the latter visited Washington in 1962.[29] He had also raised the matter with President de Gaulle in June 1961, though whether this was to Britain's advantage is highly doubtful. The French President was wary of Britain, regarding it as the Trojan Horse of Washington. Co-operation in nuclear defence could have recommended the British to de Gaulle, but this was excluded by British arrangements with the United States. Anglo-U.S. nuclear co-operation 'became a major element in de Gaulle's determination to keep Britain out of Europe'.[30] The Nassau Agreement, discussed below,

> may not have been decisive in causing his first veto, but, at the very least, it fully confirmed his basic assessment that British strategy with its dependence upon the United States clashed with a European orientation of Britain's economic policy; it also provided him with a convenient opportunity to reject Britain's application.[31]

Macmillan, Kennedy, and de Gaulle were also somewhat at odds over Berlin. The Soviet Union had put increasing pressure on the Western powers about Berlin, with proposals designed to detach West Berlin from West Germany. On 13 August 1961 the East Germans sealed off their part of Berlin and started building the Wall. Macmillan felt 'The danger is, of course, that with both sides bluffing, disaster may come by mistake'.[32] He praised the coolness of the Americans and West Germans, but thought de Gaulle seemed 'to contemplate war with equanimity'.[33] The West sent a note of protest to Moscow, and the Russians did not press their claims any further. Somehow the Berlin crisis fizzled out.

The British government was apparently not aware of another powerful adversary to Britain's admission to the EEC. Konrad Adenauer, who had been West German Chancellor since 1949, and Premier Macmillan did not get on. They were not at one in regard to the Soviet Union. Macmillan believed Adenauer and his colleagues did not understand the Russians, did not understand their wartime suffering and their post-war suspicions about West Germany. Adenauer believed, on the contrary, it was Macmillan who did not understand the Russians; he felt he was inclined to make concessions to the Soviet Union for electoral purposes, and was too ready to suggest German concessions in Britain's interest. He is said to have described Britain as the exploiter of 'us poor dumb Continentals'.[34] The German Chancellor had told de Gaulle that Macmillan had offered economic union to the United States –

without success. Adenauer was also worried that sterling was weak, that the administrative apparatus of the EEC could not yet integrate Britain and the other applicants, and that Britain was hoping to undermine Franco-German unity. Britain and the Federal Republic were also at odds over the cost of stationing British troops in Germany. De Gaulle fed Adenauer's suspicions. He claimed to the Chancellor that Macmillan had sought to include the Commonwealth in the EEC, and feared the United States would be next in line for admission. Adenauer is reported to have concluded his discussion with de Gaulle on the issue by saying, 'No three cheers for a British entry'.[35] The negotiations, led by Edward Heath, had been started in October 1961, and were broken off in August 1962. Finally, on 14 January 1963, President de Gaulle held a press conference in Paris, at which he declared that his country would veto the United Kingdom's entry into the EEC, come what may. The other members of the Community would have, in principle, welcomed Britain's admission. The same was true of many members of the West German Establishment and the opposition Social Democrats of Willy Brandt.

If Macmillan did not get on with his European counterparts, men a Conservative leader might have been expected to get on with, he did get on with Kennedy, whose sister Kathleen had married Macmillan's wife's nephew. Nevertheless, their friendship was somewhat remarkable, given the differences of age, style, background, and ambitions of the two statesmen and, not least, because Kennedy claimed to be the leader of the party of hope, rather than the party of nostalgia. Yet it was with Macmillan that the young President had his closest relationship with a foreign leader. Kennedy found Macmillan had

underneath his affectations and mannerisms . . . a sharp, disillusioned mind, a vivid sense of history and a strong desire to accomplish certain objectives during his term of office. Possessed of a genuine horror of nuclear war, he was determined to press for a test ban and to search without cease for a *détente* with the Soviet Union . . . Kennedy, with his own fondness for the British political style, liked Macmillan's patrician approach to politics, his impatience with official ritual, his insouciance about the professionals . . . They found the same things funny and the same things serious.[36]

Perhaps Macmillan clung even more to the United States after the failure of his European bid. At Nassau in December 1962, when failure in Europe was surely in sight, Macmillan got Kennedy to agree to the sale of Polaris missiles for launching British nuclear warheads from British-built submarines. Polaris replaced the Skybolt missile, the development of which, jointly by Britain and the United States, had been cancelled because of mounting costs. In some quarters this gave some renewed credibility to the government's claim to have a British, independent deterrent, and to the claim to having a 'special relationship' with the United States. Though not conceived for that purpose, it gave badly needed prestige to a government which appeared to be increasingly in trouble both abroad and at home.

Macmillan's last major initiative in external affairs was his successful efforts to bring about a nuclear test ban treaty. This was signed in Moscow in August 1963 by Britain, the Soviet Union, and the United States. The treaty banned nuclear explosions in the atmosphere, outer space, and underwater, but not, alas, underground. Many other states immediately signified their readiness to sign the treaty; unfortunately, France and China were not among them. Macmillan could be proud of the outcome, limited though it was, for he had sought it longer, and with greater zeal, than any other statesman.

Macmillan's purge

By early 1961 the British economy started to show signs that it was entering the 'stop' part of the 'stop-go' cycle which was becoming a permanent feature of the post-war economy. At home output was rising slowly, abroad the pound was under pressure and the balance of payments remained in the red. In April, Selwyn Lloyd, who had replaced Amory as Chancellor in July 1960, introduced a politically damaging Budget – a combination of increases in the insurance stamp and in health charges, reductions in surtax, and a pay pause in July. More action followed in July. This included raising bank rate from 5 to 7 per cent, a surcharge on purchase tax, cuts in public expenditure, and the prospect of a 'pay pause' and a long-term planning of the economy. Within a month Britain had been granted a large credit by the IMF. In February 1962 the Chancellor announced a 2 to 2½ per cent 'guiding light' for pay settlements.

A new feature of government policy to counter Britain's economic weakness was the setting-up of the National Economic Development Council (NEDC), proposed by the Chancellor in July. Its task was to examine British economic prospects, stretching five or more years into the future. Its membership consisted of the appropriate ministers, civil servants, academics, and management and unions in industry. Among the eight industrialists on NEDC were Reay Geddes, Managing Director of Dunlop; F. A. Cockfield, Managing Director of Boots; Lord Robens of the Coal Board, a former leading Labour politician; and Dr Richard Beeching of the British Transport Commission. Beeching became the target of popular wrath for his plans severely to prune the railways. On the trade union side were Frank Cousins, William Carron, Sid Greene of the National Union of Railwaymen, and Ron Smith. George Woodcock, General Secretary of the TUC during 1960–69, was also a member. Remarkably, Woodcock was one of the few professional economists on NEDC. A former Lancashire spinner who started work at twelve, he gained a first-class honours degree in economics at New College, Oxford. After an interlude in the civil service, Woodcock worked as senior economist to the TUC for ten years.

Harold Macmillan had been in favour of 'planning' during the 1930s and had published a book, *The Middle Way,* which advocated what became known as indicative planning. But NEDC was not the product of Macmillan's fertile mind. A group of somewhat unorthodox industrialists led by Sir Hugh Beaver of Guinness, and reinforced by Reay Geddes, had convinced Selwyn Lloyd of the idea.[37] They, and some others, including economic journalists and academics, had been impressed by French experience. Despite wartime devastation, colonial retreat, labour unrest, and severe political turmoil, France was achieving higher economic growth than Britain. The French claimed to take economic planning seriously, so it was thought; Britain should follow their example.[38] One idea behind NEDC was the need for an economic forecasting and advisory body independent of the Treasury. There was a good deal of scepticism about the quality of the Treasury's advice and the crisis of 1961 strengthened that scepticism. According to Samuel Brittan, by the time Selwyn Lloyd announced his austerity measures, which led Britain into a recession, the balance of payments was once again in surplus.[39] The NEDC was also designed as a body through which the two sides of industry could work out a strategy for the future. It was sold to the public as planning by consent. In terms of what the Conservatives had been saying about planning for over ten years at least, it represented a dramatic shift in policy. As the Conservative journalist Henry Fairlie put it in *Encounter* (September 1962), it represented,

almost the exact reverse of the attitude of 'Set the People Free', which was Conservatism in 1951; of 'Conservative Freedom Works', which became Conservatism before and after 1955, and of 'I'm all right, Jack', which was Conservatism in 1959.

As could be expected, there was some dismay in certain Conservative circles, and a majority of the Cabinet opposed it.[40] Another measure conceived to help the country's limping economy was the National Incomes Commission announced by the Prime Minister in July 1962. This was presented as an impartial review body on pay, but it never got off the ground because the trade unions did not regard it as such.

'Neddy' and 'Nicky', as the NEDC and the Commission became

known, did nothing to help the Conservatives' sagging fortunes. From June 1961 Labour led the Conservatives in the polls and a number of by-elections warned the government of its likely fate in a general election. The most dramatic of these was the loss of the safe Conservative seat at Orpington in March 1962. The interesting aspect of this result was that the seat went to the Liberals, not to Labour. A mainly middle-class outer London suburb, Orpington was certainly not normal Labour country. But the result formed part of a trend of rising support for the Liberals. There was much speculation at the time that this new Liberal support marked a more permanent trend towards the Liberals. This proved not to be the case. The new Liberal voters were, in very many cases, part of the white-collar revolt against the Conservatives rather than positive conviction that the Liberals had anything much to offer. Orpington, though, was not just a flash in the pan. For one thing the Liberals retained the seat in the general election of 1964. More importantly, it highlighted a trend. Dissatisfied or bored with the two main parties, more voters have been prepared to experiment with minor parties in the 1960s and 1970s than was the case in the first ten years or so after the war. Other poor by-election results followed for the government. In June 1962 Labour took their first seat from the Conservatives since the general election, at Middlesbrough West. On the same day the Liberals pushed Labour into third place at Derbyshire West, where the Conservatives retained the seat but with a much smaller percentage of the vote than at the 1959 election. In the following month Labour retained Leicester North-East and this time the Liberals pushed the Conservatives into third place. The next day occurred what became known as the 'July massacre'.

Macmillan had been ridiculed as 'Macwonder' and 'Super Mac' by Labour. If anything, these jibes had won him popularity. Now he was christened 'Mac the knife'. The Opposition scoffed at him, though some admired his audacity in private. In his own party there was shock and anger; 'This was making enemies on a grand scale'.[41] He had embarked upon the biggest Cabinet reshuffle of the post-war period. Out went his Lord Chancellor, Chancellor of the Exchequer, Minister of Defence, Ministers of Education and Housing and Local Government, and a number of others of lesser importance. Lord Mills, Minister without Portfolio, also departed, though he had wished to go. Those so slain had not formed any 'anti-party group' against Macmillan, nor could they be said to represent the Right or the Left of the Party. In the main they seemed to be 'fall guys' for policy failures like Selwyn Lloyd (Exchequer), Charles Hill (Housing and Local Government), and David Eccles (Education). In two major areas the vacancies gave

Macmillan the chance to appoint younger, reform-orientated, ministers. These were Reginald Maudling (Chancellor of the Exchequer) and Sir Edward (now Lord) Boyle (Education).

Some of the changes gave a grain of hope to some Tory reformers, but at the grass-roots level confidence was shattered.[42] The electorate was not impressed either. In November 1962, in the first by-election since the reshuffle, Labour took Dorset South and Glasgow Woodside from the Conservatives, and scored a near miss at Norfolk Central. Nor did the death of Gaitskell in January 1963 seem to alter the trend very much. It was still, however, much more a trend against the government than positively to Labour.

In addition to the economic and other problems facing the Macmillan administration, the government was confronted with a series of scandals which, taken together, and stretching over a fairly long period as they did, must have badly harmed the credibility of Macmillan and his party. First of all there was the public anger over the effects of the property boom of the 1950s and early 1960s. It has been calculated that well over one hundred people became millionaires between 1945 and 1965 as a result of their activities as property developers.[43] Jack Cotton, Charles Clore, Harry Hyams, Jack and Philip Rose, and Sir Harold Samuels became well-known for their *coups* and take-overs of property firms, and the controversy much of their redeveloping caused. War damage and economic development led naturally to the redevelopment of towns and cities. But the frenzied redevelopment of the period owed much to the repealing of the Labour government's Town and Country Planning legislation, under which development profits went to the state, and the creation of a free market in development land. The Conservatives passed legislation to this effect in 1953, 1954, and 1959. The familiar skyline of London was shattered by the high-rise blocks—in part, office blocks no one wanted, luxury flats no one could afford, and hotels which were beyond the means of the natives. Most of the developers kept within the law. Some did not. One notorious case, which became a symbol of the time, was that of the landlord Peter Rachman. He had bought run-down property for redevelopment. His problem was sitting tenants who would not move. He therefore used any number of brutal and illegal means to get them out. Sir Basil Spence, as President of the Royal Institute of British Architects, was reported by the *Financial Times* (17 June 1960) as saying:

The speculators are cornering the limited supply of building land in town and country and holding the community up to ransom. The money that should be going into better architecture and higher standards is being taken by people who have contributed nothing to the building process. This has grown to the dimensions of a public scandal, and threatens to make good planning and city reconstruction prohibitively expensive.

There were also a number of other scandals connected with law and order and security which cast their shadows over the affluent society and the Conservative Party. The holding-up of the Glasgow–London mail train and robbery of £2.5 million on 8 August 1963 must rank as one of the most spectacular crimes in history. Clearly Macmillan could not be blamed for this. However, it did appear to be one more indication that Britain was as out-of-date and Edwardian as Macmillan's image. It came at the tail-end of a number of spy and security affairs. There was the Portland (Underwater Weapons Establishment) spy scandal in March 1961.[44] There was the case of John Vassall, a Foreign Office clerk who had been blackmailed into spying for the Russians and was convicted in November 1962. There was the conviction of the double agent George Blake, who had betrayed many British operatives behind the Iron Curtain. In January 1963 Kim Philby, former Middle East correspondent of the *Observer,* and former head of the Soviet section of Britain's Secret Intelligence Service, reached the safety of the Soviet Union, for whom he had been working for many years. Worst of all for Macmillan was the Profumo affair. John Profumo, Secretary of State for War, a minister not in the Cabinet, had had an affair with Christine Keeler, a twenty-year-old model, who was having a simultaneous affair with Captain Eugene Ivanov, assistant Soviet naval attaché and an intelligence officer. The two men, when visiting their friend, 'did, no doubt, narrowly miss one another on occasions'.[45] Profumo's big mistake was to deny his association with the girl. This untruth, which he had pronounced in the Commons, was later exposed by the *Sunday Mirror.* Lord Denning was asked to investigate the whole affair, which he did during June–September 1963. He criticized Macmillan in his report: 'It was the responsibility of the Prime Minister and his colleagues, and of them only, to deal with this situation: and they did not succeed in doing so'.[46] Lord Denning concluded that the events had led some to believe there had been a decline in the integrity of public life in Britain. 'I do not believe this to be true. There has been no lowering of standards'. The difference was that, compared with the past, 'Scandalous information about well-known people has become a marketable commodity'. Doubtless this was so, but many people thought the affair revealed the hypocrisy in high places if nothing more. An editorial in *The Times* (4 July 1963) had already summed up what many disillusioned white-collar workers, ex-Conservatives, and Liberal protest voters felt during this period:

The kind of affluence that all too much of Conservatism has seemed to encourage has been the pursuit of money for its own sake, the acquisition of wealth with the least effort and by whatever means are handiest, the jealous protection of capital gains at a time of firm control of wages, the rewarding of smartness instead of industry.

And the same leader warned: 'The tawdry cynicism that the worst Conservatives flaunt needs to be exorcized'. Ronald Butt, writing in the *Financial Times* (20 September 1963), blamed the 'pay pause' and the Profumo affair for the decline in Conservative support. He believed 'a large section of the middle-class' had come to think the government was not 'fair'. Pounded from all sides, and suffering from an illness which was not just diplomatic, it was obvious that Macmillan could not last much longer. The end came in October 1963. Macmillan is reported by Maudling to have said that 'he never thought he could be "brought down by two tarts" '.[47]

Lord Home becomes Prime Minister

Veteran political correspondent James Margach saw four potential leaders in the Conservative government in February 1963: Maudling, Macleod, Edward Heath, and Quintin Hogg (Lord Hailsham). He also saw in Butler a potential caretaker Prime Minister. He asked a shrewd question, 'Have Mr Butler, Mr Heath or Mr Maudling the fire, the political devil and the rumbustious fervour to get the Tories back on their feet . . .?' (after their likely election defeat!) He went on to comment that he felt Hailsham and Lord Home, the Foreign Secretary, had a good deal of support, but were disqualified by virtue of being in the Lords rather than the Commons.[48] The removal of this disqualification was made possible by the Peerage Act, which was given all-party support and became law on 31 July 1963. Under the Act a peer can disclaim his peerage for his lifetime. The campaign for the change in the law, it must be mentioned, was led by Anthony Wedgwood Benn, a Labour MP, who succeeded to his father's title in November 1960.

When the Conservative Party met at Blackpool for its annual conference, the atmosphere was 'ugly'.[49] Lord Home read out Macmillan's letter of resignation, which caused 'consternation, confusion and intrigue'.[50] All the contestants for the fight were there. Many still felt Butler must get the leadership or if not Butler, then Maudling.

Reginald Maudling (1917-79) was regarded by some qualified observers as 'the ablest Chancellor the Conservative Party has produced in ten years'.[51] Brought up in Bexhill and London, his family was 'upper- or middle-middle-class . . . My father was a consulting actuary . . . We led a comfortable life'.[52] After preparatory school, Merchant Taylors as a day boy, classics at Merton

College, Oxford, he qualified as a barrister. The war was spent in RAF intelligence. An unsuccessful contestant in the 1945 election, he worked in the Conservative Research Department until elected as MP for Barnet in 1950. He served at the Ministry of Civil Aviation and at the Treasury before becoming Minister of Supply (1955-57) and Paymaster-General (1957-59). He was promoted to the Cabinet in September 1957. From 1959 to 1961 he was President of the Board of Trade, and then spent a year as Colonial Secretary, before becoming Chancellor in 1962.

Also at the conference was Lord Hailsham (Quintin Hogg, b. 1907). In an open bid for the leadership he announced, without warning to his Cabinet colleagues, that he was renouncing his peerage. He had the backing of Macmillan, the Prime Minister's son Maurice, Julian Amery, Churchill's son Randolph, and the latter's brother-in-Law, Christopher Soames.[53] His flamboyance enthralled some delegates just as it put off some of his Cabinet colleagues. The son of an Attorney-General and later Lord Chancellor under Baldwin, he had entered the Commons himself in 1938 after a celebrated by-election win at Oxford, and had been a staunch supporter of Chamberlain's foreign policy. A former Scholar at Christ Church, Oxford, and President of the Oxford Union, he had been a fellow of All Souls, and was called to the Bar in 1932. He served in the army in the Middle East during the war, and after being wounded in 1941, and another period in Palestine, did battle again in Parliament. He was a noted member of the Tory Reform group. His major appointments were First Lord of the Admiralty, Minister of Education, Lord President of the Council, and Minister of Science. He had also been Chairman of the Conservative Party (1957-59).

At the time of the leadership crisis there were two joint Chairmen of the party, Iain Macleod and Lord Poole. Macleod was thought to be out of the race because he was said to be 'too left-wing, too tired'.[54]

At the conference much heat was generated, much lobbying went on, and much bitterness resulted, but no leader was elected. In fact the conference had no authority to elect a leader. As Reginald Maudling has recorded, 'The decision did not lie in the hands of the Conference but in the rather mysterious channels of communications within the Party . . . And so the voices were collected. The traditional yet mysterious process continued. I am not quite sure to this day what happened'.[55] Lord Butler tells us that what happened was that Macmillan switched his support to Home, ignored the mounting opposition within the Cabinet to Home, and advised the Queen to ask him to form a government.[56] Both Hailsham and Maudling had withdrawn in favour of Butler, but to no avail. In the interests of party unity Butler was once again asked to sacrifice himself. He did so.

The row over the new Prime Minister did not end there. Macleod and Enoch Powell refused to serve under the new leader. And there was a good deal of talk about altering the method of selecting the Conservative leader. Poole, Humphry Berkeley, and Lord Lambton, both MPs, had pleaded for this in July, and this eventually happened when Home's successor had to be chosen.

The Times (19 October 1963), and other serious papers, drew attention to the new Prime Minister's weaknesses, 'It is not the earl but the politician over whom the doubt arises. Except for a spell in the junior office of Minister of State for Scotland in 1951-55 Lord Home has no administrative experience of home affairs'. The Earl of Home (b. 1903) was first elected, as Lord Dunglass, to the Commons in 1931 and worked as Neville Chamberlain's Parliamentary Private Secretary (1937-39). Tuberculosis kept him out of the political arena for some time, and he was defeated in the 1945 election. He was briefly an MP again (1950-51) before succeeding as 14th earl. He entered the Cabinet as Secretary of State for Commonwealth Relations in 1955, becoming Foreign Secretary in 1960. His promotion to the Foreign Office caused a storm. He was not exceptionally hostile to the Soviet Union and went along with Macmillan's attempts to promote *détente*. On the Common Market as well, though not enthusiastic, he went along with official attempts to gain entry. On southern Africa and the Middle East he was more to the right than Macmillan. The new tenant of 10 Downing St was estimated by the *Observer* (20 October 1963) to be owner of 96,000 acres of farmland, forest, and grouse moor in Scotland. This empire included 56 large farms and many other properties. Home had married the daughter of his old headmaster at Eton, a lady with a reputation for having a social conscience. He disclaimed his earldom, becoming plain Sir Alec Douglas-Home, and was duly elected as MP for Kinross and West Perthshire.

In his speech to the conference R. A. Butler had talked about the Conservative Society where 'there are a variety of ladders to the top and ... positions of responsibility are not reserved for one coterie or class or band of education'.[57] To be sure, he was postulating an ideal, something to be aimed at, but it is surely not unfair to ask what progress the Conservatives had made towards realizing this society? We need not dwell on the fact that it was certainly not true of the Conservative Cabinets of Harold Macmillan or Sir Alec: out of twenty-three members of Douglas-Home's Cabinet ten were old Etonians, only three had not been to public schools. If one looks at the background of Conservative candidates in the election which followed, one is forced to the conclusion that either 'Rab' Butler was a voice crying in the wilderness, or merely a politician engaging in empty demagoguery, mouthing the rhetoric of the time to win back Mr Orpington. Out of 304 Conservative MPs elected in 1964, 229 were products of public schools, 97 of them from Eton, Harrow, and Winchester. More than half had been at Oxbridge. Perhaps more significant still was the fact that the replacements for Conservative MPs who either had died or had retired during 1960-64 were of exactly the same background as the MPs they replaced. Thus, for instance, 16 old Etonians retired, but another 16 found seats in the Commons.[58] Christopher Hollis wrote in 1961: 'It is estimated that between 30 per cent and 40 per cent of Trade Unionists vote Conservative. Yet there is only one bona fide Conservative trade unionist Member, Mr Mawby'. This was no longer quite true in 1964; a second representative of Conservative trade unionism reached the Commons, Sir Fred Brown, who was a member of ASSET the white-collar trade union. What was true of education was also true of occupation. Bank employees, computer-operators, local government officers, draughtsmen, works managers, white-collar civil servants, GPs, and all the rest – hardly any of these occupational groups, 'Orpington man', were likely to be found on the Conservative benches. Yet the majority of the more traditional of these groups had always voted Conservative, and in the affluent society their numbers were increasing. Did it, does it, matter? Reginald Bevins, Macmillan's Postmaster-General, believed it does. In 1965 he wrote:

A Party that cannot gain power without a big share of the working and lower middle classes' vote cannot afford to be led predominantly by a group of Old Etonians, however gifted they may be. This makes a bad joke of democracy and nowadays it is seen that way, especially by the younger generation. It is also dangerous because when a majority of our leaders come from the same social strata, far removed from ordinary life, they are unlikely to make decisions which are acceptable to ordinary people ... The notion that some people are born to rule, or even know how to rule, must be destroyed.[59]

Expansion in education

With an election at most a year away Sir Alec Douglas-Home had little choice but to carry on with most of the policies initiated by his predecessor. One piece of new legislation was pushed through, however, and it caused an outcry within the Conservative Party which nearly robbed the government of its majority. This was the abolition of resale price maintenance (RPM). Edward Heath, as Secretary of State for Industry, Trade, and Regional Development, was responsible for this. The Act abolishing RPM was designed to increase competition in the retail trade and thus contribute to keep prices down. The small shopkeepers who were regarded as solidly Tory felt they needed RPM to help them resist the supermarkets. At one stage the government's majority on the Bill dropped to one. It was the closest that a government had come to defeat on an important measure since 1951 and did not augur well for the general election, by this time (March 1964) a maximum of seven months away.

One important measure which Sir Alec's regime agreed to implement was the expansion target set by the Robbins Committee on higher education. The Committee had been set up by Harold Macmillan in December 1960 under the chairmanship of Lord Robbins, a professor of economics. The government announced on 24 October that it would accept the target set for expansion over the next ten years. This was probably the most important single domestic reform embarked upon by the Macmillan–Home governments. Robbins urged the doubling of university places to 218,000 within ten years, with 390,000 places in higher education as a whole. His Committee had examined higher education in the United States, the Soviet Union, West Germany, France, and certain other countries, and it was by no means critical of what had been achieved in Britain. Staff/student ratios were better in Britain, few students failed to make the grade, and more students were assisted from public funds than in most countries. Yet it was felt that many more Britons could benefit from higher education, and many more graduates would be needed if Britain was to maintain its place in the modern world. It was particularly concerned about technology, applied science, and management. The report recommended that the existing Colleges of Technology be developed as technological universities. It also recommended the setting-up of five special institutions to promote technology. It was influenced by the lack of any parallel in Britain of the Massachusetts Institute of Technology and the technical universities of Zurich and Delft. The Committee found that education for management was not satisfactory. There had been criticism of this both from the business community and the NEDC. The Committee therefore recommended that at least two major postgraduate schools should be established in major business centres. It also stressed the need for foreign-language courses for those at technological universities. Another innovation Robbins wanted was a National Council for Academic Awards to award degrees to students studying in institutions other than universities. It was also felt necessary to improve the conditions of university staff, not just their pay, but also promotion prospects, which had declined compared with pre-war, accommodation, and other facilities. Finally, the Report wanted a separate Minister of Arts and Sciences. This latter recommendation was not accepted by the government.

The Robbins Report was the fifth to be published on some aspect of education since February 1959. It was a sign of the great public interest in the issue. Parents were more anxious than ever before that their children should be given the chance to develop their potentialities. Politicians were forced to respond to this – which is not to say there were not genuine reformers among the politicians. There was also the aspect stressed by Robbins: Britain's need for a trained cadre to enable it to hold its own in the world of science-based industry. The McMeeking Committee, which had reported in February 1959, wanted improvements in technical training, more apprenticeships, and so on. The Crowther Report, published later in the same year, wanted, among other things, the school-leaving age raised to sixteen, and part-time education for those who had left school. A government White Paper published in January 1961, when Sir David Eccles was Minister of Education, recommended more and better technical education with new courses, high standards of entry, extension of day-release opportunities, and more sandwich courses. Finally, the Newsom Committee was established to consider the education of children of average or less than average ability in the thirteen to sixteen age-groups. It reported in October 1963 and it too advocated the raising of the school-leaving age. It wanted an alternative to the GCE ordinary level.

Sir Edward Boyle did announce the raising of the school-leaving age in line with the Newsom recommendation. This was to be in 1970-71, but it was postponed for economic reasons. That was a hope for the future, but the Conservatives could claim many achievements in office. Since 1951 the number of students in higher education had more than doubled. Seven new universities had been established, others were projected. The number of teachers in training had risen from 28,000 in 1955 to 55,000 in 1963. The Willis Jackson Report on *The Supply and Training of Teachers for Technical Colleges,* published in May 1957, had set targets which had been greatly exceeded. There had also been an explosion in the numbers of young people taking GCE 'O' and 'A' levels –impressive, but not impressive enough for many parents, teachers, and experts in the field of education. There were those, like Dr Jacob Bronowski, Director-General of the National Coal Board's process development department, and a well-known writer on scientific affairs, who believed that unless Britain thoroughly, and rapidly, upgraded the status of science and scientists, it would soon be 'relegated to the status of a third-class power'. Speaking, not for the first time, in September 1963, he wanted to see changes in education and more scientists in boardrooms and in politics.[60]

Others were concerned with the injustices of the system caused by the divisive nature of secondary education. Much of the argument centred on the 11-plus exam, the introduction of comprehensive schools, and the continued existence of the private sector in education.

The 1944 Education Act had established secondary schooling for all, but it was based, in theory, on selection at eleven for one of three types of education: modern, technical, or grammar. The technical schools remained few. As it was, the great majority of working-class children went to modern schools and the majority of pupils in the grammar schools were from the middle class. At first, as the 11-plus was supposed to test intelligence, it was presumed that most working-class children were less intelligent than their middle-class peers. However, after 1951 doubts were raised about the validity of these tests. In that year the GCE replaced the School Certificate as the academic examination which would eventually lead to the university. It was presumed that 'modern' pupils would not take it. Later some secondary-modern headmasters started to introduce a GCE stream in their schools with surprising results. The numbers of modern pupils achieving GCE results similar to those of grammar-school entrants, though a minority of those taking the exam, were significant enough to lead to serious doubts about the usefulness of the 11-plus.[61] The 11-plus came to be seen as a test which discriminated heavily, if not deliberately, against the working class. With the increasing demand for paper qualifications in the 1950s, middle-class parents whose children were 11-plus failures demanded a chance for their children to take the GCE, so the number of moderns offering GCEs rose. But critics of the system pointed out that these schools suffered from poor staffing ratios, poorer qualified teachers, and poorer facilities, as compared with the grammar and public schools. If selection at eleven was an arbitrary, often unfair, method, with great variation according to which part of the country one lived in,[62] then this unfair distribution of resources in secondary education could not be justified. It discriminated against the great majority of the country's children, especially those from working-class homes. Both the discrediting of the 11-plus and the maldistribution of resources provided powerful arguments in favour of comprehensive schools which were supposed to provide equal opportunities for all children, allowing individual children to rise as far as their abilities would take them. The comprehensive system was also supposed to give the child a greater sense of security and self-esteem than the selective system which marked so many children as failures. The government itself was not prepared to take action to force through comprehensive education, and doubtless many Conservative politicians were not convinced of the need for a change. Sir Edward Boyle, who became Minister of Education in the summer of 1962, was sympathetic towards reform. In an interview he commented,

The boys or girls of 15 who made a good start at primary school but then find themselves in the 'B' stream of a secondary modern, feel they're at a socially inferior school – if they believe they're second-class children, then they react by behaving as second-class children. You must never make children feel they are being divided into sheep and goats.[63]

He welcomed the London County Council's decision to end the 11-plus. But powerful groups within the Conservative Party remained wedded to selection and the tripartite system of secondary education, and no one thought of dealing with the problem of the private sector.

The other big issue in secondary education was the future of the private sector, both the direct-grant grammar schools, which received some support from local authorities, and the more exclusive public schools. The public schools generated a good deal of anger and annoyance in left of centre circles because their pupils did so well at getting university places, and because they almost monopolized the foreign service, the higher ranks of the legal profession, Sandhurst, and many other institutions. If socialists and Liberals were angry about the situation, Tory reformers were embarrassed. As Sir Robin Williams of the Bow Group, the reform wing of the Conservative Party, put it,

The public schools – as at present organized – therefore attract a degree of envy and resentment which is unhealthy in a stable democracy. Even if only to divert this potentially destructive emotion, Conservatives ought to consider the desirability of broadening the basis of recruitment to the public schools.

He also admitted,

it is as a caste that they are often regarded both by others and by themselves. Secondly, since the pupils at these schools come with limited exceptions from well-to-do homes (irrespective of their fathers' starting points in life) and mix with children of similar backgrounds, they have little chance of learning about the way of life and habits of mind of those different from themselves. The lack of this knowledge means that the understanding which must form the basis of 'the social unity which makes all men brothers' is also absent. Although such is not the intention of those who run the public schools, they are in fact a divisive factor in society.[64]

Sir Robin wanted the problem solved by the establishment of a system of Queen's Scholarships to the public schools, so that, he wrote, 'grant-aided pupils at leading public schools will eventually comprise 35 to 50 per cent of admissions'.[65] Not all of them would be Queen's Scholars, some would have been selected by local authorities, some would be admitted because they were 'in need of boarding education'.[66] As Sir Robin pointed out, a few local authorities had been successfully buying places at public schools for some time. Although there are a number of objections and ambiguities in the scheme proposed by this Bow Group pamphleteer, especially from the advocates of egalitarianism, it could have been made to work in some form or other. The fact is, the Conservatives were not prepared to tamper with this area of vested interest so important to the upper echelons of their electoral clientele. It was left to the Opposition to promise to deal with the situation.

The Labour Party set out its proposals in *Signposts for the Sixties*. Labour advocated the setting-up of an Educational Trust and 'After full consultation as to method and timing, with the local authorities and with the schools themselves, the Trust will recommend the form of integration that will enable each of them to make its best educational contribution'. Some would become sixth-form schools,

others could remain as secondary boarding schools for children whose parents' circumstances make this type of education necessary. Still others could serve the needs of those areas where geographic or economic reasons make it impossible for local authorities to provide schools with a sufficiently varied range of courses.

A few would do sub-university work with the 18-21 age group.[67] This had been Labour's policy under Winchester-educated Hugh Gaitskell and it remained the policy under its new, grammar school-educated, leader Harold Wilson.

Wilson elected Labour's leader

Harold Wilson was elected Leader of the Labour Party in February 1963 when he beat George Brown on the second ballot by 144 votes to 103. In the first round of the contest James Callaghan had come bottom of the poll with only 41 votes and had therefore been forced to retire.[68] As is customary in the Labour Party, only Labour MPs took part in the election process. Wilson had clearly won, and won with many votes from the Centre and Right of the Party as well as from the Left. Yet his election was regarded by many on the left and the right as a shift of the Labour Party to the left. If one had studied Wilson's career carefully, one would have concluded that his stance had been slightly left of centre, but nothing more. As President of the Board of Trade he had resigned from the Attlee Cabinet with Bevan, not as an anti-rearmer, but for the very sensible reason that he believed the degree of rearmament would cripple the nation's economy. When Bevan resigned from the shadow cabinet in 1954, Wilson took his place. His attacks on the government's economic policies, which displayed an impressive analytical skill, knowledge of economics, ability to deal with statistics, and, not least, the ability to make people laugh at the right time, earned him a reputation for professionalism both inside and outside the Commons. His reward was advancement both in the shadow cabinet and in the constituency section of the NEC. In November 1960 he stood against Gaitskell in the election for the party leadership, losing by 166 votes to 81. It was not that he was a unilateralist, he claimed it was because he disagreed with Gaitskell's intention to fight, and fight again, against the conference decision. Thus he got the applause, and the votes of the Left. On the Clause IV issue he took up a nicely ambiguous position. He wanted to unite on policy, not divide on theology. He wanted to forget Clause IV and concentrate on producing a (moderate) statement on public ownership for the next election. He had hardly, if ever, advocated public ownership on socialist grounds, but purely on the grounds that an industry or a firm was 'failing the nation'. He had further strengthened his image with the Left by his advocacy of increased trade with the Communist world, and with all sections of the Party by his support for a campaign against world poverty, on which he had written a book. For years he had had a respected place on the executive committee of the Fabian Society, which included intellectuals from both wings of the Party. Finally, like his close political companion Richard Crossman, he was a friend of Israel, which was not without significance in the Parliamentary Labour Party. So much for Wilson the platform figure. What was he off the platform?

Harold Wilson's father was an industrial chemist by profession, a Lib-Lab by political conviction, and a Baptist by religion. Wilson junior was born in Huddersfield in 1916. His family were prosperous enough to own a motor-car, prosperous enough to send Harold and his mother for a visit to his uncle in Australia. In 1932 the family moved to Merseyside and lived in 'pleasant semi-rural surroundings'.[69] Harold Wilson's next move was to Jesus College, Oxford with a scholarship from Wirral Grammar School. He read philosophy, politics, and economics and had a most successful undergraduate career. He then became a lecturer in economics at New College, where he came into contact with Sir William Beveridge. When war came, Wilson was drafted into the civil service, soon becoming head of the Manpower, Statistics, and Intelligence Branch of the Ministry of Labour. In 1940 he became Secretary of Beveridge's Manpower Requirements Committee. In 1941 he was moved again and put in charge of the economic and statistical services, first of the Mines Department of the Board of Trade, which later became the Ministry of Fuel and Power. His contribution was significant enough to be mentioned in the official history produced after the war.[70] Thus when the war ended, he was in an excellent position to choose the civil service, academic life, or politics as a career. He won Ormskirk for Labour in 1945, and by 1947 was youngest member of the Cabinet and President of the Board of Trade. In 1940 Harold Wilson had married Gladys (Mary) Baldwin, the daughter of a Congregationalist Minister from Cambridge. They had met in 1934 when she was working as a typist at Port Sunlight.

Like Home, Wilson was limited by what he inherited and by the knowledge that a general election could not be far off. The Party too realized that it was facing an election within the year and it responded to this challenge. The ginger groups of Left and Right, Victory for Socialism and Campaign for Democratic Socialism, disbanded and put themselves at the disposal of the new leader. With the possibility of a Labour victory apparently strong, the energies of some CND activists were transferred to Labour, and the movement moved, once again, to the outer fringes of the political scene.

If Wilson believed in anything, he certainly believed in the influence of the mass media. And he was determined to exploit them to his own, and Labour's, advantage. On the basis of research done by Dr Mark Abrams's opinion-polling agency, it was decided that most of Labour's publicity should be aimed at the 'target voter' and especially those in the marginal constituencies. Target voters were thought to be roughly one-sixth of the electorate, who might be expected to change their views and, just as important, actually bother to vote. On some issues like nationalization and defence, they inclined towards the Conservatives, on others, like housing and education, their views coincided more nearly to those of Labour. Luckily for Wilson, they were not too interested in defence or nationalization, but they were interested in Britain's general standing in the world. John Harris, the Labour Party's Director of Publicity, had recruited a small, unpaid, team of Labour supporters who were engaged professionally in public relations and the media. This team worked with Mark Abrams. In May 1963 Labour started a major advertising campaign based on Abrams's findings. This was conducted through a number of national dailies. A portrait of Wilson featured prominently in this onslaught, together with a campaign symbol and slogan – a thumbs-up sign and the invitation, 'Let's GO with Labour and we'll get things done'. This campaign was something entirely new for Labour. Harold Wilson could thank the Gaitskellites for it. Most of the unofficial publicity team, if they had had strong preferences, had been Gaitskellites. Wilson does not seem to have hesitated about using their specialized skills.

The Conservatives were old hands at public relations and, independently of Labour, they too started a publicity campaign in

May 1963. Happily for them, they did not concentrate on Macmillan, more on what they considered to be the achievements of their government, and the failings of their opponents. Moreover, they had more to spend than Labour. Once the leadership issue had been settled, they went over to popularizing the new Prime Minister.

The new Prime Minister had problems. Party unity was not entirely achieved under his leadership. The dramatic and mysterious circumstances surrounding the death of President Kennedy in November 1963 could have been bad for Labour. To some extent Wilson was trying to present himself as a British Kennedy; with the hero dead, would voters fall back in shock to a more traditional leader? For Sir Alec the new President represented a problem; no two leaders in an alliance could have been so different in background, style, temperament, and method. The New Year found the new leader of the Conservatives facing army mutinies in Africa, rioting in Southern Rhodesia, fighting between Greeks and Turks in Cyprus, and increasing conflict in Vietnam. At home Sir Alec was faced by more traditional worries. By February the Prime Minister had received a special memorandum from the Treasury warning of a sharp deterioration in the prospects for Britain's balance of payments. Unless remedies were applied quickly, there would be another serious payments crisis in October.[71] In an interview with the *Financial Times* (7 February 1964) Maudling, the Chancellor, admitted that Britain was going to have a 'tight situation in the latter half of the year, though I would not assume that there will necessarily be a current account deficit'. Strangely, in view of this developing situation, the Conservatives decided to hold on until the autumn. There were dangers in doing this. The economic situation could suddenly deteriorate, the electorate could rightly feel they were holding on in the party rather than national interest, and treat them accordingly. On the other hand, there could be advantages. Sir Alec could have more time to project himself, a good summer could have a soothing effect upon the electorate, the Opposition could run out of steam or simply bore the electorate to death by campaigning during the summer-holiday period. This turned out to be a good gamble. Labour wisely abstained from too much campaigning in the summer, but the summer was good and it did seem to help the government.

Election 1964

The election was set for 15 October 1964. Labour's hopes were dashed on 27 and 30 September when two polls, first Gallup and then NOP, put the Conservatives ahead – for the first time in three years! Labour looked destined for the role of perpetual opposition. How was it possible that the Conservatives had made such an apparently total recovery? Did Sir Alec perhaps have a certain charisma after all? Certainly Tory ladies loved the 14th earl, and some women felt he looked in need of help – he brought out their maternal instinct – and they were prepared to give it. Certainly deference, among men as well as women, was not yet dead by 1964. Wilson was a much better speaker, on any platform. His rhetoric contained a certain similarity to that of Kennedy, but there the similarity between the two leaders ended.[72] Their backgrounds had nothing in common, for instance. They were born within a year of each other, but there was no physical resemblance between either Wilson and Kennedy or Wilson and the two aspiring *ersatz* Kennedys – Willy Brandt and Pierre Trudeau. Wilson's rhetoric of science, efficiency, meritocracy, new frontiers, the New Britain, and his very able television performances, led many of his political friends to overlook his lack of height, his utterly non-athletic appearance, and his lack of any sartorial style. In some respects the government, almost any government, had the advantage. They could claim to be *doing* things, getting on with the job, while the Opposition was merely talking. They could cast doubts on Labour's ability to rule, its lack of experience after nearly thirteen years in the wilderness. They could claim Wilson's team was really a one-man band. They could also allege that Labour's programme was impracticable and would cost too much, was a menu without a price list. This had happened in 1959. Then Hugh Gaitskell had made a slip about income tax. Having promised many welfare improvements if Labour were returned, he had also promised there would be no increase in income tax to finance them. Many people just could not believe it. A similar incident occurred in 1964. In answer to a question on housing asked at an uneventful meeting in a small village school in Derbyshire, George Brown talked in terms of a possible 3 per cent rate of interest for new borrowers seeking home loans. The rate of interest charged by building societies at the time was 6 per cent. The *Sunday Express* translated Brown's words into a definite commitment. Briefly tempers flared, the campaign livened up, then somehow the controversy died down again.[73] Yet the Conservatives were not having it entirely their own way. On 30 September there was bad news for them too: Britain was in deficit on its overseas trade for the second quarter of the year. Sir Alec was more confident when dealing with defence than with domestic issues and he used much of his time worrying and warning the public on Labour's alleged defects in this direction. But most people were more interested in prices and the balance of payments than in prestige and the balance of terror. Hogg's interventions, in which he proclaimed that anyone voting Labour was 'stark staring bonkers', did the Conservatives no good. When the polling-stations closed, it was anyone's guess, and it was still anyone's guess hours later after most of the results were out. Even when Harold Wilson had arrived back in London at lunchtime the next day, he could only comment, 'It's getting more like the Kennedy story all along. We'll get the result from Cook County soon'.[74] His long relentless pursuit of supreme political office ended at 3.50 in the afternoon of the same day when he got the call from Buckingham Palace. Labour had a majority of four.

It has been estimated that had 900 voters either not voted for Labour or abstained, Mr Wilson would have lost the election.[75] 'If there had been no postal vote, Labour's overall majority would certainly have been 20 and possibly 40'.[76] Ironically, it was Attlee's government which had introduced this device and it always told against Labour. Labour's poor organization and Liberal interventions had also cost a few seats. Yet, all in all, it was a rather disappointing result after such high hopes. The Labour Party had to ask itself why it had lost working-class support. Certainly in a few areas, most notably in Smethwick, it was due to fears of unrestricted Commonwealth immigration which had come to be associated with Labour. But this was not the whole explanation. The parties had to ask themselves what factors lay behind the lower turn-out compared with 1959. Did it indicate greater contentment with the state of Britain, or did it mean greater disillusionment with both major parties? No satisfactory answers were found to these questions. The 1964 result was a harbinger of the unsettled state of opinion, the more questioning, more doubting, more cynical attitude of the 1970s, which has distinguished the 1970s from the 1945-59 period.

Notes

1 Nigel Fisher, *Iain Macleod* (London, 1973), 26
2 Harold Macmillan, *Pointing the Way 1959-61* (London, 1972), 23.
3 C. A. R. Crosland, *The Future of Socialism* (London, 1956), 79.
4 As quoted in Vernon Bagdanor, 'The Labour Party in Opposition, 1951-1964', in Vernon Bagdanor and Robert Skidelsky, eds., *The Age of Affluence 1951-1964* (London, 1970), 98.
5 Mark Abrams, Richard Rose, Rita Hinden, *Must Labour Lose?* (London, 1960), 100.
6 ibid., 31.
7 ibid.
8 ibid.
9 ibid., 34.
10 ibid.
11 ibid., 100.
12 ibid., 26.
13 ibid., 13, 16.

14 Margaret Stewart, *Frank Cousins: a Study* (London, 1968).
15 Stephen Haseler, *The Gaitskellites: Revisionism in the Labour Party 1951-64* (London, 1969), 189.
16 Stewart, op. cit., 101.
17 ibid., 102.
18 ibid., 103.
19 Haseler, op. cit., 217.
20 *The Campaign Guide 1964,* 584-5.
21 *Report of the Sixty-first Annual Conference of the Labour Party,* 157.
22 ibid., 159.
23 *Sunday Pictorial,* 7 October 1962.
24 Willy Brandt, *People and Politics: the Years 1960–1975* (London, 1978), 161.
25 *Report of the Sixty-first Annual Conference,* 246.
26 The four Labour MPs were technically independent because they had had the Whip withdrawn because of their earlier opposition to the Parliamentary Labour Party's defence policy. Much of the argument that went on at this time over the EEC in Britain is given in Lord Windlesham, *Communication and Political Power* (London, 1966).
27 Arthur M. Schlesinger Jr, *A Thousand Days: John F. Kennedy in the White House* (New York, 1965), 720.
28 ibid.
29 ibid.
30 Joseph Frankel, *British Foreign Policy 1945-1973* (London, 1975), 306.
31 ibid.
32 Macmillan, *Pointing the Way,* 393.
33 ibid., 394.
34 Terence Prittie, *Konrad Adenauer 1876-1967* (London, 1972), 268.
35 ibid., 293.
36 Schlesinger, op. cit., 340-1.
37 Samuel Brittan, *Steering the Economy: the Role of the Treasury* (London, 1969), 150.
38 See Thomas Wilson, 'Planning And Growth,' *Crossbow,* Supplement No. 3 (New Year, 1962). This gives some clues to the government's 'rethinking' on economic planning and outlines French experience. Christopher Dow's *The Management of the British Economy 1945-60* (Cambridge, 1964) was also influential, as were the writings of Shonfield.
39 Brittan, op. cit., 159.
40 ibid., 152.
41 Reginald Bevins, *The Greasy Pole* (London, 1965), 137.
42 ibid.
43 Stephen Aris, *The Jews in Business* (London, 1970), 163.
44 Gordon Lonsdale, the spy in question, gives his version in *Spy: Twenty Years of Secret Service* (London, 1965). Philby's activities are chronicled in Bruce Page, David Leitch, Phillip Knightley, *Philby: the Spy who Betrayed a Generation* (London, 1968).
45 Donald McL. Johnson, *A Cassandra at Westminster* (London, 1967), 148. Dr Johnson was a Conservative MP at this time; he gives a large extract from the Denning Report.
46 The *Guardian,* 26 September 1963.
47 Reginald Maudling, *Memoirs* (London, 1978), 124; two young women featured in the affair.
48 The *Sunday Times,* 17 February 1963.
49 William Rees-Mogg, The *Sunday Times,* 13 October 1963. Rees-Mogg was then an aspiring Conservative, more recently editor of *The Times.*

50 Lord Butler, *The Art of the Possible* (London, 1971), 242.
51 Rees-Mogg, op. cit.
52 Maudling, op. cit., 19.
53 Butler, op. cit., 242; see also *Observer,* 13 October 1963.
54 *Observer,* 13 October 1963.
55 Maudling, op. cit., 128.
56 Butler, op. cit., 248.
57 ibid., 244.
58 D. E. Butler and Anthony King, *The British General Election of 1964* (London, 1965), 239.
59 Bevins, op. cit., 156-7.
60 *The Times,* 17 September 1963.
61 Brian Simon, *Intelligence Testing and the Comprehensive School* (London, 1953). David Rubinstein and Brian Simon, *The Evolution of the Comprehensive School 1926-1972* (London, 1973), 56.
62 J. W. B. Douglas, *The Home and the School* (London, 1964), 24.
63 *Sunday Times,* 9 September 1962.
64 Robin Williams, *Whose Public Schools?* (Bow Group, London, 1957), 21.
65 ibid., 58-9.
66 ibid., 55.
67 Labour Party, *Signposts for the Sixties,* 31.
68 The votes on the first ballot were Wilson 115, Brown 88, Callaghan 41.
69 Gerard Eyre Noel, *Harold Wilson and the New Britain* (London, 1964), 27.
70 ibid., 48-9.
71 See William Rees-Mogg and Anthony Vice, 'Treasury warns Sir Alec of a balance of payments crisis', in *Sunday Times,* 16 February 1964.
72 Kennedy's influence on Wilson is discussed in David Nunnerley, *President Kennedy and Britain* (London, 1972), 232-4.
73 Anthony Howard and Richard West, *The Making of the Prime Minister* (London, 1965), 163-72.
74 ibid., 235. Cook County, in the district of Illinois whose marginal vote for Kennedy in 1960 swung the state and therefore the United States in his favour.
75 ibid., 225.
76 Butler and King, op. cit., 226.

7 The Wilson Years, 1964-66

Wilson's Cabinet

The Soviet leader Nikita Khrushchev had once remarked on a visit to Britain that if he were British, he would be a Conservative. Strangely, on the very day that Sir Alec Douglas-Home was being overthrown by the ballot-box, Khrushchev was overthrown by a palace intrigue. Harold Wilson reflected later, 'It was an open question whether, if the news from Moscow had come an hour or two before the polls closed, there would have been an electoral rush to play safe and to vote the existing Government back into power'.[1] But 'a little bewildered, more than a little lonely'[2] Wilson had too many real nightmares to contend with to lose any sleep over what might have been.

The first problem for Wilson was rapidly to assemble his Cabinet. Like any other Prime Minister, he had to consider that he must try to gratify the ambitions of his leading colleagues, at least two or three of whom regarded themselves as potential holders of his office. Again, like his predecessors he had to try to strike a balance between the various sections of his party, and disarm potential rebel groups by finding posts for as many of their leaders as possible. Wilson achieved a fair degree of success in all of this. Whether he always made the best appointments for particular posts is another matter. He showed commendable loyalty to Patrick Gordon Walker, who had been defeated at Smethwick, by offering him the Foreign Office. Gordon Walker (b. 1907), educated at Wellington and Oxford, had served Attlee as Secretary of State for Commonwealth Relations (1950–51), and had been a leading Gaitskellite. Gaitskellites got the other important offices as well. George Brown (b. 1914) was given the new post of Secretary of State at the Department of Economic Affairs (DEA). The son of a London chauffeur/van driver of Irish descent, who was victimized for taking part in the general strike, Brown left school at fifteen to become first a ledger clerk, and then a fur salesman. By the time he was twenty-two he was working for the TGWU, later becoming a district organizer. In 1945 he became the TGWU-sponsored MP for Belper. He too had held office under Attlee – as Minister of Works (1947–51). Brown had, of course, been a rival of Wilson's for the leadership, and there was no love lost between them.[3] He was one of the most colourful characters in the Labour leadership, but was feared somewhat for his fits of temper and damaging slips of the tongue in public.[4] But Crossman, no friend of Brown's, commented in his diary, 'One must never underestimate Brother George, particularly his ability to get a grip on the real situation when he is in good form'.[5] Wilson appointed James Callaghan (b. 1912) Chancellor of the Exchequer. It has been said,

By setting up the Department of Economic Affairs as a rival to the Treasury the Prime Minister guaranteed that George Brown and James Callaghan would be always at each other's throats. An even more potent problem posed for Callaghan was that Wilson ostentatiously paraded the fact that he himself was the real Chancellor and Treasury overlord.[6]

Against this it must be said that Wilson had a problem finding jobs with enough status for all his top colleagues, and that the idea of the DEA had been part and parcel of Labour's armoury for some time before the election. The other economic ministry went to Douglas Jay, an experienced economist and old Gaitskellite. Sir Frank Soskice (b. 1902) had been Attlee's Solicitor-General and, briefly, Attorney-General; Wilson made him Home Secretary. The Earl of Longford (b. 1905), a scion of the Anglo-Irish aristocracy, old Etonian banker, publisher, prominent Catholic, friend of Gaitskell, and, as Lord Pakenham, Attlee's Minister of Civil Aviation, and then First Lord of the Admiralty in 1951, became Lord Privy Seal. The Ministry of Defence went to Denis Healey (b. 1917) who was tasting his first experience of office. Regarded as a distinguished, if orthodox, commentator on defence and foreign affairs, Healey had been in charge of the Labour Party's International Department before he became MP for Leeds in 1952. The son of a technical college principal, he had gone from Bradford Grammar School to Oxford, and achieved distinction there and served in the army during the war. After flirting with communism, he had appeared at the 1945 Labour conference as an extreme leftist, but the Cold War soon converted him into an extreme moderate. His keen interest in defence did not recommend him to subsequent Labour conferences. A former schoolteacher, graduate of Durham University, MP for Workington since 1945, Fred Peart (b. 1914) was appointed Minister of Agriculture. One of the few Labour MPs really interested in agriculture, Peart had been PPS to the Minister of Agriculture in Attlee's administrations. He too was a Gaitskellite. A man with a reputation for toughness and blunt speaking, Ray Gunter (1909–77), a former official of the Transport Salaried Staffs

Association, was given the Ministry of Labour. The new Minister of Education and Science was Michael Stewart (b. 1906), who had been Under-Secretary for War (1947–51).

What of Wilson's friends, his old Bevanite comrades who had done so much to help him succeed? Barbara Castle (b.1911), a product of an old ILP family, Bradford Girls Grammar School, and Oxford, was named Minister of Overseas Development. Mrs Castle, good-looking and always charming as well as intelligent, had been a member of Labour's NEC since 1950. Her record as a woman in post-war politics had so far been rivalled only by Mrs Thatcher. Anthony Greenwood (b. 1911), the son of Arthur Greenwood, a noted left-winger, took over as Secretary of State for Colonial Affairs. Educated at Merchant Taylors and Oxford, Greenwood had been in the Commons since 1946, and a member of the NEC since 1954. Arthur Bottomley (b. 1907), whom Wilson made Secretary of State for Commonwealth Affairs, was another MP associated with left-wing causes. He was one of the working-class members of the Cabinet and had been Secretary for Overseas Trade (1947–51). James Griffiths (1890–1975) was another, but he had been more of the Centre–Right. One other working-class Cabinet Minister, and an unexpected member of the Cabinet, was Frank Cousins, who was given the new Ministry of Technology. Richard Crossman (1907–74) took over Housing and Local Government. After a brilliant academic career at New College, Oxford, Crossman had worked on psychological warfare during the war. He was returned as MP for Coventry East in 1945 and took up a position similar to that of Wilson in the Labour Party. As we have seen, he was a bitter critic of Attlee's Palestine policy and, near the end of his life, told the author that he regarded his advocacy of Zionism as his most outstanding political contribution. Crossman had supported Wilson for the leadership in 1963 and on earlier occasions. The architect of Wilson's 1963 victory was George Wigg (b. 1900). MP for Dudley since 1945, Wigg had had a remarkable career as a professional soldier rising through the ranks to become colonel in the Education Corps. He had been prominent in debates on security and defence in the Commons, and had done more than anyone else to bring down Profumo. In Wilson's first administration he served as Paymaster-General. This did not carry with it Cabinet rank. In his memoirs Wigg commented on the composition of Wilson's first Cabinet as follows:

I counted among its members eight who had voted for Callaghan, seven for Brown and six for Wilson. From the moment of his election as Leader of the Opposition until the day he ceased to be Prime Minister in 1970, Wilson seemingly forgot the existence of his enemies within his own Party. Indeed, the more violent and loud-mouthed an opponent had been, the better was his chance of being included in the Wilson administration. That was a characteristic I never quite understood. Forgive, yes – forget, not bloody likely! Many times I told Wilson he was a modern counterpart of Richard III, who advanced his enemies, forgot his friends, and 'got done' for his trouble.[7]

Wilson had a Cabinet of twenty-three – the same size as that of Sir Alec Douglas-Home. Ten had attended Headmasters' Conference schools and Oxford; one, the Prime Minister, a maintained grammar school and Oxford. Two others had gone from non-public schools to provincial or Scottish universities, and ten had not received higher education.

The tiny majority in the Commons was obviously a major headache which no one had really contemplated. In theory it would have been possible to come to some kind of arrangement with the Liberals. The difference between them and the Labour Party on many issues was not all that great. It could also have been argued that they had earned the right to some kind of recognition and consultation, as their vote had increased from 1.6 million in 1959 to over 3 million in 1964. This represented over 10 per cent of the votes. Yet they still had only 9 votes to deliver in the House of Commons. For Wilson this course was, in practice, virtually impossible. Any kind of agreement with the Liberals would have aroused the worst suspicions of most of the rank-and-file of the Labour Party, recalling the times of Ramsay MacDonald. Wilson does not seem to have hesitated in deciding to see it through with only the meagre Labour forces available to him. That was undoubtedly the right decision. With or without the Liberal votes ministers and backbenchers alike were going to be under tremendous pressure. In some respects, the Opposition had the initiative and could pounce at any time. The slender majority must have caused some difficulties with many of the top civil servants. They would have been less than human had they not considered the new administration as less than permanent. No doubt, as Marcia Williams, Wilson's political secretary and confidante, put it, the civil servants at 10 Downing Street gave Labour a cold reception when they arrived there, 'We were treated as ships passing in the night'.[8] No doubt the civil servants regarded Mrs Williams and what came to be known as Wilson's 'kitchen cabinet' as interlopers. This was a small group around Harold Wilson, the key figure of which was Mrs Williams.

It is impossible to understand the real Wilson and ignore Mrs Marcia Williams, whom he later created Lady Falkender. For more than twenty years she remained the greatest political influence in his life ... I doubt very much whether Harold Wilson would ever have become Party leader and Prime Minister but for the ambitious thrust provided by Mrs Williams. Of one thing I am certain: she had much the better political flair. Her tragedy was that she was not prepared to conceal it,[9]

so wrote James Margach. In Wilson's own account of the period her name does not appear. But his later press secretary, Joe Haines, believes, 'Any future historian's appraisal of Harold Wilson's role as Prime Minister and Leader of the Opposition will be incomplete unless he comprehends the full extent of her sway'.[10] George Wigg and Richard Crossman wrote in the same way.[11] The 'kitchen cabinet' included, in addition to Mrs Williams, George Wigg, Professor (later Lord) Kaldor, Professor (later Lord) Balogh, both academic economists, Peter Shore, journalist and later MP, Gerald Kaufman, and one or two others at various times.[12] Clearly, any Prime Minister can have aides and advisers, individuals he knew in opposition, whose judgement he trusts. But there are dangers. First, the civil service can start to feel underrated and gradually become demoralized. Secondly, the Prime Minister's Cabinet colleagues can feel that their legitimate influence and power are being undermined, that their ideas and contributions are not wanted, and that they can either resign or simply become yes-men. Thirdly, the public can feel that the politicians they have elected are being outmanoeuvred by shadowy figures hovering in the background. This can help to undermine public confidence in the government and the democratic process. It is only fair to say that in the case of the Wilson administration, all three happened to some extent. It was all part of Wilson's view that, in the age of mass communications, Britain was getting in fact, if not in theory, a presidential-type system of government. As we shall see, it did not always work out happily for Britain or the Labour Party. George Brown felt this, and gave it as the reason for his resignation from the government in 1968.

I resigned on a matter of fundamental principle, because it seemed to me that the Prime Minister was not only introducing a 'presidential' system into the running of the Government that is wholly alien to the British constitutional system – others have been tempted to do it that way too – but was so operating it that decisions were being taken over the heads and without the knowledge of Ministers, and far too often outsiders in his entourage seemed to be almost the only effective 'Cabinet'.[13]

As far as Wilson's 'kitchen cabinet' is concerned it would be wrong, however, not to emphasize that he had come to office carrying on as Prime Minister almost on a day-to-day basis, and that he had inherited a bad economic situation, which needed immediate attention. These two factors, as much as his distrust – of the civil service, of many of his old Gaitskellite rivals, of sections of the mass media – and his Kennedy complex, must have greatly determined his political style.

In his diaries Richard Crossman also complains about the lack of discussion on important policy issues[14] and about the unsatisfactory nature of official records of Cabinet meetings. 'Another big surprise was the discovery that Cabinet minutes are a travesty, or to be more accurate, do not pretend to be an account of what actually takes place in the Cabinet. The same applies to the minutes of Cabinet Committees'. His conclusion was that 'The combination of this kind of Cabinet minute (which provides the main directive for Whitehall) and official committees enormously strengthens the Civil Service against the politicians'.[15]

One other aspect of the governmental system under Harold Wilson deserves mention. Despite all the brave talk about modernizing, streamlining, about sweeping away the 'Edwardian establishment mentality',[16] despite the crippling official schedules of ministers, again and again one finds Wilson going along with outmoded rituals, archaic ceremony, what Crossman called the 'mumbo jumbo'. He describes the unnecessary ceremony attached to the official appointment of Cabinet ministers, the so-called 'kissing of hands':

I don't suppose anything more dull, pretentious, or plain silly has ever been invented. There we were, sixteen grown men. For over an hour we were taught how to stand up, how to kneel on one knee on a cushion, how to raise the right hand with the Bible in it, how to advance three paces towards the Queen, how to take the hand and kiss it, how to move back ten paces without falling over the stools – which had been carefully arranged so that you did fall over them. Oh dear! We did this from 11.10 to 12.15.[17]

The balance of payments deficit

The massive and mounting balance of payments deficit, the biggest since the war, was the Wilson administration's first major problem. It was dealt with by the Prime Minister and a few others, probably James Callaghan, George Brown, and Douglas Jay. The action taken was not put up for full and free discussion in the Cabinet; on the contrary, 'Cabinet as a whole had no advance notice so we simply had to accept the *fait accompli* or resign'.[18] Wilson tells us that it was the central problem of his administrations during 1964–70, 'It was this inheritance which was to dominate almost every action of the Government for five years of the five years, eight months we were in office'.[19] He decided that devaluation of sterling was not going to be part of the new administration's plan to deal with the deficit. It was felt this would have been politically damaging for the Labour government, reviving memories of the earlier devaluation under Clement Attlee. Wilson himself has commented:

There would have been many who would conclude that a Labour

Government facing difficulties always took the easy way out by devaluing the pound. Speculation would be aroused every time that Britain ran into even minor economic difficulties – or even without them. For we were to learn over the years that it was all too easy for those so minded to talk the pound down on the most frivolous of pretexts.[20]

Labour could have devalued and rightly blamed the situation on the outgoing administration. It chose not to do so.

On 11 November, James Callaghan introduced a crisis Budget, a package containing the stick and the carrot. National insurance contributions were raised, up too went the duty on petrol, and it was announced that income tax would go up in the spring. For Labour supporters part of the carrot was the announcement of a capital gains tax and the replacement of the existing income and profits taxes on companies with a corporation tax. This side of the Budget also included increased retirement pensions and the abolition of prescription charges for drugs. Earlier in October the government had placed a surcharge on imports at the rate of 15 per cent. Finally, it had promised to examine ways of cutting public expenditure. The surcharge attracted criticism abroad, even though the government had made it clear it was only regarded as a temporary expedient. The surcharge was, in any case, inherited from the Conservatives, who had been planning something similar. Neither the October measures nor the November Budget did anything to assuage the fears of sterling-holders abroad and the pressure on the pound continued. On 23 November bank-rate was raised to a record 7 per cent, and Lord Cromer, Governor of the Bank of England, was sent to get assistance from foreign central banks. This mission was completed by 25 November when pledges of massive support stabilized the situation, leaving the country dazed and deeply in debt.

That the country was not exactly enthusiastic over Wilson's policies was indicated by two by-elections on 21 January. Both were in safe Labour seats and both were caused by the need to get Patrick Gordon Walker and Frank Cousins into the Commons. Both previous MPs had been hustled off to other pastures to make way for the new ministers. Understandably the voters in the two constituencies were not very impressed by this procedure and some probably protested by not voting. In Leyton, where Gordon Walker was the candidate, Labour organization was weaker than usual. But few expected the result – the defeat of the Labour candidate. At Nuneaton, Cousins was returned with a much-reduced majority. If the electorate was less than enthusiastic about the new administration, this was not because it favoured the Opposition. The Conservatives too did badly in by-elections. On 24 March, David Steel, an unknown young Liberal, took a seat from the

Conservatives at Roxburgh, Selkirk, and Peebles.

Callaghan's April Budget was more deflationary than the special crisis Budget. Cigarette-smokers and whisky-drinkers had to pay more, and Callaghan delighted his own backbenchers by abolishing entertainment allowances for businessmen except when *bona fide* overseas buyers were being entertained. Higher-purchase regulations were also tightened. Milder, on the other hand, were the capital gains tax and corporation tax. Foreign financial centres were not impressed and the end of June found Callaghan having talks with the American Secretary of the Treasury, Henry Fowler, on further help for Britain's ailing currency. He had set the scene to impress his American host by again toughening higher-purchase controls earlier in the month, balancing this with a lowering of bank-rate in an effort to avoid industrial recession. Less than a month later the Chancellor announced the severest package of restrictions so far introduced by the Wilson administration – still more tightening-up on higher purchase, delays in or cancellation of government projects, and restrictions on local-authority borrowing. By September there was greater optimism because of the activities of George Brown rather than those of the Chancellor.

Despite the difficulties involved in setting up a new ministry, and despite the tug-of-war with the Treasury and the Bank of England in the shape of James Callaghan and Lord Cromer, Brown had moved with enthusiasm and resource in the weeks following his appointment. In December he produced the 'Joint Statement of Intent on Productivity, Prices and Incomes' signed by representatives of the government, the TUC, and the employers' side of industry. Trade unions and management agreed to ensure that increases in all incomes would be related to increases in productivity. The government promised to prepare and implement a general plan for economic development, providing for higher investment, improving industrial skills, modernization, balanced regional development, higher exports, and for the largest possible sustained expansion of production and real incomes. The NEDC was to be the vehicle through which all this was to happen.[21] In February the National Board for Prices and Incomes (NBPI) was established, headed, perhaps surprisingly, by a former Conservative MP, Aubrey Jones. Jones, a director of Guest, Keen and Nettlefolds and chairman of Staveley Industries, had been a minister in the outgoing government. At this stage the NBPI had very little power. The brave words of the statement of intent were not translated into practice, and incomes had gone ahead of productivity in the first half of 1965. The Americans were putting on the pressure. Fowler doubted whether the voluntary prices and incomes policy which George Brown had negotiated would be able to withstand the pressure for wage increases to which we were subject. While he did not attempt in any way to make terms or give us orders, he was apprehensive that if further central bank aid were required it would be difficult to mount if we had no better safeguard against inflation than the voluntary system. It was in these circumstances that we began first to think in terms of statutory powers.[22]

Whether or not orders were given, the situation was regarded as critical enough to recall the Cabinet early from holiday.[23] Back came George Brown from the south of France to go into conclave with the TUC leaders. The result was that the TUC agreed to accept statutory control of prices and incomes. The NBPI was made a statutory body, with the Secretary of State having the right to refer any price or wage proposal to it. He had the power to enforce its decisions by ministerial order, and to defer the implementation of any wage or price settlement while the Board's investigations were continuing. The legislation provided for an 'early-warning' system for price increases and wage and salary settlements. Two weeks after his success at the TUC conference, which ratified the agreement between Brown and the TUC leaders, the Secretary of State published, on 16 September, his department's National Plan. The plan set the annual rate of growth at 3.8 per cent. This seemed reasonable to most people, though it was a higher rate than Britain had been achieving. As the summer drew to a close, the Prime Minister and his colleagues felt reasonably happy about progress on the economic front. They were less happy about the developing situation abroad.

Ian Smith's UDI

On 11 November 1965 the expected happened. Ian Smith, Prime Minister of Southern Rhodesia, proclaimed his country independent of Britain. Southern Rhodesia had enjoyed internal self-government since 1923, but was still technically a British colony. Out of a population of approximately 5.3 million only the 252,000 or so whites had any say in the running of the country. In April 1964 the white electors had voted overwhelmingly for Smith's white supremist Rhodesia Front party. Between October 1964 and November 1965 Wilson had worked hard to promote a settlement with Rhodesia. He had met the Rhodesian leader at the funeral of Sir Winston Churchill in January 1965. Smith had visited London again in October 1965, expressly to parley with Wilson. In between these two meetings Arthur Bottomley and Lord Gardiner, the Lord Chancellor, had visited Rhodesia to study the situation on the spot. In the summer another British emissary, Cledwyn Hughes, had visited Rhodesia. There does not seem to have been the least chance of any settlement. The Labour government had stated five principles which had to be fulfilled before it could agree to formal independence. The first, and most important, of these was 'The principle and intention of unimpeded progress to majority rule, already enshrined in the 1961 constitution, would have to be maintained and guaranteed'. The second was a guarantee against retrogressive amendment of the constitution. Third, Britain sought an immediate improvement in the political status of the non-white population. Fourth, 'There would have to be progress towards ending racial discrimination'. Finally, Britain wanted to be sure that any agreement on independence was acceptable 'to the people of Rhodesia as a whole'.[24] Implementation of these principles would have required a radical change in Rhodesia, a change not just in a constitution, but in the way of life of the whites. This the majority of them were not prepared to contemplate. When judging Wilson's response to the problem, it must be remembered that his predecessors had left no contingency plans for dealing with a unilateral declaration of independence (UDI), though it was not unexpected. After taking office the Labour government had done nothing to prepare to meet a problem which Wilson had simply sought to solve by personal diplomacy. Crossman believed that Wilson had felt so appalled by the prospect of UDI that 'he convinced himself that by his personal intervention he could prevent it. Only this can explain his astonishing readiness to go to any lengths in order to delay that final decision'.[25] Perhaps Wilson thought that his offensive of words would be a positive advantage with the British public and would cost the country very little. There was a danger, of course, in making himself look ridiculous over what could be interpreted as a policy of appeasement. Wilson's public interventions on the issue appear to have won him public esteem, and he succeeded in splitting the Conservative Party over Rhodesia. Yet many of his parliamentary colleagues, and some in the Cabinet, remained sceptical. Mrs Castle, in particular, according to Crossman, wanted the Prime Minister to take firm action against the Smith regime; 'even if her influence hasn't prevailed, her conscience has haunted him and made him uneasy and unsure of himself . . . she got under his skin in a quite extraordinary way'.[26] The governor was instructed to declare the Rhodesian government dismissed and the regime illegal—without practical effect. A policy of mild sanctions was also adopted: expelling Rhodesia from the sterling area, loss of Commonwealth preference on Rhodesian exports, and a ban on the purchase of Rhodesian sugar and tobacco. George Wigg thought sanctions were:

a soft option. Wilson, who throughout had cherished the idea that Smith would be less racialist than the more extreme members of his Government, defied history as well as reason when, at Lagos on January 11, 1966, he expressed the view that sanctions would be effective in a matter of weeks.[27]

Richard Crossman also felt more could have been done by means of 'black propaganda or subversive organization to put pressure on Smith'.[28] Callaghan too thought stronger measures could be used.[29] It was certainly a mistake to have announced *before* UDI that Britain would not use force. Wilson is said to have admitted that 'A criticism made against me is that had I threatened to use British troops I would have prevented UDI. Perhaps the criticism is justified'.[30] But Wilson had to try to satisfy so many different constituencies. At the United Nations the African and other non-aligned states, backed by the Soviet bloc, were pressing for immediate action, including the use of troops and the imposition of a new constitution based on immediate majority rule. At home many influential groups were against any such action. Even the *Daily Mirror,* normally for Labour, warned Wilson against military action. The government also had to consider Rhodesian action against Zambia, on which Britain was dependent for 40 per cent of its copper. Wilson believed that interruption of this supply would have caused widespread dislocation in British industry and 2 million unemployed.[31] On 20 November the U.N. Security Council called on all states to sever economic relations with Rhodesia and for an oil embargo. In April 1966 the United Kingdom secured authority to prevent by use of force if necessary the arrival of tankers bringing oil to Rhodesia at Beira, in Portuguese Mozambique, on the grounds that the continuation of the illegal regime was a threat to peace. As we all now know, this particular operation was largely window-dressing. As with his economic policy, so with Rhodesia, and in his relations with the United States, Harold Wilson was walking the tightrope.

Rethinking nuclear defence

Like many in the Labour Party, Harold Wilson had been strongly critical of American policy in the Eisenhower era, especially over foreign policy. He had also been strongly critical of the sale of British companies to American interests and of the evolution in Britain of an 'Americanized society'.[32] The arrival of Kennedy at the White House brought about a change in Wilson's appraisal of the United States. He early identified himself with Kennedy and saw little to criticize in the Kennedy administration's policies. By the time Wilson was in Downing Street, Lyndon Baines Johnson had taken over the White House. Within six weeks of assuming office Wilson was off to confer with President Johnson. It seems clear that Johnson wanted to avoid devaluation of the pound, fearing unpleasant repercussions in world trade. In return for financial help the Americans sought to get all they could from Wilson in the way of support for the Johnson administration's defence and foreign policies.[33] The President wanted as much help as he could get in South-East Asia. According to Wilson, he was asked by Johnson to involve British forces in Vietnam, but he resisted this.[34] Wilson did offer a British jungle-training team from Malaya and 'also our teams for anti-subversive activities'.[35] The Wilson–Healey–Gordon Walker team were also urged by Johnson to keep up their commitments east of Suez. Healey is reported to have told the Cabinet that although the Americans did not want Britain to maintain huge bases, they wanted it 'to keep a foothold in Hong Kong, Malaya, the Persian Gulf, to enable us to do things for the alliance which they can't do'.[36] Wilson was ready to oblige the Americans. The Prime Minister had ideas of Britain's, and his own, importance, out of all proportion to the real situation of the country's finances. Informing his colleagues about his trip to the United States he said, 'They want our new constructive ideas after the epoch of sterility. We are now in a position to influence events more than ever before for the last ten years'.[37] Drew Middleton, the distinguished American correspondent, writing in 1965, commented that Wilson's first remark on becoming Prime Minister was, ' "Britain is a world power, a world influence or she is nothing". Which sounds like any Tory statement'.[38] He went on, 'The fact is that the retention of a façade of world power costs Britain too much in money and manpower'. When Labour took over, defence expenditure was about £2,000 million, of that about £357.1 million was spent overseas. 'This tremendous diversion to defence naturally reduced Britain's competitive commercial position vis-à-vis her rivals'.[39] Middleton continued: 'Both the Kennedy and Johnson Administrations encouraged the British to maintain these bases. Did this advantage to the United States in terms of world stability outweigh the risk of encouraging a steady decline in the British economy?'[40] Labour looked like falling into the same trap as its political opponents had done.

One other major defence problem confronted the Wilson administration when it took office – what to do about Britain's nuclear force. The party faithful had been led to believe it would give up a weapon which Wilson had claimed was neither independent nor a deterrent. Wilson thought he could appear to be doing that, without in reality doing so, by participation in an Atlantic Nuclear Force (ANF). Such a force would serve a second purpose. It would serve as a counter-proposal to the American-backed Multilateral Nuclear Force (MLF), which had been talked about for years. When presented to NATO in 1960 by the Americans, it meant, 'a force of Polaris missile submarines to be jointly owned and operated . . . and to be manned by crews of mixed nationality'.[41] The MLF would add to NATO strength, help the United States financially by the NATO allies' financial contributions, and 'funnel the Federal Republic's supposed nuclear appetite, and . . . court her away from France by forging new German–American links'.[42] Neither the Conservatives nor Labour had been enthusiastic. There were strong doubts about whether mixed manning would be practical. There was some fear of a German finger on the nuclear trigger, and that this would weaken Britain's 'special relationship' with the United States. The outgoing Conservatives had had an alternative to the MLF, which was brushed up by Wilson and Healey and taken with them to Washington, to become known as ANF. For various political reasons the Americans were, by December 1965, losing their enthusiasm for the MLF and gave Wilson the go-ahead to explore his ANF idea, which would have been based on existing U.S., British, and possibly French nuclear forces, with a small 'mixed-manned' element to assuage German feeling. It became official British policy to 'internationalize' the United Kingdom nuclear force in the ANF, or something like it. Accordingly, the 1966 Defence White Paper states it was the 'aim to internationalize our nuclear strategic forces in order to discourage further proliferation and to strengthen the alliance'.[43] After early 1965 the great debate on the British deterrent 'came to a standstill as the issue faded away'.[44] It can rightly be asked, after the fierce controversy within the Labour Party in 1960, how Wilson was able to achieve this retention of the British bomb with so little fuss. A number of factors contributed to this end. First, key unilateralists were prisoners in the government – Cousins, Castle, and Greenwood. Second, Wilson's tiny majority helped to keep the Left in line. Third, most Labour MPs and activists felt Wilson had a steadier trigger-finger than Douglas-Home or any other likely Conservative Premier. Fourth, the government used the argument that the Polaris submarine fleet was already too advanced to turn back, and that it was creating jobs in an industry badly needing them. Fifth, it was hinted that Britain's bomb could be used to protect democratic India against Mao's China, for China had carried out its first nuclear explosion on the day of the British election. Sixth, it was argued that Britain's abandonment of the bomb would be an empty gesture when it looked likely that any number of states would soon have it – China, Israel, possibly India. Two other arguments, which did not appease the quasi-pacifists, but carried conviction with those worried about costs and the practical side of Britain's nuclear force, were that the Polaris submarines, unlike the earlier V-bombers, were cheap, and that possible co-operation with France could be used as a ticket of admission to the EEC. Wilson was also helped by the noisy opposition of the Tory Right when it was suggested that Britain would internationalize its nuclear force. This helped to make Wilson's proposal appear more radical than it really was. The innovatory appointment by Wilson of a Minister for Disarmament, Lord Chalfont, was also another factor in his favour, though Chalfont's complete lack of any connection with the Labour Party weakened the effect of the move.

One other practical defence problem which the Cabinet had to decide during this period was the future of the TSR-2, the tactical strike and reconnaissance aircraft. This was apparently cancelled by the Cabinet, after much debate and a simple vote, on the grounds of cost, and on the understanding that Britain could buy the American F-111-A should the need arise.[45] Some Cabinet members were worried about this decision because of the precarious state of the aircraft industry. The Anglo-French Concorde was saved from a similar fate, because it was argued cancellation would have meant not just breaking a commercial contract but a treaty.[46] No doubt, possible admission to the EEC also played a significant role in this decision.

Sir Alec goes

On 22 July 1965 Sir Alec Douglas-Home announced that he was giving up the leadership of the Conservative Party. After the 1964 election there had been brave attempts to patch up the unity of the Party, but these had never quite succeeded. Sir Alec's supporters could, and did, claim that the narrow majority won by Labour indicated that the Conservative leader had done an excellent job of restoring the Party's fortunes in the short time available to him. The fact was, however, that he trailed Wilson in the opinion polls after October 1964. The loss of the Roxburgh seat in Douglas-Home territory by a Home-type candidate, in March 1965, gave ammunition to the critics of the 14th earl. As Reginald Maudling put it, 'As usually happens in the Conservative Party the old rules of public life applied, namely that there is no gratitude in politics, and you should never kick a man until he is down'.[47] The Conservatives faced the problem that an election could not be far off and they had to settle the leadership question, one way or the other, as soon as possible. This time they had an election procedure which was similar to that of the Labour Party. On 20 July, Edward du Cann, Chairman of the Conservative Party, had dismissed talk of Sir Alec giving up;[48] yet it was on that day that the leader was making his final decision. One key factor is believed to have been an NOP poll which indicated that voters took Wilson as superior to Sir Alec on almost every quality mentioned, including sincerity.[49] Having lost their old leader, the Conservatives did not take long to decide on a new one. There were three candidates, Edward Heath, Reginald Maudling, and Enoch Powell. Powell, already something of an *enfant terrible* of the Party, did not expect to win. He was merely testing the ground to see how much support there was for his peculiar brand of *laissez-faire* anti-Establishment Conservatism. It was thought by some that the publication, shortly before the poll, of a book of his speeches, would have helped him. In a review of this book in the *Spectator,* none other than Iain Macleod had written: 'Enoch Powell has the finest mind in the House of Commons. The best trained and the most exciting'.[50] For the other two candidates, however, the only question of interest in Powell's candidature was from whom would he take the most votes, Maudling or Heath? The *Daily Mail* and the *Daily Express* predicted a Maudling victory and opinion polls indicated his popularity. Yet when the votes of the 298 Conservative MPs were counted on 26 July, Heath was clearly the victor. He had gained 150 votes to 133 for Maudling and only 15 for Powell. In Edward Heath the Conservatives had decided for a Macmillan-type Conservative, that is as far as his policies were concerned; in other respects, he was almost a carbon-copy of Harold Wilson.

Many later saw in Heath the cold, uninspired technocrat, all brain but no heart. This was not Willy Brandt's view, 'I never felt Edward Heath's reputed lack of personal warmth'.[51] Heath was, nevertheless, something of a loner. His close political colleague Macleod felt he did not know Heath much better after their twenty years as colleagues than when they had entered the Commons together on the same day in 1950. Macleod did not feel anything for Heath's non-political interests, music and sailing.[52] Cecil King noted in his diary on 20 June 1966, 'Ted Heath to lunch today. I am beginning to see what people mean when they call him cold. He is not cold, but he is certainly not forthcoming, when he has every reason to be just that'.[53] He was to write again on 14 May 1970,

People say Ted is cold, unfriendly, unapproachable, and all that kind of thing. But he is easy to talk to, warm, friendly and forthcoming. I think it would be fair to say that he is no politician and certainly no Leader of the Opposition. He is essentially an able civil servant, but the Tories have no one better.[54]

In addition to choosing a new potential Prime Minister the Conservatives were, in other respects, trying to prepare themselves for a renewed electoral struggle. Under Lord Blakenham, party Chairman until replaced by Edward du Cann, in January 1965, two important committees of investigation were set up. One, under

Lord Chelmer, looked into the status and remuneration of constituency agents; the other, chaired by Iain Macleod, examined the role of the Young Conservatives. The Chelmer report advocated improved pay and training for agents, and a system of subsidies for highly marginal constituencies to enable them to attract better agents from the safer seats. It also wanted an enhanced status for the agent *vis-à-vis* the candidate or MP and the constituency chairman. The agent was to be raised from a relatively lowly technician, to being a co-manager, even managing director, of the local party. The Macleod committee wanted more political discussion in the Young Conservatives. It also recommended that the upper age limit be raised to 35, with special emphasis on work among the 25-35 age group. There were also changes in the Conservative headquarters during this period, and efforts to give the Party a younger, more modern image by changes in the leadership and among the parliamentary candidates. Edward Heath was forty-nine when he became leader, Edward du Cann was forty. Both had been at Oxford, neither had been at public schools. Not without some pain the list of approved parliamentary candidates was completely overhauled. It was hoped there would be a trend against the preference for landowners, retired businessmen, and service officers. This, it should be stressed, was done under the old leadership and was not an innovation of the Heath era. The results of this reform were by no means spectacular. Butler and King in their survey of the 1966 election concluded:

The educational pattern remains much as in previous years though the slight decline in Etonian Conservatives continued (there were 84 candidates in 1966 compared to 94 in 1964) ... A classification of the first or formative occupation of each candidate yields much the same proportions as in 1964.[55]

The other problems the Conservative leadership tried to deal with were finance (there was more emphasis on the need to collect a large number of relatively modest subscriptions rather than relying too much on big business donations), market research, and policy. Great efforts were made to extend the discussion over party policy. Heath had become chairman of the advisory committee on policy after the 1964 election, and his committee, aided by many advisory groups, eventually produced a policy document entitled *Putting Britain Right Ahead*. It was a limp and limited document which concentrated on relatively few areas. There was talk about new incentives, especially for those identified by the Party whose 'vigour and initiative' were needed to improve the competitive ability and prosperity of the nation. Reform of legislation relating to trade unions was advocated with a new range of industrial courts. In the field of social security the Conservatives wanted the extension of occupational pension schemes as widely as possible, rather than reliance on the new state pension scheme. The Conservatives were moving in the direction of selective benefits to those who really needed them rather than universal benefits irrespective of need. They also wanted to see more of the burden of social security being placed directly on the employers in the belief that this would encourage the more efficient use of Labour. Finally, the Conservatives wanted to see Britain in Europe at the first available opportunity. Planning, and education, so dear to the heart of Harold Macmillan, appeared to have been forgotten. In fact the document hid any number of differences over policy among the leading personalities of the Party. The most dramatic revelation of these differences came over Rhodesia rather than economic policy. The official party line on oil sanctions against Rhodesia was to abstain. But at the end of the Commons debate on the issue on 21 December 1965, 48 Conservatives led by Julian Amery divided the House; another 31 voted with the government.

Wilson's 1966 victory

Speculation about a general election ended when Harold Wilson announced on 28 February that polling-day would be 31 March 1966. Mike Randall, editor of the *Daily Mail,* commented to Richard Crossman on 9 March that people were not interested in the election, 'and it is not going to warm up or be anything more than a titular election because the decision has already been taken by ordinary people'.[56] Few sparks flew in the campaign which followed. Heath and his team got in first with their manifesto, *Action Not Words,* which was basically the policy set out in the earlier document. In addition, it promised 500,000 houses, and retention of the bases east of Suez and of the Territorial Army, under threat of axing as an economy measure. Wilson went in to bat with *Time For Decision,* which offered planned growth of incomes, the setting-up of a Ministry of Social Security, steel nationalization, regional planning, and a national transport plan. It too offered 500,000 houses, and a major effort to improve education and medical services. The 1964 stress on the scientific revolution was gone. Labour held many of the best cards in the 1966 election. They could point to the inherited balance of payments problem. They appeared to have some good ideas, like the DEA, option mortgages, and the NBPI, which needed time and a clear majority to enable them to develop. Third, Labour had not proved the disaster the Conservatives had predicted; hence the Labour slogan 'You *know* Labour Government works' had some appeal. Unemployment was low and incomes were rising, though much of this was due to the improvement in world trade. Finally, Wilson was much better established than Heath as a popular figure. On TV 'Mr Wilson showed his accustomed mastery in his final appeal – no partisan gibes but only the apotheosis of his family doctor manner'.[57] Immigration was a potential hazard for Labour, but it did not develop as an election issue. Smethwick was won back by Labour, as was Leyton.

Labour's majority increased to 96 over all other parties. There was a fairly general swing to Labour and the Party could well be pleased. The only disappointment was that the victory was achieved on the lowest turn-out of voters since 1945. Labour appeared to suffer more than the Conservatives from abstentions. As in 1964, Labour appeared to increase its support higher up the social scale, especially among the young. It gained even more support among the unskilled and the very poor.[58] The Liberals had a crumb of comfort by increasing their parliamentary strength from 9 to 12, but their vote and percentage of the poll fell. Their dream of forming some kind of Lab-Lib alliance, which had been talked about since 1959, faded overnight. Crossman, in a sober analysis of the result, commented on 1 April,

If we had carried on without the election in March and gone right forward to the municipals in April and May we would have had a disastrous defeat. With rates going up and rents going up, our candidates would have been swept away . . . then there would have been no chance of going to the country in May or June. The election would have been pushed off until October and by then we might have had the most appalling crisis blowing up . . . As it was we have given the electorate time to get to like our style and see how active we were. But they haven't had enough time to see our actions put into effect and recognize them as failures. From now on we shall never again be able to look back at the Tory thirteen years and contrast them with our eighteen months.[59]

Notes

1 Harold Wilson, *The Labour Government 1964-70: a Personal Record* (London, 1971), 2.
2 ibid.
3 Richard Crossman, *The Diaries of a Cabinet Minister*, vol. I: *Minister of Housing 1964-66* (London, 1975), 601. Cecil King, *Diary 1965-70* (London, 1972), 38.
4 Anthony Sampson, *Anatomy of Britain* (London, 1962), 102 recalls the Khrushchev dinner incident. Brown is reported to have said 'I react emotionally not intellectually'.
5 Crossman, op. cit., 601.
6 James Margach, *The Abuse of Power* (London, 1978), 177.
7 Lord Wigg, *George Wigg* (London, 1972), 259.
8 Marcia Williams, *Inside Number 10* (London, 1972), 27.
9 Margach, op. cit., 141-2.
10 Joe Haines, *The Politics of Power* (London, 1977), 157.

11 Wigg, op. cit., 316. Crossman, op. cit., 582.
12 ibid.
13 Lord George-Brown, *In My Way* (London 1971), 161.
14 Crossman, op. cit., 582, 202, 198.
15 ibid., 198-9.
16 Harold Wilson, *The New Britain: Labour's Plan Outlined* (London, 1964), 9. This volume includes all the radical, Kennedy-style, modernizing rhetoric; there is no plan as such. Marcia Williams, op. cit., 17 contains a telling passage about Wilson's first visit to the Palace after the election, 'It struck me at the time as an ironic beginning to the white-hot technological revolution and the Government that was to mastermind it'.
17 Crossman, op. cit., 29.
18 ibid., 28.
19 Wilson, op. cit., 5.
20 ibid., 6.
21 Samuel Brittan, *Steering the Economy: the Role of the Treasury* (London, 1969), 204 gives full text.
22 Wilson, *The Labour Government*, 131.
23 Crossman, op. cit., 315.
24 *The Labour Government*, 143.
25 Crossman, op. cit., 378.
26 ibid., 378.
27 Wigg, op. cit., 326.
28 Crossman, op. cit., 379.
29 ibid., 382.
30 King, op. cit., 45.
31 *The Labour Government*, 183.
32 Paul Foot, *The Politics of Harold Wilson* (London, 1968), 207. He used this term in a speech in 1960.
33 Joseph Frankel, *British Foreign Policy 1945-1973* (London, 1975), 205.
34 *The Labour Government*, 48.
35 Crossman, op. cit., 94.
36 ibid., 95.
37 ibid.
38 Drew Middleton, *Crisis in the West* (London, 1965), 90.
39 ibid., 91.
40 ibid.
41 Andrew J. Pierre, *Nuclear Politics: the British Experience with an Independent Strategic Force* (London, 1972), 244.
42 ibid., 245.
43 ibid., 290.
44 ibid., 291.
45 Crossman, op. cit., 191.
46 ibid., 57-8.
47 Reginald Maudling, *Memoirs* (London, 1978), 134.
48 *Guardian*, 21 July 1965.
49 *Sunday Times*, 25 July 1965.
50 Andrew Roth, *Enoch Powell; Tory Tribune* (London, 1970), 328.
51 Brandt, *People and Politics* (London, 1978), 249.
52 Fisher, *Iain Macleod* (London, 1973), 315.
53 King, op. cit., 71.
54 ibid., 326.
55 D. E. Butler and Anthony King, *The British General Election of 1966* (London, 1966), 207-8.
56 Crossman, op. cit., 475.

57 Butler and King, op. cit., 123.
58 ibid., 265.
59 Crossman, op. cit., 489.

8   The Wilson Years, 1966-70

Seamen's strike

Labour's victory in 1966 was remarkable for a number of reasons. It was the first time that a twentieth-century Prime Minister had led his party to a second electoral victory with an increased majority. For Labour it was only the second time that the Party had achieved a comfortable majority since the Labour Representation Committee had been established in 1900. But it was important, for it proved that 1945 was not just a special case caused by the exceptional, and not to be repeated, conditions of war. It was a slap in the face for those who had predicted, after the defeat of 1959, that Labour could not achieve victory by itself and therefore needed an alliance with the Liberals. Some of those political soothsayers began predicting the demise of the Conservative Party, believing the election showed that Labour had, at last, become the natural party of government. There was even a certain relief in the financial world about the Labour victory. The Conservative Party's image in that, normally Conservative, quarter was still tarnished as a result of its financial failure in 1964.[1] As for the Conservatives themselves, they were of course demoralized by the prospect of a long period in the wilderness. The role of Opposition still did not come easy to them. Some felt the change in leadership had been a mistake, even though Heath had not done badly in the campaign. The more gullible Conservatives, those who believed their own propaganda about Wilson being an 'old-fashioned' or 'full-blooded' socialist, were horrified at the thought of the large doses of socialist medicine they would have to swallow during the five years to come. Some full-blooded socialists, again the more gullible, on the contrary, were in a state of shocked ecstacy. Suddenly their wildest dreams looked like becoming reality. The long, sometimes bitter, often sterile, arguments about resolutions on party policy, the long hours in dingy, half-empty assembly halls, in shabby, smoke-filled, committee rooms, canvassing in wind and rain, had not been in vain. Uncannily, even before all the election posters had been superseded on the hoardings, socialist dreams were turning into nightmares.

179

Wilson made few government changes. James Griffiths and Sir Frank Soskice left the government, Sir Frank becoming Lord Stow Hill. Richard Marsh joined the Cabinet as Minister of Power and was given the job of preparing and piloting through the Bill to nationalize steel. This went through and the British Steel Corporation was established in 1967. It had the difficult job of modernizing and streamlining the industry, a task not yet completed. The Queen's Speech contained, in addition to steel nationalization, reference to a number of other measures concerned with industrial policy. Some of them had been held over from the previous session. One of them was legislation to create the Industrial Reorganization Corporation (IRC). This body had been established in January 1966, but an Act of Parliament was required to provide it with funds. It was 'a kind of government-sponsored merchant bank, to encourage efficient firms to take over the less efficient, to encourage mergers and help finance them, to be, in effect, a stimulator of change by the mere fact of its existence'.[2] Its first chairman was Frank Kearton who, according to George Brown, whose responsibility it was, 'did an absolutely fantastic job there while still having his own job as chairman of Courtaulds. How he managed to find the time for both has always puzzled me'.[3] The most notable take-overs helped by the Corporation were GEC's takeover of AEI and English Electric, and the merger of Leyland Motors with the British Motor Corporation. The idea was not just to bail out ailing industries, nor simply to subsidize prestige projects, as the Conservatives had done in the cases of Concorde and the ocean liner *Queen Elizabeth II*. It was to provide Britain with large companies which could compete effectively in international markets. Thus British Leyland, it was hoped, would be able to take on the state-owned Renault, and Volkswagen, which had been developed from public funds. British Leyland, formed in 1968, continued to have troubles, results of inefficient plant location, overmanning, and poor industrial relations, and was only saved from collapse by nationalization in 1975 on the recommendation of the Ryder Report. The ailing computer industry was also helped, and after a series of shake-ups International Computers Limited (ICL) finally emerged as the only British computer firm. This measure had been tackled since 1965 by the Ministry of Technology. The Wilson administration also tried to encourage industry by introducing the Queen's Award to Industry, and more industrialists were given recognition in the honours list than previously. Finally, industrial training boards were established to assist in the training of staff in modern methods. Training boards were soon in operation for the road transport, hotel and catering, civil air transport, and petroleum industries. Others followed. The boards approve levy and grant schemes which provide financial incentives for the improvement and extension of training. They have also established their own training centres. One other measure of modernization which affected both industry and banking was decimalization. In December 1966 the Decimal Currency Board was created under the chairmanship of Sir William Fiske to prepare the introduction of decimal currency in 1971. Appropriate legislation was approved by Parliament in 1967.

One other item foreshadowed in the Queen's Speech of April 1966 was legislation on prices and incomes. This led to the resignation of Frank Cousins on 3 July, the day before the Bill was published. He was replaced by Anthony Wedgwood Benn.

The most notable feature of the Budget which followed just after the election was the introduction of the Selective Employment Tax (SET), in effect, a payroll tax paid by employers for each of their employees. The brunt of the tax was to fall on the service industries, as there was to be a remission of the tax in manufacturing industry. The tax was acceptable to both the Treasury and the DEA – to both Callaghan and Brown. The strategy behind it was that labour was to be encouraged to move out of the service industries, catering, for instance, and into manufacturing industries and thus, it was hoped, into firms producing exports. The Treasury liked it as an anti-inflationary measure which would bring in revenue. Apparently

when Callaghan started discussing this tax in Cabinet there was bewilderment and consternation. Nobody could quite follow what he was saying and he had the easiest time in the world . . . it seems . . . to make an absolute mockery of Cabinet government and Cabinet responsibility to introduce S.E.T. in this way and tell none of us about it until it is too late to do anything.[4]

The tax proved unpopular with trade unions and employers alike; it could be argued that much of catering was an export industry, and that many of those engaged in it, or in other affected industries, would not be likely to migrate to manufacturing industry. The Conservatives and the trade unions attacked it as something likely to put up the cost of living. The Budget did not involve any new burdens, such as increases on the duties on beer, spirits, and tobacco – as had been expected – and thus Callaghan redeemed his election pledge. Many felt he was simply putting off the evil day. Equally, the international banking community were not impressed, for they felt that as the Labour government was now free from electoral considerations, it could have done more to put its house in order. In June sterling again ran into trouble. Whether this was in any significant respect due to the seamen's strike is impossible to say, but the strike certainly did not improve the situation.

The strike called by the National Union of Seamen (NUS) began on 16 May and lasted until 2 July. Only half British shipping was affected by it. The union wanted a pay increase larger than the government's 3–3½ per cent norm. The seaman's wage was low, his work was hard, his conditions of service were Victorian – or worse! Wilson himself later recognized much of this:

If the union was militant . . . this was in large part due to a generation of union complacency. For years the NUS had been little more than a companies' union, and the shipowners and union officials had an equal responsibility for the utter frustration of union members . . . Frustrations outside the field of wages and conditions related to such matters as the failure to press for the modernisation of the 1894 Merchant Shipping Act. In 1960 an unofficial strike . . . should have acted as a sharp warning to both sides . . .But the warning went unheeded.[5]

Cecil King commented in his diary at the time, 'I should have thought the Government has chosen to fight – or been forced to fight – on unattractive ground'.[6] The government had allowed handsome salary improvements for judges and some other groups. In depressed mood Crossman recorded on 19 May:

The Cabinet is formally committed to breaking the strike in the way we didn't break the doctors', the judges' and the civil servants' strikes . . . We listen to George Brown telling us to resist to the death. We listen to James Callaghan telling us to resist to the death, although it would cost us a small fortune in foreign exchange. Only Dick Marsh disagreed and said that he thought the strike was no issue to fight on, since the men had a very strong case. But after he had finished no one gave him very much support.[7]

As the strike continued, with all the drama of a national emergency having been declared giving the government sweeping powers, Crossman got more depressed.[8] His mood, as he himself recognized, was shared by very many in the Labour movement, from MPs down to humble party members. By not allowing the employers to settle the dispute the government were really undermining their own policy on prices and incomes. They seemed to have a double standard, one for the better-off, and another for the poorer, or less well-organized, section of the working classes. The only chance for such an incomes policy to succeed was to be fair and to be seen to be fair.[9] It could be claimed, as Crossman said so often about the administration of which he was a member, that they never thought ahead, never anticipated difficulties, and had simply to react to an immediate situation. If this was so and the government were merely reacting instinctively, then it was an indication of how far apart were the instincts of most of the Cabinet from those of their followers. The strike ended as a technical victory for Harold Wilson. He used the fear of Communist influence in the NUS to torpedo the strike, a tactic often denounced by Labour spokesmen in the past. No doubt the Communists had increased their influence in the union as a result of the bad conditions prevailing, but, as we have seen, Wilson has admitted that the union leadership had failed their membership. The ordinary seamen supported the stoppage, but the leadership advocated a return to work, pressurized by government and media as being dupes of a Communist plot. It is doubtful whether the Prime Minister convinced any of his own rank-and-file by this tactic that his incomes policy was a just one. More likely, it marked the beginning of real and sustained disenchantment with a hitherto popular leader.

Economic crisis, 1966

The position of sterling did not improve with the ending of the seamen's strike. The pressure continued. On 14 July, Bank Rate was raised from 6 to 7 per cent, a harbinger of the gathering economic storm. The triumvirate of Wilson, Callaghan, and Brown looked increasingly unable to steer the economy into a peaceful harbour. Callaghan, and Wilson, wanted to avoid devaluation of sterling if possible. Brown preferred devaluation to deflation. Wilson chose to back the Treasury call for more deflation rather than the DEA call for devaluation. He announced in the Commons that deflationary measures would be announced in two weeks time. He still insisted on playing his world role and flew to Moscow to act as a go-between for President Johnson over the escalating war in Vietnam. Within hours of Wilson's return, the Cabinet met to discuss the austerity package. The package, prepared by top civil servants headed by Sir Burke (now Lord) Trend, Secretary of the Cabinet, himself an old Treasury man, was discussed by the Cabinet on 19 and 20 July, 'And Cabinet was a desultory affair. Nothing had been adequately prepared. Nothing thought out properly. We were fixing things once again, horribly inefficiently, at the last moment'.[10] The package included ten measures which together were regarded as the toughest deflation since 1949. Hire purchase, as usual, was hit, with down-payment on cars, motor-cycles, and caravans raised to 40 per cent. There were higher down-payments on other items and shorter repayment periods. The 'regulator' was invoked, a device introduced by Selwyn Lloyd in 1961 under which a Chancellor could raise or lower indirect tax rates by 10 per cent. Callaghan used it to increase taxes on drink, oils, petrol, and purchase tax. Certain postal charges were increased. There was an increase of 10 per cent on the year's surtax liabilities. More controls on building were introduced, except in the development areas. Big cuts were made in investment programmes in the nationalized industries and local and central government; but housing, schools, hospitals, government-financed factories, including advance factories built in development areas, were excluded from the cuts. There was a tightening-up of foreign-exchange controls. What probably had the greatest psychological sting was the six-months freeze on wages, salaries, 'and other types of income', to be followed by a period of severe restraint. One other item was a proposed cut in overseas civil and military expenditure. Of particular concern were the costs of maintaining the British forces in Germany; the Chancellor flew to Germany immediately to emphasize that concern.[11] As Wilson later wrote, he faced 'the roughest House any Prime Minister had faced for a very long time. But it was nothing to the evening that lay ahead'.[12] Wilson's difficult night was in no small measure the result of George Brown's announcement that he was going to resign. He was, however, persuaded not to do so by his Cabinet, and, above all, parliamentary colleagues. It was a most unusual situation caused by a most unusual politician.

Brown had to make his contribution by incorporating proposals for the wage freeze into his prices and incomes legislation. This was included in Part IV of the Bill and it contained an element, perhaps no more than a threat or a hint, of compulsion. In the case of a deliberate breach of the pay standstill, an Order in Council could be laid before Parliament, to impose penalties of up to £500.[13] When the Bill came before Parliament on 4 August, 25 Labour MPs abstained. In the circumstances the government could consider itself very lucky.

On 24 July, Richard Crossman had recorded in his diary that the week had been one catastrophe after another, ending in 'the tragi-comic incident of George Brown's semi-resignation this week'. He went on to assess Harold Wilson's position: 'I suppose it is the most dramatic decline any modern P.M. has suffered. More sudden than Macmillan's'.[14] This was probably an emotional reaction to immediate events rather than a cool assessment of the Prime Minister's prospects. Wilson was able to get the TUC General Council to 'acquiesce', by a majority vote of 20 to 12, in the incomes policy, subject to the proviso that 'social equity' was preserved.[15] He was given strong public support when he visited President Johnson on 28 July. During a speech in which he had mentioned the greatness of Shakespeare, Milton, and Churchill, the President said Britain was 'blessed with a leader whose own enterprise and courage will show the way. Your firmness and leadership have inspired us deeply in the tradition of the great men of Britain'.[16] Finally, Wilson's luck had not quite run out. He returned to see Britain beat West Germany in the World Cup at Wembley. This event certainly did a little to restore the nation's confidence, for the moment at least, and no doubt it did Britain's image some good abroad as well.[17]

Having apparently succeeded, Wilson reshaped his Cabinet. George Brown was relieved of the burdens of the DEA and given the opportunity to show his skills at diplomacy. Michael Stewart swopped the Foreign Office with Brown for the DEA. Richard Crossman was promoted to Lord President of the Council and Leader of the House, Anthony Greenwood succeeding him at Housing and Local Government. Greenwood's place at the Ministry of Overseas Development was taken by Arthur Bottomley, who in turn handed over the Commonwealth Relations Office to Herbert Bowden. The latter's responsibilities went to Crossman. Bowden (b. 1905) was regarded as less hostile to Smith than was Bottomley,[18] and Wilson was still hoping to find a way of settling the dispute with Rhodesia by negotiation. As for Brown's new office, Wilson believed:

> The Foreign Office, at the same time, could do with a shake-up and a little more dynamism. We seemed to be drawing nearer to the point where we would have to take a decision about Europe, and George Brown seemed to me the appropriate leader for the task which might lie ahead.[19]

By promoting Crossman, Wilson probably believed he was making the former Housing Minister more dependent on him. He was also giving him the unpleasant task of disciplining the Parliamentary Labour Party, thus forcing the former rebel to become a policeman.[20] Greenwood, another former rebel, was given Housing and Local Government because, it was felt, he had the necessary charm needed to deal with local authority representatives.[21]

Rhodesia

Wilson's final major trial in the eventful summer of 1966 was the meeting of Commonwealth leaders. Inevitably, the main item on the agenda was the situation in Rhodesia. The conference very nearly led to the breaking-up of the Commonwealth because the great majority of the African states wanted to commit Britain to NIBMAR – no independence before majority African rule. The British Prime Minister was not prepared to agree to this. He stuck to his earlier five principles (above, p.168) to which he added a sixth, 'just as, in the period *before* majority rule, there must be no exploitation of the majority by the minority, in the period *after* majority rule was reached the minority must equally have built-in guarantees against exploitation by the majority'.[22] He succeeded, a remarkable feat, in getting the conference to agree to a communiqué embracing the six principles and calling on Rhodesia to restore the authority of the governor. If the Smith regime did not do so, the British government would not be prepared to submit to the British Parliament any settlement involving independence before majority rule. Backed by the Commonwealth, the communiqué ended, Her Majesty's Government would sponsor in the U.N. Security Council a resolution providing for effective and selective mandatory sanctions against Rhodesia.[23] The illegal regime had until the end of November to call off the rebellion. Apparently on the advice of the governor, who had remained in Rhodesia, Wilson agreed again to see Smith. He had been advised that there was a reasonable chance of a settlement.[24] It was Crossman's view that the Cabinet was desperate for a settlement, 'we recognize we are clutching at a straw', he wrote on 28 November.[25] The British government, according to this source, feared what it would be called upon to do if no settlement was reached. It feared the economic consequences of possible confrontation with South Africa.

The meetings of the Prime Minister and the Rhodesian leader and their aides took place between 2 and 5 December. Rather dramatically, they took place on board the cruiser *HMS Tiger,* which went 'round and round in circles' in the Mediterranean.[26] The fact that the meetings were held on a warship was perhaps meant to recall the conference of Churchill and Roosevelt in Placentia Bay; if so, they did not. The 1966 conference was, at best, a sad parody of that earlier seaborne meeting. Though Wilson was prepared to agree to Rhodesian independence on terms which would have meant black majority rule would have been a very long way off, the talks failed to produce a settlement. The leaders held further fruitless talks, this time on *HMS Fearless,* moored at Gibraltar, in October 1968. Even so, in the spring of 1969 the farce continued with further 'desultory exchanges'[27] between London and Salisbury, but Rhodesia drifted more and more in the direction of South Africa, acquiring all the trappings of an authoritarian racist regime. Undoubtedly some domestic opinion was appeased by all the Prime Minister's efforts to reach an agreement with white Rhodesia. Many people, though, did see the need for economic sanctions.[28] And it could rightly be asked,

if troops could be sustained in the jungles of Borneo, if the Zambian economy could be sustained by an airlift and an emergency road service, why should the communications problem of tackling Rhodesia have been too much for the British defence machine? . . . our defence forces, at a cost of £2,000m a year, were apparently deemed incapable of keeping the law. The challenge that was too much for them came from a white population the size of Harrow . . . the last chapter in the history of the British empire could be written either as a sell-out to racialism or as a patent – and probably successful – determination to defeat racialism . . .[29]

If Wilson's many efforts to come to terms with Smith won him some brief improvement in his image at home, they surely weakened Britain's image abroad. So fond of recalling Dunkirk, Wilson was inviting comparison with Chamberlain rather than with Churchill.

It is convenient here to mention the Wilson government's wavering over its policy towards South Africa. In Opposition, as leader of the Labour Party, Harold Wilson had spoken with some eloquence in condemning the apartheid regime of the Republic of South Africa. He had promised that the Labour Party in office would not sell arms to South Africa. In 1963 he said:

Under Hugh Gaitskell's leadership we condemned the supply of arms to South Africa as long as apartheid continues. That is the policy of the Labour Party today. It will be the policy of the Labour Party when we are called upon to form the Government of this country. And lest there be any doubt, we shall apply exactly the same policy in respect of arms supplied to the Portuguese Government for the use in territories they control in Africa.[30]

Wilson reaffirmed this stand in June 1964.[31] However, he refused to go further, to a general boycott of trade with South Africa. The argument used was that such a policy would hit the black South Africans harder than the white minority. On paper it looked a fairly clear and straightforward policy.

The problem of trade in military hardware to South Africa was never satisfactorily solved by the Wilson administration. On the one hand, Wilson had to square anything his government undertook in this direction with the clear commitments given before October 1964. On the other hand, he was under pressure, at a time when the economy was particularly vulnerable, to allow industry to sell as much as possible overseas. He was also under pressure from the Ministry of Defence and, some of the time, Foreign Office, because of the Simonstown Agreements. These dated from 1955 and provided for co-operation between Britain and South Africa in the defence of the sea routes round the Cape of Good Hope, regarded by defence experts as vital for the West's supplies of strategic raw materials. Primarily, South Africa would need naval equipment, including naval aircraft, to fulfil this defence commitment. Soon after taking office Wilson weakened the effect of the arms embargo by agreeing that existing contracts would be honoured; under this loophole, sixteen low-flying Buccaneer strike bombers already on order would be delivered. Trade seems to have been as important as defence in this case.[32] In this earlier period Vauxhall Motors was given permission to sell four-wheel-drive chassis for armoured cars or motor lorries for the South African army.[33] Clearly, this was equipment which could be used for internal repression. A crisis blew up over the question of arms sales to the republic in December 1967. According to Wilson, the strains caused by this issue in the

Cabinet were 'strains more serious than any other in our six years of Government'.[34]

Wilson, in Cabinet, was being pressed by a group led by Brown, Healey, Callaghan, and Gordon Walker to lift the ban on the sale of arms to South Africa. This he felt he could not do and he was given strong backing by Castle, Greenwood, Shore, and some others. After much heat and anger, and the decision had been put off more than once, the Cabinet decided on 18 December against any change of policy.[35] The Labour government did allow a deal between Rio Tinto Zinc and the South African government on uranium-mining which virtually gave the republic a nuclear capability.[36] This was not, apparently, discussed at Cabinet. Finally, on arms shipments, it should be added that Britain was under an obligation, as a member of the United Nations, to carry out the resolution of 18 June 1963 banning such supplies.

Under Wilson general trade with South Africa grew. Indeed, in February 1966 it was given official encouragement by the setting-up of the South African Section of the British National Exports Council, an official body established in 1964 by the then Conservative government.[37] Remarkably, the system of imperial preference was still in operation for trade between the two states, even though the republic had left the Commonwealth in 1961 (above, p. 111). One other consideration touched Britain's trade with South Africa: the possible effect such commerce would have on trade with other areas. By the 1970s, for instance, exports to black Africa exceeded those to South Africa.[38]

Yet another difficult and painful African problem was the civil war in Nigeria. From its birth Nigeria had been plagued by tribal rivalries. Never far below the surface, these were a key element in the civil war which erupted in July 1967. Colonel Odumegwu Ojukwu proclaimed the independence of the eastern (Ibo) region of Nigeria. At first the new state, Biafra, had considerable success against the military forces of the junta which ruled Nigeria. In autumn 1967 the federal government requested military supplies from the United Kingdom. The British government responded favourably to this request, and eventually the federal forces prevailed over the Biafrans. The official British position was that it did not want to assist, by neutrality, the Balkanization of Africa. Secondly, Britain was worried that if it failed to assist Federal Nigeria, the Soviet Union would. In fact some Soviet military supplies were sent to Nigeria. The British government was also worried about British investments and supplies of oil. Ten per cent of Britain's oil came from Nigeria at this time, when Britain's other supplies were less than certain because of the situation in the Middle East. One other factor was that most other African states were against Biafra, which was in strange company with Zambia, Tanzania, Rhodesia, South Africa, and Portugal, for their different reasons, sympathizing with it. Outside financial interests were providing Biafra with arms from France, and the infant state's backers launched a highly successful publicity campaign. Biafra was presented as a long-suffering nation caught between the alternatives of liberation or genocide.[39] In December 1968 the Gallup Poll showed that the great majority of British people were emotionally involved with Biafra.[40] In the Labour Party the respected former Colonial Secretary James Griffiths supported Colonel Ojukwu's regime. There was considerable support for Biafra in the Parliamentary Labour Party and in the Cabinet. Wilson paid a brief visit to Nigeria and certain other African states in March 1969 in an attempt to urge moderation on the Nigerian government and offer his services as a mediator. Little came of the visit. In Britain the government and independent organizations offered relief aid to both sides. The controversy ended only with the defeat of Biafra in 1970.

Britain had failed effectively to promote peace in Nigeria just as it had failed to promote peace in the war between India and Pakistan in 1965. On that occasion the leaders of the two belligerent states went not to London but to Tashkent for the Soviet Union's help in settling the dispute. It was a measure of Britain's decline and the decline of the British government's credibility in the world at large. Potential tragedy turned to farce when Britain sent a detachment of troops and metropolitan police to the rebellious island of Anguilla, in the Caribbean, one of the left-over bits of the ill-fated Caribbean Federation. The occupation of the island of roughly 6,000 inhabitants in 1969 meant that, in Wilson's own words, 'The musical-comedy atmosphere, the mock-gunboat diplomacy, the colourful personalities of some of the leading police, made it the joke of the year. The cartoonists inevitably had the time of their lives, and who could blame them?[41]

Labour's idealistic hopes of the late 1950s and early 1960s for the Commonwealth were shattered in another way. The Party had advocated greater assistance to the developing countries. Wilson had set up a new Ministry of Overseas Development, with Mrs Castle in charge, to emphasize this interest. As we have seen, Bottomley replaced Castle in August 1966. Both were in the Cabinet. When Bottomley left the Cabinet a year later, the new minister, Reg Prentice, was not included in the Cabinet. Nor was his successor, Mrs Judith Hart, in 1969. This marked the downgrading of this priority. Net official assistance from Britain to the developing countries fell under the Labour administration:[42]

	£m.	% of GNP	£m. (1970 prices)
1964	176	0.53	201
1970	186	0.36	186

Though the Labour leaders kept up the rhetoric about the Commonwealth, many of them had decided, quite early on in the life of the Wilson administration, that Britain needed a new, European, orientation in its relationships.

Wilson's EEC attempt

Labour had said little about Europe in the election of 1966, but there had been clear indications after October 1964 that the Wilson administration was considering its options. EFTA was not proving adequate for British purposes, and some form of associate membership of the EEC did not seem a real possibility. Britain's trade pattern was changing. In the period 1959-66 exports to the EEC states had increased annually by 9.6 per cent, to EFTA countries by 9.5, to the United States by 6.4, to Australia, New Zealand, and South Africa by 3.8, and to the less-developed countries by 1 per cent. There had been big percentage increases in exports to Japan and eastern Europe too, though these areas were not very significant as trading partners. In 1966, Britain still sold 24.5 per cent of its exports in the less-developed countries, with the EEC coming second (19.2 per cent), EFTA third (14.9), the United States fourth (11.8), and Australia, New Zealand, and South Africa taking 12.3 per cent.[43] The decline in the relative importance of British trade with the old Commonwealth states and South Africa took place in an environment of preferential tariffs and high national income growth-rates. Trade with the EEC had improved in spite of trade barriers which would get worse if Britain remained outside. Some politicians had thought in terms of a North American Free Trade Area as an alternative route for Britain, but this was a purely academic concept, not even under consideration by the United States. It was with these kind of figures that the members of the Wilson Cabinet, together with a number of key officials, went to Chequers in October 1966. Brown, Stewart, and Callaghan were fundamentally in favour of joining the EEC, Jay and Peart were fundamentally against, and most of the rest were in-between. There was a 'really furious row',[44] but the meeting ended by agreeing that Wilson and Brown should go on a grand tour of the EEC to test the ground. This they did and Britain formally applied to join the Community in May 1967. On 10 May the government managed to get an impressive vote in favour of the application – 488 to 62. Among the 'Noes' were 35 Labour MPs. Another fifty or so had abstained. The Wilson–Brown attempt to get into Europe ended on

27 November 1967 when de Gaulle once again vetoed Britain's application. He talked about Britain's economic weaknesses, but his real motive was that he saw Britain as still an American satellite with undue pretensions to grandeur. The fault was not of course all with the President. The British economy *was* weak, the British government *did* at times sound like the Voice of America in relation to Vietnam, and British leaders still seemed to be living in a world which was not quite real. Willy Brandt, a friend of British entry, then Bonn's Foreign Minister, recalls how he visited George Brown in December 1967: 'I was greeted by the perplexing and dis-illusioning plea: "Willy, you must get us in so we can take the lead" '.[45] It is unlikely Brown was teasing Brandt. In his book *In My Way*, published in 1971, he could still write:

All this I feel absolutely convinced, means that Britain's future rests upon her emergence as the leader of a new bloc in the world: not General de Gaulle's old 'third force'; I'm not suggesting a neutralized Europe, but a new European bloc which would have the same power and influence in the world as the old British Commonwealth had in days gone by.[46]

Brandt was sufficiently amused, saddened, or dismayed to quote this passage. The British government knew that the French President was still the same man who had put paid to Britain's previous application. In those circumstances they would probably have done themselves, and the country's prestige, more good by sounding out the possibilities through the normal diplomatic channels, and through George Thomson, who had been given special responsibilities in this direction. As Crossman recorded on 9 February 1967, 'Here we have Harold and George who should be concentrating on vital domestic problems like prices and incomes gallivanting round Europe and occupying the time of the very important officials'.[47]

Callaghan prepared his 1967 Budget amid a mood of optimism. The last quarter of 1966 had produced a decent surplus on the balance of payments, and there would be a small surplus on the first quarter of 1967. Backed up by expert opinion, including that of the Bank of England, Callaghan expounded to the Commons the view that it would be possible to earn a series of payment surpluses in the years up to 1970, at the existing rate of exchange. He estimated a growth-rate of 3 per cent (against 4 per cent promised by Brown).[48] The only notable feature of the Budget was a Regional Payroll Subsidy (REP) designed to create jobs in the development areas, as against areas of low unemployment such as the West Midlands.[49] In May sterling started to come under pressure again. A set of bad trade figures, tension in the Middle East; 'but probably the most important reason for the disquiet was Britain's second application

to join the EEC . . . Even in the preliminary soundings the French –
and to some extent the EEC in Brussels – had stressed the sterling
area and the British balance of payments as obstacles'. High
officials in the Treasury also believed that if Britain were to join the
EEC, the parity of sterling at $2.80 could not be maintained.[50]
Britain was also hit by recession in the United States and West
Germany, and by the war in the Middle East in June 1967. Yet the
Chancellor did not seem to be clear about the precarious situation
of sterling. In June he eased higher-purchase restrictions. He also
announced various social-benefit improvements for later in the
year. Undoubtedly, a factor in his calculation was that
unemployment had reached the highest level for twenty-seven
years.

At the end of August the Prime Minister announced another
government reshuffle. Out went anti-Marketeer Douglas Jay,
sacked in the station-master's office at Plymouth.[51] Out too went
Arthur Bottomley and the Wilson-loyalist Herbert Bowden. The
most significant change, however, was that the Prime Minister had
decided to act as 'overlord' at the DEA, handing over the
day-to-day running to his close associate Peter Shore. Wilson has
claimed that, although Michael Stewart had done a good job at the
DEA, he wanted him for a 'full-time co-ordinating role',[52] with the
title First Secretary of State. Cynics have claimed[53] that Wilson took
over the running of the DEA because he was still optimistic about
the economy. Certainly, a week later the Prime Minister insisted
that the balance of payments was 'in a position of basic balance and
growing strength'.[54] Samuel Brittan has seen the change as 'Mr
Wilson's final attempt to use detailed industrial intervention as an
alternative to devaluation. Whether or not this could ever have
been feasible, it was three years too late . . .' He should 'have taken
over responsibility for economic and industrial policy three years
before in 1964, and left the role of world statesman until Britain's
external finances were stronger'.[55] Days after the Prime Minister's
optimistic pronouncement, a bad set of trade figures for the second
quarter of 1967 was issued, which largely excluded the effect of the
closure of the Suez Canal (from June). What the voters thought
about the situation was revealed by Conservative gains from
Labour at Cambridge and Walthamstow West on 21 September.
This meant the government had lost four seats since the election,
the earlier two being at Carmarthen (to the Welsh Nationalists),
and Glasgow Pollok (to the Conservatives). Local election results
earlier in the year had also been demoralizing for the government.
In October Callaghan bravely faced his critics at the Labour Party
conference at Scarborough. His critics were many, ranging from
Michael Foot and Frank Cousins on the left, to Christopher

Mayhew and Woodrow Wyatt on the right. Wyatt was not against a prices and incomes policy; he was for a tough one, but he was strongly for expansion as well, and he saw devaluation as inevitable:

we are continually being crucified for a couple of hundred million quid – and that is what it is. Everybody knows that this year we are not going to have a surplus. We will probably be several million, or hundreds of millions, on the wrong side and we will be forced to have devaluation.[56]

Despite the many voices raised against him, Callaghan was given a standing ovation by the delegates after he had defended his policies. He avoided answering Wyatt's prognostications. Yet as the delegates cheered, he must have wondered whether, as on a previous occasion at Scarborough, some of those who cheered a Labour leader would then support the resolutions against him. This did not happen. The closest conference got to formally criticizing the government's policies on this issue was a resolution which, while it agreed with the principle of prices and incomes policy, urged the government 'to redress the present grossly unjust distribution of wealth'.

Callaghan had won the skirmish at the Labour Party conference, but he lost the battle to banish devaluation. Throughout October sterling deteriorated. A dock strike did not improve matters, though it should not be exaggerated. Clearly, further attempts to defend the existing rate of exchange would have been self-defeating in terms of the necessary deflation this would have meant. Even the Prime Minister had come to recognize that he had got to surrender. It was a defeat for the government. It was a disaster for the Prime Minister and for his Chancellor. One further incident made a bad situation worse. With rumours flying around, and sterling draining away, the Chancellor gave an ambiguous and evasive reply to a question on the financial situation put by the Labour MP Robert Sheldon. The result was a massive stampede to ditch sterling. Hundreds of millions were lost in a single day.[57] The Cabinet formally agreed to the measure on 16 November: a devaluation of 14.3 per cent. At the same time bank rate went up to 8 per cent and there were to be severe cuts in bank lending. The official announcement was made on the evening of Saturday 18 November. Wilson broadcast on television the following day. Even he was shaken. How else can one explain his assertion that 'Devaluation does *not* mean that the value of the pound in the hands of the British consumer, the British housewife at her shopping, is cut correspondingly. It does not mean that the money in our pockets is worth 14 per cent less'?[58] Wilson attempted for some time to pretend that it was not a defeat but merely a well-prepared withdrawal to previously prepared positions, thus giving his troops

193

the chance of a massive counter-stroke, 'an export-led expansion', but few believed him. It seemed Callaghan had become the scapegoat. On 30 November he was sent to the Home Office. Home Secretary Roy Jenkins became the new Chancellor. Wilson stayed where he was. Crossman lamented, privately, on 26 November, 'I don't see the remotest chance of Harold going. It's much more likely that he will drag us further down until, in two or three years' time, there is a landslide of 1931 dimensions'.[59] The Conservative lead, according to Gallup, had been 7½ per cent before devaluation. It jumped to 17½ per cent.[60] By-elections at Hamilton, Leicester South-West, and Manchester Gorton confirmed the downward trend in the government's popularity. In the first two, Labour lost seats to the Scottish National Party and the Conservatives respectively. In the third, Labour scraped home. All three polls were held in November before devaluation.

The cutting of Britain's defence commitments

It was not until 16 January 1968 that other measures were taken to deal with the economic malaise. Labour stalwarts at all levels had to swallow many a bitter pill. Most of the soothing words spoken by the leadership at the previous party conference became just one more catalogue of broken promises. Prescription charges, which had caused so much anger in the Labour Party, out of all proportion to their effect, were reintroduced. The national insurance stamp charge was increased. The number of houses to be built was decreased. Free school milk for secondary school pupils was ended. The raising of the school-leaving age, demanded for so long, was deferred until 1973. This last measure was too much for Lord Longford, who resigned from the government, Mr Wilson's only casualty in the Cabinet. The Conservatives could gloat, but they too saw some of the things dear to many a Tory heart being destroyed in the financial holocaust. The Territorial Army was virtually to disappear and so was Civil Defence. The order for the F111A aircraft was cancelled. Millions had to be paid in compensation, but nevertheless, hundreds of millions of pounds were saved by the cancellation. Going too were Britain's commitments east of Suez.

Labour MPs had argued for years that the United Kingdom should give up its remaining global commitments in defence; now this was happening, but for the wrong reasons – simple financial expediency. The whole business began to look like a series of panicky pullbacks caused by a collapsing currency. In February 1966 Christopher Mayhew had resigned as Minister of Defence (Royal Navy) because he felt it was absurd pretending to hold on east of Suez, yet denying the forces the tools to do the job, especially, in this case, aircraft-carriers.[61] In October 1966 Wilson was talking about Britain's frontier being on the Himalayas.[62] A new Anglo-American base in the Indian Ocean was mooted. In March 1967, 63 Labour MPs had been severely rebuked by Wilson for voting against the Defence White Paper, which contained renewed justification for staying east of Suez. The Middle East war of June 1967 had revealed Britain's inability to influence events in that area in any way. Yet it took some time for the lesson to sink in. Wilson was later to admit, 'I was one of the last to be converted'.[63] At Scarborough in October 1967 both Brown and Callaghan had spoken strongly against an early withdrawal from east of Suez. Callaghan had argued emotionally, 'many people cheered Harry Lee . . . a Socialist who in Singapore is endeavouring to cope with the consequences of British withdrawal in the middle 1970s. Are we going to walk out and leave them flat? You know very well you cannot'.[64]

The next financial crisis came a short time later and could easily have resulted in another devaluation. It was more notable for its, accidental, political consequences than any economic ones. The U.S. dollar was weak because of the United States' deficit on the balance of payments. In the last three months of 1967 U.S. payments losses were running at an annual rate of about $7 billion. 'In other words, as many dollars flowed abroad in the last three months of the year as in the first nine months'.[65] This sort of thing had been going on for some time. Clearly the United States was in no position to lecture the British on good housekeeping. By March the situation was desperate. Johnson decided to close the London gold market, reaffirm the dollar parity with gold, and take other steps to redress the situation.[66] It was imperative, he warned his allies in Europe,

that we cooperate in order to avoid financial disorders that could 'profoundly damage the political relations between Europe and America and set in motion forces like those which disintegrated the Western world in 1929 and 1933'. I also told them: 'The speculators are banking on an increase in the official price of gold. They are wrong'.[67]

He found willing co-operation in Downing Street. Wilson hurriedly called a meeting of the Privy Council to issue an Order in Council proclaiming a bank holiday. Somehow Brown was not informed of the meeting and felt, not for the first time, slighted and dejected. An ugly scene took place in 10 Downing Street and he resigned on 16 March, to be replaced at the Foreign Office by Michael Stewart. Before Labour MPs could recover their composure, they were hit again. When the Budget proposals were announced on 19 March, they must have believed their 1964 programme had been sentenced to death by a thousand cuts. The Budget 'turned out to involve the most swingeing increases in taxation the country had ever faced on one single occasion'.[68] Tax on petrol, cigarettes, and whisky, road fund licences, corporation tax, SET, betting tax – all were increased. Income-tax allowances were cut so as to neutralize the previous family allowances except for the poorer families. As a sop to the Left there was to be a special surcharge on large investment incomes. The only consolation was that income tax was not going up. When the voters were given their chance to show what they felt about it all, they threw out Labour from Meriden, Acton, and Dudley. All went to the Conservatives on 28 March.

Brown's departure had surprisingly little impact on the Party in Parliament and the Prime Minister decided on further changes. Ministers were moved around in April, with Barbara Castle taking on a new importance as First Secretary of State for Employment and Productivity. Gordon Walker (Education and Science) and Fred Lee (Board of Trade) joined the growing company of ex-ministers. At the beginning of July, Ray Gunter, the outspoken right-wing trade unionist, joined them. There were rumours in the press and at Westminster of a 'Wilson must go' campaign led by the 'émigré' ex-ministers, and even calls for a 'national' government, but the rumours seem to have remained largely rumours.

Enoch Powell

The economy apart, 1967-68 was a sad and frightening period in other respects too. War had flared up once again in the Middle East in June 1967. With the closing of the Suez Canal this brief war had considerable negative economic consequences for Britain. Happily Britain did not get involved in the conflict, but the sympathies of the government and the media were largely with Israel and this did Britain's relations with the Arab states no good. In May 1968 an unexpected crisis blew up in France. Student protests at the University of Nanterre, just outside Paris, over conditions there spread to Paris. Students occupied university buildings and set up 'counter universities'. Peaceful demonstrations soon became violent confrontations with armed police. The streets of Paris were lit up at night by blazing cars. Students at other universities in France took similar action. Then, to the astonishment of their own leaders, workers started to go militant. Strikes and factory occupations spread like wildfire throughout the country. Suddenly it looked as though de Gaulle would fall and France would be plunged into civil war. It was only after the government had given in to most of the economic demands of the workers, and called new elections, that the republic returned to some sort of normalcy. If anything, the French students had learnt the art of protest, 1960s-style, from the Germans and Americans. German students were incensed by the successes during 1966-69 of the extreme right-wing nationalist NPD, which appeared an effective political force at that time. In the United States the protests were about racial discrimination and America's increasing involvement in the Vietnam War. Britain too experienced its own more modest, and more moderate, form of student protest in 1968. There were protests about living conditions at universities, about their hierarchical structures and methods of teaching. The most extreme protests were at the London School of Economic and Political Science (London University) and Essex University, though there were occupations of offices, stealing of confidential papers, and other actions at many other universities and polytechnics. Some reforms followed these actions. Students also took to the streets over the Vietnam War and the activities of far right groups in Britain. Left-wing students were angered by the Labour government's general support for the United States over Vietnam. The horrors of the Vietnam War were seen nightly on television and many felt sympathy for a small nation which seemed to be the hapless victim of power politics. The Soviet invasion of Czechoslovakia in August 1968 briefly united all shades of opinion in Britain, including the Communists, in condemnation of this aggressive act against another small country. In February 1967 the extreme right-wing National Front came into being, gaining support largely on the immigration issue. Indeed, 1967-68 was a period in which immigration and race looked like becoming dangerous obsessions.

Fear of the extent of coloured Commonwealth immigration had led the Macmillan administration to introduce the Commonwealth Immigration Act of 1962. There had long been small numbers of such immigrants in Britain. More were encouraged to come during the war to help Britain make up the shortages of labour. The post-war migration began in 1948 with the arrival, on the steamer *Empire Windrush,* of several hundred West Indians. With little thought about any possible consequences, Britain sought to ease its labour shortage. The West Indians, a considerable number of whom were ex-servicemen, sought to escape the poverty and other restrictions in their colonial homelands. In the following year the Royal Commission on Population did express concern, recommending that migrants 'could only be welcomed without reserve' if they 'were of good human stock and were not prevented by their religion or race from intermarrying with the host population and becoming merged with it'.[69] Clearly there could be much argument about who did, and who did not, meet the requirements. Year after year other migrants continued to flow into Britain. As British prosperity grew, so Britain became a more attractive place to settle in, while West Indians found their opportunities to emigrate to the United States curtailed. Apart from a number of medical practitioners and tiny numbers of other professional and clerical personnel, the immigrants were doing jobs which native Britons did not wish to do. By the second half of the 1950s considerable numbers of Indians and Pakistanis began to arrive. The British government got the two Asian governments to agree to restrict the flow. However, neither government was able to impose effective restrictions. Reluctant to act out of loyalty to the old imperial idea, the government had to think again after anti-immigrant clashes in Nottingham and Notting Hill in London. Sir Oswald Mosley, who had wasted his many talents in the 1930s organizing the British Union of Fascists, sought once again to use the problem of strangers, to rally support for his minuscule Union Movement. Once again Mosley found himself in a political *cul-de-sac*. Race did not appear to be an issue in the 1959 election, but the government felt compelled to restrict the flow. The main thrust of the government's case was that Britain was an overcrowded island. The other part of its argument was that

It cannot be denied that the immigrants who have come to this country in such large numbers have presented the country with an intensified social problem. They tend to settle in communities of their own, with their own mode of life, in big cities. The greater the numbers coming into this country the larger will these communities become and the more difficult will it be to integrate them into our national life . . .[70]

Hugh Gaitskell argued passionately and cleverly against the 1962 Act. He regarded it as a measure of appeasement of racism. He did not believe that free entry would lead to larger numbers arriving than could be found jobs, and he thought that the answer was dispersal of immigrants throughout the country, better housing and education for all, including immigrants, and more attention to fighting prejudice. The Labour Party supported him in this view, though some had their private doubts. At the election of 1964 Labour's policy was not entirely clear. They seemed to be saying they would keep the Act, but try to work out a system of effective voluntary controls with the Commonwealth states. The Act would then be repealed. Once in office Wilson sent Lord Mountbatten, who had the advantages of being a member of the royal family and having friends in, and experience of, the Indian subcontinent, on a mission to the appropriate Commonwealth states. His discussions did not produce a satisfactory alternative system of controls and the Labour government felt it could retain the 1962 Act with good conscience.

198

Under the 1962 Act immigrants were admitted under a voucher scheme. There were those who had been offered definite jobs (Category A), and those who had certain specific skills which were in short supply in Britain (Category B). There was also a third Category C, made up of those who did not qualify under the other two. This third category was dropped in 1964. In July 1965 the Wilson administration placed a ceiling of 8,500 on the total number of vouchers to be issued. Of this total a thousand were reserved for Maltese. The net total number of non-white Commonwealth immigrants was officially estimated at 42,700 in 1955. It fluctuated downwards to 21,850 in 1959, jumping up to 57,700 in 1960. There was an upsurge in 1961-62 because of the impending legislation. Over 240,000 came in those two years. Though numbers fell away, the average for the three years 1963-65 was over 53,000. The majority of those entering in these years came in as dependents.[71] Obviously, the Act was not being as effective as its authors had expected.

In 1968 a new problem aggravated the situation. Substantial numbers of Asians had gone to East Africa when that area was under British colonial rule. They became of key significance in the commercial life of those territories and in the professions. When the three territories in this area became independent as Tanganyika (1961, later Tanzania), Uganda (1962), and Kenya (1963), special provision was made for these Asians. Those born there would become citizens of the newly-independent state, providing at least one parent had been born in that state. Those not so covered remained citizens of the United Kingdom and colonies or British protected persons. These then had the option of remaining British passport-holders or applying, within two years, for the citizenship of the state where they lived.[72] Increasingly these states put pressure on their Asians. They were pursuing a policy of Africanization and wanted to rid themselves of these foreign communities. In 1967 the pressure was on in Kenya. The numbers of Asians coming to Britain from this source started to increase. Britain sent Malcolm MacDonald to try to persuade the Kenyan government to moderate its policy, but to no avail. The result was that further restrictive legislation was passed after little discussion and much heart-searching. Crossman saw it as another Cabinet 'balls-up', 'Already in 1965 we should have known all about the Kenya Asians because a paper was put up to Cabinet raising all the issues'.[73] He put the blame on the Cabinet Secretariat 'which is supposed to be a kind of super progress-chaser and keep a look-out for all Cabinet decisions and watch that they're adequately carried out'.[74] Even had the Secretariat done so, the dilemma which faced the government and the Commons would not have been solved: should Britain break its pledge to these Asians or run the risk of racial violence in the future? The government decided it could not take the risk and a Bill was rushed through Parliament towards the end of February 1968. It extended the operation of the 1962 Act to those possessing citizenship of the United Kingdom and Colonies if they were without substantial personal connection with this country. This was defined in terms of birthplace of parents or grandparents. The Liberals, a small number of Conservatives, including Iain Macleod, and some Labour MPs voted against the Bill. The official Opposition line was to abstain.

To its credit, the government did not deal with the problem of immigration merely by imposing restrictions. It did make a start to providing equality for those already in Britain. Two Race Relations Acts were placed on the statute book. The first, in 1965, made it unlawful for any person to practise discrimination on the grounds of colour, race, or ethnic or national origins against anybody seeking access to or facilities or services at restaurants, cafés, pubs, theatres, cinemas, dance halls, and all other places of public entertainment or recreation. It also covered public transport and places maintained by local authorities. The Act set up a Race Relations Board, with local committees to hear complaints and attempt conciliation. Where this was not possible, civil proceedings could be instituted by the Attorney-General. The Act of 1968, the result of the investigations of a committee under Professor Harry Street, was much wider in scope and extended the law to employment and housing. The government hoped to appease the anti-restrictionist minority in Parliament as well as the immigrants. It realized that legislation would not change attitudes overnight, and put the emphasis on conciliation rather than compulsion. Divided on the issue, the Conservative Party voted against the 1968 Act though about twenty Conservatives, led by Sir Edward Boyle, abstained. The Wilson administration also sought to take the heat out of the immigration question by providing extra help for those local authorities with high concentrations of immigrants. The immigrants made up, in 1966, about 3.2 per cent of the population of Greater London, about the same in the West Midlands, 1.8 per cent in West Yorkshire, and 1 per cent in South-East Lancashire. However, within those areas there were particular boroughs where the concentrations were higher. In the London boroughs of Brent and Hackney they were over 7 per cent, in Wolverhampton and Huddersfield, Birmingham and Bradford, over 4 per cent.[75]

Depending on one's point of view, the government had, by its new restrictionist policies, either taken a realistic stand or appeased the racists and the ignorant. At any rate, it looked as though it had got the problem of the Kenyan Asians under control. At this time television viewers were given nightly a reminder of the horrors of racial tension from the United States. Martin Luther King, black civil rights leader and Nobel Prize-winner, had been assassinated on 4 April 1968. Severe racial tension and violence exploded in the days which followed. In Washington 'entire blocks of buildings were going up in smoke . . . Before the holocaust was over, forty other cities had experienced similar tragic outbreaks . . . from coast to coast'.[76] It was in this situation of remorse and fear that Enoch Powell, Defence spokesman of the shadow cabinet, used his considerable skills of oratory to make a widely publicized speech on immigration and race relations, on 20 April before the passage of the second Race Relations Bill. He wanted to stop or virtually stop the inflow of immigrants, and promote the maximum outflow, 'with generous grants and assistance'. He opposed the Bill as something which 'is to be enacted to give the stranger, the disgruntled and the *agent provocateur* the power to pillory [Britons] for their private actions'. He also opposed it because, 'Here is the means of showing that the immigrant communities can organize to consolidate their members, to agitate and campaign against their fellow-citizens, and to overawe and dominate the rest with the legal weapons which the ignorant and the ill-informed have provided'. If the views he was expounding were extreme by the standards of the Conservative front bench, his rhetoric and emotion laden examples were even more extreme. 'Those whom the gods wish to destroy, they first make mad. We must be mad, literally mad, as a nation to be permitting the annual inflow of some 50,000 dependents . . . It is like watching a nation busily engaging in heaping up its own funeral pyre'. He spoke of the formerly 'quiet street' which had become 'a place of noise and confusion' where lived a single old white lady, who was abused by her immigrant neighbours, and had 'excreta pushed through her letter-box'.[77]

Powell found he had struck a popular chord. Hundreds of letters of support poured in. In London a group of dockers and meat porters marched to Westminster to congratulate him. Edward Heath sacked him and called the speech racist.

Why had Powell done it? It was not the first time that the two men had differed in their attitudes and policies. They had been rivals for the leadership. Was Powell seeking by a single, sharp, blow to overturn Heath by a popular movement from below which would force Conservative MPs to re-examine their loyalties? In some ways it was reminiscent of Wilson's challenge to Gaitskell, but with very different results for the challenger.

It could be said of Powell (b. 1912) as of Heath (b. 1916) that his mother made him. Powell's mother was a teacher, Heath's had been in service. Powell's father too was a teacher, Heath's was a carpenter who set up his own business. Powell had the grit of the Black Country in him, Heath grew up in the more placid atmosphere of Broadstairs. Like Heath, Powell was a scholarship boy. Heath was at Balliol, Oxford; Powell spent his undergraduate days at Trinity College, Cambridge. In 1934 he became a Fellow. As young men they were both austere loners. Heath was a highly successful organist and student politician, Powell pursued his scholastic ambitions and became the youngest professor of Greek in the British Empire, holding the chair at Sydney University. Both were anti-appeasement Tories before the war, and both enjoyed the war when it came. Powell ended his service career as a brigadier in Intelligence, Heath was a major in the Honourable Artillery Company. Before entering Parliament in 1950 Heath was a temporary civil servant, news editor of the *Church Times,* trainee banker, and, when he had the time, lieutenant-colonel in the Territorial Army. Powell also reached the Commons in 1950. Before that he had worked with Maudling and Macleod as a Conservative back-room boy. The two young politicians soon got reputations as frugal, hard-working bachelors. Neither of them smoked, neither drank much. Powell married his former secretary in 1952, Heath remained unmarried. They also differed politically. From the start, Powell was a rather doctrinaire right-wing Conservative, his future rival was a pragmatist of the Centre–Left. Enoch Powell was one of the Suez Group of Conservative imperialists. Edward Heath was an early European. Powell served Harold Macmillan as Financial Secretary to the Treasury and as Minister of Health. From July 1962 to October 1963 he was in the Cabinet. Heath too had been in the Cabinet; he was Chief Whip (1955-59), Minister of Labour (1959-60), Lord Privy Seal attached to the Foreign Office, and Secretary of State for Trade and Industry (1963–64).[78] As we have seen (above, p. 173), Powell had been defeated in the leadership election of 1965. Had he decided in 1968, at a time when Heath's leadership was being questioned, to seek to remove him by dramatizing and exaggerating his, no doubt, genuine concerns about immigration? We see a similar sort of development in respect of his views on Europe. In 1965 he appeared to be a European. Most of the anti-EEC vote in the leadership election went to Maudling.[79] Yet later Powell emerges as the leading anti-marketeer in the Conservative camp. Perhaps Powell's Birmingham speech was part of the provincial revolt against the accepted complacency of Establishment London, or simply a reflection of a fatal maverick streak, a protest against the polite consensus politics aimed always at the middle ground where passion is dead and the clash of principles is replaced by the calculations of pollsters, psephologists, and speech-writers. Whatever its origin, the speech could not have done race relations, law and order, or, in the long run, its tormented author any good. It indicated a lack of understanding of the Conservative Party, for, if anything, it strengthened Edward Heath. It certainly strengthened Harold Wilson. On 2 May he gave a forthright and eloquent answer to Enoch Powell which did much to restore, temporarily at least, his sagging popularity with his own supporters. Finally, the speech marked the beginning of the widening gulf between Powell and the Conservative Party.

Eruption in Northern Ireland

On 17 April 1969 a remarkable young woman was elected to Parliament—Bernadette Devlin, a 21-year-old student, and a left-wing, independent, Irish republican. She had beaten the Ulster Unionist candidate at a by-election in the Mid-Ulster constituency. This was the culmination of a struggle which had begun over two years before, and, some would say, it was part of a larger struggle which had been going on for centuries.

In 1921 the British government and Irish nationalist representatives signed a treaty under which Ireland was to become a self-governing dominion of the British Commonwealth, similar in status to Canada, and styled the Irish Free State. Northern Ireland, six counties, was to be free to stay out of the new dominion and remain part of the United Kingdom. The two parts of Ireland, the predominantly Catholic South, and the predominantly Protestant North, already had parliaments set up under the Government of Ireland Act of 1920. The treaty of December 1921 brought to an end years of armed conflict between the forces of the British Crown and the Irish Republican Army – a somewhat different body from the ones using that title today. Total peace did not come to either part for some years, mainly because the extreme republicans could not be satisfied with anything less than a republic, free of Britain, and incorporating the whole of Ireland. Various forms of discrimination against the Catholics in the North, who make up roughly one-third of the population, have meant that no chance has been given to allow for the development of non-sectarian politics. The Catholics have felt that they could never achieve their full rights in the mini-quasi-state of Ulster ruled permanently, as it has been, by the Ulster Unionist Party, the political vehicle of the mass of the Protestant majority. For their part, the Protestants in the North have felt under siege, as the state based on Dublin has never relinquished its claims to the six counties making up Northern Ireland. The constitution of 1937 claims to be for the whole of Ireland. In 1949 the Catholic state formally became the Republic of

203

Ireland, thus severing all remaining constitutional ties with Britain. The Irish Republican Army (IRA), the handful of militant irreconcilables, had been ruthlessly suppressed in North and South during the world war, and it was some years before the organization was capable of any action again. An armed campaign during 1956-62 against partition had been a failure. With greater prosperity in both parts of Ireland fewer young men could be recruited for such romantic gestures. By the 1960s the IRA are said to have sold their weapons because they had come to see the future struggle as political rather than military.[80] It began to look as though sectarian attitudes were breaking down on both sides.[81] The coming to office of Captain Terence O'Neill, as Prime Minister of Northern Ireland, in 1963 was a sign of this. O'Neill was regarded as a moderate and embarked upon a programme of modest reform. For the first time since the partition the leaders of the two Irish political entities met in 1965. There were, however, rumblings of discontent among the more extreme elements in the Protestant community. Prominent among them was the Rev. Ian Paisley. In August 1966 O'Neill warned Wilson of the need 'for a short period for Ulster to assimilate his earlier reforms'.[82] By this time the Catholics too were stirring. In 1967 the Northern Ireland Civil Rights Association was formed through the earlier work of Dr Conn and Mrs Patricia McCluskey, who were keenly interested in securing for Catholics a fair share of new council housing so long denied them. They were influenced by the changing political climate in both Britain and Ireland, and by the example of the successful civil rights campaigns in the United States. On 5 October 1968 a civil rights march, attended by three Labour MPs from London, went ahead in Londonderry as planned, even though it had been banned by the Northern Ireland Minister of Home Affairs, William Craig. The marchers were attacked along the route, and police used 'needless violence'[83] against them. Backed by the British government, O'Neill was prepared to step up the implementation of the reform programme, including a development commission to replace the Protestant local authority in Londonderry, and an ombudsman to investigate particular grievances. O'Neill was, however, outflanked by the right wing of his own party. He dismissed Craig, and two other ministers subsequently resigned. He called an election in February 1969, hoping his moderate policies would be endorsed. This tactic was not entirely successful. For the first time in 24 years his own constituency was challenged and O'Neill was returned on a minority vote with Paisley coming close to beating him. There was no kind of understanding between the Catholic civil rights candidates and moderate Unionists. The victory of Miss Devlin in April was another blow in that it aroused the extreme protestants even more. More demonstrations and disorder took place, and bombings of public utilities seemed to indicate the inability of O'Neill's Stormont government to maintain order. Accordingly, he announced his resignation on 28 April. Major James Chichester-Clark replaced him. Another factor in O'Neill's downfall had been his determination to introduce universal adult suffrage for local elections. Northern Ireland still retained franchise laws restricting voting to persons with statutory qualifications as property-owners or tenants. The result was that about one-quarter of persons eligible to vote in Westminster elections were not eligible to vote in local government elections, and plural votes could be claimed by people with multiple property qualifications. This hit Catholics more than Protestants.[84] The new Prime Minister, no doubt with one eye on London, agreed to implement this measure of reform and proclaimed an amnesty for political offenders.

Miss Devlin's maiden speech held the House of Commons 'spellbound by a tremendous performance', but both Wilson and Crossman recalled they found her negative and uncompromising in her approach.[85] No doubt the new MP believed the Commons understood little and cared less about Ulster, which at that time still seemed far away. She knew the reality behind the statistic that there the unemployment rate was always above the United Kingdom average, being three times higher for Catholics than for Protestants. She and her lonely Belfast colleague Gerry Fitt knew the reality of the discrimination against educated Catholics which drove them out of the province to find jobs, of the discrimination in the shipyards where the bulk of those employed were Protestants. Crossman remarked on how little the Cabinet knew about the conditions in Ulster and quotes Healey as admitting the same.[86] He called both O'Neill and Chichester-Clark inarticulate, upper-class, landowners and this did seem to be part of the problem. O'Neill, it could be claimed, knew the world, and was refreshingly open to outside influences, but did he know Ulster? Both he and his successor were set apart from the bulk of their own party by education, speech, manners, life-style, and wealth. Such men could only maintain their leadership as long as they mouthed the traditional shibboleths of Unionism, but they proved incapable of leading their flock into the new, non-sectarian, pastures. As the Ulster crisis deepened, they were put aside. Chichester-Clark went in March 1971. Ian Paisley came more and more into prominence as an authentic leader of a considerable section of Protestant opinion. Unfortunately, his colourful personality and oratory were put to destructive, rather than constructive, purposes.

In August 1969 there was renewed violence. The annual (Protestant) Apprentice Boys of Derry March led to Catholic fears of a violent passage through their territory, Bogside. Barricades went up. For 48 hours Catholics hurled abuse, stones, and petrol bombs at the Royal Ulster Constabulary, who retaliated with tear-gas. The Irish Republic's tricolour flew over Bogside and 'Free Derry' was proclaimed. All this led to tension in Belfast. There too barricades went up and firing broke out (it is not clear who started it)[87] between the police and Catholics. Five Catholics and two Protestants died. Catholics were forced out of their homes which were then burned.[88] James Callaghan, as Home Secretary, sent in British troops to restore order and establish truce lines. He visited the devastated areas himself. More promises of reform followed. Official investigations substantiated Catholic complaints. The Cameron Commission of September 1969 concluded that civil rights grievances had a 'substantial foundation in fact and were in a very real sense an immediate and operative cause of . . . disorders'.[89] The Hunt Report in October recommended the disbandment of the B Specials, a predominantly Protestant auxiliary police force, and the disarming of the regular police. The British government implemented these recommendations together with the setting-up of the Ulster Defence Regiment, which was to be a non-sectarian body to support the civil power. Unfortunately, many Catholics saw it as merely the B Specials in military uniform. The Protestants were angry about the loss of the 'Bs' and riots took place. On 11 October the British army intervened to crush fierce Protestant riots in the Shankhill, Belfast.

The humiliation of the Protestants, and their anger, were deep and bitter. The Catholics, for their part, knew that they had won a victory, but did not know how to exploit it, and also dreaded a counter-attack . . . the militants among the Catholics, and a great many of the young, were little disposed to settle for a hum-drum package of reforms, the objectives of 1968. They wanted more, much more. But more of what, exactly?[90]

Not even the IRA agreed on what they wanted; this body split during the 1960s into the official, or 'Red and Green', IRA and the provisional, or 'Green', IRA. There is also a third group, the *Saor Eire,* or Free Ireland. The difference of doctrine of the three groups need not concern us; what is of interest is that they can, with a minimum number of recruits, and a minimum cover, inflict so much damage on life and property in Northern Ireland. It is also possible to pose the question, but not to answer it, as to whether the British government could have prevented the worst by earlier intervention, including power-sharing in Ulster. Easter 1970 saw vicious rioting between troops and the Catholic inhabitants of the Ballymurphy housing estate on the edge of West Belfast. For the first time since the Second World War British troops were again in conflict with Irish republicans.

Industrial Relations: *In Place of Strife*

As inflation mounted in Britain, so did strikes. There were 2,116 disputes in 1967 and over 2.7 million working-days lost. In 1969 the number of disputes had risen to 3,116 and over 6.8 million working-days were lost. Britain's record was still better than the United States, Canada, Italy, Ireland, and a number of other industrial countries, but much worse than West Germany and Sweden. Japan had improved its position relative to Britain, so had France, except for the year of the massive strikes of 1968. Most of Britain's strikes remained unofficial, and they continued to hit the headlines as well as the economy. The government had set up a Royal Commission on Trade Unions and Employers' Associations under the chairmanship of Lord Donovan, a Lord Justice of Appeal and former Labour MP, in 1965. The Commission reported in June 1968. It drew attention, once again, to the problems caused by the large number of trade unions, and their different shapes and sizes. This meant fragmented bargaining between employers and employees in individual firms, inter-union rivalry, leap-frogging in pay claims, and unofficial strikes. The Commission was reluctant to put much emphasis on legal sanctions as a means of improving industrial relations. The reason for this view was that such sanctions would be difficult to enforce and would make a difficult situation worse. The conclusion was based on foreign experience and the reluctance of employers in Britain to go to court. The Commission did, nevertheless, make a number of recommendations related to the law affecting industrial relations. First, it wanted a special Industrial Law Committee to keep the law under review. Second, it recommended compulsory registration of trade unions with the Registrar of Friendly Societies, replacing the system of voluntary registration. Third, a majority of the Commission recommended that section 3 of the Trade Disputes Act 1906 should no longer apply to persons and combinations other than trade unions and employers' associations on a proposed new register. This would have put unofficial strikers at risk of legal sanctions. Fourth, a majority recommended the repeal of section 4 of the Trade Union Act 1871 which precludes the direct legal enforcement of various kinds of trade union agreement. Finally, another important recommendation was that section 2 of the Trade Disputes Act 1906, relating to picketing, should be amplified so as to make lawful the peaceful persuasion of customers not to deal with an employer in dispute.

Meanwhile the Conservatives had been thinking out their proposals on industrial relations and had published them in April, under the title *Fair Deal At Work*. Clearly the government was under considerable pressure to initiate legislation from the public, the Opposition, and, not least, from Britain's creditors abroad. Ray Gunter had been keen to complete this work, but now Barbara Castle faced this task, for which there were certainly no political rewards in the Labour Party. Her proposals were published on 17 January in a White Paper which was cunningly called *In Place of Strife,* a title recalling Bevan's *In Place of Fear.* But Mrs Castle needed much more than a cunning title and her very high standing in the Labour movement. As Wilson put it, 'From the day when *In Place of Strife* was published ... there had been sharp reactions from the Labour movement, the TUC, the Parliamentary Party and particularly its Trade Union group – and the NEC'.[91] At the end of the debate on the White Paper it was approved by the Commons by 224 votes to 62 of whom 53 were Labour members. The Conservatives abstained. The Industrial Relations Bill which followed foresaw the setting-up of a permanent Commission on Industrial Relations to carry on a variety of functions in relation to trade unions and employers. It would have also established an Industrial Board to hear certain types of case against employers, trade unions, and individual employees. It was by no means merely designed to restrict the activities of trade unions. It contained many proposals which would have strengthened employees' rights. For instance, it sought to establish the principle that no employer had the right to prevent or obstruct an employee from belonging to a trade union. It sought safeguards against unfair dismissal and greater rights for employees under the Contracts of Employment Act 1963. It proposed giving trade unions the right to have certain sorts of information from employers, subject to safeguards for confidential information. What worried trade union leaders were certain proposals which, in the words of Vic Feather (later Lord Feather), would 'introduce the taint of criminality into industrial relations'.[92] Under the proposed legislation the Secretary of State could, by Order, require those involved to desist for up to 28 days from a strike or lock-out which was unconstitutional or in which for other reasons adequate joint discussion had not taken place. The Secretary of State would also have had the power to order a ballot where an official strike was threatened. Included was another proposal which required all but the smallest unions to have professional auditors, and to make new provisions with regard to superannuation funds for members. One other clause about which some trade unionists had their doubts was that enabling the proposed Industrial Board to hear complaints by individuals of unfair or arbitrary action by trade unions. Finally, the Bill would have included the Donovan proposal withdrawing the immunity of unofficial strikers from legal sanctions. This was the proposal which ran into most trouble. It soon became clear that the government had no chance at all of securing passage of the Bill. Richard Crossman recorded on 22 May that most of the Cabinet 'didn't declare themselves' and Callaghan hoped that Wilson, Castle, and Roy Jenkins would destroy themselves politically by pursuing it.[93] By 17 June he was recording that 'The history of this Bill has been a history of improvisation'.[94] Even had the Bill gone through, therefore, and irrespective of the rights and wrongs of it, it would have been something of a disaster. On that day Crossman was present at 'the most devastating Cabinet meeting I have attended',[95] at which most of his colleagues indicated their opposition to the Bill. A face-saving formula was then worked out and agreed on 19 June 1969. The TUC General Council agreed to a solemn and binding undertaking, setting out the lines on which they would intervene in serious unofficial strikes. The government would not continue with the proposed legislation during the current session of Parliament, but would continue its discussions with interested parties about possible future legislation.

Fulton on the Civil Service

In another direction the government's efforts at reform also came to nothing: its attempt to reform the House of Lords. The upper chamber had a built-in Conservative majority, because of the hereditary principle, which had been dented, but not destroyed, by the introduction of life peerages in 1958. It offended most Labour activists in the country and many Labour MPs, who wanted it abolished. Since the creation of life peerages it had become a little less unpopular with the Labour Party because a number of radical individuals who had agreed to go there had remained radical in spite of the temptations. There was renewed anger about the Lords when in June it rejected the Southern Rhodesia (United Nations) Sanctions Order, 1968. Wilson later wrote that 'not since the Parliament Act of 1911 had the Lords deliberately set themselves out to frustrate in this way the executive actions, and in this case actions to fulfil international commitments, of the elected Government'.[96] But he did not seek to abolish the Lords. In November 1968 the government published its White Paper on Lords Reform, the result of all-party talks which had been going on for some time. At that time there were roughly 736 hereditary peers by succession, 122 hereditary peers of first creation, 155 life peers, 23 serving or retired law lords, and 26 bishops.[97] The White Paper proposed that the hereditary basis of membership should be eliminated and that no one party should possess a permanent majority in the Lords. There was to be a two-tier system of membership. Those with the right to vote would be restricted to hereditary peers of first creation and all life peers, the law lords, and the bishops, plus a few of the hereditary peers by succession who, by their previous record, had shown their interest in the activities of the chamber, and would now be made life peers and thus join the voting members. The rest would have the right to speak, but not to vote. To enable new blood to be brought into the upper chamber there was to be a retiring age of seventy-two. Such peers would still be able to attend, but again, not to vote. The government of the day would always be assured of a majority. The Bill to reform the Lords was defeated by a strange alliance of left-wing and Conservative backbench opposition led, respectively, by Michael Foot and Enoch Powell. From the point of view of the Left, the Lords would have been still grossly undemocratic in its composition. They feared, though, that a revived second chamber would exercise more power and authority. The government had proposed that the power of delay for non-financial Bills would be cut from one year to six months. Some Conservatives were worried about the power of patronage which would go to the Prime Minister under the proposed reforms. Powell himself remained an unashamed believer in the principle of primogeniture in the House of Lords.

MPs were invited to put their own House in order during the years of the Wilson regime. New and younger Labour MPs felt that the Commons' hours and methods were inefficient and downright inconvenient. An experiment, introduced in the session 1966–67, of holding sittings of the Commons in the mornings proved a failure because most Conservatives, having outside professions, were against it.

More successful was the experiment with specialist committees. These had been advocated for a number of years by those, both inside and outside the Commons, who believed the backbencher had little chance effectively to examine the work of government. Experiments were started with the Select Committee on Estimates by dividing it into six sub-committees covering various aspects of public policy from Defence and Overseas Affairs to Technological and Scientific Affairs. These committees met in private. After the 1966 election more experiments took place because of the greater interest in this subject by the new intake of Labour MPs, among whom was John Mackintosh, a former professor of politics, who had long been an advocate of such committees. A Select Committee on Agriculture was set up at the end of 1966 and wound up again a year later. Labour MPs had not been very interested in its work. More permanent, and more successful, were the Committees on Education and Science, Race Relations and Immigration, and the Select Committee on Scottish Affairs. These Committees produced some useful reports, but it is doubtful whether they have increased the backbenchers' power *vis-à-vis* the executive.[98]

The years 1964–70 were what could be called a golden age of Royal Commissions. Apart from those already mentioned there were Commissions on the civil service, on local government, and on the public schools. The second and third of these are discussed below (pp. 226–7, 259). Here discussion will be confined to the Fulton Commission on the Civil Service. In the period before the Fulton Commission was set up in February 1966, there had been a good deal of concern about the civil service. Members on both sides of the House had come to believe that civil servants wielded a great deal of power and that power was slipping away from the politicians and into the hands of the civil servants. Before taking office Crossman had written in his introduction to Bagehot's *The English Constitution,* 'In our new kind of civil service, the minister must normally be content with the role of public relations officer to his department, unless the Premier has appointed him with the express purpose of carrying out reforms'.[99] From the other side of the House, Reginald Bevins wrote, after retiring from office, that the civil service is 'seriously affected by its self-importance and its judgement . . . [is] sometimes corrupted by its excessive power'.[100] Others, like Attlee and Maudling, have rejected this view.[101] Even so, Maudling admits he was forced to 'beat a hasty retreat' when, at the Board of Trade, over the issue of a promotion, he had the Secretary of the Cabinet, Sir Norman Brook, breathing down his neck.[102] The influence of the top civil servants must be great with most ministers, most of the time. How can we expect a politician, in office for the first time, who has been moved from Overseas Development to Transport and then to Employment, all within 5½ years, to have exercised much influence on the work of those departments, or, as a Cabinet minister, on government policy in general? Both Left and Right believed that as government had become a major influence on the country's economy, the civil service must accept a major part of the blame for its failure. Critics have alleged three major weaknesses in the top end of the civil service, the Administrative Class. First, a lack of professional expertise. Second, an educational and social exclusiveness which limits the value of their judgements about a complex industrial society which is also a political democracy. Third, a lack of experience of industry, commerce, and local government, producing the same effect. All these criticisms were made by the all-party Estimates Committee in its sixth report in 1965, which produced evidence to justify much of this criticism. Of particular interest, in view of the discussion about social change in Britain since the war, was the revelation that the proportion of Oxbridge entrants to the Administrative Class had risen from 78 per cent (1948–56) to 85 per cent (1957–63), and that the proportion from local authority maintained and aided schools went down from 42 to 30 per cent. Those whose fathers were manual workers dropped from 22 per cent to 15 per cent. The proportion who took degrees in classics went up from 21 per cent to 24 per cent, while social sciences fell from 24 per cent to 17 per cent, and only 3 per cent recruited were mathematicians, scientists, and technologists. Finally, the proportion of successful candidates with first-class honours fell from 40 per cent to 30 per cent. At a time when the fields of university recruiting were widening, the proportion of Administrative Class recruits from these wider fields, instead of rising, was actually falling. In 1965, J. R. Colville, formerly Joint Private Secretary to Sir Winston Churchill (1951–55), felt the government had been let down in 1964 by the lack of a proper statistical service: 'A first class statistical service would, I suspect, be of greater value . . . than any number of young men with first class honours degrees thinking all day long about "the big underlying issues". This is surely a job of Ministers'.[103] The Fulton Commission went over the same ground, making the same criticisms. Its report, published in 1968, contained language that hurt the mandarins of Whitehall: 'The Service is still essentially based on the philosophy of the amateur . . . Today this concept has most damaging consequences . . . The cult is obsolete at all levels and in all parts of the Service'. Fulton wanted more professionally qualified entrants, more training within the civil service, abolition of the class system with better prospects of promotion from the lower ranks, more entrants with 'relevant' degrees from a wider variety of universities, and more secondment from the civil service to other parts of the public service and private industry. Sir William Armstrong became head of the Home Civil Service in 1968; as such he was responsible for introducing the reforms which could conceivably have been the most important single reform of the Wilson administration. In 1978 Lord Crowther-Hunt, who drafted much of the Fulton Report, commented, 'In general, the Civil Service implemented those parts of Fulton that it liked and which added to its power, and failed to implement the ideas that would have made it more professional and more accountable to Parliament and the public'.[104] A training college had been established, the number of qualified accountants had risen from 309 in 1968 to 367 in 1978, but secondment had not developed on any great scale. The Oxbridge pattern of recruitment had been maintained, at well over 60 per cent.[105] In 1976 the figures for the Home Civil Service were as follows:[106]

	Applicants	*Successes*
Oxbridge	500	102
Non-Oxbridge	1896	58
Polytechnics	190	1
Others	50	—

The Parliament of 1966-70 also attempted to make the administration more responsible to the public through the Commissioner for Administration Act 1967. The Parliamentary Commissioner, or Ombudsman, has the task of investigating written complaints made to MPs by members of the public who claim to have sustained injustice in consequence of maladministration. The idea of establishing such an institution had been discussed during the Macmillan era, but rejected on the grounds that it would seriously interfere with the prompt and efficient despatch of public business. It was considered that MPs were the appropriate people through whom grievances could be put right. This reform, though useful, has had only a limited impact compared with similar offices in other countries. The Commissioner's jurisdiction is severely limited. He is not empowered to deal with complaints about local government, National Health Service hospitals, personnel matters in the civil service and the armed forces, the nationalized industries, and the police. In addition, his work gets little publicity and many MPs prefer to investigate complaints themselves rather than use the services of the Commissioner. In 1978 there was a big increase in the number of complaints lodged, which seems to indicate the office served a genuine need.

One other Act, relevant to the coming general election, was the Representation of the People Act 1969. Its main provision was the lowering of the voting age to eighteen. The majority of Conservatives voted against this on a free vote. Both these measures were in line with developments in other advanced industrial societies.

The Parliaments of 1964-70 passed four other Bills which were also in keeping with the trends in other advanced industrial societies. They were not party political measures, but it is unlikely that a Conservative-dominated Commons would have approved them. The first was the abolition of capital punishment, due to the untiring efforts of Sydney Silverman, who introduced his Murder (Abolition of the Death Penalty) Bill in 1964. It was passed in July 1965. The Lords then carried a Conservative amendment that the measure should lapse automatically after five years unless both Houses passed motions for permanent abolition. Such motions were approved in December 1969. MPs decided to risk running counter to public opinion on this issue. (Interestingly, the former executioner, Pierrepoint, had come to the conclusion that capital punishment was not a deterrent.)

In July 1967 the Sexual Offences Act legalized homosexual practices, in private, between consenting adults in England and Wales. This was a private Member's measure introduced by Leo Abse, a Welsh Labour MP. In October of the same year the Abortion Act became law. This had been introduced by Liberal MP David Steel. The Act made abortion much easier. It permits the termination of pregnancy on the following grounds: first, that the continuation of the pregnancy would involve risk to the life of the pregnant woman, or injury to the physical or mental health of the pregnant woman or any existing children of her family, greater than if the pregnancy were terminated; or second, that there is sub-stantial risk, that if the child were born, it would suffer such physical or mental abnormalities as to be seriously handicapped. Supporters of this measure later complained that it was far more difficult in some areas than in others to get an abortion, and this because of the attitude of doctors. A strong pressure group, mainly based in the Catholic community, continued to oppose the Act. In 1975 there was some tightening-up of its practice. This was because of complaints about high fees charged by private nursing-homes with inadequate facilities to foreign women seeking abortions in Britain. The number of abortions greatly increased after the passing of the Act. The Theatres Act 1968, introduced by Labour MP George Strauss, ended censorship of plays in London, and no doubt made it easier for writers to put on more honest, controversial, and, dare one say it, 'adult', plays in Nottingham and Leicester as well as in London. Parliament also modernized the law on divorce in 1969. The irretrievable breakdown of the marriage became the sole reason for granting divorce. In line with other countries where divorce was available Britain was experiencing an explosion of divorce before the Act. Between 1959 and 1969 the annual number of petitions for divorce and annulment in England and Wales had increased by something like 133 per cent. This trend continued. The secularization of society, the improving education of women, and the increase in the number of married women at work were probably the main causes for this development. The term 'women's liberation', or simply 'women's lib', erupted into the mass media about 1968.

Also in keeping with the trend towards 'women's lib' was the National Health Service (Family Planning) Act 1967, which enabled local health authorities to provide a family-planning service for all who seek it either directly or by way of a voluntary body. The advice is provided free, the contraceptive devices are charged for according to the means of the recipient.

The legislators resisted change in one area of non-partisan controversy – drugs. Drug-taking, trafficking, and offences continued to cause mounting concern. Dangerous-drug offences doubled between 1969 and 1972. The causes of this development remained uncertain and somewhat obscure. All these measures, which recognized the changes in society and attitudes, and in turn helped to produce change, were seen by some as a dangerous lurch in the direction of the permissive society, by others as moves towards a more honest and more humane Britain.

June election, 1970

When Harold Wilson appeared on a TV sports programme as a football fan, there were those who thought the election could not be far away. It was announced on 18 May 1970 and polling-day was on 18 June. Everything pointed to another Labour win. The local election results in May had gone Labour's way. The opinion polls gave Labour a good lead. Top people – Cecil King the newspaper magnate, Lord Renwick and Norman Collins of ATV, Lord Crowther of Forte, Lord Shawcross, former Attlee minister turned TV tycoon (Thames Television), Paul Chambers of ICI, Lockwood of EMI, and McFadzean of Shell, and others too – met together and wondered how they could use their mouths and their money to scotch Wilson. King commented gloomily, 'On television Wilson lacks all authority but looks genial and confident; Heath looks a nice man but is just not convincing – it is hard to say why'.[107] Money wages were up and the balance of payments looked not unhealthy. Wilson wanted to play it cool, avoid fireworks. All was not well, however, among Labour's rank and file. Individual membership had fallen every year since Labour had been in office. The Parliamentary Labour Party was divided. In May, Labour MPs had once again demonstrated their disagreements over the government's support for American policy in Vietnam. Wilson no doubt thought he could appeal to the voters over the heads of Labour MPs and ordinary party members. In spite of all the setbacks ownership of consumer durables and home ownership had continued to rise during Labour's period of office. In some respects, discussed below, Britain was a franker, freer, place to live than it had been in the early 1960s. But none of the great plans for reform had come off. Wilson had certainly not put back the 'Great' in Great Britain, Britain's standing in the world had certainly not risen. The government had been driven helplessly from one improvisation to another. For Labour supporters, those who had to man the creaking, run-down, constituency machines, these had been years of frustration and failure.

On 19 June at 4 a.m. Crossman and his wife motored home. It was the 'cool, delicious dawn of an exquisite June morning'.[108] Politically, it was the delicious dawn of the man with the boat rather than the man with the pipe. To everyone's amazement Heath, the most despised politician in post-war Britain, the punch ball of the media men, had made it. The Conservatives had fewer votes than in 1951, 1955, or 1959, but they had gained a majority of 43 over Labour. The quiet election with the lowest turn-out since the war had proved to be Wilson's undoing.

Notes

1 Henry Brandon, *In the Red: the Struggle for Sterling, 1964-66* (London, 1966), 115.
2 Brian Lapping, *The Labour Government 1964-70* (London, 1970), 43.
3 Lord George-Brown, *In My Way* (London, 1971), 95.
4 R.H.S. Crossman, *The Diaries of a Cabinet Minister*, vol. I: *Minister of Housing 1964-66* (London, 1975), 510-11; see also Cecil King, *Diary 1965-70* (London, 1972), 69.
5 Harold Wilson, *The Labour Government 1964-70: a Personal Record* (London, 1971), 227.
6 King, op. cit., 69.
7 Crossman, op. cit., 524.
8 ibid., 533-4.
9 ibid., 547; see Mrs Castle's remarks.
10 ibid., 578.
11 Wilson, op. cit., 259.
12 ibid., 260.
13 Crossman, op. cit., 577.
14 ibid., 581.
15 Wilson, op. cit., 262.
16 ibid., 265.
17 This was the writer's impression in Austria and East Germany.
18 David Butler and Michael Pinto-Duschinsky, *The British General Election of 1970* (London, 1971), 15.
19 Wilson, op. cit., 272.
20 Richard Crossman, *The Diaries of a Cabinet Minister*, vol. II: *1966-68* (London, 1976), 17.
21 Wilson, op. cit., 273.
22 ibid., 278.
23 ibid., 286-7, 138.
24 Crossman, *1966–68*, 138.
25 ibid., 140.
26 Marcia Williams, *Inside Number 10* (London, 1972), 170.
27 Wilson, op. cit., 577.
28 Lapping, op. cit., 62.
29 ibid., 62-3.
30 Michael Foot, *Aneurin Bevin 1945–60* (London, 1975), 272.
31 ibid., 272.
32 Crossman, *1964–66*, 54.

33 Foot, op. cit., 275.
34 Wilson, op. cit., 470.
35 ibid., 474.
36 Joseph Frankel, *British Foreign Policy 1945-1973* (London, 1975), 141.
37 Foot, op. cit., 274.
38 Frankel, op. cit., 267.
39 Wilson, op. cit., 556-7.
40 Lapping, op. cit., 67.
41 Wilson, op. cit., 626.
42 *Pears Cyclopaedia 1976-1977* (London, 1977), G33.
43 D.G.M. Dosser, 'Britain and the International Economy', in *Westminster Bank Review* (May 1968).
44 Crossman, *1966-68*, 83.
45 Brandt, *People and Politics* (London, 1978), 161.
46 George-Brown, op. cit., 209.
47 Crossman, *1966-68*, 231.
48 Samuel Brittan, *Steering the Economy: the Role of the Treasury* (London, 1969), 222.
49 ibid., 224.
50 ibid., 226.
51 Wilson, op. cit., 427.
52 ibid., 426.
53 Andrew Alexander and Alan Watkins, *The Making of the Prime Minister 1970* (London, 1970), 36.
54 ibid., 36.
55 Brittan, op. cit., 228.
56 *Report of the Sixty-sixth Annual Conference of The Labour Party,* 189.
57 Crossman, *1966–68*, 576. Alexander and Watkins, op. cit., 39.
58 Wilson, op. cit., 464.
59 Crossman, *1966-68*, 592.
60 Alexander and Watkins, op. cit., 43.
61 Mayhew's own views are given in Christopher Mayhew, *Party Games* (London, 1969).
62 Patrick Gordon Walker, *The Cabinet* (London, 1972), 127.
63 Wilson, op. cit., 243.
64 *Report of the Sixty-sixth Annual Conference,* 200.
65 Lyndon Baines Johnson, *The Vantage Point: Perspectives of the Presidency 1963-69* (New York, 1971), 317.
66 ibid., 318. Johnson uses the expression 'We finally decided to close the London gold market'.
67 ibid., 318-19.
68 Alexander and Watkins, op. cit., 45.
69 Lapping, op. cit., 110.
70 Frank Field and Patricia Haikin, *Black Britons* (London, 1971), 8-9.
71 ibid., 12
72 Humphry Berkeley, *The Odyssey of Enoch: a Political Memoir* (London, 1977), 77-8.
73 Crossman, *1966-68*, 733.
74 ibid., 734.
75 Field and Haikin, 15-16.
76 Johnson, op. cit., 175.
77 Berkeley, op. cit., contains the speech in full.
78 For biographies of Heath and Powell see: Andrew Roth, *Heath and the Heathmen* (London, 1972); George Hutchinson, *Edward Heath: a Personal and Political Biography* (London, 1970); Paul Foot, *The Rise of Enoch Powell*

(London, 1969); Berkeley, op. cit.; Andrew Roth, *Enoch Powell: Tory Tribune* (London, 1970); T. E. Utley, *Enoch Powell: the man and his thinking* (London, 1968).

79 Roth, *Enoch Powell,* 329.

80 Martin Dillon and Denis Lehane, *Political Murder in Northern Ireland* (London, 1973), 35.

81 This was the impression gained by the writer on a visit to Northern Ireland in 1963 when he interviewed Captain O'Neill, Gerry Fitt, and some others.

82 Wilson, op. cit., 670.

83 Lord Cameron, *Disturbances in Northern Ireland* (Belfast, 1969), Cmd 532, para 51.

84 Richard Rose, *Governing without Consensus* (London, 1971), 441.

85 Richard Crossman, *The Diaries of a Cabinet Minister,* vol. III: *1968-70* (London, 1977), 451. Wilson, op. cit., 674; for Devlin's own views see Bernadette Devlin, *The Price of my soul* (London, 1969).

86 Crossman, *1968-70,* 478-9.

87 Rose, op. cit., 106.

88 James Callaghan, *A House Divided: the Dilemma of Northern Ireland* (London, 1973), 74. This is Callaghan's account of his own activities in regard to Ulster; he remarks about his visit that he was impressed by the fact that only Catholic houses had been destroyed.

89 Rose, op. cit., 107.

90 Conor Cruise O'Brien, *States of Ireland* (London, 1972), 183.

91 Wilson, op. cit., 626.

92 Peter Kellner and Christopher Hitchens, *Callaghan: the Road to Number Ten* (London, 1976), 96.

93 Crossman, *1968-70.*

94 ibid., 520.

95 ibid., 523.

96 Wilson, op. cit., 537.

97 Frank Stacey, *British Government 1966-1975: Years of Reform* (London, 1975), 73.

98 ibid., 21-37.

99 Walter Bagehot, *The English Constitution* (London, 1963), Introduction by R.H.S. Crossman, 51.

100 *Guardian,* 21 June 1965.

101 Lord Attlee, the *Queen,* 30 June 1965. Reginald Maudling, *Memoirs* (London, 1978), 177.

102 ibid., 77.

103 *Sunday Times,* 12 September 1965.

104 'A Failure To Reform?' *Sunday Times,* 19 March 1978.

105 ibid.

106 *Civil Service Recruitment of Graduates 1977* (Civil Service Commission, n.d), 2, Table 2.

107 King, op. cit., 327, 330-1.

108 Crossman, *1968-70,* 949.

9 Britain under Heath, 1970–74

Heath's trouble with the press

Edward Heath's Cabinet was not one of new faces. It contained few surprises. It was reassuring for Conservatives right of centre to find Sir Alec Douglas-Home returning to the Foreign and Commonwealth Office. At the Home Office 'Reginald Maudling's placid bulk could cool the law-and-order brigade and straddle the bipartisanship needed on Northern Ireland . . . Heath had to put up with Quintin Hogg, so he dressed him up as Lord Chancellor, renamed him Hailsham and sent him back into "exile" in the Lords on the Woolsack'.[1] As expected, Iain Macleod went to the Treasury. Thus all, but one, of Heath's old rivals were safely in the Cabinet. It would have been difficult for Heath to have found any suitable office for Powell. Not quite so well known to the public was the new Minister of Labour, the Cambridge-educated metallurgist and industrialist Robert Carr (b. 1916), who was supposed to succeed with the unions where Barbara Castle had failed. Another key appointment was that of Anthony Barber (b. 1920) as Chancellor of the Duchy of Lancaster with special responsibility for negotiating Britain's third attempt to get into the EEC. He had been Minister of Health under Sir Alec. Farmer and landowner William Whitelaw (b. 1918) became Leader of the House, and Peter Walker (b. 1932), the self-made millionaire and chairman of Lloyd's insurance brokers, took over the Ministry of the Environment. Among the other significant appointments were Sir Keith Joseph (b. 1918), deputy chairman of Bovis Holdings Ltd, as Secretary of State for Social Services, and James Prior (b. 1928), a Cambridge-educated farmer and land agent, as Minister of Agriculture, Fisheries, and Food. One other appointment of great significance, though it was not really seen as such at the time, was the appointment of Margaret Thatcher (b. 1925) as Minister of Education and Science. Essentially, Heath's Cabinet was a fairly moderate and meritocratic team. If it did not represent, in social terms, the mass of ordinary party members in the constituencies, it did represent a shift from the upper-class emphasis of previous post-war Tory Cabinets to the more middle-class elements of the Party. One rough indicator of this was the fall in the number of Old Etonians from eleven under Sir Alec to three under Mr Heath – Douglas-Home, Hailsham, and Carrington.[2] The last-named went to Defence. There were only eighteen members of Edward Heath's Cabinet. One Kennedy-style innovation was the setting-up of a 'think-tank' under Lord Rothschild, known as a Labour supporter, to advise the government on possible future policy initiatives.

Heath suffered his first piece of bad fortune within weeks of taking over. On 20 July his neighbour at 11 Downing Street suffered a heart attack and died. Suddenly, without warning, one of the most able, and most likeable, of Heath's colleagues was gone. Macleod was replaced by Anthony Barber at the Treasury, and Geoffrey Rippon took over as 'Mr Europe'. John Davies, former Director-General of the CBI, with only a few weeks of Commons experience behind him, became Minister of Technology.

Heath's second difficulty was to a considerable extent of his own making – his bad relations with the press. Like Gaitskell, Heath has certain unfortunate facial characteristics which make him an ideal target for the cartoonists. His accent, it has been said, sounds as if it owes more to the elocution master than to any natural evolution. Yet in many respects he came across as a civilized and decent man. Before 1970 he did seem to get a rough deal from most of the media men – whatever their politics. Perhaps the fact that he appeared to have confounded their predictions, as well as those of many of his colleagues, by winning the 1970 election, had given him a certain defensive arrogance, behind which the 'real' Ted Heath was condemned to remain hidden. At any rate, according to James Margach, 'When Prime Minister he became authoritarian and intolerant'. At 10 Downing Street 'The shutters were fastened and the door opened only to a select few by a Government which was the most secrecy-conscious since the war. Downing Street became the most closed society in all my experience. Heath had the shortest honeymoon of all with the political correspondents'.[3]

Cuts in government expenditure

Politically Heath was both moderate and radical at the same time. In opposition his party had developed policies which not only challenged some of those being pursued by the Wilson regime, but also represented a break with those of Macmillan and other post-war Conservative administrations. The aim was to break with the state-interventionist and consensus welfare policies of previous Labour and Conservative governments, and set the compass to travel towards a neo-capitalist El Dorado. In some respects it was influenced by the Republican Right in the United States and by a somewhat false impression of what the Christian Democrats were about in West Germany. The state, so the theory went, would interfere less in the economy, but would also give fewer hand-outs to industry. Firms would have to become more efficient or perish. As John Davies told the Conservative Party conference in October 1970, 'I will not bolster up or bail out companies where I can see no end to the process of propping them up'.[4] Government expenditure would be cut, individuals would find less taken from their pay packets, but they would have to do more for themselves. Those who could not would be caught in the safety net of selective benefits, benefits for those who really needed them.

The object ... is not to destroy the social services but to restrict provision to those areas where it is most efficient. The aim is to free as many people as possible from the need to rely entirely (or even mainly) on public authorities, to restore a greater degree of family responsibility expanding the amount of private provision. At the same time, by reducing the pointless redistribution of funds where no net benefit is secured, it should be possible both to lower administrative costs and concentrate help where it is most needed.[5]

How did all this work out in practice?

Doctrinaire Conservatives could chuckle with delight at the announcement that Thomas Cook and Son, the successful state-owned travel agency, was to be sold, that the National Coal Board was to be encouraged to sell its brickworks, British Rail its hotels, and the nationalized gas industry was to be stopped from pursuing its exploration of the North Sea gas and oil fields. Smiles of joy at such measures disappeared when the government was faced with the alternative of breaking its pledge on 'lame ducks' or letting Rolls Royce, a symbol around the world for British engineering skill, go to the wall. Heavily committed to a costly programme of development on the RB 211 engine for the Lockheed TriStar, the company needed immediate financial help to avoid bankruptcy. The government felt it had no choice but to step in with a loan. When the company collapsed three months later, the government nationalized it. Given this approach, it was only to be expected that the Industrial Reorganization Corporation should be closed down.

Like the government it had succeeded, Heath's administration was worried about inflation. It was not, however, quite sure what to do about it. Barber introduced a mini-Budget in October 1970 which cut government expenditure on school milk, council house subsidies, prescription costs, and dental treatment. Income-tax cuts were promised in six months time. There was some restriction on credit. These measures could easily be attacked by the Opposition as socially divisive, and even inflationary. The main ones to carry the burdens would be the working classes, thus giving rise to increased wage claims. The same could be said for the Housing Finance Act of 1972.

The aim of this legislation was to cut subsidies to council-house tenants by introducing a 'fair rent' policy. It meant considerable rent increases for very many tenants and a rise in their cost of living. Those who could not afford the new rents could get rent rebates. Over 30 per cent of British families lived in council houses or flats at that time. The experiment was started of encouraging local councils to give their tenants the opportunity to buy the homes in which they lived. Apart from being regarded as a step along the road to the old Conservative goal of a 'property-owning democracy', it was thought it would generate more funds for new council-house building. Critics claimed it merely reduced the stock of cheaper housing for the less well-off. House prices did leap up between 1970 and 1972 by about 30 per cent *per annum*. This also increased inflation.

In opposition the Conservatives had opposed Wilson's attempt at a prices and incomes policy. When they were returned to office, they abandoned such attempts. The National Board for Prices and Incomes was abolished, only to re-emerge later. Heath and his colleagues sought some kind of voluntary agreement with the trade unions and the Confederation of British Industries (CBI). This did not work to the government's satisfaction and in November 1972 a 90-day standstill was imposed upon wages and salaries, dividends, rates and rents, and on all prices other than imports and fresh foods. Offenders were liable to be fined. In April 1973 this was replaced by a more flexible form of restraint known as Stage Two. Under new legislation two bodies were established; a Price Commission and a Pay Board. Though there were to be exceptions, the total annual increase for any group of employees should not exceed £1 a week plus 4 per cent of the current pay-bill excluding overtime. The Pay Board had to give its prior approval for settlements involving more than a thousand employees, in other cases it had to be notified. It became an offence to strike or threaten to strike to force an employer to contravene an order of the Pay Board. Price increases were limited under Stage Two, but there were a fair number of exceptions. Large firms had to give prior notice to the Price Commission, medium firms had to report regularly, and small firms had to keep price records. Imports were one of the exemptions and the price of goods from abroad went up rapidly in 1973. Stage Three of the pay policy was introduced in October 1973 and under it there were only modest increases allowed with a limit of £350 a year on the amount to be received by any individual. Again there were important exceptions for such things as 'unsociable hours', and progress towards equal pay for women. Threshold payments were also introduced, allowing modest, automatic, increases in pay for each jump in the cost of living index.[6] These measures did not keep down the rate of inflation, the biggest single factor being the soaring cost of imported raw materials, oil, and food.

Industrial Relations: '. . . all hell will be let loose'

The government had hoped that new legislation relating to trade unions would have played an important part helping the economy. Accordingly it introduced the Industrial Relations Bill in 1971. It was passed in spite of strong TUC opposition. Once again the Heath administration was indicating it was not afraid of breaking out of the old consensus framework. The Bill had many similarities with the earlier proposed legislation of Barbara Castle. Under it trade unions were forced to register or forfeit the legal immunities available to registered unions. Registration did, however, bring with it obligations. The rules of registered trade unions had to set out clearly which officers had authority to instigate or direct industrial action; they had to deal with ballots and elections, dues and discipline, and members' complaints against the union. As one authority on the subject put it at the time, 'Almost every union in the country will be compelled to redraw its rules in accordance with these guiding principles and they will have to do it quickly because a timetable is laid down and it is a pretty brisk one'.[7] The 'guiding principles' would be those of the registrar. The new law introduced the concept of unfair industrial action, under which the threat of a sympathetic strike or other sympathetic industrial action was included.[8] Also included under this concept was industrial action by an unregistered union, a strike to bring about a closed shop, or action designed to induce changes in collective agreements. The legislation established a system of industrial tribunals and a National Industrial Relations Court (NIRC). The Act included a number of items which every trade unionist would favour, such as the statutory right to belong to a trade union, and protection from unfair dismissal. One of the main arguments against the Act was that Britain's industrial relations were much better than those of the United States, with its wealth of labour legislation, from which the framers of the Act had borrowed much. Even more important, it would, certainly in the short run, embitter the relations between government and the unions at a time when the maximum co-operation was needed. Heath and his colleagues simply ignored the experience of his predecessor and crashed on. Industrial relations deteriorated throughout the Heath period and a considerable part of this deterioration was due to the Industrial Relations Act. In February 1971 there was an impressive display of trade union opposition to the Act when over 100,000 members demonstrated in London. In the following month 1.5 million engineering workers staged a one-day strike against the legislation. Other similar strikes followed. Nevertheless, in August the Act came into force. The TUC continued to oppose compulsory registration and subsequently 32 unions were suspended for registering. The Transport and General Workers' Union, the largest, was fined for contempt by the NIRC in March 1972 and again in April. On 21 May 1972 five dockers were committed to prison for contempt by the NIRC. Vic Feather, Secretary of the TUC, had warned 'As soon as the first trade unionist goes to prison, all hell will be let loose'.[9] This did not happen, but opposition to the Act continued. The Act probably made trade unionists more determined to oppose the government's pay policy. Certainly this was a period in which there was increasing use of industrial action in support of pay claims by a wide variety of employees. Gas and power workers, engine-drivers and miners, ambulance-drivers and hospital ancillary staff, firemen and civil servants, all contributed to the increase in days lost through industrial action.

Another major piece of legislation of this period was the Local Government Act of 1972. It stemmed from the proposals of the Redcliffe-Maud Committee, which had been set up by the previous administration. Local government in London had been reformed in 1963 and no changes were made there. The system in the rest of the country had remained virtually unchanged since the 1880s. There was widespread feeling that it no longer corresponded to the needs and realities of present-day Britain. There was an artificial distinction between town and country, there was fragmentation of services, and councillors were highly unrepresentative of the communities they served. The Act set up 46 counties in England, with a two-tier system. In six predominantly urban areas new authorities, metropolitan counties, were established. Within them were a number of metropolitan district authorities forming a second tier. In the rest of England existing county boundaries were retained as far as possible with the new counties having authority over the formerly independent county boroughs. The former county boroughs and district councils then became the second tier. Wales was divided into eight counties with a similar, but not identical, structure to the English two-tier system. The local government structure in Scotland was suitably modified under legislation passed in 1973. Another feature of the Act, designed to make it easier for a wider range of individuals to serve on local councils, was the introduction of a flat-rate attendance allowance. Under the Local Government Act 1948 a financial loss allowance had been introduced, but it covered only loss of earnings claimed. The new allowance was a step nearer to actually paying councillors a salary. The aldermanic system, under which a proportion of council members were indirectly elected by fellow councillors, was abolished. This had been introduced in 1835 as a sop to the House of Lords, and had led to a situation where, occasionally, parties defeated at the polls were able to hang on to power with the help of their aldermen who were not yet up for re-election. These measures failed to produce more representative councils or raise the low level of participation in local government elections. In 1964 over half the county council seats had not been contested, many remained uncontested after the Act came in. The Act did not solve the problem of the relations between local and central government or the problem of finance. No change was made in the rating system. Massive increases in rates took place in 1974. Some of these had, of course, nothing to do with the Act, some were indirectly caused by it, and some were directly the result of it. 'The expense of the new system and how to meet it were questions not adequately faced'.[10]

The lack of competition in local government elections, with small groups of individuals from one party exercising unchallenged power on local councils for many years, was undoubtedly an important cause of a degree of corruption which came to light during this period. The key figure in this was John Poulson, an unqualified architect with the largest architectural practice in Europe. In the 1960s he was said to be earning £1 million *per annum* in fees. He controlled four companies, one with his wife, and was declared bankrupt in 1971. Local authorities claimed negligence over a number of contracts he had fulfilled. And when his bankruptcy was being investigated, it was discovered he had paid £334,000 to MPs, local councillors, and civil servants. Superficially, Poulson was a highly respectable man. He was a Commissioner of Taxes. He was also Chairman of the Executive Committee of the (Conservative satellite) National Liberal Party. His wife was a JP and Chairman of the Yorkshire Women Conservatives. However, he showed no political prejudice when seeking business favours from local politicians and others in official positions. His two best-known associates were Alderman Andrew Cunningham and T. Dan Smith. Cunningham was Chairman of Durham County Council, Felling Urban District Council, Durham Police Authority, Northumbria River Authority, Tyneside Passenger Transport Authority, and the North-Eastern Regional Airport Committee. He worked as regional organizer of the General and Municipal Workers' Union. For a time he represented that union on the National Executive Committee of the Labour Party. Smith was, among other things, leader of the controlling Labour group of Newcastle upon Tyne City Council and a member of the Redcliffe-Maud Committee. Poulson,

Cunningham, Smith, and some others were jailed for their activities. Other trials followed connected with Poulson's affairs, involving officials of British Rail, the National Coal Board, South-Western Metropolitan Hospital Board, and some other councils.[11] Up and down the United Kingdom, particularly in London, Glasgow, Yorkshire, and Wales, there have been convictions for corruption in local government during the 1970s not connected with Poulson. In South Wales, for instance, there were nineteen corruption trials connected with local government in 18 months during 1976–77. Altogether, thirty people, including twenty businessmen, were found guilty in the Welsh cases. Twelve were sent to prison.[12]

Heath had one casualty in the Poulson affair. Reginald Maudling, Home Secretary, had been a business associate of Poulson. As Home Secretary he was also in charge of the Metropolitan Police, who were investigating the architect's activities in London. As Maudling later wrote, he felt he 'had no option but to resign'.[13] He decided not to accept an alternative political appointment offered by Heath, and was replaced in July 1972 by Robert Carr.

Another modernizing Act which affected local government was the Water Act 1973. Local authorities lost their functions as suppliers of water and sewerage services. These became the responsibility of ten regional water authorities and a National Water Board.

In July 1973 the National Health Service Reorganization Act became law. Under the Labour government Kenneth Robinson, Minister of Health, and Richard Crossman, as overlord of social services, had recommended changes in the National Health Service. These plans came to nothing after the Conservatives were returned to office. Sir Keith Joseph adopted a 'managerial' approach to reform of the NHS. Under the 1946 Act setting up the NHS, hospitals were run by appointed boards responsible to the minister, general-practitioner services were run by Executive Councils also responsible to the minister, and the local authorities were responsible for ambulances, midwifery services, and a variety of clinics. Under the 1973 Act Area Health Authorities were set up with boundaries in line with those of the new counties. The Crossman proposals advocated an element on these authorities elected by the local government bodies. Joseph rejected this proposal and the idea of having district bodies below the Area Health Authorities. The local authorities have retained their services and family doctors and hospital doctors have got better representation on various statutory committees. The Area Health Authorities are linked with the university medical schools by university representatives on the authorities. The main criticism of the new system is that it produced a bureaucratized NHS rather than a democratic one. Neither the 1973 Act nor the limited changes which have taken place since the return of Labour in 1974 did anything to put right the other difficulties of the NHS. There has long been dissatisfaction with the financial provision for the service. Waiting lists for non-urgent surgery have tended to grow rather than diminish. Disquiet about the treatment of long-stay patients in hospitals, of the elderly, and of patients in mental hospitals has continued. Infant mortality rates throughout the United Kingdom have fallen greatly in the period since 1945, but greater progress has been made in some of the neighbouring countries of Europe and Britain now lags behind many of them. Proportionate to population, Britain has fewer medical practitioners than many other European states, and fewer hospital beds. The NHS is also highly dependent on Asian immigrant doctors to keep the hospitals manned.[14]

Northern Ireland's continuing conflict

Heath's administration certainly did not take over a happy situation in Northern Ireland. On 3 July 1970, 2,000 troops of the British army were sent into the Lower Falls Road area of Belfast to search for arms. The troops found 50 pistols, 26 rifles, 5 submachine-guns, and a great deal of ammunition in the 3,000 homes they searched.[15] The Catholics retaliated to the raid by stone-throwing, answered with tear-gas. A curfew was introduced in an attempt to get the situation under control, but the violence escalated. In the five years of O'Neill's government only three persons died in disorders.[16] In the years that followed the death toll mounted. In 1973 alone 250 people were killed in Northern Ireland: 171 civilians, 66 army or Ulster Defence Regiment personnel, 13 police. Since the beginning of the present troubles 927 had died up to the end of 1973, 207 of them British troops.[17] Reginald Maudling has written about the government's dilemma at the time:

If action were taken, such as searching houses for arms . . . it could be very easily regarded by the whole Catholic community as a victimization of them as Catholics and, therefore, would bolster the support that they gave to the Provisional IRA. If, on the other hand, these vigorous actions were not taken . . . there was always the danger of a violent Protestant reaction . . . There was no doubt in my mind that the Catholic community had had less than their fair share in governing their own country, and that there was severe discrimination against them.

But the more the IRA used violence, the greater the reaction among the Protestants against concessions. 'We were really trying to walk up an escalator that was moving down'.[18] The Heath government accepted the package of reforms announced by the Wilson administration, but it would take time and patience to implement them, and time it did not have. It was faced with the delaying tactics of the more reactionary Ulster Unionists. The reforms had to be implemented through the Stormont regime: 'It was uphill work, and the progress, if progress at all took place, was exceedingly slow; too slow, in fact if we were to obtain our objective of peace and reconciliation'.[19] On the advice of Brian Faulkner, who had replaced Chichester-Clark as Prime Minister in March 1971, London accepted in August the introduction of internment without trial in Northern Ireland. At the same time it negotiated with friends and neighbours to explore the possibility of a settlement. In September 1971 Edward Heath had talks with Brian Faulkner and Jack Lynch, Prime Minister of the Irish Republic. These talks did not appear to lead anywhere and the bombings and the assassinations continued. One particularly bad incident occurred in Bogside, Londonderry, on 30 January 1972. A civil rights march against internment took place in spite of a ban on all marches. There was strong disagreement about what actually happened, but the march ended with thirteen Catholics dead and sixteen wounded, killed by British troops. No British fatalities had been suffered. On 30 March 1972 the Northern Ireland constitution was set aside and all legislative and executive functions were transferred to London. William Whitelaw was appointed Secretary of State for Northern Ireland with special authority to deal with the situation. Exactly one year, and many bombs, later the government published a White Paper, *Northern Ireland: Constitutional Proposals.* This proposed a new system of devolution based on elections by proportional representation. An Executive would exercise the powers previously exercised by the Stormont government except, that is, for law and order. This would remain the responsibility of the Secretary of State. A referendum, boycotted by all the Catholic-supported parties, produced a 57.4 per cent vote of the total electorate in favour of retaining the union with Great Britain. Elections for the new assembly were held in June 1973. Negotiations were then carried on by the Official Unionists, the Alliance Party, and the Social Democratic and Labour Party to set up a Northern Ireland Executive. When Whitelaw was replaced by Francis Pym in November 1973, the situation was beginning to look hopeful. One matter remained outstanding, the proposal in the White Paper to establish a Council of Ireland. A conference was held at Sunningdale, Berkshire, in December attended by representatives of the London government, the Northern Ireland Executive-designate, and the government of the Irish Republic. It was agreed to create a Council of Ireland which, though it would have a mainly consultative role, would have certain functions to do with tourism, agriculture, and the environment. Direct rule ended on 1 January 1974. During 1973 the death toll had been 250 as against 468 in 1972.[20] This was the situation when the Conservatives left office. Britain had committed about 20,000 troops to deal with the problem, about the number Britain had used in 1921 to deal with the 'troubles'.[21] One other aspect of the situation in Northern Ireland was the damage to Britain's image abroad. Internment brought with it accusations of torture by the British forces. By 10 November 1971, 980 men had been detained without trial. Some of them alleged ill-treatment or torture by the security forces. The British government asked the Parliamentary Commissioner, Sir Edmund Compton, to investigate. He dismissed the charge of torture, but he and his colleagues concluded, referring to eleven cases of 'interrogation in depth', 'We consider that the following actions constitute physical ill-treatment; posture on the wall, hooding, noise, deprivation of sleep, diet of bread and water'.[22]

What were perhaps even more disturbing for the government than bombs in Belfast were bombs in London. On 12 January 1971 bombs shattered the peace at Robert Carr's home in Hertfordshire. No one was injured, but Detective Chief Superintendent Roy Habershon, who investigated the crime, believed 'that those who were responsible either intended to kill the Carrs, or had such a reckless disregard for them that it amounted to the same thing'.[23] Some jumped to the conclusion that the bombs were the work of extremist trade unionists protesting about the Industrial Relations Bill.[24] This was certainly not the case. In fact, they were the work of a new group outside any known political circle, which made the work of detection so much more difficult. It revealed itself to the press the following day as the Angry Brigade, Britain's tiny contribution to a worldwide phenomenon of youthful revolt against the urban, capitalistic, mass-communications society, whether hidden behind the Western democratic or Soviet façade. Its members were influenced by the Vietnam War, the Paris students' revolt, the ideas of Raoul Vaneigem and Guy Debord, and the slums of Notting Hill and Stoke Newington. Mainly of middle-class backgrounds, they were the products of either Essex or Cambridge universities. It became clear that they had been responsible for a number of earlier bomb attacks, and other attacks followed that on the home of Robert Carr. The Ford Motor Company offices, the Territorial Army Centre at Holloway, the flat of John Davies, and the Biba boutique, Kensington High Street, were among their targets,

Life is so boring there's nothing to do except spend all our wages on the latest skirt, or shirt. Brothers and Sisters, what are your real desires? Sit in the drugstore, look distant, empty, bored, drinking some tasteless coffee? or perhaps BLOW IT UP OR BURN IT DOWN. The only thing you can do with modern slavehouses – called boutiques – IS WRECK THEM.[25]

They saw fashion as a means of manipulating and enslaving the mind with useless irrelevancies from the past. They opposed secret files on students at universities, the census, social security files, computers, TV, passports, work permits, insurance cards, in short 'bureaucracy and technology used against the people'.[26] Their efforts were rewarded with sentences of ten years imprisonment. The sentences would have been longer had not the jury, regarding them as misguided idealists, put in a plea for leniency.

Even with the Angry Brigade out of the way after August 1971, other bombs disturbed the peace of England. The IRA remained active. In February 1972 seven people were killed by an IRA bomb in Aldershot. Bombs exploded in central London in March 1973, killing one and injuring 238. In August 1973 letter-bombs were received in London and two people were injured at the Stock Exchange. In the following month there were thirteen injured by bombs in London underground stations. A bomb also exploded at Chelsea barracks. On 18 December sixty were injured by further bomb explosions in London. The bombings continued in January 1974. Happily, there was no reaction against Britain's sizeable Irish community.

Immigration and Rhodesia

In their election manifesto the Conservatives had promised that 'for the future, work permits will not carry the right of permanent settlement for the holder or his dependents' and that 'future immigration will be allowed only in strictly defined special cases'. The Immigration Act of 1971 was designed to redeem these pledges. Under it, work permits replaced the former employment vouchers and enabled the holder to remain in Britain initially for one year only. Dependents of immigrants already in Britain before the Act continued to have rights of entry free from control, but those admitted with work permits had no such automatic right to bring their wives or children. The Act also created a new category of immigrant – Patrials – individuals having close ties with Britain, by birth for instance, who can come without restrictions. The Act strengthened the law to prevent illegal immigration and introduced a scheme of financial assistance for immigrants seeking voluntary repatriation.

In another area of Commonwealth policy the government of Edward Heath was unable to redeem its election pledge. It sought a settlement with Rhodesia without success. In 1970 Rhodesia had declared itself a republic and introduced a new constitution which permanently denied Africans a majority in its parliament. Douglas-Home nevertheless went to Salisbury and signed an agreement with the rebel regime. He achieved certain limited concessions on the widening of the African franchise, reduction of discrimination, and promotion of racial harmony. Britain offered £50 million in aid. The settlement would only come into effect when the British government was convinced that the majority of Africans supported it. The government accordingly sent Lord Pearce on a fact-finding mission to assess the state of black Rhodesian opinion. In May 1972 he reported that black Rhodesians were generally not favourable to the terms of the proposed settlement, which therefore lapsed.

If the black Commonwealth states were not too happy about Britain's handling of the Rhodesian situation, they were even less understanding about Britain's relations with South Africa. Once again the issue of arms to South Africa became a controversial issue. It dominated the Commonwealth heads of state conference held in Singapore in February 1971. The British government accepted an obligation under the Simonstown Agreement of 1955, signed by Britain and South Africa, to supply South Africa with naval equipment, for it believed that Anglo–South African naval co-operation was necessary to keep open the sea lanes to the Persian Gulf and the Indian Ocean. Under the Agreement Britain had supplied naval vessels and helicopters for anti-submarine patrols. As we have seen, Harold Wilson had his problems over the Agreement. In effect, the Heath government was merely continuing the policy of its predecessor. It agreed to sell spare parts for the helicopters and consider requests for replacements. It was also prepared to consider requests for other naval equipment to fulfil what it considered to be its obligations under the Agreement. Heated words were exchanged at the Singapore conference over the issue. Heath denied such arms sales would give a certificate of respectability to the South African regime. Britain, he said, condemned apartheid and racial discrimination, and, he pointed out, there were many examples in history of a country allying itself with another whose system of government and treatment of its people it disliked; thus opposition to the Russian system did not prevent Britain and America allying themselves with the Soviet Union in the Second World War. A split was narrowly averted at the conference and all the heads of government agreed a declaration of principles which included the passage, 'We recognize racial prejudice as a dangerous sickness threatening the healthy development of the human race and racial discrimination as an unmitigated evil of society. Each of us will vigorously combat this evil in our own nation'.[27]

One experienced analyst of British foreign policy commented on the arms row,

The high-sounding phrases of the traditional world role sounded hollow when Sir Alec referred to Britain's responsibility in the Indian Ocean in the face of Soviet penetration as the reason for the government's decision to resume the sale of arms to South Africa. A more fundamental reason for this decision could be sought in the government's narrower objective of not being pushed around by the Africans or, for that matter, by the Americans, or the French, or anybody else.[28]

Battle for Common Market entry

On 28 October 1971 the House of Commons voted on the principle of British entry into the EEC. The motion in favour of entry was carried by 356 to 244 with 22 abstentions. One in five MPs had rebelled against their party leadership. It was the biggest revolt since the vote preceding Chamberlain's resignation in 1940. Supporting the government on entry were 69 Labour MPs. Another 20 Labour MPs abstained. The government watched 39 of its own supporters join the Opposition in voting against, two other Conservatives abstained. Emlyn Hooson parted company with his fellow Liberals and voted against.

After negotiations which had turned out not to be as tough as expected, Britain signed for entry on 22 January 1972. Also signing the treaty of accession at Brussels were Ireland, Denmark, and Norway. To the pro-Marketeers it lightened the gloom of an otherwise bleak month with the start of a miner's strike, unemployment breaking through the, psychologically damaging, one million barrier, and violence continuing in Northern Ireland culminating in the tragedy of Londonderry on 30 January.

The battle for Common Market entry caused both party leaders problems with their followers, but Wilson suffered more than Heath. The Labour government had failed to gain entry in 1967 because of de Gaulle's veto. In 1969 the general resigned and Georges Pompidou was elected French President. Pompidou turned out to be less Gaullist than his former master, whom he had served as Prime Minister. The Wilson administration had decided to have a second attempt in 1970, only to be prevented from completing its negotiations by electoral defeat. Labour's election manifesto had stated that entry was the aim and had referred to the negotiations in progress. If anything, Labour's parliamentary representatives returned in 1970 were slightly more pro-EEC than those in the previous Parliament.[29] Pro-Marketeer George Brown, defeated at Belper, was replaced as deputy leader by the equally pro-EEC Roy Jenkins. Pro-Marketeers like Shirley Williams were elected to the shadow cabinet. Harold Wilson decided that discretion was the better part of valour and said very little on the subject, only occasionally warning about getting in on the right terms. In May 1971 one hundred Labour MPs signed a pro-EEC advertisement in the *Guardian*. These included Denis Healey and Anthony Crosland, and other members of the shadow cabinet. However, there was much confusion in Labour's ranks and the anti-Market forces were gathering momentum. Probably thinking of their political futures Healey and Crosland wavered and wobbled. The public was treated to the spectacle of former ministers of Wilson's Cabinet like Peter Shore and Barbara Castle strongly opposing what they had been committed to in government. It was not really Labour's finest hour. By a majority of one, strangely the vote of Shirley Williams, the Party's National Executive Committee decided to call a special one-day conference to debate the issue. Held in London, the July conference allowed the Party to let off steam and proved that Labour had a vast number of effective, even eloquent, speakers among those not destined for the corridors of power. Technically the conference had only consultative status and therefore both sides could afford to be more comradely and adopt the 'more in sorrow than in anger' approach to their opponents. The party's normal annual seaside jamboree was held, as usual, in October. The cudgels were out with threat of disciplinary procedures from Chairman Mikardo against pro-entry MPs. The conference voted overwhelmingly for the Executive's resolution which 'opposes entry into the Common Market on the terms negotiated by the Conservative government . . .' It claimed the government had refused to give the public the facts and called for a general election. The revolt of the pro-entry MPs which followed on 28 October was even more dramatic because it was in defiance of a three-line whip. Heath had given his colleagues a free vote. More drama was to come with the resignation of Roy Jenkins, George Thomson, and Harold Lever from the shadow cabinet in April 1972. The break had come over the issue of whether Labour should demand a referendum over EEC entry.

Heath had said during the election campaign that no British government could take the United Kingdom into the EEC against the wishes of the British people. Throughout 1971 polls conducted on the issue showed apathy, indifference, or opposition to entry into the EEC. Only briefly were there small majorities in favour. In political circles both pros and antis agreed the issue was one of fundamental importance for Britain—so why not let the people decide, if not in a general election, then by a referendum? Heath and Wilson opposed the idea. They claimed it was against British traditions, and continental experience with referenda had not been good; it was a device favoured by dictators. Yet if the pro-Marketeers were claiming Britain should turn away from its old ways, they appeared to be very conservative on this issue. The main protagonists of the idea were Tories Enoch Powell and Neil Marten, and Socialists Anthony Wedgwood Benn (or Tony Benn as he preferred to call himself) and Michael Foot. Heath stood firm and rejected the idea; Wilson gave in and the shadow cabinet voted for the proposal, which led to the resignation of Jenkins and the others. Apart from the inconsistency of his colleagues, Jenkins feared the reactionary potential of this idea in paving the way for referenda on all types of issue. 'By this means we would have forged a more powerful continuing weapon against progressive legislation than anything we have known in this country since the curbing of the absolute powers of the old House of Lords'.[30] It nevertheless became firm Labour Party policy. Heath remained content that he had succeeded in gaining Commons approval for both the principle of entry and for his negotiated terms, even though, on occasion, his majorities on the implementing legislation fell to five, six, and even four.[31] No doubt Wilson felt cheated, by the accident of electoral defeat, of taking the laurels in this particular venture. He did not take up the offer to join Heath, Macmillan, and Brown at the accession ceremony in Brussels.

With Britain's entry into the EEC the earlier Anglo-American intimacy was bound to decline still further. This did not worry Heath too much, for he,

unlike his predecessors whether Conservative or Labour, never had a special emotional attachment to the United States . . . And so in contemplating the virtues of the special relationship with the United States, Heath who had hardly acquired the taste for it, had already lost it. He did not believe in perpetuating a myth in which neither he nor the Americans any longer saw real profit . . . in the view of Prime Minister Heath Britain's first interest was to help make the European Community into a new European power.[32]

He did, however, have good personal relations with Richard Nixon, United States President since 1969.

Oil crisis

On 6 October 1973 the world political scene changed, when Egyptian forces successfully crossed the Suez Canal and stormed the Mannerheim-style defences of Israel's Bar Lev line, determined to retake Egyptian territory lost in the 1967 encounter with the Zionist state. The Syrians also attacked Israel, hoping to avenge

1967. With the Americans pouring arms and prestige into Israel, and Soviet weapons and prestige at stake in Egypt, anything could happen. Once again the forces driving the world towards Armageddon were brought to a halt. Before the end of the month this fourth Arab–Israeli war was over. The battle honours were about even, but when the, by now traditional, U.N. ceasefire came into effect, the Israelis were holding some 1,500 square kilometres of Egyptian soil beyond the Canal compared with only 500 square kilometres retaken by the Egyptians in Sinai.[33] Perhaps as many as 20,000 Arabs had given their lives in this latest round. Some 2,500 Israelis were killed.[34] As during the previous Middle East wars the political temperature in Britain went up several degrees. Once again the pro-Israeli organizations got into top gear to raise money, gain friends, and influence politicians. Traditionally the Jewish community is better represented among Labour's ranks than among the Conservatives in the Commons. In any case, many on the Labour side still regarded Israel as an embattled socialist state. The government could, therefore, expect a lot of Opposition criticism over its Middle East policy. Its difficulty stemmed from the fact that for many years Britain had been supplying arms to Israel and to Jordan. Heath's government wanted to supply ammunition and spares to neither of these countries during the war, claiming this was a policy designed to minimize the conflict. It would be changed if Israel's existence were in danger. As Douglas-Home put it to the House on 18 October, 'I say solemnly on behalf of Her Majesty's Government – and I repeat this – that we cannot, of course, allow any risk to the security of Israel and the State of Israel, which is recognised in the United Nations as an entity in its own right'.[35] Sir Alec had quickly realized that the Middle East, with possible Soviet–U.S. confrontation and danger to oil supplies, could provide the most serious problem which Britain or the West had faced since 1945.[36] He gave an implicit warning to the considerable pro-Israeli faction, 'I will listen always to the voices of Israel and the Arab countries . . . but my concern must be with the British interest as it affects our own future and may affect our future for many years to come, both economically and politically'.[37] Wilson admitted the Palestinians and the Egyptians had a case, but he put his weight behind Israel – 'a democratic socialist country . . . a country which, despite her prodigious arms burden, has established a remarkable record in the social services and care for people, especially her children'.[38] He reached his old form when dealing with the oil threat, frothing at the mouth with synthetic indignation.

We must not be blackmailed by oil sanctions. No one underestimates the gravity of what is happening on this front – the cost, simply, of the increase in prices and its effect on inflation in this country. We had to face the same situation in 1967. I hope that I may show a little more understanding to the problems of the present Prime Minister than he did then, because that was a most important factor leading to the devaluation of 1967 . . . We must decide what is right as a nation, as a Government, as a Parliament, and abide by it. Danegeld is Danegeld, whether exacted by pillagers from the Kattegat or by the oil-rich monarchs and presidents.[39]

Jeremy Thorpe, the Liberal leader, believed, 'No one will buy British arms for his self-defence if he believes that the minute they are needed for self-defence he will not have the ammunition to make them operational'.[40] The government also came in for a good deal of sharp criticism from some of its own backbenchers. Hugh Fraser, John Gorst, Tom Iremonger, and Philip Goodhart all rose to urge the government to change their policy of preventing arms supplies from Britain reaching Israel. Sir Henry d'Avigdor-Goldsmid spoke 'As a supporter of the State of Israel' and as a Conservative condemned the government's policies. He spoke with obvious pride of Israel's military achievements,

They had the idea that overwhelming scientific knowledge, technological sophistication in modern weapons and well-trained and brave soldiers are the answer. They may be the answer, but their aim cannot be achieved without much and huge suffering such as that which is going on.[41]

The Arabs had few friends in the House on that October day. Andrew Faulds, who had won back Smethwick for Labour in 1966, braved the indignation of many of his colleagues to say, 'It is Israel's intransigence which has made the fourth round of the Arab–Israeli conflict inevitable'. The Arabs were only reoccupying their own territory. Would anyone have called the D-Day landings to liberate Europe aggression, he thundered.[42] He voted with the government at the end of the debate, as did one or two other Labour MPs. In addition to Fraser, Gorst, Iremonger, Goodhart, and Sir Henry, a number of other Conservatives voted with the Opposition: Michael Fidler from Bury, Geoffrey Finsberg of Hampstead, Major-General Jack d'Avigdor-Goldsmid, and 'Mad Mitch', Lt. Colonel Colin Mitchell, formerly of the Argyll and Sutherland Highlanders, and some others. The revolt failed, however; the government carried the House by 251 votes to 175. The vote in the Commons did nothing much to alter events beyond Britain's shores which were to have a dramatic impact upon the economy and the government.

On 17 October the Organization of Arab Petroleum Exporting Countries (OAPEC) decided to cut back oil production by an immediate 5 per cent, with a further 5 per cent reduction to be imposed each month until a full settlement was reached with Israel on the lines of U.N. resolution 242 which, in part, called for an

Israeli withdrawal from the occupied Arab lands, but also called for the Arabs to make peace with Israel. Coincidentally with this and of much greater importance, a meeting of the Gulf states of the Oil Petroleum Exporting Countries (OPEC), including Iran, also decided to denounce earlier price agreements and impose new, much higher, price levels—a measure that had been coming for some time. It was partly the result of the realization by the exporting countries of the value of their assets and the fact that oil was virtually the only asset they had. New militant nationalist regimes had gained power in Algeria and Libya as well as earlier in Iraq and it was only a matter of time before they changed their relations with companies exploiting the oil. Libya shook the oil world in 1971 with a sudden decision to nationalize BP's Sarir concession. Market conditions had given the governments of the exporting countries a better chance to impose their will on the importing states. The Yom Kippur War of October 1973 speeded up the process. Continued American support for Israel led even the conservative, Western-orientated King Feisal of Saudi Arabia to favour the use of the oil as a weapon. The Shah of Iran, not involved in the Arab–Israeli quarrel, saw that his country's oil could be used to help him achieve his grandiose ambitions for Iran's economic development, and for his own role as a world statesman. Suddenly the industrial nations of the Western world seemed sentenced to a slow death, for increasingly their prosperity had been based on cheap oil from the Middle East. Attempts at intervention would have been met with Arab sabotage of the pipelines—with disastrous consequences. The Arabs pursued a policy of differentiating between states according to their attitude to the Arab cause. The British policy of neutrality helped the United Kingdom compared with some other European states. But oil prices soared and Britain was in a weaker position than many other industrial states to pay the extra cost.[43] Two-thirds of its oil came from the Middle East.

Heath's February election

Even without the oil crisis, Britain's economic situation was not good. Once again the balance of payments was in the red, inflation was worse than under Wilson, unemployment was higher. The pay policy had somehow staggered on to Stage Three. On 10 October the National Coal Board offered the miners 13 per cent. This they rejected and an overtime ban followed. Not only the oil-producers were growing aware of their power. The government had last faced confrontation with the miners in 1972 and had lost – after a costly strike. The industry had been declining for years. Its workforce had been cut from 593,000 in 1960 to 269,000 in 1973. Now suddenly it

237

looked as though mining was important again. The miners felt they could enforce higher rewards for the tough and still dangerous work they performed. In March 1973 seven miners were killed by floodwater at Lofthouse colliery. Another seven died in May in a pit collapse at Seafield colliery, Kirkcaldy. On 30 July eighteen miners lost their lives in a pit-cage accident at Markham colliery in Derbyshire. In 1973, 40,000 miners were suffering from 'The Dust' – pneumoconiosis,[44] accepted as incurable. Poor eyesight is another hazard in mining and there is a good chance of breaking a limb. Though they were no friends of the government, it is doubtful whether many wanted to strike – if they could avoid it. Strikes cost strikers money, strikes cost unions money, and strikes mean extra work for union officials. Joe Gormley (b. 1917), Irish-Lancastrian President of the National Union of Miners, and a Catholic, was not looking for trouble.

Mick McGahey (b. 1925), Vice-Chairman of the NUM, had got near the top without giving up all his genuine anger and determination to change the system. The son of a Scots miner, he was, like his father, a Communist. Gormley had beaten him for the chairmanship of the NUM, so he had to be content with the chairmanship of the Communist Party. He became a bogyman for the Conservatives, who greatly overestimated his influence.[45] The constant obsession with the Communists was probably an important factor in clouding the government's judgement and leading to its downfall. According to one serious account, Sir William Armstrong, who was very close to Heath, suffered greatly from this kink about Communists. He also suffered a nervous breakdown during the crisis.[46] Some of the other leading actors in the drama had their problems. William Whitelaw, tired from his ordeal in Northern Ireland, took over the equally vulnerable post of Secretary of State for Employment in December 1973. He was certainly no reactionary in Conservative terms, but equally he did not know much about the trade union movement. Heath himself was keeping up a killing pace, involved with Europe and Northern Ireland as well as domestic political problems in December. Len Murray was new to his job as General Secretary of the TUC and new also to top-line negotiating in private and media diplomacy in front of millions.

On 2 January 1974 the three-day working-week was introduced. Certain cuts had already been made in November in street-lighting, floodlighting, and television. A State of Emergency had been declared. Britain seemed to be sinking day by day. It was in this situation that on 9 January the TUC offered a possible way out: the government to treat the miners as a special case; other unions not to use the miners' settlement as an argument in trying to get better settlements for their own members. For the TUC this represented a big concession, one which could involve union leaders themselves in difficulties later. For the government it was not watertight. The Chancellor turned it down. Nevertheless, talks between the government and the NUM went on; but the gap between them was not bridged. On 24 January the miner's executive asked for a strike ballot of their members. On the same day the Pay Board published its report on relativities. This suggested a long-term arrangement for considering special cases left behind in the pay race. Neither the Board nor Whitelaw felt the miners' case should be investigated, as this would put too much pressure on the Board. Whitelaw later admitted he believed this was a mistake.[47] By 30 January, Heath was indicating that if the miners resumed normal working, their case could go to the Board. It was too late. The mood of the miners was revealed on 4 February when it was announced that almost 81 per cent of them had voted for a strike. Further talks and manoeuvres failed and on 7 February it was announced that a general election would take place on 28 February.

Evidence seems to suggest Heath wanted to avoid an election. He did not want one fought on the issue of the unions versus the government. He feared a massive Conservative victory would make his party reactionary.[48] Many Conservatives, though, not men like Whitelaw, Prior, or his speechwriter Michael Wolff, eagerly sought an election to isolate the miners. Had Heath been more resolute, events might have been quite different. In view of the energy crisis and the hard lot of the miners the government could have resolved early on to give the miners a good settlement and to be tough with the less deserving and less decisive. Practical people were coming to the conclusion the cure was worse than the disease. The coal strike began on 10 February.

No one could complain that there was no choice in the election of February 1974. When the nominations closed on 18 February, the total was 2,135 compared with 1,837 in 1970 and 1,868 in 1950, the previous record.[49] In addition to the three main parties, there were 54 National Front candidates, 44 Communists, Welsh Nationalists contesting all Welsh constituencies, there was a confusing array of candidates in Northern Ireland, and the Scottish National Party fielded 70 candidates. Labour was challenged by independents from its own ranks. On the right Dick Taverne was standing as a Social Democrat in his old constituency of Lincoln, four others who agreed with his views were standing elsewhere. On the left Eddie Milne stood for the constituency he had long represented—Blyth.

Labour could not have felt too happy about the election. It feared union unpopularity would drag it down. This could easily have happened, but, on the other hand, some felt Heath was being unnecessarily stubborn and bloody-minded. Was all the chaos really worth it, it was asked. As the campaign developed, a number of incidents strengthened this view. Bank profits announced during the month led to the feeling that Heath's society was an unfair society. On 19 February the National Westminster Bank announced a 50 per cent increase in its profits. Two days earlier Wilson appeared to have played a trump by revealing that he had succeeded in concluding a 'social contract' with the trade unions. This turned out to lack much substance, but it was good propaganda. Another blow was delivered against Heath on 26 February from a source which he least expected. Campbell Adamson, Director-General of the CBI, told a conference of managers he would like to see the next government repeal the Industrial Relations Act. (He had not realized his speech was being recorded!) How much influence Powell's remarks and advice to the electors had it is difficult to say. He campaigned against the Common Market. This was not, however, the main issue of the election. Speaking at Shipley on 25 February he advised Conservatives opposed to the EEC to vote Labour. The following day he admitted on television that he had already used his postal vote to support Labour; 'It would have been strange indeed if I had voted in any other way than the way in which I have advised the country to vote'.[50]

The strain of waiting was even worse than in 1964. For a time it looked as if Labour might be heading for a clear majority. By midnight such hopes for Labour had been dimmed. In the end Labour had to be content with less than a clear majority, having won 301 seats to 297 for the Conservatives. The Liberals were up from 6 to 14. The nationalists gained 9 seats and the extreme Ulster loyalists 11 of the 12 Northern Ireland seats. Gerry Fitt of the SDLP was also returned. The election gave something to all the politicians. The Liberal vote had gone up from 7.5 per cent in 1970 to 19.3 per cent. The Conservatives remained slightly ahead of Labour in actual votes. The nationalists had done well. Labour had improved its position over all and, after some days of manoeuvring with Thorpe, Heath was forced to concede that the man with the boat had this time been thwarted by the man with the pipe. The incumbents in Downing Street changed: the problems remained the same.

Notes

1 Andrew Roth, *Heath and the Heathmen* (London, 1972), 210.
2 Howard R Penniman, ed., *Britain at the Polls: the Parliamentary Elections of 1974* (Washington D.C., 1975), 5.
3 James Margach, *The Abuse of Power* (London, 1978), 160–1.

4 Penniman, op. cit., 11.
5 Angus Maude, *The Common Problem: a policy for the future* (London, 1969), 187; one of the most fluent expositions of the Conservative position.
6 *Pears Cyclopedia*, G54.
7 A.H. Thornton, *The Industrial Relations Bill For and Against* (University of Nottingham, 1971), 9.
8 ibid., 10.
9 ibid., 30.
10 Peter G. Richards, *The Local Government Act 1972: Problems of Implementation* (London, 1975), 156.
11 *Keesing's Contemporary Archives*, 24 June–30 June 1974, 26583A. Reginald Maudling, *Memoirs* (London, 1978), 196; see also Edward Milne, *No Shining Armour* (London, 1976), an MP's account of his fight against corruption in the north-east.
12 *Sunday Times*, 4 December 1977.
13 Maudling, op. cit., 193.
14 Frank Stacey, *British Government 1966-75* (London, 1975), 157–75 gives an account of the various proposals for NHS reform.
15 Richard Rose, *Governing without Consensus* (London, 1971), 111.
16 ibid., 112.
17 David McKie, Chris Cook, Melanie Phillips, *The Guardian/Quartet Election Guide* (London, 1978), 159.
18 Maudling, op. cit., 183.
19 ibid., 185.
20 McKie, Cook, Phillips, op. cit., 159.
21 Charles Townsend, *The British Campaign in Ireland 1919-1921* (London, 1975), 212.
22 Sir Edmund Compton, *Report of the inquiry into allegations against the security forces of physical brutality in Northern Ireland arising out of events on 9th August 1971,* Cmnd 4823 (HMSO, November 1971), 71.
23 Gordon Carr, *The Angry Brigade: the Cause and the Case* (London, 1975), 15.
24 Cecil King, *Diary 1970-74* (London, 1975), 79: 'Presumably this is the work of trades-union militants on the extreme Left'.
25 Carr, op. cit., 104.
26 ibid.
27 *Keesing's Contemporary Archives*, 13–20 February 1971, 24441.
28 Joseph Frankel, *British Foreign Policy 1945-1973* (London, 1975), 330.
29 Uwe Kitzinger, *Diplomacy and Persuasion: How Britain Joined the Common Market* (London, 1973), 293.
30 ibid., 392.
31 ibid., 396.
32 Henry Brandon, *The Retreat of American Power* (London, 1972), 167–8.
33 Henry Stanhope, *The Times*, 26 October 1973.
34 David Downing and Gary Herman, *War Without End, Peace Without Hope* (London, n.d.), 245.
35 Hansard (Commons), vol. 861, col. 424, 18 October 1973.
36 ibid., col. 426.
37 ibid., col. 426.
38 ibid., col. 440.
39 ibid., col. 441.
40 ibid., col. 449.
41 ibid., col. 479.
42 ibid., col. 498–9.
43 This is all covered in Christopher Tugendhat and Adrian Hamilton, *Oil the*

Biggest Business (London, 1975).
44 *Sunday Times,* 29 April 1973.
45 'The Fall of Heath: Part 2', by Stephen Fay and Hugo Young, *Sunday Times,* 29 February 1976.
46 *Sunday Times,* 7 March 1976.
47 *Sunday Times,* 29 February 1976, 7 March 1976.
48 *Sunday Times,* 22 February 1976.
49 David Butler and Dennis Kavanagh, *The British General Election of February 1974* (London, 1974), 89.
50 ibid., 105.

10 Labour's minority governments, 1974-79

Wilson's new Cabinet

Harold Wilson became Prime Minister once again on 4 March 1974. Heading Britain's first minority government since the Labour government of 1929-31, he faced a daunting prospect and he needed all his native wit and accumulated experience to master the situation. Labour had received its lowest share of the poll since 1931, and the Conservatives their lowest for over 50 years. His 1964 experience stood him in good stead and he resolved, once again, to act as if he had a working majority. He knew that the other parties would think twice before forcing another election on the country. His Cabinet was a talented one, the majority having had previous experience. He was able to bring back some well-known figures the country was used to: Healey as Chancellor of the Exchequer, Callaghan at the Foreign Office, and Roy Jenkins at the Home Office. Fred Peart took over once again the Ministry of Agriculture and Fisheries. Edward Short (b. 1912), the former Durham headmaster and wartime captain in the Durham Light Infantry, became Lord President of the Council and Leader of the House. He left this position and the Commons in 1976 to become Lord Glenamara. Anthony Crosland (1918-77), famous for his *Future of Socialism,* was put in charge of the Ministry of the Environment. The son of a senior civil servant and of a Plymouth Brethren family, Crosland went from Highgate School to Trinity College, Oxford where he gained a first in PPE. After wartime service as a captain in the Parachute Regiment, he became a Fellow of Trinity and lecturer in economics. He served Wilson at the Board of Trade, Local Government and Planning, and Environment. Crosland was a protégé of Hugh Dalton and a personal and political friend of Roy Jenkins. Jenkins, however, had very different antecedents. Born in 1920, he is the son of Arthur Jenkins, a Welsh miners' MP who had acted as secretary to Attlee. Like Crosland, Jenkins took a first in PPE at Oxford and during the war he served as a captain in the Royal Artillery. A highly successful author of biographical and historical works, including books on Attlee and Asquith, he was also director of operations for the John Lewis Partnership. First elected to Parliament in 1950, he had already served Wilson as Minister of Aviation, Home Secretary, and Chancellor. In 1976 he left British politics to become the President of the EEC Commission.

One small advance for women was that for the first time in British politics two women were included in the Cabinet, Barbara Castle and Shirley Williams. This too was reminiscent of the 1920s, in that MacDonald had appointed the first woman Cabinet Minister, Margaret Bondfield, in 1929. Mrs Castle took over Social Services and Mrs Williams was appointed to the new post of Secretary of State for Prices and Consumer Protection.

Shirley Williams (b. 1930) is the daughter of the late Sir George Catlin, the well-known academic and author. After attending St Paul's Girls' School and Somerville College, Oxford, she did postgraduate studies at Columbia University, New York. She worked on the *Financial Times* and as a teacher in Ghana before becoming the General Secretary of the Fabian Society. Mrs Williams began her political career at Oxford, where she was the first female President of the Labour Club. She stood as a Labour candidate at a by-election in 1954 and in the elections of 1955 and 1959, before her successful campaign in 1964. Prominent in Gaitskellite circles, she was also a pro-Marketeer and was Chairman of the Labour Committee for Europe. Before attaining Cabinet rank she had served in the ministries of Labour, Education, and at the Home Office. A Catholic and divorcee, Shirley Williams has a reputation for getting into fierce political arguments without making enemies.

The key left-wing figures in the government were Tony Benn and Michael Foot. Benn became Secretary of State for Industry, Foot was persuaded to tackle Employment. Both were the products of families with Liberal political traditions. The *bête noire* of Conservatives and Labour right-wingers alike, Tony Benn (b. 1925) is the son of William Wedgwood Benn, who was for many years a Liberal MP before joining Labour in 1927. William Wedgwood Benn was MacDonald's Secretary of State for India (1929-31). Created Viscount Stansgate in 1941, he served as air commodore in the RAFVR and was briefly in Attlee's government. Tony Benn also served in the RAFVR as a pilot officer. A former President of the Oxford Union, he worked as a BBC talks producer before being elected to the Commons in 1950. As mentioned above (p. 143), he fought to remain in the Commons when his father died in 1960. Benn was not regarded as a leftist during his earlier parliamentary career. Unlike most politicians, he seemed to move somewhat to the left in office (he was Wilson's Postmaster-General (1964-66) and Minister of Technology (1966-70)); the Left really started to love him, however, after 1971. He spoke out strongly for workers' participation and in favour of more public ownership. Because of this he was moved by Wilson from Industry to Energy in March 1975. Benn had been an early opponent of the Common Market, but in 1970 he was preaching in favour of British entry.

The world is so small that Britain alone cannot separate itself from world influence nor prevent its destiny being affected by what happens abroad ... Of course we can stay out and stand alone, but we will still find that European, American and Russian decisions will set the framework within which we would have to exercise our formal parliamentary sovereignty.[1]

As a member of the Wilson government he changed his mind again and became a key campaigner against entry. Michael Foot appears to see in him a future leader of the Labour Party.[2]

Michael Foot (b. 1913) is the son of Isaac Foot, the Liberal MP, and the brother of two Liberals who subsequently joined the Labour Party. He has remained consistently 'Bevanite' throughout his political career. He was educated at Wadham College, Oxford and was President of the Oxford Union in 1933. He earned his living as a journalist for Lord Beaverbrook and later became editor of the left-wing Labour weekly, *Tribune.* Though elected to the Commons in 1945, he lost his seat in 1955. He was subsequently elected in Bevan's old seat at Ebbw Vale in 1960, and wrote an important biography of Bevan. Though strongly in favour of public ownership, Foot has always been a libertarian socialist who has never shown any sympathy for any totalitarian states.

One other anti-Marketeer prominent in the government was Peter Shore (b. 1924), Secretary of State for Trade. A product of Quarry Bank High School in Liverpool and King's College, Cambridge, Shore served as head of the Labour Party Research Department at Transport House from 1959 to 1964. Responsible for the Labour publication *Twelve Wasted Years,* an attack on the Conservatives' record in office, he had been Deputy Leader of the House in 1969-70.

To the uninitiated Wilson must have seemed like a miracle-worker. Within a few days of his first Cabinet meeting the miners' strike was over, the nation was put back working full-time, and the State of Emergency was ended. The balance of payments deficit was larger than any before, though a considerable part of this was due to the increase in the price of oil, and therefore beyond Heath's or Wilson's control. An early Budget was required and Healey presented it on 26 March, with an increase in income tax and corporation tax. Up too went the duties on 'sin' – on cigarettes, wine, beer, spirits, and betting. Most people had expected a stiff Budget and such taxes on 'vice' could even be regarded as slightly morally uplifting. Harder was the announcement of price increases in the nationalized industries. These increases were designed to make the country more fuel conscious and make the industries concerned pay their way. Even the extension of value-added tax (VAT) to petrol and diesel oil could be seen as necessary and justified in view of the energy crisis. But was it necessary for Healey to put VAT on ice cream, soft drinks, and sweets? Healey's Budget was not all punishment. The old-age pensioners were promised the biggest increase ever and social security benefits were increased. Considerable food subsidies were also introduced and there was promise of stricter price control from Mrs Williams. The government took a hard look at prestige projects. The controversial scheme for a third London airport at Maplin was dropped and so was the Channel Tunnel scheme. Somehow Concorde was allowed to struggle onto the runway and eventually take to the air. Crosland took steps to discourage the sale of council houses, a rent freeze was introduced, and mortgages for owner-occupiers were subsidized because of the threat of increased interest charges. To a great extent the government appeared to be acting decisively to end irrelevant, divisive, and inflationary policies, and giving some help to the great mass of people at what was a difficult time. The attempt by Reg Prentice, Secretary of State for Education, to speed up the development of comprehensive education was less than universally popular, though many working-class parents saw it as offering their children a better chance in life.

The miners' strike was over, yet the government still had to prove it could successfully operate its Social Contract with the unions. It abolished the Pay Board, but allowed Stage Three of the pay policy, which came to an end in July, to run its course. It managed to steer clear of trouble with the engineering workers and, on the whole, there was relative peace in industry for the next few months. Not so in the National Health Service. In May nurses turned to strike action against low pay. They were given a substantial award of up to 30 per cent. In July hospital workers also turned to industrial action to reinforce their claim against poor pay. The government managed to get the Industrial Relations Act abolished and set up a Conciliation and Arbitration Service (ACAS) headed by Jim Mortimer, a socialist, former draughtsman, and trade union official with a degree in economics from London University. Except for the troubled motor-car industry, there appeared to be a reasonable chance that government and unions could co-operate. This was especially so after the September conference of the TUC at which the Prime Minister and unions agreed on moderate wage settlements for the coming year. Healey had introduced a second Budget on 22 July, cutting VAT and announcing help for ratepayers. It was a good Budget for an approaching election without being an obvious bribe.

Northern Ireland was very troublesome again in 1974. As we have seen, at the general election, the friends of Ian Paisley had almost swept the board for Ulster's Westminster seats. This encouraged the extreme Protestants to greater militancy. On 15 May the authorities were apparently taken by surprise by a massive strike of Protestant workers against the proposed Council of Ireland. Probably Merlyn Rees, the minister responsible, made a mistake by not receiving the strike leaders. The Northern Ireland Executive collapsed and direct rule was reintroduced. The bombings continued, provoking fear and anger. In May a bomb exploded in a car park at London's Heathrow Airport. On 17 June another went off beside Westminster Hall, injuring eleven people. In the following month there were explosions in Birmingham and Manchester and again at Heathrow. The bomb which went off at the Tower of London on 17 July killed one person and injured forty-one. In October two bombs in crowded pubs at Guildford killed five and injured seventy. There were other explosions later in the year. All these outrages were attributed to, or claimed by, the Provisional IRA. The Prevention of Terrorism Act, given the Royal Assent in November, was the frightening response to a frightening situation.

One other terrorist attack which did not succeed was the attempt to kidnap Princess Anne in London on 20 March. Only the quick reaction and bravery of her personal bodyguard, James Beaton, foiled the plot in which four people were injured. Beaton himself was severely wounded in the attack. Perhaps as a result of this particular failure, kidnapping did not increase in Britain.

The situation abroad looked as tense, changeable, and dramatic as at home. In Israel, Golda Meir and her Cabinet resigned in April. This marked a weakening of the hold of the Israeli Labour Party on the government of the state which they had ruled continuously since 1948. In May, Willy Brandt, the Social Democratic Chancellor of West Germany, resigned because one of his aides was exposed as an East German agent. Helmut Schmidt, also a Social Democrat, replaced him. In France, President Pompidou died suddenly and Valéry Giscard d'Estaing was elected in his place in May, an event to be of some significance, though it should not be exaggerated, in the growing closeness of Franco-German relations; Schmidt and Giscard are reputed to be close personal friends. More dramatic still was the resignation in August of President Nixon after a long campaign against him because of the Watergate scandal. His successor as 38th President of the United States was Gerald Ford. Nixon and Heath had been political allies. Also of importance was the *coup* which led to the overthrow of the Portuguese dictatorship, which had managed to maintain itself, resisting the winds of change, since 1926. This was rapidly to change the situation in southern Africa because the new regime immediately started to bring to a close the disastrous colonial war and to dismantle its African empire, with grave consequences for the Smith regime in neighbouring Rhodesia. Another apparently permanent feature on the international scene was turned out by his armed forces in September – Haile Selassie of Ethiopia. This too had consequences for East and West, for the Russians and the Americans, in Africa. Of more direct importance for the British government was the overthrow of Archbishop Makarios of Cyprus in July. Later in the same month the island was invaded by Turkish troops. The British government attempted to mediate between Greece and Turkey over the issue, with only moderate success. The government cancelled Royal Navy visits to Greece and Chile, states where the democratic governments had been overthrown by the military. If anything, this raised Britain's prestige abroad, especially as in Greece the military regime collapsed. It certainly helped the government with its own backbenchers who were offended by a Royal Navy visit to South Africa and by the government's agreement to honour a contract for a destroyer for the Chilean Navy. Undoubtedly the government's main initiative abroad was its renegotiation of Britain's terms of entry into the EEC, started by Callaghan in April.

October election, 1974

The Conservatives faced a dilemma after February 1974. They risked public indignation if they appeared too partisan, if they appeared to be trying to bring down the government merely for narrow party reasons. Yet not to fight the government was to demoralize their own supporters still further. Heath tried to justify the Party's tactics in Parliament as follows:

What is the point of giving the present government the opportunity of having a general election? Say we had been able to defeat them . . . and a general election was called before the country itself realised the disastrous direction in which the Labour Party is leading us, what is the point in that?[3]

This explanation did not recommend itself to the great majority of his supporters. The Conservative leader, never in an unassailable position, was under pressure from his opponents within the Party to resign. One factor which held them back was the near certainty of an early election. Nor was Heath helped by the loss of some prominent members of his team. Sir Alec, Anthony Barber, and Christopher Chataway, the former athlete and TV journalist who had reached Cabinet rank under Heath, all announced their retirement from politics. They all gave personal reasons, but their departure appeared to cast doubt on their belief in an early Conservative return to office.

The inevitable election came in October. Both major parties were on the defensive. The Conservatives, it could be claimed, had run away from office in the first place and thus brought the country to its present pass. Labour was suffering from splits and defections. The members of the government were at twos and threes over the EEC, with ministers more or less contradicting each other in public. Christopher Mayhew gave up a safe seat to fight Bath for the Liberals. On 22 September, Lord Chalfont defected, claiming the Left had taken over the Labour Party. His loss was not as great as that of Mayhew, but he was one of Wilson's discoveries and protégés who had, before his ministerial appointment in 1964, been Defence correspondent of *The Times*. He had never really had any connection with the Labour movement. This was true of another casualty, Lord Brayley, Under Secretary for the Army, another of Wilson's protégés, a self-made businessman who died of cancer before allegations of financial irregularities in respect of his company could be cleared up. Wilson's name was mentioned in connection with his one-time office manager, Anthony Field, brother of Marcia Williams, who was involved in a 'land reclamation' scheme in the north-west. Some felt this was the kind of land deal which Labour had long denounced. Mrs Williams herself was rewarded for her hard work on behalf of Wilson by a peerage, which had been announced in April. This was also the period when Alderman Cunningham and T. Dan Smith were facing trial and conviction for their activities (above p. 225). The impact of it all was lessened by the exposure of forgeries connected with allegations against Harold Wilson and Edward Short. Nevertheless, the whiff of scandal probably helped to make Labour supporters more apathetic. As for Wilson, he appeared to be guilty of only one fault, bad judgement of men; but this was a serious fault in a leading politician.

The smaller parties were not all that happy about the election: for them it meant substantial expenditure they could not afford. The Liberals had to fear that, as so often when there is a Labour government, right-of-centre waverers turn away from them to the Conservatives. Only the various anti-power-sharing Ulster Unionists could go into the campaign with confidence; come what may, most of them would be returned once again to Westminster. This time they had the added attraction of Enoch Powell, who had joined them as the candidate for the safe Unionist seat of South Down. This did not stop him from once again letting it be known that he would vote Labour because Labour stood for a referendum on the EEC.

On 10 October, polling-day, the sky was overcast and there were showers in various parts of the country, 72.8 per cent of the electorate, 5.3 per cent fewer than in February, braved the grey and gloom to record their votes. They gave the Conservatives 35.8 per cent – their lowest percentage vote since 1935 – and put Labour back with a majority over all the other parties of just three. This majority was based on winning back three seats from rebel ex-Labour MPs in Lincoln, Sheffield Brightside, and Blyth. Labour's vote was up by 2.1 per cent, giving them 39.2 per cent. As for the Liberals, neither their greatest hopes nor their worst fears were realized. They lost 1 per cent of their vote and (net) one seat. Surveys had shown there was some confusion about what the Liberals stood for, and within the Party there were sharp divisions: 'Was the party on the "left", as many of its activists insisted or in the "moderate centre" as most of its MPs suggested? The party's vote was, if anything, drawn more from the Conservatives than from Labour, and its policies were also closer to the Conservatives'.[4] With a hundred more candidates the Liberal vote was actually three-quarters of a million less. The anti-immigrant, reactionary, National Front fielded ninety candidates, without success. It seemed to take votes from all parties equally and gained most support in the East End of London. The only parties which could count the election as a real victory were the anti-power-sharing Ulster Unionists – though they lost one seat on a recount – and the Scottish National Party. Both increased their support, the SNP dramatically so. Eleven SNP representatives were returned to the Commons, four more than in February; their gains were at Conservative expense. In Wales the nationalists, Plaid Cymru, increased their representation from two to three. They took one seat from Labour, but were Labour-orientated in their outlook on most issues. It was difficult to be certain what the electors expected or wanted. Clearly they did not have much time for the Conservatives, but they were not all that enthusiastic about Labour either.

Sociologically speaking, British politics had not changed much since 1945. The Conservatives still had a majority among women voters, but only just. Women, 52 per cent of the electorate, had pretty consistently saved the Conservatives from defeat in 1951, 1955, 1959, and 1970. In terms of social class the Conservatives still commanded the support of 63 per cent of the middle class (to Labour's 12) and 51 per cent of the lower-middle class (to Labour's

24). Labour's greatest support in social-class terms was still among the unskilled and 'very poor', 33 per cent of the voters, 57 per cent of whom declared for Labour as against only 22 per cent for the Conservatives. In terms of age the Conservatives had a majority of 49 per cent to 37 per cent for Labour among the over 65s, 20 per cent of the electorate. Labour enjoyed its greatest advantage among the 18-24 age-group, who formed only 11 per cent of the electorate. Labour also enjoyed a massive majority among the 2 per cent of 'coloured' voters, a category which did not exist in any significant numbers before 1964.[5]

In terms of the background of MPs one could, once again, ask of the Conservatives, 'Whatever happened to the Tory trade unionists? Whatever happened to Mr Industrial Charter?' Just two Conservatives out of 277 MPs were listed as skilled workers. In terms of occupation 55 were barristers, 38 were company directors, 23 company executives, and 23 farmers. Labour still returned 89 MPs who could be classed as workers, including five clerks, among its 319 MPs. Many of these were former trade union officials. Indeed, one estimate puts the decline of the genuine worker representation as from 27.6 per cent in 1945 to 12 per cent in 1974.[6] Labour MPs were much better educated than in 1945. The percentage of graduates had increased from 43.2 per cent in 1945 to about 56 per cent in 1974. Among the Conservatives 64.7 per cent were graduates in 1945 and over 67 per cent in 1974.[7] Labour's graduates, however, represented much more the expansion of higher education since 1945. Of the 182 Labour university-educated MPs, 102 were from non-Oxbridge institutions, as against only 35 of the 190 Conservative graduates. Labour is in danger of becoming a party of the provincial lower-middle class, drawn especially from the teaching and, to a lesser extent, the legal profession. The Conservatives remain largely the party of the middle and upper-middle classes, particularly from the southern half of England. In neither case do MPs represent the great variety of professions and skills of the advanced industrial society which Britain is. In neither case do they really represent the great majority of voters who are manual or white-collar workers. No one would suggest they become a microcosm of Britain's trades and professions. But are there not dangers when Parliament is so unrepresentative? In one other sense Parliament is unrepresentative: in Britain since 1945 women have provided only a fairly consistent 4 per cent of MPs. This compares with around 22 per cent in Sweden and Finland, and about 2 per cent in France, Canada, and the United States.[8] Labour has consistently given more women their opportunity to be legislators than the Conservatives, or Liberals.

Britain's EEC referendum

One of the first problems for the new Wilson administration was how to resolve the explosive issue of Britain's membership of the EEC. It could not renege on its promise to put the results of the renegotiation before Parliament and people. A White Paper on the renegotiations was published on 27 March. The four main areas of negotiation were the Common Agricultural Policy; the level of contributions to the EEC budget; relations with the Commonwealth and developing states; and Britain's ability to pursue its own regional and industrial policies. Some concessions were gained. A plan was agreed under which member states would be eligible for reimbursements on their contributions to the budget on the basis of their gross national product and economic growth. Britain also managed to negotiate concessions on sugar, beef, and New Zealand dairy products. The renegotiated package was presented to Parliament in April. The Commons then voted by 396 to 170 in favour. The government had to rely on the Conservatives and Liberals to get the legislation through. Only 135 Labour MPs voted in favour. The pro- and anti-Marketeers in the Cabinet had agreed to differ. Seven Cabinet ministers rejected the renegotiated terms – Castle, Benn, Foot, Ross, Shore, John Silkin, and Varley – because they thought EEC membership would be 'markedly unfavourable' from the economic point of view. 'But the gravest disadvantages are political'. They saw these as the inevitable shift of power from the elected Commons to the non-elected Commission and Council of Ministers in Brussels. And they claimed:

Timid voices and vested interests will now combine in seeking to persuade us we have no choice; that Britain outside the Common Market would suffer great disadvantage. Do not believe them. On the contrary, a far greater danger to our legitimate economic interest, to the continued unity of the UK, and to the practice of democracy in this country arises from our continued membership of the EEC.[9]

Powell also saw the central issue as political:

Opinion has been right to fasten upon sovereignty as the central issue. Either British entry is a declaration of intent to surrender this country's sovereignty, stage by stage, in all that matters to a nation, and makes a nation, or else it is an empty gesture, disgraceful in its hollowness alike to those who proffer and to those who accept it.[10]

Labour's promised referendum took place in June. Only 64.5 per cent of the electorate bothered to vote. They gave the pro-EEC forces a two-to-one majority in favour of the renegotiated terms: 17.3 million voted 'Yes', 8.4 million 'No'. The 'Yes' vote represented 43 per cent of the total eligible to vote. The Labour Party special conference had voted overwhelmingly on 26 April against EEC membership. Delegates were not convinced by the argument that the socialists were the biggest group in the European Parliament and that, together with the Communists and left Christian Democrats, there was likely to be a majority in favour of the working classes in that Parliament. But it could be argued the European Parliament is weak without effective powers. During the referendum Michael Foot joined Enoch Powell to oppose the Market. The Communists and the Welsh and Scots Nationalists also joined the anti-EEC camp. They were opposed, however, by a powerful alliance of the Establishment, most of the press, and big business. Both sides were given free facilities to send their views to each voter, and both had equal time on television. Most of the ordinary voters appeared baffled by the arguments about wine lakes and butter mountains, about sugar and sovereignty, beef and bureaucrats, New Zealand cheese and Italian Communists. Some were persuaded that without an empire Britain needed new friends, others that having joined, Britain would have to pay a heavy penalty for leaving; more by the possibility of emulating the 'economic miracles' of western Europe; and still more by the smiles or frowns of their favourite politicians when the EEC was mentioned. Many members of the 'silent majority' felt that if Benn, Powell, and the Communists were against the EEC, it must be a good thing. Many trade unionists, despite Vic Feather's argument to the contrary, believed that if BP, ICI, the big banks, and Uncle Sam thought Britain ought to join, then it could only be bad for Britain. The more thoughtful reflected on what would happen to a lonely Britain nearing the year 2000 faced with high trade barriers, built by mighty new states armed with cheap labour and modern technology, capable of waging fierce trade wars for political as well as economic reasons. They believed it would be better to co-operate with states with similar values, similar standards, and similar problems than to be forced to rely on the goodwill of totalitarian or unstable regimes, of Japanese corporations, or even their American cousins.[11]

The high hopes of the pro-EEC European movement on British entry had not really been achieved by the end of 1978. Lord Thomson, pro-EEC Cabinet minister under Harold Wilson, and later a member of the Commission of the EEC, wrote in July 1977,

These early years in the Community were a dispiriting experience . . . We found when we arrived an immense fund of goodwill, affection and underlying respect for British capacity and character. The following three years – 1973 confrontation; 1974 renegotiation; 1975 referendum – have substantially run down our working capital of goodwill.[12]

Thomson claimed that the uncertainty about Britai s intentions both put off West European investors from transferring capital to the United Kingdom and made it difficult for British industrialists to plan their investment. A Conservative Party publication soberly assessed developments:

The UK's accession to the EEC . . . offered great opportunities to British exporters, by opening up an enormous free trade market for manufactured goods. It was unfortunate that a major slump in world trade should occur so shortly after the UK's accession . . . Confidence in the export industries was shaken, and British exports have been insufficient to balance the increased penetration of the UK market by our EEC partners . . . The competitive advantage gained from sterling's depreciation, and the trend towards self-sufficiency in oil, should enable the UK to achieve a favourable balance in our total trade with our EEC partners.[13]

That is the hope; so far, the reality has been a heavy British deficit on trade with the EEC. This deficit had grown from £191 million in 1971 to £2,412 million in 1975. It fell to £1,733 million in 1977. In that year Britain's total deficit was £1,709 million on all its world trade.[14] The EEC's Common Agricultural Policy (CAP), designed for economies with relatively large agricultural sectors, continued to work to Britain's disadvantage. As one pro-EEC Labour Party writer put it, 'There is certainly evidence to show that because about 70 per cent of the Community budget is spent on agriculture, and because Britain is a large importer of food and other commodities, she gets less return on her budgetary contributions than other member countries'.[15] The same writer went on to point out that Britain paid less than her gross domestic product share on agricultural levies to the Community,

but more (over 20 per cent) on customs duties because she is a large importing country. Though she ranks seventh when it comes to GDP per head, in 1976 Britain was the third highest contributor per head (£3.90) following Germany and Belgium. By 1982 Britain could be the largest net contributor to the Community despite her comparative poverty.[16]

On a positive note, Britain has received over £1,500 million in loans at favourable interest rates from the EEC and over £500 million in grants during its period of membership.[17] Another controversial area of EEC policy was aid to and trade with the developing countries. In February 1975 the Lomé Convention had been signed by the EEC states and 46 developing countries: most of Africa as well as Caribbean and Pacific countries. According to Judith Hart, Labour's Minister of Overseas Development at the time, it 'reflects a new relationship which replaces paternalism by co-operation'.[18] Since then another 10 developing countries have negotiated their accession to the Convention. As Britain and the other EEC states approached the first direct elections to the European Parliament, polls reflected apathy among the voters in the majority of the Community states, including Britain.[19]

Problems with industrial management

One of the key items in the Queen's Speech on 29 October 1974 was the proposal for a National Enterprise Board, subsequently set up under the Industry Act of 1975. The NEB became a state holding company to administer government holdings of shares in companies, acquire additional ones, and give financial assistance to businesses in trouble. It removed restrictions on the Secretary of State for Industry, included in the Conservatives' Industry Act of 1972, which prevented him acquiring more than 50 per cent of the equity share capital, and required him to dispose of any share acquired as soon as it was practical to do so. The Act gave the NEB a budget of £1,000 million, and it was not long before the NEB had a long line of customers asking for loans. Under the British Leyland Act of 1975 the NEB acquired 95 per cent of the equity of that ailing motor giant. Ferranti Ltd followed, with the NEB taking 50 per cent of the ordinary voting shares. Rolls-Royce (1971) Ltd, already publicly owned, became part of the NEB empire. Other firms were subsequently assisted. Among these was the American-owned Chrysler company, which needed, and got, over £162 million in order to avoid a total shut-down with the loss of about 27,000 jobs. Chrysler was not taken over. The government did, however, take over the ailing aerospace and shipbuilding industries after being forced to drop nationalization of ship-repairing companies in order to get its legislation through. Though the Conservatives tried to denounce much that the government did in this direction as doctrinaire socialism, it is doubtful whether they would have done much else, judged by the record of Heath's administration. Had the government not intervened, unemployment would have gone much higher and so would the cost of unemployment relief. As it was, the government was hoping to rationalize these long-troubled industries as well as nationalize them. It did get involved in what amounted to denationalization by selling off a profitable block of shares acquired by British Petroleum, itself partly owned by the state, during the earlier rescue operation for Burmah Oil; this was to placate Britain's creditors abroad and allowed some cutting down on borrowing. In November 1975 the government held a meeting at Chequers of union chiefs and industrialists to look at the problems of industry and government policy on them. This led to an agreement which identified 30 sectors of industry deserving of government attention and help, either because they were intrinsically likely to succeed, or because state assistance could make the difference between success and failure, or because they were thought vital to the success of others. It looked sensible enough, concentrating the limited resources where they could do the most good. But in practice it proved not so simple. The government also recognized the importance of the small firm to the economy. Whether it was a result of inspiration provided by E. F. Schumacher in his book *Small is Beautiful* or merely an indirect attempt to make life with the Liberals and Nationalists more tolerable is not clear.

Britain's difficulty as a manufacturing nation was highlighted by a calculation of Dr Frank Jones, industrialist and inventor. According to Jones, in 1976 total assets per employee in manufacturing industry stood at £7,500. In Japan the total assets supporting each employee in manufacturing industry amounted to just over £30,000 at the 1976 rate of exchange. The figure for West German industry was about £23,000 per employee.

The discrepancy in assets per employee of between three and four times has been crucial in enabling the Japanese and German employee to manufacture at two or three times our productivity. Much the same situation applies in the US industry where the asset figure per employee lies between the German and Japanese figures with productivity about three times that in the United Kingdom. The gap gets wider each year and to bring our industry into line . . . would even now mean finding a way of usefully employing a further £100,000 million of assets whilst maintaining only the present labour force.[20]

The problem has been to identify the reason for the missing £100,000 in investments. Jones put it down to government tax policies taking too much from industry. As we have seen, others claim that too much capital has been exported over a long period. The banking system has also been criticized in this respect. John Carrington and George Edwards, writing in *Management Today* (December 1978), a publication of the British Institute of Management, believe British banks should learn from Japanese banks and from British building societies on improving methods to ensure the financing of long-term loans to industry. While not claiming that this was the sole cause of Britain's poor industrial performance, they wrote: in France, Japan, and West Germany

which transfer saving into industrial investment more efficiently than we do in the UK, government acts as a long-stop guarantor (via the central bank) against a run on the banks, so ensuring their liquidity. Second, government, having acted as the long stop and confidence giver, leaves it to the banks' financial expertise to decide where loans should be placed. Funds are, in fact, placed after the banks have carefully analysed, not what assets are available to cover the loan, but what the chances are of the investment facilitated by the loan generating sufficient cash flow to service the debt and to produce a further margin. . . . This is perhaps the key difference between an expanding (Japan) and a static (UK) economy . . .

British building societies, they argued, operated in ways similar to foreign banks by

lending long from short-term deposits, and thus reduce the cash-flow cost of debt while retaining flexible interest rates that do not overtly inconvenience borrowers, but do ensure a continued inflow of deposits. If such a mechanism were adopted by the banks in Britain for their industrial customers, under the umbrella of arms-length guarantees of liquidity by government, as in Japan, Britain would stand to reap considerable growth benefits similar to those long experienced by both Japan and West Germany.

Controversy about British management and its contribution to the so-called 'British sickness', economic malaise, has continued from at least the early 1950s, and was even seriously discussed in the late nineteenth century. There was a feeling that British employers were less well qualified than their West German, American, or Japanese rivals, and that they understood their employees less. There was also the feeling that foremen, technicians, and professional engineers were less well qualified and undervalued. Three writers who had studied German firms put this point about foremen, in *Management Today* (March 1978), emphasizing that compared with his British colleague, the German *Meister* was better qualified and enjoyed a higher status. The Select Committee on Science and Technology, in its third report (October 1976), could not come to any firm conclusions about the reasons for British manufacturing industry's poor performance. But it felt that the mutual suspicions of industry and universities towards each other were a reason why not enough able people were going into industry. It also believed that there were still far too many directors of British companies who were unqualified in the appropriate field.

Certainly evidence has been produced to show that in the 1970s university engineering students were less well qualified at the start of their courses than students in other disciplines.[21] The standard of engineering graduates has also been criticized and the lack of co-operation between industry and the universities has been blamed as a factor in this. It has also been suggested that the low status of the professional engineer is to blame for the failure to attract more, and more talented, applicants. An expert committee of inquiry, set up by the Conservative Party, commented in July 1978,

The title 'engineer' is much misused in Britain. It has never been reserved to

257

denote exclusively a person of high professional skills and competence. Anyone may style himself an engineer without the need for any test of ability. The results are not difficult to foresee. At the present time the engineering profession in this country is accorded little prestige by comparison with, for example, those of law and medicine although the training is just as demanding and frequently lónger. It is not surprising therefore that the more able school-leavers turn away from engineering as a career and look elsewhere for what they regard as more attractive and prestigious outlets for their abilities.[22]

In Britain many managers, top executives, and businessmen have not received a higher education. In Japan, by comparison, 'A university education constitutes, with few exceptions, the single most important prerequisite to qualify for managerial rank'. However, preference is given to graduates of certain leading universities, with corporation executives recruiting the next generation of bosses from their own old universities.[23] In Germany too a university education is normal for the executives of large firms. Ten years ago Graham Turner, then the economics correspondent of the BBC, believed, after three years' research, that

One of the more obvious reasons why many British companies perform unimpressively is that the men who run them lack the will to do better. They aim low and are satisfied with modest performances; exhibit a marked lack of the self-critical faculty; and put a quiet (though not ostentatious) life high on their list of priorities.[24]

Turner rejected the view that high taxation was responsible for this situation, recalling that in 1901 an observer of British management had listed 'indifference' as one of the major problems of British management.[25]

A Brookings Institution team headed by Professor Richard E. Caves of Harvard came to much the same conclusion in 1974. They claimed:

Nowhere else does the middle class make such extensive use of private schools and bear such financial burdens to avoid sending children to state-supported schools. Whatever may be said in favour of Britain's private schools, one result of the system is to create two distinct social groups that share no common educational experience. The economic life of the nation cannot be separated from the social context, and lack of common schooling inevitably hampers the kind of communication needed to improve industrial relations.

The prevalence of private schools undoubtedly reinforces the prejudice against being 'in trade'. Although Britain is an urban industrial society, the social ideal of many Britons is still the country squire living on his lands.

The middle-class and upper-class disdain for industry is matched by a curious reluctance among lower-class people to take advantage of what opportunities exist to rise through the management hierarchy, normally an important channel of social mobility in advanced countries.

The team gave British management low marks for professional quality. For instance, the study concluded that overmanning was mainly the fault of management, not the unions, and that financial controls were often deficient. The investigation did, however, point out that Britain's poor growth-record went back a hundred years. 'Industry's chronic reluctance to invest is not due to a lack of savings or of company liquidity, and has not responded much to tax incentives'.[26] If all of this was only half right, it was a sad indictment. It was also the kind of survey which did Britain's image no good and helped to undermine confidence in the British economy and currency. The alleged social exclusiveness of much of management had, of course, been attacked by the Royal Commission on the Public Schools in the 1960s:

Some have expressed a more extreme view to us. Britain, they say, cannot flourish without leaders, and leadership could not flourish without the public schools. Public school headmasters are among those who blush for the philosophical, historical and sociological naïveté that such a proposition enshrines. Have other nations without such a system of education – the Israelis, the Japanese, the Swedes – no leaders? Have we no other source of leaders? The Robbins Report is only one of the more recent studies to demonstrate the abundant reserves of talent in this country. Much of this talent is only gradually beginning to surmount the handicaps imposed, first, by home circumstances and, secondly, by a restrictive system of secondary schooling. Justice and efficiency both demand that nobody of character and ability should be denied the chance of achieving professional competence which is the prerequisite of leadership. Our country would prosper more if greater efforts were made to attain this ideal.[27]

Margaret Thatcher

Having lost three elections out of four it was inevitable that Edward Heath should have been under great pressure to vacate the leadership of the Conservative Party, or at least submit himself for re-election. He accepted the challenge by accepting the recommendations of a party committee, the Home Committee, that when the Conservative Party was in opposition, there should be an annual election for the leadership. This was put into effect on 4 February when Heath was opposed by Mrs Margaret Thatcher and Hugh Fraser, the MP for Stafford and Stone. The result revealed the erosion of Heath's support. He was only able to muster 119 votes to Thatcher's 130, and Fraser's 16. Heath decided to throw in the towel and retire to the backbenches. The nagging doubt remains that if he had been determined to fight it out, he might well have beaten Margaret Thatcher on the second ballot. Some later doubted that a woman could really lead the Conservative Party to victory, and Heath certainly remained a shadow over Mrs Thatcher during the next four years. On the second ballot for the leadership there were no less than five candidates, perhaps a sign of the doubts about Margaret Thatcher. She nevertheless emerged as the clear winner with 146 out of 271 votes cast. William Whitelaw received 76, Sir Geoffrey Howe and James Prior 19 each, and John Peyton only 11. Fraser had decided not to stand. In 1975 Margaret Thatcher had thus made history, becoming the first woman to lead a major British political party.

She burst on to the political stage in 1959 when she was elected MP for Finchley. She had already unsuccessfully sought a par-liamentary seat. Her victory at Finchley was quite a feat in that the Conservative Party has shown itself less sympathetic to women than Labour, and Labour's record is by no means good. Margaret Thatcher already had a number of achievements behind her, far more than most women of her age and social class. Her father was a grocer who became mayor of Grantham. She made her way on scholarships from Kesteven and Grantham Girls' School to Som-merville College, Oxford, where she read chemistry and gained a BSc and MA. Not content with this, she read law and was called to the Bar in 1954. Married to a businessman since 1951, she was able to get her childbearing over quickly by having twins, a boy and a girl, in 1953. Obviously she had tremendous dedication, drive, and determination, as well as intelligence, to go on climbing up and up the ladder. Having a constituency in London was some help, given even the minimum of domestic responsibility. The comforts of a well-off home were clearly important. Even more important was an understanding husband; 'both of us have been so interested in work that it was always accepted that, somehow, work had to come first'. He 'was always *there* – anything I wanted he could provide, and he was always *there*. His being older may have had a lot to do with this'.[28] Just as important was being well organized: 'I make lists of things to do and get lots of pleasure ticking them off'.[29] Mrs Thatcher dresses so that 'one gets the impression that she has worked hard to achieve a look guaranteed never to offend or distract'. This is certainly not true of her political utterances. On education, defence, immigration, and, most recently, trade unions, she has taken aback her more moderate colleagues. One of her weaknesses is that she has not held any of the great offices of state, but then that was equally true of Harold Wilson in 1964. It was also true of Edward Heath, though he had had more experience than Thatcher when he became leader in 1965. Another of her weaknes-ses is the impression of trying hard to convey the image of a suburban housewife from the stockbroker belt. Shirley Williams, from a far more privileged background, and a product of the same college of the same university, had in the 1970s a much younger, more classless aura about her.

Thatcher retained the services of that experienced champion of moderation William Whitelaw. Lord Hailsham soldiered on in her cause, as did John Davies. Lord Carrington (b. 1919), who had been Heath's Minister of Defence, led the Party in the Lords. James Prior, formerly Lord President of the Council and Leader of the House, came into prominence as shadow employment minister. Sir Geoffrey Howe (b. 1926), who had served as Solicitor-General, and then as Minister for Trade and Consumer Affairs (1970-72), also played a prominent role in Mrs Thatcher's team, as shadow chancellor. A barrister, Queen's Counsel, he went from Winchester to Trinity Hall, Cambridge. The son of a coroner, Howe had long been associated with the liberal wing of the Conservative Party. This was also true of the spokesman on education, Norman St John-Stevas (b. 1929), a barrister, prominent Catholic, and former President of the Cambridge Union. Among the more rugged right-wingers appointed by Margaret Thatcher was Airey Neave (1916-79), an old Etonian company director and Second World War Colditz hero, to cover Northern Ireland. The other lady in the Tory team, Mrs Sally Oppenheim (b. 1928), is the daughter of a diamond-cutter and Sheffield tycoon. Educated at RADA, she became spokesman on consumer affairs. The one other prominent member of the shadow cabinet was the dark and brooding figure of Sir Keith Joseph, a senior member of the Macmillan, Home, and Heath governments. Businessman, barrister, and former Fellow of All Souls, Oxford, Sir Keith seemed to want to tilt the Conservative Party away from the consensus politics of Macmillan towards a more doctrinaire, right-wing Conservatism. In this he sounded more like Mrs Thatcher than Whitelaw.

Callaghan becomes Prime Minister

Just over a year after Heath's departure, his great adversary decided to go. It was a shock for the Parliamentary Labour Party to learn on 16 March 1976 that Harold Wilson had resigned. He claimed that he had made up his mind to do this when he took office in March 1974. He could claim that thirty years on the front bench was long enough for anyone. He was proud of the fact that he had served for eight years as Prime Minister – longer than any other post-war Prime Minister. He claimed he wanted to give others their chance, and the new Prime Minister the possibility to establish himself before going to the country. Wilson's sudden departure, nevertheless, caused speculation that there were perhaps other reasons for his resignation – running away from escalating economic problems for instance; after all he was only sixty years old.

One other aspect of Harold Wilson's resignation was baffling: his final honours list. Somehow he did not seem quite right in his Knight of the Garter attire. But the chuckles and derisive laughter at this were nothing compared with the anger caused, among Wilson's own colleagues and supporters, and the press, by the ennoblement of the show-business tycoons Lew Grade and Bernard Delfont, the Gannex raincoat-manufacturer Sir Joseph Kagan, and Sir Max Rayne, the property millionaire. The knighthood for James Goldsmith, the City of London financier and contributor to Conservative Party funds, caused equal anger and derision. In 1978 Lord Kagan fled to Israel after a warrant had been issued for his arrest for tax and currency offences. *The Times* asked, 'Who could wish for inclusion in a roll call giving rise to universal astonishment and derision?'[30] It was a sad ending to such a long career in politics. Certainly, Sir Harold had had more than his fair share of suffering from the 'slings and arrows of outrageous fortune', but he had suffered just as much from self-inflicted wounds, and this was just one more of them.

As Wilson was no doubt aware, there was no shortage of would-be successors. Six candidates stood in the first round. On the first ballot Michael Foot led with 90 votes, James Callaghan secured 84, Roy Jenkins did less well than expected with 56, Tony Benn did reasonably well with 37, Denis Healey got a disappointing 30, and Anthony Crosland flopped with only 17. The second ballot produced 141 for Callaghan, 133 for Foot, and 38 for Healey. The final outcome was Callaghan 176 to Foot's 137. Foot's performance must have been very satisfying for him. It reflected the improvement in the position of the Left in the Parliamentary Labour Party as compared with the old Bevanite days. It was, however, in part a mark of his personal standing. Many who did not always agree with him admired his great ability, his personal integrity, and his loyalty to the Commons and to the Labour Party. One other factor came into it. The wounds of the Common Market campaign had not yet healed, and this had certainly gone against Jenkins on the first ballot. Foot probably picked up some votes on the third ballot because of his strong opposition to the EEC.

Sensibly, the new Prime Minister recognized Foot's strength in the Party and appointed him Lord President and Leader of the House. Crosland took over from Callaghan at the Foreign Office; Peter Shore then replaced Crosland as Environment Secretary. Albert Booth in turn replaced Foot at Employment. Healey soldiered on at the Treasury and Jenkins for the time being at the Home Office. Somewhat surprisingly, Mrs Castle was dispensed with, replaced by David Ennals. The only other major change in the personnel of the government before the general election was the promotion of the almost unknown medical practitioner David Owen (b. 1938) to be Foreign Secretary in place of Crosland, who died suddenly in 1977. Owen was the youngest Foreign Minister since Anthony Eden. When Callaghan took over, he had been one of two Ministers of State at the Department of Health and Social Security. He was later moved as a junior to the Foreign and Commonwealth Office. His subsequent appointment caused annoyance among Labour MPs, as there were many more experienced, and able, politicians waiting for promotion. The controversy increased when, in almost his first act, Owen announced the appointment of the Prime Minister's son-in-law, Peter Jay, as British Ambassador to Washington. Owen's handling of the Rhodesian issue gained him few friends on left or right, though the emergence of Soviet-backed regimes in the former Portuguese territories on the borders of Rhodesia reduced British influence on a settlement still further. Owen later came in for criticism over his utterances about Iran. He expressed strong support for the despotic regime of the Shah, which fell shortly afterwards. Some of his own backbenchers seemed to be far better informed than he and his American colleagues. The French dealt with the situation far more shrewdly.

Few would have predicted during the early 1950s that James Callaghan would one day lead the Labour Party as Prime Minister. Admittedly, his measure of popularity among his colleagues was shown by election to the shadow cabinet throughout the 13 years of Conservative rule. Nevertheless, he did not have the brilliance of a Crosland, the charisma of a Bevan, the obvious sincerity of a Gaitskell, the rhetoric and repartee of a Wilson, or the style and sophistication of a Jenkins. He had kicked over the traces briefly when he first entered the Commons in 1945, notably over the American loan and that great issue of principle, the price of cocoa in 1947. After that, he settled down to a happy marriage with the leadership as a dependable advocate of party unity. He was usually to be found somewhere just right of centre. It is true he managed to work himself up over Suez, South Africa, and Cyprus. However, even this was not much more than the routine anger of Labour orthodoxy on these issues. The basic elements of his success were his original discovery by Laski and Dalton, his trade union connection, his unity stance, accident, and his own very real determination to succeed. Given his background, he needed more of this last quality than most of his colleagues.

James Callaghan's father was a chief petty officer and later coastguard, of Irish descent, who died young. Callaghan has summed up the years that followed thus, 'I was conscious we were very poor'.[31] Hard work and maternal encouragement got him through the School Certificate, the equivalent in those days of GCE 'O' Level, and into the security of the Inland Revenue as a junior clerk. Callaghan then rose up through the ranks of the Association of Officers of Taxes, reaching the executive committee in 1934 and becoming a full-time official in 1936. He took up a fairly left-wing position on the issues of the 1930s, and came into contact with, and impressed, Professor Laski. When war broke out, Callaghan chose not to remain in his reserved occupation, volunteering instead for the navy. He had a quiet war in Naval Intelligence. He was elected MP for Cardiff South-East in 1945. Some Conservatives felt Callaghan presented them with a new difficulty. The former Conservative Minister Peter Walker, claimed in 1977, 'We have a Prime Minister, who is good on television; who looks like Stanley Baldwin; who lives like Stanley Baldwin; and Stanley Baldwin with the vote of the Labour Party and North Sea oil is a very formidable opponent'.[32]

The Liberals also changed their leader in the life of the 1974-79 Parliament. The change in the leadership of the Liberal Party in May 1976 was the result of one of the strangest affairs in recent British politics. Jeremy Thorpe had been leader for nine years, having replaced the much-respected fellow old Etonian Jo Grimond in 1967. The Party had certainly improved its performance over the years, but this was due more to the electorate's boredom, frustration, and disgust with the other parties, especially the Conservatives, than to identification with Liberal policies. The Liberals had enjoyed the advantage of not having been in office. They were certainly not more united than the other two parties. The radicalism of Peter Hain's Young Liberals – Hain later defected to Labour – Cyril Smith's Northern populism, Trevor Jones's community politics, Lord Gladwyn's right-wing Liberalism, were all different from each other as they were from Thorpe's – what? It was difficult to be certain. A not inconsiderable number of Liberals believed he was not a serious politician and concentrated too much on showmanship rather than on policy. His social style and dress – expensive, flamboyant, and rather deliberately out-of-date clothes – caused much adverse comment.[33]

The son of a Conservative MP and King's Counsel and himself a barrister and television journalist, Thorpe was elected to the Commons on the second attempt in 1959. He soon established himself as a personality, and as an effective debater in the Commons. As leader of the Liberals, however, he never managed to escape from the shadow of the previous leader, who remained in the House. There was another shadow he could not escape from. This was his friendship with Norman Scott, a former male model who alleged he had had a homosexual relationship with Thorpe. It was the persistence of these accusations which finally finished him. He had already been undermined to a considerable extent by his association with a fringe bank, London and County Securities, which was charging 280 per cent on second mortgages.[34] After revelations about its activities the bank fell like a house of cards. Thorpe's fall took longer.

Of the new leader David Steel (b. 1938), Cyril Smith is reported to have said, 'You could not make a bang if you had a firework in each hand'.[35] Yet Steel, elected by the most democratic procedure of the three main parties, seemed refreshingly different from Thorpe. Educated in Nairobi and at Edinburgh University he was the son of a clergyman. Like Thorpe he had been a television journalist, and was the youngest member of the 1964-66 Parliament (above p. 165). He had been a supporter of liberal causes such as Shelter and the Anti-Apartheid Movement. He led the Liberals into the 'Lib-Lab' pact of March 1977. Under this arrangement the Liberals promised to sustain the government, which was by then in a minority, in return for consultations on government legislation. The pact brought the Liberals nearer to office than they had been at any time in the post-war period. It did not stop their further decline. They had lost deposits up and down the country in by-elections before it, and continued to do so after it. It was the old story of floating right-of-centre voters returning to the Conservatives during a period of Labour government. The charm and intelligence of David Steel could do nothing to alter this. After arguments and recriminations within the Party, with Smith leading the assault, the pact was terminated in the summer of 1978. By this time its termination made little difference to the government.

Bullock on industrial representation, and North Sea oil

The government had been forced to put a brave face on one by-election reverse after another. In June 1975 it lost Woolwich West to the Conservatives. In November 1976 Walsall North fell. There a special factor had helped the Conservatives. The former Labour MP and former Cabinet minister, John Stonehouse, had been convicted of corruption and fraud and sentenced to seven years imprisonment. In the following March, Birmingham Stechford, Roy Jenkins's old seat, was won by the Conservatives. A greater blow was the fall of Ashfield, a mining constituency, in April. The Conservatives also took Ilford North in March 1978. The government was in the doghouse because, like its predecessor, it could not control the economy. And, like its predecessor, it had made promises in opposition which it was unable to fulfil in office. Britain had reached a state of stagflation – a stagnating economy with high unemployment which was nevertheless hit by high inflation. Britain's rate of inflation in the 1970s was higher than the other EEC states, except for Ireland and Italy; higher than Austria, Sweden, Switzerland, the United States, and Japan. Unemployment reached new post-war peaks, nearing the 1.5 million-mark. In opposition Healey had said, 'Unemployment in Britain today is by far the biggest single cause of avoidable human misery and suffering'.[36] Yet in 1977 it was higher than in other leading Western industrial nations – the United States, Japan, West Germany, France, Italy – except for Canada. This unenviable record was due to a considerable extent to Healey's deflationary measures of the previous year, which in turn were the result of the sterling crisis of that year. At the beginning of the year the pound had stood at $2.024. By the last days of September it was down to $1.637. The pound appeared to be dying. Only massive borrowing abroad prevented it from doing so. Then suddenly the pound was climbing up once again, towards the 2-dollar mark. The heavy dose of public-spending cuts, the greater stability afforded the government by the 'Lib-Lab' pact, the expectation of oil revenues from the North Sea fields, all helped to reverse the trend. The freeing of the pound from its previous linkage with the dollar also helped, especially as the dollar crisis deepened, caused by America's large deficit on its overseas trade.

It was all too easy to blame the government or 'Socialism' for this state of affairs, but this explanation was hardly convincing. The Social Democrats had been in government in West Germany, the most successful industrial state, since 1966, and had led that country since 1969. They had led the equally successful Austria since 1970, and had been in government there throughout the post-war period except for 1966-70. France apart, Labour's European sister parties had been in government in most of the other West European industrial states for most of the previous ten years. Another easy target was the trade unions. In the first two years of the Labour government there was a great improvement in industrial relations; after that there was a turn for the worse. In the five years 1973-77 Britain's record was better than Australia, Canada, Ireland, Italy, Spain, and the United States. It was true of course, in the 1970s as in the 1960s, discussed in chapter 5 above, that Britain suffered from an archaic trade union structure. At the end of 1977 there were still something like 485 trade unions in Britain.[37] In 1977 there were still 74 unions with memberships of under a hundred, compared with 126 in 1967. Those with memberships between a hundred and 499 had actually increased from 136 in 1967 to 144 in 1977, but making up only 0.3 per cent of total union membership. Nearly 63 per cent of British trade unionists were organized in the 11 biggest unions. But the situation was far from satisfactory. The unions did themselves no good, as far as popular esteem was concerned, by failure to have postal voting for important union elections, and secret ballots for strikes. In the 1970s trade unions seemed to enjoy less public approval than at any time since the war. This is remarkable considering the growth of unions and the fact that they were more representative than ever of the 'workers by hand and by brain'. Indeed the growth areas had been among the white-collar, supervisory, and technical employees. In 1977 there were 12.6 million members of trade unions in the United Kingdom, which probably means they and their members make up half the population.

Britain's industrial relations continued to look very bad indeed compared with those of West Germany. For many of the politically interested sections of the population West Germany remained the state to study and to follow. The TUC had belatedly come round to the view that perhaps there was something in West Germany's system of co-determination, employee participation in management. Under pressure from his own backbenchers Wilson had set up the Bullock Committee, under the chairmanship of Lord (Alan) Bullock, to investigate the possibilities. In its report published in January 1977, it commented that in West Germany

many of those we met saw a strong and direct connection between the success of the West German economy since World War II and the presence of employee representatives on supervisory boards. West German industrialists, though opposed to parity representation, were largely in agreement that board level representation provided a system of legally enforced communication between managers and employees which led to an earlier identification of problems involving changes for employees and to a more thoughtful and farsighted style of management.[38]

The Committee also reported favourably about similar developments in Sweden. It might also have considered the position of trade unions in Austria, where they have the right, among other things, to pass judgement on every important draft Bill before it is presented to Parliament.[39]

The main proposals of the Bullock Committee were that in an enterprise employing more than 2,000 people the unions would have the right to call for a ballot of the workforce on proposals for trade union directors. If the ballot were favourable, with a minimum of 50 per cent of the employees voting, the unions involved would form a Joint Representation Committee (JRC). The company board would then be reconstructed, comprising two equal groups appointed respectively by the shareholders and the JRC, and a third smaller group co-opted in agreement with the other two. There would also be an Industrial Democracy Commission which would give advice and decide the composition of boards in the case of deadlock. A minority of the Bullock Committee rejected these proposals in favour of more modest representation at below board level. The Bullock majority, and minority, proposals died without leaving much of a heritage behind them. It is doubtful whether the government was ever very serious about them. The Committee had been conceived originally to stop a Private Member's Bill, proposed by Labour MP Giles Radice, on industrial democracy. The Conservatives opposed Bullock, so did the employers' organizations, and so did some trade union leaders as well. Certainly there would have been difficulties in trying to establish a framework for industrial democracy, but it appeared that the leaders of British politics and industry were not yet ready to break new ground away from old-fashioned, authoritarian structures towards co-operation through participation. Only in the nationalized industries was a limited experiment embarked upon.

One ray of hope in the otherwise gloomy 1970s was the emergence of Britain as an oil power. The first discovery of oil in the British sector of the North Sea was made in 1969 and the first oil was landed in 1975. By mid-1978 nine fields in the British sector were producing oil: Brent and Forties, two of the largest offshore oilfields in the world; Argyll; Auk; Beryl; Claymore; Montrose; Piper; and Thistle. It is estimated that by the early 1980s Britain will be among the top ten leading oil-producing countries. Under the Petroleum and Submarine Pipe-lines Act, 1975 a public corporation was set up – the British National Oil Corporation (BNOC) – with powers to explore for, produce, transport, and refine petroleum; store, distribute, and buy and sell petroleum; and provide advisory services and carry out research and training.[40] BNOC took over the British offshore interests previously held by the National Coal Board, and those of the Burmah Oil Company. Majority participation agreements had been signed between BNOC and all the companies operating North Sea fields. There was of course controversy about the state's involvement in the oil industry, with the Conservatives preferring to leave things largely to private companies. However, the Labour government's schemes for a public sector plus participation agreements were modest compared with those of many oil-producing states, from Austria to Mexico. Britain was expected to be self-sufficient in oil by 1980. North Sea gas expanded rapidly in the late 1960s and early 1970s and was also making a major contribution to Britain's energy requirements.

Referenda in Scotland and Wales

This book opened with the brief local success of a Scottish Nationalist candidate in the Motherwell by-election of 1945. The general election of July 1945 seemed to indicate that the Scottish voters had consigned the Scottish National Party to the waste-paper basket of history. It was to take another 22 years to achieve another brief success, this time at the Hamilton by-election in 1967. The Nationalists lost it again in the subsequent general election, but on this occasion they got a consolation prize – the Western Isles. A second seat was won in the by-election at Glasgow Govan in November 1973 when the winsome Margo Macdonald defeated the Labour candidate. As we have seen above, the breakthrough came for the SNP in the elections of 1974. In October of that year the SNP gained 11 seats and 30.4 per cent of the vote in Scotland. In any European country that vote would entitle it to be called a major party. In Wales, Plaid Cymru won 3 seats and 10.8 per cent of the vote. It came as an apparent shock to many English people that so many voters in Scotland and Wales were so dissatisfied as to vote for parties which seek to establish separate states, states enjoying relations with England little different from those existing between the United Kingdom and the Irish Republic. In both cases a powerful ingredient of this nationalist vote has been the apparent failure of the two main parties to deal with real economic and social difficulties existing in the two countries. In both Scotland and Wales unemployment rates remained higher than the average for Great Britain. Migration had long been the only alternative for many to the dole queue. Housing too remained a problem in the 1970s. In 1976 the stock of housing in Wales was older than that of England. Doubtless this was also the case in Scotland. A Department of the Environment report showed Clydeside had 90 per cent of the most concentrated areas of urban deprivation in the United Kingdom.[41] The situation of the rural communities and small farmers was another cause of discontent in both countries. There was a feeling of being forgotten and neglected. With Britain in a state of economic crisis under both Labour and Conservative governments it was easy for the nationalists to preach political and economic sovereignty as a solution. They could claim their countries were being exploited by England and offer themselves as something new, yet traditional, parties of hope and nostalgia, radical but also respectable.

The two nationalist parties had been fighting since before the Second World War to achieve separation from England. In neither case could it be argued that this was not feasible on the grounds of either size or their economies. Wales had a population of 2.7 million in 1976 and Scotland 5.2 million. Thus Scotland was bigger in population than Denmark, Finland, Ireland, and Israel (among many others), and Wales was bigger than Iceland, Jamaica, Lebanon, Luxembourg, and Singapore (among others). Economically, most of Britain's oil is off the eastern coast of Scotland, Wales 'exports' drinking-water on a massive scale to England. Scotland already had a fair degree of autonomy through the Scottish Office which, set up in 1885, took over most Home Office functions, and education. Since 1892 the Secretary for Scotland has had a seat in the Cabinet. In 1939 the Scottish Office was opened in Edinburgh, and now covers most aspects of government. Scotland had always maintained its own system of law. Under Harold Wilson the Cabinet post of Secretary of State for Wales was created, with wide powers. In the case of both Scotland and Wales more public expenditure per head went to them than to England throughout the 1970s. The Welsh Language Society protested about the lack of recognition of Welsh, but BBC Wales television and radio devoted much of their output to programmes in the Welsh language. According to the census of 1971, only 1.3 per cent of the inhabitants of Wales spoke only Welsh, a further 20.8 per cent spoke Welsh and English.

What kind of policies would the nationalists pursue if they came to power in their respective countries? Plaid Cymru would like to set up a co-operative economy of 'living associations of free people' in contrast to Labour's state capitalism and Conservatism's private capitalism.[42] The SNP wanted an Industrial Development Corporation to stimulate industry and Scottish participation in the oil companies rather than nationalization.[43] In foreign policy the two parties had opposed the EEC and took up a quasi-pacifist line on defence problems.

The Kilbrandon Commission on the Constitution which reported in 1973 advocated devolution in Scotland and Wales, but only devolution consistent with the preservation of the essential political and economic unity of the United Kingdom. Back in office, Labour, who had originally set up the Kilbrandon Commission, gave the people of Wales and Scotland the chance to vote on proposals to establish assemblies in the two countries. These referenda in February 1979 produced an anti-devolution majority in Wales and only a narrow victory for devolution in Scotland based on a low poll.

Northern Ireland peace hope

As Britain moved towards the 1980s, Northern Ireland continued to be the most intractable and urgent political problem. The Labour government tried again in 1974 to find a constitutional solution. A White Paper of July 1974 announced the setting-up of a Constitutional Convention to work out a new political framework for

Northern Ireland. The two conditions laid down were that there must be power-sharing, and that there must be recognition of an Irish dimension. The Northern Ireland Act, 1974 set up a 78-member Convention to work to this end. Elections held in May 1975 gave the various anti-power-sharing Unionists nearly 55 per cent of the votes and 46 seats. The SDLP and the other Catholic groups got 26.2 per cent, and the moderate unionists, Northern Ireland Labour Party, and Alliance Party – all power-sharing parties – nearly 19 per cent. Thus there had been some improvement in the fortunes of the moderate groups since October 1974. The majority report wanted to return to a system very similar to that of the old Stormont constitution, with no power-sharing. After various further discussions and attempts by Merlyn Rees, Secretary of State for Northern Ireland, the Convention was formally dissolved in March 1976. The government had run out of ideas.

Hopes were raised that at least the violence would end after talks between British government officials and Provisional Sinn Fein representatives, the political wing of the Provisional IRA, led to a cease-fire in February 1975. Rees ordered the British forces to keep a low profile. Certainly there was much less IRA activity against the security forces, but there was no end to the sectarian killings. In summer 1975 the cease-fire broke down completely. Some thought the IRA had only called it in the first place because it wanted time to refurbish its resources. In January 1976 elements of the Special Air Services (SAS), tough troops trained in irregular warfare, were sent to reinforce the army. This represented a hardening of the government's policy. On the other hand, Rees had pursued a policy of releasing detainees held without trial. By Christmas 1975 all had been released.

There was renewed hope once again in August 1976 when there were spontaneous mass demonstrations for peace in Northern Ireland. These had been brought on by the killing of three children by a terrorist car which was out of control. A Peace Movement came into existence headed by Mrs Betty Williams, Miss Mairead Corrigan, and Mr Ciaran McKeown. They took part in similar demonstrations up and down the United Kingdom and Ireland. They braved denunciations by the IRA and, as Airey Neave put it, 'The Women's Peace Movement, courageous and sincere, certainly brings hope to a tragic community'.[44] Neave was echoing worldwide sentiment. The Movement was awarded the Nobel Prize for Peace. Peace, however, did not break out. In 1976 a total of 296 individuals were killed in Northern Ireland, the total for 1977 was 112. Between 1968 and 1978 about 2,000 civilians and soldiers had died as a result of the disorders. Just about the worst of vicious crimes in this sad story was the activities of the 'Shankhill butchers', a group of Belfast Protestants who after heavy drinking seized individual Catholics off the street at random, and tortured their victims before cutting their throats with butchers' knives. The ringleader, William Moore, admitted eleven murders of this type. In February 1979 eleven Protestants were given a total of 42 life sentences for 19 murders and other serious charges. All were judged sane by medical experts.[45]

Without ideas, the government struggled on in Northern Ireland. It was not prepared to think the unthinkable, to contemplate withdrawal from that troubled land. It is difficult to think of any case where a government has succeeded in bringing such a war to a successful conclusion. Its continuation endangers the British army both individually and collectively, as well as innocent civilians. It also poses a continuing threat to law and order in the rest of the United Kingdom, and possibly to the democratic order itself. Yet would there be any disgrace in calling in a peace-keeping force from the Commonwealth, from lands the Irish know well such as Canada, Australia, and New Zealand – or from NATO, Canada, Denmark, and Norway? It would then be clearly up to the people of Northern Ireland, up to the leaders of the separate communities, to come to terms with the reality of their situation.

England continued to be plagued by the senseless violence of Northern Ireland. As mentioned above (p. 247), the Wilson government had to deal with escalating terrorism in 1974, culminating in twenty deaths when bombs went off in Birmingham pubs on the night of 21 November. Under the Prevention of Terrorism Act, passed one week later, the IRA became an illegal organization in Great Britain; the Home Secretary was given power to 'exclude' suspected individuals from Great Britain; and the police got power to detain suspects for up to seven days without a charge being made. Necessary though this legislation was, it looked like a step towards *1984*. The Commons refused to be panicked into introducing the death penalty for terrorism when the issue was raised in 1974 and 1975. On both occasions a majority of Conservatives voted in favour of the death penalty for terrorist crimes. Mrs Thatcher commented, 'I personally believe that those who commit these terrible crimes against humanity have forfeited their right to live'.[46] One crucial argument against the death penalty for this sort of crime was that it could easily lead to an escalation of violence, including kidnappings and reprisals.

Crime and police computers

In common with other industrial societies, east as well as west of the river Elbe, Britain suffered from increasing rates of crime of most kinds during the 1960s and 1970s. There were the crimes which resulted from increased temptation and opportunity, like shoplifting, and crimes, the causes of which baffled the experts, such as vandalism and football hooliganism. And there were more serious crimes such as assault, muggings, and the use of firearms. To meet this challenge more police had to be recruited and more civilians to assist them. To meet this challenge more police had to be recruited and more civilians to assist them. The police became better trained, more professional, organized in larger units, and, perhaps, more discontented. In 1949 there were 58,990 policemen in England and Wales and 1,176 policewomen. The totals for 1959 were 70,156 and 2,338 respectively. In 1969 the totals of those serving were 87,342 men and 3,492 women. By 1976 there were 101,042 men and 6,997 women serving in the police forces of England and Wales. The authorized strength was 116,880, so that these forces were over 8,000 below strength.[47] Throughout the post-war period the police had been under strength. London presented a particular problem. Compared with the early post-war period the police service today looks like a centralized force. In 1949 there were 127 police forces in England and Wales. Today there are only 43. Officially, however, they are still run by committees of local government representatives and magistrates. Some in the police service believe the 43 units do not correspond to the needs of efficiency. Though great strides have been made in training, it is doubtful whether the police have enough specialists to deal with particular types of crime which appear to be more prevalent than a few years ago. Fraud and corruption certainly seem to be growth areas and need highly trained detectives to deal with them. Offences connected with drugs have been another growth area, with the need for the police to try to infiltrate drug organizations, no easy task when these are based on ethnic groups such as the Chinese. Race relations present the police with a special problem, as surveys have indicated that young immigrants felt they were likely to be unfairly dealt with by the police.[48] Undoubtedly the greatest challenge to police ingenuity has been in the field of urban terrorism. This was virtually unknown in Britain during the 1950s, but not before that. Britain's 'political police', the Special Branch, was established originally to deal with Irish Republicans during the 1880s. Among the terrorist targets at that time were Nelson's Column, underground stations, Scotland Yard, the Tower of London, and London Bridge.[49] The IRA engaged in a bombing campaign in England at the start of the Second World War, and there have been other minor outbreaks. Urban terrorism and the increasing use of firearms by criminals, have forced the police to give greater attention to training in the use of firearms, and to the development of special units to deal with these crimes. Public attention in the 1970s has focused a great deal on violence connected with political demonstrations and trade disputes. The Red Lion Square riot between left and right extremists in 1974, and the demonstrations and picketing connected with the Grunwick industrial dispute in 1977, are notable examples of these developments. Too much should not be made of this rowdy dimension. As Sir Robert Mark, former Commissioner of the Metropolitan Police, has pointed out: one had to consider

whether social violence has increased in this country or whether that is an illusion created, even if unintentionally, by newspapers and television. Violence has always been a natural aspect of society and, indeed, many social changes now regarded as wholly acceptable have been achieved by it. Local self-government, social legislation and parliamentary reform all owe something to social violence. The trade unions did not emerge without it. The Chartist movement between 1837 and 1848 laid the foundation of what we now regard as constitutional democracy. The suffragette movement between 1905 and 1914 resorted to violence to a degree now largely forgotten or unremarked. There was violence during the General Strike and during the hunger marches of the thirties: but violence had tended to diminish as the claims which inspired it have been conceded.[50]

Sir Robert went on to emphasize that there was nothing new in squatting, sit-ins, demos, and even home-made bombs. He was warning against over-reaction to the activities of violent minorities and recommended the minimum use of force to contain them. 'In a free society such as ours, government must be by consent. The forcible suppression of a minority . . . is the negation of freedom and can only be achieved by overwhelming resources of manpower willing to enforce undemocratic laws'.

Two aspects of the development of the police since the mid-1960s worried some observers of the British scene. One was the apparent increase in corruption, the other was the 'Big Brother' aspect of police organization and surveillance. In the 1960s there were a number of cases of police misusing their powers. One led to the conviction of two Sheffield policemen for severely beating up suspects, another involved Detective Sergeant Challenor of the Metropolitan Police, who had acted illegally in 24 cases. Among other things he had planted evidence on left-wing political demonstrators. At his trial he was found unfit to plead through insanity. Three others were sentenced on charges of perverting the course of justice in connection with the Challenor affair.[51] There were also a number of cases where immigrants were the victims. The spectacular case of corruption in the 1970s was that involving members of Scotland Yard's Obscene Publications Squad, who had taken large bribes from proprietors of pornographic bookshops. They were jailed in 1977 for offences which had been committed over a considerable period. In 1976 Sir Robert Mark revealed that in the four years he had been Commissioner, 82 officers had been required to leave the Metropolitan Police after formal proceedings. Another 301 had left voluntarily amid criminal or disciplinary inquiries. Of 72 officers tried by jury 36 had been acquitted.[52] In the decade before Mark was Commissioner an average of 16 officers had been eased out of the service. Was there more corruption about? Or was it that Mark set higher standards than his predecessors? Or was it that a greater press and public awareness of corruption and malpractice was forcing matters into the open? It is difficult to be sure. But Mark had taken over with the brief to clean up Scotland Yard's CID, and there had been corruption cases at the Yard in the 1930s. Part of the trouble, it has been suggested, is laws on gambling, prostitution, licensing, pornography, and drugs, which are not really enforceable and which therefore put police officers in temptation.[53] Another reason why some police officers broke the rules was, as in the case of Sheffield, the pressure they were under to get results. The Police Act 1976 was an attempt to help to restore public confidence in the police by setting up a Police Complaints Board with functions relating to complaints from the public against the police. The chairman and his deputy (or deputies) are appointed by the Prime Minister. 'The members of the Board shall not include any person who is or has been a constable in any part of the United Kingdom'.[54] The Minister for the Civil Service has general oversight of the Board's activities. The Board replaced the much-criticized system under which the police dealt with complaints from the public themselves.

Another aspect of police work which has worried particularly civil rights workers has been the development of the Police National Computer (PNC). This is just part of the computerization of information in recent years by banks, credit firms, insurance companies, employers, local authorities, and the NHS. The Committee on Privacy, under the chairmanship of Sir Kenneth Younger, which reported in 1972, felt the computer as used by the private sector was not then a threat but could possibly become one in the future. The White Paper *Computers and Privacy* of 1975 recognized the possible dangers from the storage of information in this way: inaccurate, incomplete, or irrelevant information being stored; the possibility of access to information by people who should not or need not have it; the use of information in a context or for a purpose other than that for which it was collected.[55] By the end of the 1970s Britain was behind some other countries – Canada, Norway, Denmark, France, Sweden, the United States, and West Germany – in providing a legal framework to protect its citizens from malpractice in this increasingly significant field.[56] A committee chaired by Sir Norman Lindop reported on the whole issue in December 1978. It dealt, among other things, with the PNC, which holds five major files: the index to national records in the Criminal Records Office; a file of vehicle-owners; a file of stolen and suspect vehicles; an index to the national fingerprint collection; and a file of wanted or missing persons. The advantages of this to police work are too obvious to need further comment. The Lindop Committee, while supporting the police in their use of the PNC, urged 'that the best way to avert any fears and suspicions of such systems would be for them to be subject to the data protection legislation which we propose'.[57] The storage of information on patients by the NHS was another sphere which caused concern.

The other 'Big Brother' aspects of police and security work which many of those concerned with civil rights found disquieting were the ease with which the Home Secretary could deport 'undesirable aliens', the apparently increasing use of phone-tapping, the vetting of juries, and the complete secrecy surrounding these and certain other operations of government and police activities.

A decade of 'women's lib'

If the rise of Margaret Thatcher was a sign of the progress made towards the equality of the sexes in political and social life, this progress should not be exaggerated. In the Parliament elected in 1974 there were 27 women MPs. A decade earlier there were actually 29 women elected, and a decade before that, in the 1955 election, 24. At the beginning of our period, 1945, 21 Labour ladies, one Conservative, one Liberal, and one Independent had been returned to the Commons. Clearly, the impact of women on politics since the war has not been staggering. At the end of the 1970s women could still complain about their low pay as compared with that of men. Women's gross hourly earnings as a percentage of men's in 1970 were 63.1 per cent. In 1977 they had advanced to 75.5 per cent. And in the decade of 'women's lib', roughly since 1968, the advance of women into the key professions had not been so dramatic:[58]

Women	1968	1977
	%	%
barristers	5.8	8.2
GPs	9.7	13.5
accountants	1.5	3.1
schoolteachers	57.3	59.5
electrical engineers	0.2	0.5

There are still few women university lecturers, but more women bus-drivers than there used to be. The numbers of women in the police and the armed forces have not changed greatly, but today they play a more active role in those services. The decade saw, for the first time, women becoming jockeys, Lloyds underwriters, and RSPCA inspectors. Dame Rosemary Murray became the first woman Vice-Chancellor of Cambridge University and Dame Josephine Barnes the first woman President of the British Medical Association. But were these really signs of deep changes in the social position of women or merely momentary concessions to a passing mood, the spectacular exceptions? The number of women filing divorce petitions would lead one to believe that women were certainly in revolt. In 1968 husbands had filed 20,600 petitions, wives 34,400. In 1976 the figures were 42,866 and 100,832 respectively.[59] Perhaps the decline in religious wedding ceremonies in the 1970s was due more to the change in women's attitudes than in men's. In 1971, 41 per cent of marriage ceremonies in England were held in register offices, in 1976, 50 per cent.[60] In formal legal terms women's rights were advanced during the 1970s. The Guardianship of Children Act 1973 gave mothers equal rights with fathers to make decisions about a child's upbringing, whereas previously the father's rights had been paramount. The Domicile and Matrimonial Proceedings Act 1973 enabled a married woman living apart from her husband to have a legal domicile of her own. The Criminal Justice Act 1972 ended the property qualification for jury service, thus enabling more women to serve on juries – significant, because even in 1977 only 6.5 per cent of home loans were granted to women, and only 39.5 per cent of home loans were based on two incomes.[61] The Sex Discrimination Act 1975 makes it unlawful to discriminate on grounds of sex in employment, and in the provision of educational facilities, housing, goods, services, and opportunities. It is also unlawful to discriminate in advertisements in these areas. It created an Equal Opportunities Commission to investigate discriminatory practices. The battering of women by their male partners also became an issue in the 1970s. The result was the Domestic Violence and Matrimonial Proceedings Act, sponsored by Jo Richardson, Labour MP, which gave women who were not in the process of separating from their husbands the power to get injunctions against their spouses or co-habitees to prevent them from entering the house.

By the last years of the 1970s a gentle conservative trend seemed to be establishing itself in Britain, as elsewhere, in social attitudes, including attitudes towards 'women's lib'. But, as one liberationist consoled herself, 'more women are wearing the trousers now and nobody is noticing any more'.[62]

Racial discrimination and immigration continued to be an issue throughout the 1970s. Roy Jenkins, when Home Secretary, pursued a liberal course, granting an amnesty to illegal immigrants who had got into the country before 1 January 1973. This measure, to remove the threat of blackmail and exploitation from this group, was attacked by the Opposition. He also, in an attempt to even out the flow of Asians who held British passports from Africa, increased the number of United Kingdom passport-holders allowed into the country in any year from 3,500 to 5,000. Jenkins also gave Commonwealth or foreign husbands of British women the same right of entry as wives of British men. This too was attacked by the Conservatives. Matters were made worse by confusion, which led to controversy, about the reliability of Home Office statistics on the number of immigrants entering the country. Under Merlyn Rees as Home Secretary, there was again some tightening-up of entry rules. Meanwhile Parliament also had to decide what to do about ensuring equal treatment for those already in Britain, especially the generation which had been brought up or even born in the country. There were fears that black youth, living in the decaying ghettos of the inner cities, undereducated, unemployed, and dispirited, could become a permanent pool from which the criminals and subversives would be recruited: one of the main reasons for the Race Relations Act 1976, which attempted to deal with discrimination over a broad field, and established the Commission for Racial Equality. For one thing, the 1976 Act extended previous legislation to most clubs, which was opposed by the Conservatives as an infringement of the rights of the citizen in the private sphere.

One other issue which continued to cause bitter strife was education. As with race, so with education, the parties proclaimed their abhorrence of discrimination and their desire to achieve high standards for all. They differed on their means to these ends. The Labour Party (one was not always sure about its leaders) was for the comprehensive system and opposed to fee-paying schools. The Conservatives claimed they favoured improving all schools and that the retention of the independent sector gave freedom of choice to parents. They found it difficult to deny, however, that in practice few parents had any choice. Labour's Public Schools Commission of 1968 had recommended integration of the independent schools, but nothing had come of this. The second 1974 government did, however, abolish grants to the direct-grant grammar schools, schools with high academic standards, many of whose pupils were holders of scholarships awarded by local authorities. They had to choose between joining the 'state' sector or going completely private. Most chose to do the latter. Many of the Catholic schools among them joined the 'state' system, retaining their denominational character.

Controversy also continued in educational politics about standards which some alleged were falling, and others alleged were not keeping pace with the needs of the time and the needs of industry. Some of those leading the assault believed that 'informal' teaching methods were to blame. Speaking at Ruskin College, Oxford, Callaghan paid lip-service to this widespread concern. He cautiously criticized 'informal' methods and regretted that many of the more able students preferred to stay in academic life or to find their way into the civil service, rather than go into industry. There was some truth in this, though it was really playing to the gallery, a gallery where prejudice was strong. For one thing, it underestimated the connections existing between the universities and industry. As for the civil service, its importance had grown rather than lessened. Obviously, first-class brains were needed there too. The 'informal' methods certainly needed better-trained and more resourceful teachers, with smaller classes. The assault was renewed in the 1970s on mixed-ability groups, a feature of comprehensive schools. It has been argued that by not segregating children according to ability the better pupils stimulated the less able ones. The critics of this system, on the other hand, maintained that it held back the brighter children, led the poor pupils into frustration because they could not keep up, and was particularly damaging in maths and languages. Most people were concerned about these basic subjects. Sir Alan Bullock's committee, set up to look at the teaching of English in schools, did criticize some of the students in training and called for more stringent entry requirements in this area. The committee, which reported in February 1975, also called for a more professional approach to the teaching of English. Lord James of Rusholme had already led a committee of investigation into teacher-training, which had recommended an all-graduate profession and more in-service training of teachers. Women's rights activists were disappointed by the lack of progress in providing nursery education. Many women who were forced to go out to work still had to leave their infants with expensive, untrained, babyminders. Other women who wanted to pursue careers outside the home were prevented from doing so. On the positive side, the school-leaving age was raised in 1972 to sixteen, after the measure had been postponed on more than one occasion. It is doubtful whether the great majority of schools had really been able to meet the challenge this extra year represented. There was continuing controversy about what, if any, exams these 16-year-olds should take. The GCE, introduced in 1951, and the CSE, in existence since 1965, had both proved their worth. Both catered for a wide range of abilities and interest. Both offered a wide variety of subjects outside the original hard-core academic ones. Even their overlapping at the bottom end of the GCE and the top end of the CSE was useful. More and more young people were leaving school armed with these qualifications, thus justifying the view of Robbins about the wasted talent in society. In some educational circles there was a strong feeling that these examinations should be replaced by a single one, which would be administratively tidy and would apparently give all pupils some kind of certificate; but the arguments in its favour did not seem all that compelling. There was the fear, expressed by Conservative spokesmen, that such an exam, virtually under the control of the schools themselves, would substitute subjective judgements for objective assessment. In Britain fewer young people stayed on beyond sixteen, compared with countries like West Germany, Sweden, and Japan (and the United States).[63] It is true that those who did stay on went to universities or polytechnics and obtained degrees which did not always represent skills needed by society. This, however, was true worldwide.. It was true of Western states like West Germany and the United States, it was also true of states known to the writer, like East Germany and Bulgaria, where there is far more pressure on young people to study 'relevant' subjects. Other countries too had their unemployed teachers. But did they really need to be unemployed? Were not many of them still wanted in the inner-city problem schools where much better teacher/pupil ratios were needed compared to the suburban schools? Money rather than need all too often dominated this aspect of the education scene. By the end of the decade teachers, especially in schools and universities, felt less happy than in the days of hope of the early 1960s. The pay of university staff, even more than school-teachers, had lagged behind that of comparable professions. It was not just that, like everyone else in times of high inflation, they needed the money. They felt that once again Britain had failed to recognize the contribution of higher education. In this respect the polytechnics were better served. They were, to a considerable extent, trying to abandon their distinctive role of putting on more practical, more vocational, more 'relevant' degree and other courses, and attempting to match the universities. Some departments of some polytechnics, though, were certainly exploring their disciplines in novel and interesting ways. One great success in higher education, of which the writer has personal experience, was the Open University, an achievement of the first Wilson administrations. It offered admission to students without formal GCE qualifications. It failed to attract a large working-class clientele, originally hoped for, but it gave a second chance to thousands who had either failed to get into a university, chosen not to go to one, or had chosen non-university professional qualifications. It pioneered new teaching methods and, for the most part, achieved entirely respectable standards. It led some academics to conclude that in the 1980s the universities should be exploring, together with the government and other interested bodies, ways of encouraging older people to aim for a university education, which would benefit them, the universities, and society as a whole. This is important when one considers the difficulties of finding a place in higher education especially for the working class and women, who remained grossly under-represented in universities, polytechnics, and teacher training establishments.

Labour's incomes policy

As Britain approached the election of 1979, one would have been hard put to it to describe it as a happy, prosperous land. For some inexplicable reason the government of James Callaghan had decided that employees should get only 5 per cent more income in the next year. In summer 1978 the unions had served notice on the government that their members would not wear it, but the government simply went on. It seemed strangely out of touch with ordinary trade unionists for a Labour government. Fitters, 'ankle-deep in muck and slime', processing the excrement of a million Mancunians at Chadderton sewage-works, by working overtime, taking home £54 a week, felt after nearly four years of pay policy that enough was enough, and went on unofficial strike. It was the same for 1.4 million local-authority manual workers and NHS ancillaries. Some would have been better off on social security. Some indeed were getting Family Income Supplement (FIS), others were not. As one angry tractor-driver is reported to have said, 'But why should I go crawling for FIS when I work a 40-hour week? Percentages are a con. I'll take 5 per cent of Callaghan's wages any day'.[64] He summed up the anger of many of his colleagues. For them the Labour government had done little, for them Britain was an unfair society. On left and right opinion was divided about whether an incomes policy was either necessary or practical. Britain, like other countries, was the victim of worldwide inflation; it was a low-wage country, but also a low productivity economy. Most informed opinion agreed that incomes could not rise indefinitely ahead of productivity; but could a rigid, unfair, incomes policy work? As so often over the forty years covered in this book, the government did not appear to have any clear strategy, did not appear to have done any detailed planning, did not appear to have got in touch with grassroots opinion. Callaghan's incomes policy was not fair between high-paid and low-paid manual workers, nor could it be fair between different sections of society. At the top end of the scale there were ample ways around it:

Company car, of course – three out of five on our roads are so owned. Big meals, that's old hat. Live in the Tied Penthouse at company's expense, get medical insurance on the firm; school fees are coming into it, and not just for the far-flung Foreign Office. Go to the races in the company box, get your golf club subscription paid – good for the firm's publicity. Help with moving costs and low-interest mortgages – well, that's still money of a sort.[65]

Then there were the credit cards, free petrol, and free travel. And if you were made redundant, a golden handshake. No doubt Eric Morley, made redundant by Mecca, was not the only top executive to get £200,000 severance pay in 1978. Hard-working Mr Morley looked like a pauper compared to 26-year-old Gerald Grosvenor, son and heir of the Duke of Westminster who, because of the accident of birth,

owns all the lands of Belgravia and one-third of Mayfair – including the south side of Oxford Street and land of 33 embassies. But also has a shopping centre in Wales; shooting in Scotland; trout in Shropshire; family seats in Cheshire and Fermanagh (NI); office blocks in Melbourne; a palm-fringed hotel in Hawaii; and an island in Vancouver.[66]

That these were not just the flamboyant exceptions was clear from the official statistics. In the mid-1970s the richest 1 per cent in Britain still owned one-fifth to one-quarter of all personal wealth. In income terms the richest 1 per cent took home about the same amount as the poorest 20 per cent.[67] As the distinguished Oxford sociologist A. H. Halsey put it, 'They each had, in other words, more than twenty times as much income. These are quite spectacular inequalities . . . Over and above such wealth for use as housing and personal possessions, property for power still has a most impressively unequal distribution'.[68] However, although there is argument about the extent, most would agree that Britain was a more equal society in 1979 than it had been in either 1939 or 1959. The evidence of one's eyes is confirmed by official and academic investigations. Wigan is a different place from what it was in George Orwell's day, and nearby Bolton, 'Worktown', is quite different from how Tom Harrison found it in 1936 and 1959.[69] The same is true to a greater or lesser extent of other 'worktowns'. The great expansion in the ownership of consumer durables, the expansion of home ownership, the development of council housing, social welfare, and close to full employment for all but the last few years, have raised the level of the majority of the working class. For those who still remember life before the war or even in the 1940s, it is like a revolution. In terms of income working-class wages had gone up more between 1938 and 1976 than those of many professional people. In 1976 the factory worker's wage had 172 per cent of the purchasing power of the 1938 wage. The coal-miner's wage was worth 256 per cent of the miner's wage of 1938. The percentages for the agricultural worker and the bus-driver were 199 and 144 respectively. For the middle-class professionals the percentages were as follows: solicitor 98, graduate schoolteacher 95, general practitioner 81, and university professor 74.[70] As in other industrial societies economic changes produced social-class changes. The class structure was no longer a pyramid, it was more like a light bulb, reducing the numbers at the bottom of the pile. Even for the 1.4 million unemployed in 1979 life on the dole was infinitely better than it was for their fathers in 1939, though who can say that the psychological effects are not as devastating? As for those at the very bottom, caught permanently in the poverty trap, we, but not they, can take a crumb of comfort from the fact that,

Even the worst slums of Glasgow do not compare with the rat-infested windowless tenements of Detroit or Philadelphia, where chronic unemployment and minimal medical services combine to create poverty and ill-health from which there is no escape. In Britain the patchwork services of the welfare state manage somehow to redistribute the goods generated by economic growth to provide a minimally secure life-span.[71]

On an international standardized scale of poverty Britain had more poor than West Germany or Sweden in the early 1970s, but fewer than France, the United States, or Canada.[72]

In other respects also life in Britain was not so bad. The percentage of people who owned their homes was higher than in West Germany, though lower than in France, and 'housing standards in the United Kingdom compare well with those in other developed countries. Densities of occupation are generally lower than in other major EEC countries, for example, and the proportion of dwellings lacking amenities are substantially lower'.[73] The suicide rates had been falling in Britain during the 1960s and 1970s, and Britons were less inclined to kill themselves than were some other Europeans. They were also less inclined to kill each other on the roads.

Labour's dream of gradualist socialism, the dream of the 1940s, had not been realized by 1979. Nor had the Conservative dream of a property-owning democracy. Compared with its old enemy, Germany, Britain looked a sorry place in many respects. In material terms, it had fallen behind West Germany and the majority of other Western industrial nations. Perhaps, however, this fall was not as great as was often thought. Figures produced in 1979 by U.N. statisticians indicated that in terms of real consumption per head, 'that at any rate up to 1973, there were only a few percentage points difference between actual living standards in the UK, France,

Germany and the Netherlands. Indeed in the case of Germany, the difference is within the margin of statistical error. Italy was markedly lower in both years'. In terms of Real Domestic Product, figures showed that 'the UK has moved ahead about equally with the US between 1970 and 1975, but also that since the UK accepted the Common Agricultural Policy, France and Germany – partly perhaps for this reason and partly doubtless for others – have gained relatively to ourselves'.[74] Britain's Real Domestic Product per head as a percentage of that of the United States was 63.5 per cent in 1970 and 62 per cent in 1975. This report, however, gives no cause for complacency. It also revealed that Britain was maintaining living standards by consuming more of its (lower) Real Domestic Product than West Germany and some other states. Britain's fall relative to Germany was part of an historical process, already underway in the 1870s. It was not just that Britain was not keeping up with Germany in the newer industries. Germany was ahead of Britain in welfare and education too. In this writer's mind, Germany's colossal lead in all levels of education over Britain over a long period goes some way to explaining the resilience of that country in economic terms compared with the United Kingdom.[75]

Yet in the period between 1945 and 1975 Britain gave the world more Nobel Prize-winners for chemistry, physics, and medicine than any other country apart from the United States. In 1979 Britain had less influence in the world than it had enjoyed for centuries, and yet its people were better off than at any other time. The 'good old days' of greatness and empire were not so good for the majority of Britons. It was still an unfair society at the end of the 1970s, but somewhat fairer and freer than it had been. Would Britain be able to build on these trends, build on its best traditions of fairness and concern, tolerance and democracy, inventiveness and enterprise, and successfully confront the challenge of the 1980s?

Notes

1 Letter to Bristol constituents, November 1970, quoted in *The Campaign Guide 1977* (Conservative and Unionist Central Office, London, 1977), 677.
2 *Daily Telegraph*, 19 July 1976.
3 David Butler and Dennis Kavanagh, *The British General Election of October 1974* (London, 1975), 42.
4 ibid., 285.
5 ibid., 278.
6 Colin Mellors, *The British MP* (Farnborough, 1978), 78.
7 ibid., 48.
8 ibid., 107.
9 *Keesing's Contemporary Archives*, 1975, 27137.
10 Enoch Powell, *The Common Market: the Case Against* (Kingswood, Surrey, 1971), 119.

11 The referendum campaign is covered comprehensively in David Butler and Uwe Kitzinger, *The 1975 Referendum* (London, 1976).

12 Lord Thomson, 'The European Community – the Tortoise that Moves', *Lloyds Bank Review* (July 1977), 3.

13 Conservative and Unionist Central Office, *The Campaign Guide 1977*, 261–2.

14 Peggy Crane, 'The Credit Balance', *New Europe* (European Movement; Winter 1979), 34; her figures are from *Trade and Industry* (24 November 1978), 397. Wynne Godley and Richard Bacon of the Department of Applied Economics in Cambridge calculated that 'Each person in the United Kingdom is in effect contributing £20 to other Common Market countries'. *New Society* (8 February 1979), 304.

15 Crane, op. cit., 37.

16 ibid., 37–8.

17 ibid., 37.

18 Quoted in *Europe Left* (Labour Committee For Europe), March 1975.

19 *The Economist*, 27 January 1979, 42.

20 F. E. Jones, 'Our Manufacturing Industry – The Missing £100,000 million', *National Westminster Bank Quarterly Review* (May 1978).

21 Dr J. A. Pope, Vice-Chancellor of Aston University, in *Times Higher Education Supplement*, 22 July 1977.

22 Conservative Political Centre, *The Engineering Profession: a national investment* (July 1978), 7.

23 M. Yoshino, *Japan's Managerial System* (Cambridge, Mass., 1968), 227.

24 Graham Turner, *Business in Britain* (London, 1969), 431.

25 ibid., 435.

26 'The English Sickness', *Fortune* (Chicago), May 1974.

27 Sir John Newsom, *Public Schools Commission Report* (HMSO, 1968), vol. I, 61.

28 *Observer*, 18 February 1979.

29 *Sunday Times Magazine*, 16 September 1973.

30 Joe Haines, *The Politics of Power* (London, 1977), 151.

31 P. Kellner and C. Hitchens, *Callaghan: the Road to No. Ten* (London, 1976), 22.

32 Quoted by Malcolm Rutherford, *Financial Times*, 16 December 1977.

33 Susan Barnes, 'The Life and Soul of the Party', in *Sunday Times Magazine*, 3 March 1974.

34 ibid.

35 *Daily Mirror*, 8 July 1976.

36 Hansard (Commons), vol. 835 (20 April 1972), col. 796.

37 *Department of Employment Gazette* (January 1979), 26.

38 *Report of the Committee of Inquiry on Industrial Democracy*, Cmnd 6706 (January 1977), 57.

39 *Financial Times*, 28 October 1977.

40 *Britain 1979: an Official Handbook* (HMSO, 1979), 246–7.

41 Quoted in *The Campaign Guide 1977*, 550.

42 *Plaid Cymru: Towards an Economic Democracy* (Cardiff, 1949).

43 James G. Kellas, *The Scottish Political System* (Cambridge, 1975), 132.

44 Quoted in *The Campaign Guide 1977*, 584.

45 The *Guardian*, 21 February 1979.

46 David McKie, Chris Cook, Melanie Phillips, *The Guardian/Quartet Election Guide* (London, 1978), 117.

47 *Annual Abstract of Statistics* (Central Statistical Office, 1957 and 1976).

48 Peter Evans, *The Police Revolution* (London, 1974), 53; he quotes Marplan surveys.

49 Anthony A. Thompson, *Big Brother in Britain Today* (London, 1970), 68.
50 Sir Robert Mark, *Policing a Perplexed Society* (London, 1977), 80.
51 Barry Cox, *Civil Liberties in Britain* (London, 1975), 185–6; he fully documents several important cases.
52 The *Guardian*, 26 February 1976.
53 Cox, op. cit., 192.
54 *Police Act 1976*, Chapter 46, Part I, para 1 (2). For the police see also Roy Lewis, *A Force for the Future* (London, 1976).
55 *Report of the Committee on Data Protection*, Cmnd 7341, December 1978, 451–2.
56 ibid. See Chapter 4 of the Report.
57 ibid., 220.
58 *Sunday Times Magazine*, 1 October 1978: special feature on women's movement.
59 *Annual Abstract of Statistics 1977* (Central Statistical Office).
60 *Social Trends 9 1979 Edition* (Central Statistical Office; HMSO, 1978).
61 *Sunday Times Magazine*, 1 October 1978.
62 ibid. Angela Carter was the writer.
63 W. Kenneth Richmond, *Education in Britain since 1944* (London, 1978), 110. This is a useful review of the arguments.
64 Tom Forrester, 'The Bottom of the Heap', *New Society*, 18 January 1979.
65 Katharine Whitehorn, 'The Unfair Exchanges', *Observer*, 10 December 1978. See also Joe Irving, 'A perk is as good as a pay rise', *Sunday Times*, 5 March 1978.
66 Peter Lennon, 'The World's Richest Wedding Cake', *Sunday Times*, 8 October 1978.
67 A. H. Halsey, *Change in British Society* (Oxford, 1978), 30–1. Anthony Giddens, 'The Rich', *New Society*, 14 October 1975, using Inland Revenue statistics thought the top 1 per cent owned nearer 30 per cent.
68 Halsey, op. cit., 39.
69 Tom Harrison, *Britain Revisited* (London, 1961).
70 *Association of University Teachers Bulletin* (January 1977), 13. The material was from the Economist Intelligence Unit.
71 Michael Mann, 'The Working Class', *New Society*, 4 November 1976.
72 *The Economist*, 3 February 1979.
73 *Social Trends 9 1979*, 152.
74 Douglas Jay, 'Britons may be better off than they think', *Financial Times*, 14 March 1979.
75 There is no suggestion here that education was the only factor. After 1945 there were a number of special factors aiding German recovery as well as the mass skilled labour/management/professional manpower. West Germany too has had its problems with keeping its education system up to date. For the German influence on Britain before 1919 see the fascinating study by George Haines IV, *Essays on German Influence upon English Education and Science 1850–1919* (New London, 1969).

11 Britain Under Thatcher 1979–83

Election 1979

On 28 March 1979 the government of James Callaghan made history in a way it did not want. It was defeated on a confidence vote in the Commons by 311 to 310. It thus became the first government to be so defeated since Ramsay MacDonald's minority Labour government of 1924. The inevitable election followed on 3 May. By more careful management of its parliamentary affairs, the Callaghan administration could have avoided defeat in the Commons and would then have had just a little more time to set the scene before its meeting with the electorate which had to take place by October 1979.

In many respects the Labour government was on the defensive. Its incomes policy had created apathy, anger, disappointment and despondency among its own supporters and public sector floating voters. The same was true of its failure to check unemployment, which had peaked at 1.6 million in August 1977. Its more left-wing supporters were worried about the pact with the Liberals and Britain's increasing commitment, in practical terms, to the EEC. Callaghan's Conservative critics believed the country was drifting to anarchy, with trade union activists being allowed to undermine personal freedom and gradually cripple the economy. Labour had been savaged at by-elections losing seats at Woolwich West (1975), Walsall North (1976), Workington (1976), Birmingham Stechford (1977), Ashfield (1977), Ilford North (1978), all of which went to the Conservatives, and Liverpool Edge Hill (1979), which fell to the Liberals. These reverses had cost Labour its three seat majority and forced it into the 'Lib-Lab' pact of March 1977 (above, p. 265). Yet all was not gloom from Callaghan's point of view. There was the man himself. To some he was a complacent, fumbling, 'old woman' of limited ability. To others, a greater number, he appeared a solid, reliable, uncle-like statesman. He had presided over the 'recovery' of the pound from a low of £ = $1.56 in October 1976 to $2 in January 1979. The balance of payments had moved from deficit to surplus and the gold and dollar reserves were rising. In fact, North Sea oil had greatly contributed to this. However, if Callaghan's own party was divided so were those of his opponents. Mrs Thatcher faced open opposition from Edward Heath over her approach to economic affairs, and attacks from the right wing over her support for the government over Rhodesia. As we have seen above, (pp. 264–5), the Liberal Party was by no means united and did not appear to be any threat to Labour. But in Scotland Labour had to watch out for the SNP and the breakaway, self-styled 'Scottish Labour Party' led by Jim Sillars. In England the National Front challenged the orthodox parties with a record 303 candidates. There was also a maximum effort from the Ecology Party with 53 candidates.

Between the defeat of the Callaghan government and polling day there were five weeks for the parties to organize their resources, push their candidates and propagate their ideas. As usual the Conservatives had the advantage of the best organization in the country, as well as having the most sophisticated and coherent media strategy. In April 1978 the party had given the responsibility for all its advertising and broadcasting to Saatchi and Saatchi. The Saatchi brothers were the sons of an Iraqi Jewish businessman and had been brought up in Hampstead. Charles's 'copy-writing talents had brought him a top salary and a white rolls' by the age of twenty-four. He was 'one of the Sixties wave of innovators who copied and eventually outshone the Madison Avenue style'.[1] With his brother Maurice he had set up his own agency in 1970. Labour, spending much less money, stuck to more traditional styles of broadcasting and had a less thought-through strategy. All three party leaders featured strongly in the party political broadcasts and were given presidential treatment by the media. For instance, Callaghan was given 60 per cent of the time devoted to Labour in BBC-1 news bulletins. The percentages of their parties' viewing time for Thatcher and Steel were 63 and 69 respectively.[2] Working for Margaret Thatcher, Gordon Reece, a successful television producer, staged controlled walkabouts featuring his candidate in a variety of visually appealing locations and situations. Reece planned the Conservative campaign 'down to the last and most trivial detail. Her meetings were all-ticket affairs. . . and most of her supposedly informal meetings with the voters were minutely stage-managed'.[3] Labour was much less adept at putting on such 'media events'. In addition to getting their product across, the Conservatives attacked Labour's record on prices, jobs, high taxation, low wages and, inevitably, the 'winter of discontent'. Once again Labour faced the hostility of most of the press. Of the 'popular' daily press, the *Daily Express*, *Sun* and *Daily Mail*, with a combined circulation of about 8.4 million, called for a Conservative victory. Only the *Daily Mirror* (circulation: 3.8 million) supported Labour. Perhaps Labour gained marginally from the prolonged absence of the *Times* and the *Sunday Times* (owing to an industrial dispute). This helped to boost the circulation of the *Guardian* which wanted a Labour victory, much more than it helped the *Daily Telegraph*, which remained stoutly Conservative, and the *Financial Times* (less so). Much attention was given to Labour's alleged extremism with the *Sun* claiming on 24 April, 'How Many Reds In Labour's Bed? – Power Of The Wild Men Will Grow If Uncle Jim Is Elected Again'. The same paper also featured articles by Labour defectors – Lord George-Brown, Sir Richard Marsh, Lord Chalfont and Reg Prentice – on why they supported the Conservatives. Although the opinion polls showed that the Conservatives were more popular than Labour, Callaghan was seen as a better Prime Minister than Thatcher would be.

The 1979 election was more free from extraneous events and sensations than any other contest since the war. It was the first to be fought in April for more than a century and was unusual in that election day was also the day (3 May) on which most of the local councils in England and Wales were elected. None of these factors appears to have had any bearing on the outcome – an effective majority for the Conservatives, and a very bruising defeat for Labour. Britain's first woman Prime Minister had been elected with 339 seats (up 62 compared with October 1974). Labour won only 269 (down 50) and the Liberals 11 (down 2). Of the small parties, the SNP lost 9 of its 11 seats and the Welsh Nationalists were left with 2 out of 3. Neither the National Front, nor the Ecology Party (whose candidates stood mainly in southern, Conservative-held constituencies), achieved even any near-misses.[4] With their 43.9 per cent share of the vote, the Conservatives had a smaller percentage than in their earlier post-war victories of 1951, 1955, 1959 and 1970 and they actually received fewer votes than in either 1951 or 1959, when the electorate had been smaller. With 37 per cent of the vote Labour was only 2.2 per cent below its October 1974 total, yet it had taken a lower percentage than at any election since 1931! Its vote was slightly higher than in October 1974 but that had been its smallest vote since the war. In crude terms, ignoring the differences in the numbers of candidates, the Liberal percentage (13.8) was their highest post-war total except for the two peaks of 1974. In Scotland the SNP's 1974 high of 30.4 per cent fell to 17.3 per cent. It lost 7 seats to the Conservatives. Labour could smile at this for it was the SNP which had tabled the decisive confidence motion which brought down the government. As Callaghan had predicted at the time, the SNP were like turkeys voting for an early Christmas. In Wales Plaid Cymru's percentage fell from 10.8 to 8.1 – its lowest share of the Welsh vote since 1966 – and its leader, Gwynfor Evans, lost his seat at Carmarthen.

Who had deserted Labour? Ivor Crewe was later to write,

Labour lost through the desertion of its working-class supporters: the swing was 10–11 per cent among skilled workers, and as high as 16 per cent among younger working-class men. These deserters did not stay at home, moreover, but in the main switched right over to the Conservatives. . . . The main components of the anti-Labour swing were, in order of importance, straight conversion from Labour to Conservative, and movement to and from the Liberals (especially October 1974 Liberals reverting to their original Conservative loyalties).[5]

Professor Crewe was of the opinion that the divorce between Labour principles and working-class opinion had caused this situation. Some, especially the better paid, warmed to Conservative calls for tax cuts and action against welfare 'scroungers'. Some felt the Conservatives were right in calling for tougher action on law enforcement. Some saw Labour as being about working-class solidarity, drinking with your mates at the miners' welfare, shopping at the Co-op, being like everyone else and staying the same. Better education, the media, the exciting, if mythical, world of the advertisers and American soap opera, were all disturbing the old values and causing more and more working-class people to aspire to something else. By 1979 some felt the Conservatives, rather than Labour, were more likely to offer chances to improve their lives. As one working-class Conservative voter put it to the writer, 'People like Callaghan, Wilson and Benn want us all to be the same, and stay as we are, but they, and the favoured few, live very differently . . . with their farms and London town houses and country cottages'.[6] The Conservative policy of selling council houses to sitting tenants seemed very popular with the aspiring working class (below, p. 296).

Margaret Thatcher's first Cabinet

Mrs Thatcher's first Cabinet had 22 members, compared with 24 in the out-going Labour Cabinet. She re-organized some of the ministries. The Department of Prices and Consumer Protection (set up in 1974) was merged with the Department of Trade (and thus down-graded). The minister in charge of transport lost Cabinet status and Social Security was to be represented by one Cabinet member instead of two. Finally, the separate post of Paymaster General was re-established. The key appointments were: William Whitelaw (Home Secretary); Lord Hailsham

(Lord Chancellor); Lord Carrington (Foreign and Commonwealth Office); Geoffrey Howe (Chancellor of the Exchequer); Sir Keith Joseph (Industry); Francis Pym (Defence); Lord Soames (Lord President of the Council, Leader in the Lords); James Prior (Employment); Sir Ian Gilmour (Lord Privy Seal with special responsibility for foreign affairs); Peter Walker (Agriculture, Fisheries and Food); Michael Heseltine (Environment); Patrick Jenkin (Social Services); Norman St John Stevas (Leader of the Commons and Minister for the Arts) and John Nott (Trade). On the whole it was a team of experienced men, most of whom knew the corridors of power better than Margaret Thatcher did. However,

A few eyebrows were raised at the return of Lord Hailsham to the Woolsack as Lord Chancellor, at the appointment of Christopher Soames (who had last held ministerial office under Harold Macmillan). . .and at the occupation of the Northern Ireland Office by the Chief Whip, Humphrey Atkins, who had never been known to betray the slightest interest in the subject and did not seem (to his critics at least) to have the robustness required for the administration of that troubled province.[7]

There was shock and surprise on the Right of the party that Mark Carlisle, a moderate, had got education, rather than Rhodes Boyson, the former headmaster of a London comprehensive and a vigorous critic of the comprehensive school system. Most of the Thatcher team had served under Heath (above, pp. 219–20). The moderates, or 'Wets', as Thatcher was later to dub them, were well represented. Paul Foot, the left-wing journalist, claimed it was the 'richest Cabinet to rule us since 1822'.[8] Whatever the exact truth, they were certainly a wealthy, well-heeled lot. Whitelaw, Carrington, Soames, Gilmour, Prior, Pym and George Younger (Scottish Secretary) represented the traditional Tory gentry. Heseltine and Walker were whizz-kids of business. Sir Keith Joseph, on the other hand, had inherited his father's firm, Bovis, while his colleague Humphrey Atkins had married into wealth. Nicholas Edwards (Welsh Secretary) and John Nott had made their way as merchant bankers, while Howe and Jenkin had been successful company lawyers. There were 5 old Etonians in the Cabinet compared with 3 in Heath's smaller 1970 Cabinet. In the 1924 Conservative Cabinet there had been 7 out of a total of 21.[9] The great majority in the Cabinet of 1979 were Oxbridge educated; none had studied at a provincial university or London. Women were thin on the ground both in the Commons and in government. Indeed, the Conservative victory had resulted in a reduction in the number of women MPs from 27 to 19 (11 Labour and 8 Conservative). This was the lowest number elected since 1951. Two women, Sally Oppenheim (Consumer Affairs) and

Lady Young (Education and Science) joined the Thatcher government, both of them outside the Cabinet. One junior appointment with curiosity value was that of Reg Prentice as Minister of State for Social Security (Disabled). Mr Prentice was the first politician since 1945 to have served in both Labour and Conservative governments.

Thatcher looks abroad

Although she had undertaken study visits abroad and had a certain reputation in right-wing circles, Thatcher was in no sense an expert on foreign affairs. As she looked around the world she could not have expected a warm welcome on the international stage of summit diplomacy. In Washington Jimmy Carter, a Democrat, remained in office until the inauguration of Ronald Reagan, a Republican and soul-mate of Thatcher, in January 1981. There were lessons for Thatcher in Carter's fate. He had failed to get re-elected for a second term because of mismanagement of the economy and of the crisis of the US hostages in Iran. In Bonn the Social Democrat Helmut Schmidt, a formidable international figure, held office until 1982 when he was replaced by the moderate, conservative Christian Democrat, Helmut Kohl. France was presided over by Valéry Giscard d'Estaing who, though right-wing, was a friend of Schmidt. Giscard is reported to have said of Thatcher, '*Je ne l'aime, ni comme homme, ni comme femme*'.[10] He fell victim to his country's economic problems and was defeated at the polls in 1981 by Socialist François Mitterrand. In Canada, the Progressive Conservative Joe Clark took office in the same month as Thatcher. Only seven months later he was forced to resign after failing to get Parliament to agree to his austerity budget. Defeat at the subsequent election led to the formation of another Liberal government, once again headed by the clever, sophisticated veteran, Pierre Trudeau. In Moscow another political long-distance runner was still at the helm. Leonid Brezhnev had seen western leaders come and go since 1964; he had no intention of going and held on until his death in 1983. He was followed in quick succession by Yuri Andropov (who died in 1984) and Konstantin Chernenko (who died in March 1985). In 1985 the new man in the Kremlin was Mikhail Gorbachev who appeared to get on well with Thatcher when he visited Britain just before becoming the Soviet Union's top politician.

The background against which these actors performed was a dangerous one. The Iranian revolution of 1979, which eventually brought the Islamic fundamentalist Ayatollah Khomeini to power, brought greater instability in the Middle East. War broke out between Iran and neighbouring Iraq and in December 1979 the

Soviet Union invaded Afghanistan. The following year brought unrest in Poland leading to the setting up of the Solidarity (trade union) movement there, its banning and the imposition of military rule. In Communist China the élite fought for power and tried to rid themselves of the legacy of Mao. The U.S.A. wrestled with its conscience about what to do about revolution and counter-revolution in its client states, El Salvador and Nicaragua. The stage on which Thatcher made her début was one on which the performers could receive bullets or bombs as well as bouquets. In March 1979 the IRA struck down one of Mrs Thatcher's closest associates, Airey Neave, in London. In August of the same year they killed Earl Mountbatten during a fishing trip off the coast of Co. Sligo (Ireland). In 1981 there were unsuccessful attempts on the lives of Ronald Reagan and Pope John Paul II. President Sadat of Egypt was less lucky. Bombs killed the Iranian head of state and head of government in 1981 and the much-respected Indian Prime Minister, Indira Gandhi, fell a victim to an assassin's bullet in 1984. Most of these outrages were committed in countries with a tradition of political violence, but the world did seem to be becoming a more violent place with both government agencies – especially in Latin American countries and Libya – and rebel groups using murder, extortion and terror to achieve their political ends. This was happening increasingly in Rhodesia (below, pp. 299–301).

Thatcherism

Whatever else Margaret Thatcher did during her years in office she was unique in that she gave her name to what her friends and enemies alike elevated into a political doctrine: Thatcherism. No one had ever talked of Wilsonism, Macmillanism, Attleeism or even Churchillism. There had of course been Butskellism (derived from the names of R. A. Butler and Hugh Gaitskell) denoting dedication to the mixed economy, government regulation of major areas of economic life, 'planning', the welfare state and consultation with the unions, as all of this had evolved between 1939–51. It is true that in the late 1940s and 50s the Conservatives had used the rhetoric of free enterprise, setting the people free, and freedom of choice, but they had kept to Macmillan's 'middle way' until 1965. Heath had used this rhetoric more sharply, reinforced by the Selsdon Park conference on Conservative principles in 1970. But it could be argued that the U-turns of 1972–3 led Heath to run away from basics. When she was elected leader, few had expected Thatcher to go beyond this. But over the second half of the 1970s the Thatcher version of the New Right became fashionable in the Conservative Party. There was the strong feeling that Butskellism had failed Britain, which had achieved lower economic growth and a poorer rise in living standards than most other industrial nations. Those such as West Germany and Japan which had made a point of emphasizing free enterprise or capitalism, had done better. Those which had claimed they were socialist, such as the Soviet Union, Poland and the other states of eastern Europe, had done worse. The United States still proclaimed itself as the bastion of free enterprise, and although it had had economic difficulties, it remained the world's leading economy. To many, all over the world, it still appeared as the land of unparalleled opportunity. Certainly this view was not without plausibility even though it ignored the fact that in both West Germany and Japan the state had played an important role in economic affairs throughout the period. This was also the case in other countries which had made rapid economic progress – France, Italy, Spain and the Republic of China (Taiwan) among them. It also ignored the strong welfarism in most of these countries. Supporters of the New Right used this interpretation of recent world economic history to back their arguments, and in addition gained succour from the move to the right in the U.S.A. and from a number of intellectual sources. That they took over the Conservative Party was the result, at least in part, of the social and generational changes in party membership.

In the United States there had developed a reaction against the 'big government' of the Democrats. Barry Goldwater had unsuccessfully championed this cause in the 1960s. Ronald Reagan had taken up the fight with more success and had been elected to the governorship of California in 1966, an office which he held until 1974. The election of Richard Nixon to the White House in 1969 was in part the triumph of these ideas. They suffered a setback, to some degree, under President Carter (1977–81), only to win through again under Reagan (1981–). Nixon's men knew who they were against: 'the professional welfarists, the urban planners, the day-carers, the social workers, the public housers'.[11] Reagan's theme was 'get the government off our backs'. The idea was to 'get rid of the costly failures of the Great Society. . . . The worst offender was the welfare system, and welfare reform was my highest domestic priority'.[12] So wrote Richard Nixon. In theory, by drastic pruning of the welfare programme taxes could be cut. This would in turn give people greater choice of how to use their own money and generate more prosperity because, it was assumed, individuals could spend money more effectively or efficiently than public agencies. The freed money in private hands could be used to support a variety of private welfare schemes and privatized services (formerly operated by public bodies) and still leave more money available to spend on consumer goods and services thereby creating more jobs and less need for state 'handouts'. These ideas appealed especially to those who had started life in humble circumstances but who had subsequently found a place in the American Dream; individuals like Reagan, Nixon and Milton Friedman. Reagan and Nixon were practitioners; Friedman the guru. The son of Austro-Hungarian immigrants who became shopkeepers, Friedman 'weathered poverty, anti-semitism, academic isolation and plain abuse *en route* to an extremely comfortable retirement'.[13] He won the Nobel Prize in 1976 for his work as an academic economist. He had become popular with the economists who advised the military regimes in Chile and Argentina, with Israeli Prime Minister Menachem Begin and with Margaret Thatcher. With him is associated the term 'monetarism': the theory that it is the money supply alone which should determine the amount of spending in the economy.

Nearer home, another guru of the New Right was being rediscovered in the 1970s. Friedrich August von Hayek was born into a well-established aristocratic and academic Viennese family in 1899. He had a highly successful career at the universities of Vienna, London, Chicago and Freiburg/Breisgau. He too received the Nobel Prize for Economics, in 1974. His most influential book, *The Road to Serfdom* (London, 1944), p. 67, is a powerful attack on socialism and collectivism. Of money Hayek wrote:

It is money which in existing society opens an astounding range of choice to the poor man, a range greater than that which not many generations ago was open to the wealthy. We shall better understand the significance of this service of money if we consider what it would be really mean if, as so many socialists characteristically propose, the 'pecuniary motive' were largely displaced by 'non-economic incentives'. If all rewards, instead of being offered in money, were offered in the form of public distinctions or privileges, positions of power over other men, or better housing or better food, opportunities for travel or education, this would merely mean that the recipient would no longer be allowed to choose, and that, whoever fixed the reward, determined not only its size but also the particular form in which it should be enjoyed.

This was the kind of socialism which Stalin had introduced into the Soviet Union and eastern Europe. Hayek recognized that many socialists did not want to go that far, but he rejected just as strongly 'competitive socialism' or even 'some Middle Way between "atomistic" competition and central direction'. His book was clearly out of fashion with the prevailing thought in Britain, the U.S.A. and his native Austria in the post-war period. Nevertheless Hayek had his followers, one of whom, Anthony Fisher, founded the Institute of Economic Affairs in London in 1956. The IEA gradually grew in importance as a right-wing think tank. Two other, similar, bodies were founded in the 1970s: the Adam Smith Institute and Keith Joseph's Centre for Policy Studies (CPS). Until 1985 the CPS was headed by Sir Alfred Sherman, a former Communist who had seen the error of his ways, and Lord (Hugh) Thomas, the historian of the Spanish Civil War and of Cuba and a former Labour supporter. These bodies emboldened Thatcher to say what she had always felt: that only capitalism can guarantee real freedom for the individual; that the tide of collectivism must be rolled back; and that deregulation, privatization, wider property ownership, self-help and trade union reform were the weapons in this crusade.

As part of this crusade the government embarked on a massive privatization programme. The main arguments advanced for this were as follows: those running privatized concerns would be free to decide their strategy free from government direction and without the financial constraints imposed by the Treasury; customers would benefit from the effects that a reduction in monopoly power and increased competition would have on efficiency, prices and choice; and there would be wider share ownership.[14] There was widespread criticism that this huge sale of billions of pounds worth of assets was badly executed and did not achieve the stated objectives. The city editor of the *Observer*, John Davis, commented (4 November 1979) on the sale of BP shares,

It is ironic that in a week that has seen the Government go to great lengths to stress to the nation the need for cutting its spending to fit its pocket, it should display such profligacy over the BP offer. As someone who pays his fair dues in tax, and as such is an indirect owner of those 80 million BP shares the Government is selling, I take strong exception to having my money thrown around in such a carefree manner.

Great national assets, bought and paid for with tax-payers' money and built up at great cost, were being sold off to what was inevitably a small group of investors, big institutions and foreign buyers (though in some cases employees were given favourable terms too). After the sale of British Aerospace, Amersham International, Cable & Wireless, Jaguar, the BP shares, National Freight and certain other assets, it was reckoned that the nation had lost several billions on the deal.[15] Nor were these sales likely to lead to greater competition. Most of these concerns had faced competition before and they were not being broken up into smaller units.

The sale of council houses was in some important respects different from the sale of other assets. These were being sold to sitting tenants, many of whom were not likely to buy their own homes in normal circumstances. They were being sold below the market price, thus transferring wealth from the relatively better off to the less well off (though not the poorest). Over five years some 750,000 homes were sold.

For a hundred years at least, many of the most successful entrepreneurs in Britain had been European immigrants or from the British Empire. Many of those who made the headlines between 1965 and 1985 were from these backgrounds – the media kings Murdoch and Maxwell; the heads of great industrial concerns, Weinstock and Edwardes; Forte, the head of the great hotel and catering business, and the founders of the retail high street chains. Among the exceptions were Freddie Laker, the independent airline chief, who pioneered cheap Atlantic air fares; Clive Sinclair, the home computer inventor, and John Gunn, who as chief executive built up the great international money-broking and financial information concern, EXco. Unlike Laker and Sinclair, Gunn was a scholarship boy, who had studied German at Nottingham University before joining Barclays.[16] Thatcher thought Thatcherism was about creating a climate for enterprise. On her recommendation, Murdoch, Laker and Sinclair got knighthoods.

The Bolton Committee of Inquiry (1971) had found that the small business sector was in long-term decline. There were many who felt that some of the success of Japan, Germany and Switzerland was attributable to their relatively large number of small businesses. After 1979 there was more government encouragement for individuals to go into business on their own. Unfair dismissal and maternity leave requirements for small businesses were relaxed. The enterprise allowance scheme (1982) encouraged the unemployed to set up in business by paying them £40 a week for their first year to offset the loss of unemployment benefit. Applicants had to invest at least £1,000 of their own money. Employee buy-outs of firms were also made easier. Unlike their counterparts in Germany, many embarked on their pilgrimage with more hope than skill or knowledge; often they failed. Still winning three years into their experiment were Chris and Zahra. A redundant denim sales executive Chris and his Iranian wife went into the takeaway business. The small businesses helped to regenerate the decaying inner cities and added to the quality of life. The large number of failures was in part related to poor training, high rates and the general state of the economy.

In November 1985 the Prince of Wales joined in the call for a more enterprise-orientated society. Back from a visit to the United States he was impressed by what he had seen there. He believed too many people in Britain had got used to an 'employee related existence' and more enterprise and lots more small businesses were needed. He warned that if Britain did not change it would end up as a 'fourth-rate country'.

James Prior, Employment Secretary until September 1981, said Thatcher 'loathed the trade unions' (*Guardian*, 20 May 1985). Undoubtedly had she had a free hand their activities would have been severely curtailed. There was widespread agreement, however, among Conservatives (and others) that trade union reforms were necessary. Under the 1980 Employment Act employers were given the right to take legal action against secondary picketing and most kinds of secondary action ('blacking' etc.). All new closed shops had to be approved by four-fifths of those affected and public funds were made available to encourage unions to hold postal ballots. The Employment Act of 1982 laid down that no closed shop should be enforceable unless it had been agreed by an overwhelming majority of the employees concerned in a secret ballot. It provided compensation from public funds to people dismissed from closed shops. It also made 'union labour only' requirements in contracts illegal. Trade unions became liable for damages if they were the cause of unlawful industrial actions. Finally, it gave employers legal redress against industrial action where no dispute existed between them and their own employees, or where the action was not wholly or mainly about employment matters (i.e. strikes which could be considered political). The Trade Union Act (1984) aimed to give more power to what its authors thought were the moderate majority of trade union members. It required a secret ballot of members before strike action if a union wished to retain its immunity from civil action for damages. It also required secret ballots every ten years by unions which maintained a political fund (part of which goes to the Labour Party). From 1 October 1985 all elections for union officials were to be 'fair, free, secret and direct'. Naturally enough many trade union activists and their leaders saw the legislation as 'union bashing' and advocated ignoring it. They wanted to commit a future Labour government to its repeal. The trouble was that the majority of rank-and-file unionists (as polls indicated) favoured the legislation. And in a number of ballots between 1980 and 1983 trade unionists rejected strike calls by their leaders. The movement was split over the issue of taking government money to fund secret ballots. The electricians (EETPU) and the engineers (AUEW) supported the acceptance of such funding; the majority of the TUC did not. Political fund ballots which were held proved to be victories for the Labour Party. As in the United States and West Germany, union membership fell during this period. Membership had reached a peak of 13.3 million at the end of 1979 but then dropped steadily, and by the end of 1983 had fallen by nearly 15 per cent, even though employment had fallen by only 8 per cent (*Employment Gazette*, January 1985).

From Rhodesia to Zimbabwe

The fall of the authoritarian regime in Portugal in 1974 was followed by the rapid decolonization of its empire in southern Africa. This sudden change in the political geography of Africa greatly increased the pressures on the white settler regime of Ian Smith in Rhodesia. A guerrilla war was fought with increasing ferocity between the white Rhodesia Front and black rebels backed directly by Zambia, Tanzania, Mozambique and Cuba and, indirectly, by the other black African states. By 1976 Smith had seen the writing on the wall and knew his only option was to negotiate the best surrender terms possible. He sought an 'internal settlement' with moderate black leaders enabling the whites to retain decisive influence long after formal power had been transferred to the black majority. As part of this attempt at a solution Bishop Abel Muzorewa was installed as Prime Minister in April 1979 after one man/one vote elections. The attempt failed because of lack of recognition by the outside world. Hopes that Britain's new Conservative government would come to the rescue of the Bishop proved unfounded. A significant minority of the party would have been prepared to recognize the Smith regime and a majority would have welcomed the recognition of Muzorewa. As for Mrs Thatcher, she

instinctively favoured recognition. Although a passionate (and frequently voluble) critic of South Africa's apartheid system, Mrs Thatcher was not a politician whose heart beat in time to the tunes of racial equality, nor had she much confidence in nor sympathy towards the leaders of black Africa.[17]

However, her hands were tied by the continued opposition from most of the Commonwealth states including the Conservative government of Malcolm Fraser in Australia. Washington, the U.N. and the Organization of African Unity also gave Muzorewa the thumbs down. A great deal of back-stage diplomacy, with Carrington throwing his weight against Muzorewa but in favour of a constitutional conference at which all parties would be represented, led to tough negotiations at Lancaster House (London) where the Bishop and Smith faced Mugabe and Nkomo, the leaders of the black parties Zanu and Zapu, united in the Patriotic Front. The conference, which nearly broke down on several occasions, produced an agreement which temporarily returned Zimbabwe-Rhodesia (as it was now called) to the status of a British colony. Lord Soames was appointed Governor. A ceasefire was agreed and the guerrilla forces legalized. A Commonwealth peace-keeping force took over the policing of the ceasefire. Economic sanctions against the colony were dropped. A democratic constitution was accepted which gave the whites, who represented 3 per cent of the population, 20 per cent of the seats in parliament. Two months of electioneering followed with Zanu and Zapu competing against each other and against Muzorewa's United African National Council. Voting for the 20 seats reserved for the whites gave Ian Smith's Rhodesia Front all of them. The elections for the 80 seats reserved for the blacks gave Robert Mugabe's Zanu 57, Joshua Nkomo's Zapu 20 and the United African National Council 3. Zanu had gained 63 per cent of the vote, the Council only 8 per cent. Mugabe then formed a government which included Nkomo. On 17 April 1980 Rhodesia became the independent state of Zimbabwe with The Revd Canaan Banana as its first president.

In most quarters the Zimbabwe settlement was given a euphoric reception. There were several reasons for this euphoria. In the first place the settlement had brought to an end a war which had claimed over 20,000 lives and which had endangered peace in the whole of southern Africa. Secondly, it had got implacable enemies to compromise and even to co-operate. Thirdly, it seemed to offer certain clues to a possible solution to South Africa's vexed race relations. Fourthly, the settlement also gave the white minority in Zimbabwe at least some extra time to either learn to live with black majority rule or gradually to withdraw, saving some of their assets. Had the war gone on it seemed likely they would have lost everything. Fifthly, the settlement gave a boost to Britain's image in the Third World and, indeed, in international political circles in general. Finally, for the west, the settlement appeared to restrict the growing Soviet influence in the region. Thatcher, Soames, Carrington and Kenneth Kaunda of Zambia could be well pleased with the results of their efforts. This is not the place to narrate the post-independence history of Zimbabwe, but it is relevant to mention that its development has fallen short of the hopes of 1980. Mugabe has managed to stay in power and has been able to retain the skills of a substantial number of the white minority. However, he has repeatedly declared that his aim is a one-party state and he is well on the road to achieving this aim. He has moved against both his former white enemies and his former comrades-in-arms in Zapu. Bishop Muzorewa was jailed in 1982 and Joshua Nkomo sought refuge abroad apparently in fear of his life. In its 1984 report Amnesty International, the internationally respected human rights organization, commented, 'The state of emergency, which has been in force continuously since 1965 and which had been re-imposed at six-monthly intervals since independence in 1980, was further renewed in January and July'. The report said its representatives had received information 'confirming widespread detentions and the use of torture. . .and received convincing evidence that significant numbers of extrajudicial executions had been committed by government security forces in Matabeleland North Province'. This sad state of affairs does not mean that the Lancaster House settlement was worthless. In 1980 the British government had little room for manoeuvre. Britain was in no position to enforce a solution: it could only work with the parties concerned towards one.

Labour in turmoil

As we saw (above, p. 281) tension had been building up in the Labour movement, even before the 1979 election, owing to severe disappointment with Callaghan's policies. The former Prime Minister's kindest critics thought he was guilty of bad judgement over the pay policy and the timing of the election; the harshest believed he had betrayed the movement. The truth was that no Labour government, from MacDonald's first minority government in 1924 onwards, had ever satisfied the socialist aspirations of many of its followers. In addition, every Labour administration had made bad errors of judgement over particular policies which further fuelled dissatisfaction in their own ranks. In the 1970s, Labour's zigzag course on the EEC issue had been one of these; pay policy had been another. The myth that the annual conference of the Labour Party decided issues made matters worse. Delegates passed resolutions only to find that their leaders in government ignored them. Wilson had been guilty of this over the EEC and defence after 1964. When the stalwarts met for Labour's annual conference in Brighton in October 1979 the anger felt by many delegates was tempered only by their feeling that they needed a show of unity in face of the Conservative victory. As he sang *The Red Flag*, 'though cowards flinch and traitors sneer', at the end of the conference, Callaghan probably thought he had got off lightly. The Left, however, had scored a number of significant victories. The conference had voted for the mandatory re-selection of MPs by their constituency parties. It had vested control of the election manifesto in the National Executive Committee (elected by the conference). It had voted for a commission of inquiry into the party's finances and membership which would also make recommendations about a new way of electing the leader. The Left were well represented on this commission.

On the Right of the Labour Party too there had been rumblings of discontent under both Wilson and Callaghan. For them too the EEC debate had been a matter of fundamental importance. They were frustrated by their Party's continued opposition to the EEC which put Labour out of step with most of its sister parties in the

Socialist International. The experience of working together with political opponents on the EEC referendum (above, pp. 252–4) had made some of them favourable to coalition politics.[18] They were also alarmed by the growing influence of the Left and appalled by the apparent willingness of some Labour MPs to write for Communist publications and support Soviet positions in international affairs. The Right was also concerned about the drift to the left in the trade unions and, not least, with attempts to unseat moderate Labour MPs. One of these was Reg Prentice at Newham (who later joined the Conservatives), another was Neville Sandelson at Hayes and Harlington. A report by Reg (later Lord) Underhill, the Labour Party's national agent, seemed to confirm the fears of the Right about the growing influence of revolutionary Marxists within the party. The report, submitted to the NEC in November 1975, was not published. In the same year a right-wing pressure group, the Social Democratic Alliance (SDA) was established in an attempt to counter the Left. It was led by Douglas Eden, Stephen Haseler and Peter Stephenson, editor of *Socialist Commentary*. Meanwhile, within the Parliamentary Labour Party, a number of right-of-centre MPs had set up the Manifesto Group (December 1974) with John Cartwright as its chairman. Later, in 1977, the Campaign for Labour Victory (CLV) was proclaimed. This aimed at uniting right-of-centre Labour activists outside parliament with like-minded MPs. From the Cabinet the CLV was backed by Shirley Williams, William Rodgers and David Owen, with Roy Hattersley giving it his 'guarded support'.[19] Left-wing activists were organized in the Labour Co-Ordinating Committee and the (Marxist) Militant Tendency. This was how matters stood when Labour was defeated in 1979.

Shortly after the general election there followed, in June 1979, the elections to the European Parliament. The electorate seemed confused, bored and apathetic; only 32 per cent bothered to vote. The Conservatives gained 51 per cent of the votes in Great Britain (60 of the 78 seats), Labour 33 per cent (17 seats), the Liberals 13 per cent (no seats) and the SNP 2 per cent (1 seat). In Northern Ireland, where proportional representation was introduced, 57 per cent voted, giving the Democratic Unionists, Official Unionists and the Catholic-supported Social Democratic and Labour Party one seat each.

Thatcher in trouble

Within months of taking office the Conservative government was very unpopular. At a by-election at Southend in March 1980 a Conservative majority of 10,000 was slashed to under 500. The candidate was a well-known politician, Teddy Taylor. What had caused this dramatic fall in support? Geoffrey Howe's first budget in June 1979 had hit wide sections of the electorate. It was designed to shift the raising of revenue from income tax to VAT. The standard rate of income tax was reduced with greater relief at the top end of the scale. VAT went up from 8 or 12.5 per cent to a uniform 15 per cent. Up too went interest rates. A programme of cuts in public expenditure was announced. By November the Chancellor had put up interest rates to record levels and announced further public spending cuts affecting all departments except for the armed forces and the police. This was in part his response to the increased inflation which his earlier budget had produced. The high interest rates hit industry hard as did the strengthening pound and rapidly growing unemployment followed. In 1978 it had stood at 1.25 million or 5.4 per cent of the work force. By October 1980 it had reached over 2 million and in January 1982 stood at 2.67 million. New records were being broken as unemployment rose and production fell. 1980 saw the biggest drop in industrial activity since the 1930s.

This critical situation must have been a factor in the youth unrest which exploded over Britain in July 1981. From Liverpool, *Time* magazine (20 July) reported 'a convulsive release of pent-up hatred in a wild surge of rioting, burning and looting'. The American magazine featured this as its cover story, 'Why Britain Burns', because, of course, it was not just in Liverpool that the streets were out of control. Manchester

sank into almost nightly rioting. In London, where the incendiary madness started the previous weekend with a race riot in the district of Southall, the sparks returned to alight in at least a dozen other neighbourhoods, including Wood Green, Woolwich and Brixton, the scene of vicious riots last April. The battles pitted racist 'skinheads' against ethnic Asians, have-nots against haves, and just about everybody against the police.

Similar events occurred in Birmingham, Ellesmere Port, Hull, Nottingham, Newcastle upon Tyne, Preston and other towns. The apparently spontaneous riots were a mighty follow up to what had already taken place in Brixton and Bristol. They shocked foreign observers of Britain. The influential West German news magazine, *Der Spiegel* (20 July 1981) thought, 'At the time of the marriage of Prince Charles and Lady Diana England is on the verge of civil war'. The riots highlighted the plight of youth, the inadequacies of the police, the problems of London and other inner city areas and the difficulties of the immigrant communities.

The riots of 1981 were an important factor in the introduction of the Youth Training Scheme (YTS) in 1983 which replaced the old

Youth Opportunities Programme. As a Conservative publication freely admitted in 1983, 'Only half Britain's school leavers are trained compared with nine-tenths in Germany and four-fifths in France. Over a third of school leavers entering jobs receive no training at all, and another fifth scarcely any at all'.[20] There was much criticism of the training given and the low pay which some young people regarded as 'exploitation', but it was better than nothing. In apparent contradiction to this policy, the government had in 1981 'saved' money by abolishing 16 of the Industrial Training Boards, retaining only 7. Young people were also discouraged from staying at school after sixteen to take 'O' or 'A' levels by the fact that if they did this, they could not claim social security payments, unlike those who stayed at home and did nothing! As the universities and polytechnics were suffering severe cuts under – as many in education saw him – 'the mad axeman' of the Department of Education, Sir Keith Joseph, some young people felt it was pointless to try for public exams. By the 1980s the government had another major worry about young people – drugs.

After the Brixton riots Lord Scarman was appointed to inquire into the disturbances there. His report of 25 November 1981 called for the recruitment of more police from the ethnic minorities, longer training for recruits with more emphasis on policing in a multi-racial society and dismissal as the normal penalty for racially prejudiced behaviour (this last was rejected by the Home Secretary, William Whitelaw). Scarman also recommended more foot patrols and an 'independent element in the investigation of complaints' against the police.

Since the early 1950s Brixton had been regarded as an area of black settlement and there were by then other parts of London associated with particular ethnic groups like the Jews and the Irish. By 1982 London was in danger of becoming a series of ghettos for Jews, Irish, Cypriots, blacks, Chinese, Asians, Australasians, British working class, middle class and, most recently, those from the Middle East or Hong Kong. Immigration from 'the New Commonwealth and Pakistan' which had numbered 32,200 in 1973 and 37,000 in 1979 fell to 30,300 in 1982. Whether this was because Britain was not as attractive as it had been or a result of the tightening up of the immigration rules (announced on 14 November 1979) is not entirely clear. The harder look at applicants was designed to reduce the numbers of those who married existing residents of the UK primarily to secure entry into the country. The British Nationality Act of 1981 was also meant to clarify and restrict citizenship to those with close ties with the UK. Those seeking naturalization would have to meet a language standard and foreigners marrying British citizens would have to wait three years before they could gain naturalization. The minorities felt that they were discriminated against by the new restrictions on immigration and by society in general. The Swann report, *Education For All* (1985), made a strong plea for reforms in the education system to encourage the black community and concluded that 'ethnic minority teachers have been and are still subject to racial prejudice and discrimination, both in gaining employment and in advancing their careers'. It rejected the separate schools favoured by some Asian groups. All the political parties attempted to harness the voting power of the minorities. Although it was worried about immigration, the government did allow entry into Britain of some 10,000 Vietnamese refugees.

Horrific rioting broke out again in the Handsworth district of Birmingham and, a few weeks later, in Brixton in the summer of 1985. In the first case (mainly) black rioters smashed, looted and destroyed Asian shops killing two traders. In the second, (mainly) black rioters took to the streets after the police had shot a black mother by accident during a house raid. Similar incidents sparked off rioting in Peckham and Tottenham a few days later. Had the rioters been influenced by the scenes of violence from South Africa seen nightly on their TV screens? Would black rioting in Britain increase sympathy for the minority regime in South Africa? By 1985 there were just over 1 million people of Asian origin in Britain, just under 1 million of West Indian origin and 53 million whites.

The 'gang of four' and the SDP

The unpopularity of the Conservatives enabled many in the Labour camp to resist a sober analysis of their situation. They preferred instead to continue their civil war fought in the name of more internal party democracy. At its annual conference at Blackpool in 1980 Labour confirmed the mandatory re-selection of MPs and agreed that in future the party leader should be elected by an electoral college drawn from all parts of the movement. The conference confirmed Labour's opposition to nuclear arms and to the EEC but refused the call to leave NATO and the demand that the NEC (usually dominated by the Left) should have control over the election manifesto. Callaghan then decided to bow out, to be replaced by Michael Foot who defeated Denis Healey by 139 votes to 129 on the second ballot. Healey then was elected deputy leader. Never a Marxist, at sixty-seven Foot seemed to have moved little intellectually since the 1950s. He remained committed to unilateral nuclear disarmament, withdrawal from the EEC and extensive development of public ownership. Healey was just the opposite. Foot was to be the last leader to be elected solely by the members of the PLP. At a special conference at Wembley in January 1981 it was decided that in future the leader would be elected by a process in which the unions had 40 per cent of the votes and the PLP and the constituency parties 30 per cent each. This decision represented a victory for the Left in the shape of Tony Benn and the Rank and File Mobilizing Committee (RFMC). The RFMC was an umbrella organization uniting the Labour Co-ordinating Committee, the Militant Tendency, Institute for Workers' Control and other groups. The decision represented a defeat for Foot to the extent that he had advised equal votes for each of the three sections of the Labour Party.

All of these developments were just too much for leading ex-Cabinet ministers David Owen, William Rodgers and Shirley Williams. They decided they could no longer fight for their ideals within the Labour Party and that secession was their duty. The break came in stages. On 7 June 1980 the three – or 'gang of three' as they became known – had announced that they would leave the Labour Party if it committed itself to withdrawal from the EEC. At the annual conference in the same year Shirley Williams and Tom Bradley refused to speak in favour of the NEC of which they were both members. In November Owen announced he would not seek re-election to the Shadow Cabinet and Williams (who had lost her seat in the 1979 election) said she would not seek a Labour candidature unless party policies were changed. On 1 December the Labour Party announced that the Social Democratic Alliance was a proscribed organization, that is, its members could not be members of the Labour Party. However, the three had not just spent their time in weary retreat. They had been looking around for alternatives. As we saw (above, p. 265) James Callaghan's government had reached an accommodation with the Liberals to maintain it in office and this made it easier for the 'gang' to contemplate future co-operation with the Liberals. It also made it more difficult for the other former colleagues of the three to criticize such moves. At the Liberal Party Assembly in September 1980 David Steel had urged them to leave the Labour Party. Another factor in the situation was the return to Britain in January 1981 of Roy Jenkins, who had served since 1976 as President of the EEC Commission in Brussels. It is true, as one of his political followers has written, 'his image of grand statesmanship, high living and foreign friends threw doubt on his political future', but he was probably the most experienced British politician in 1981.[21] As President of the EEC he had been in a position of responsibility roughly equal to that of head of government and he had been deputy leader of the Labour Party, Home Secretary, Chancellor and Minister of Aviation. In his Dimbleby Lecture on BBC TV in November 1979 he had questioned Britain's existing political arrangements and proposed a much stronger 'radical centre' which, he believed, would bring into politics 'many people of talent and goodwill' who were alienated by 'the sterility and formalism of much of the political game'.[22] He was in touch with Liberals and Labour Euro-dissidents and his associate, David Marquand, former Labour MP for Ashfield who worked with Jenkins in Brussels, made suitable noises at the Liberal Assembly in September 1980. Thus it was that the 'gang of three' became the 'gang of four' when Jenkins joined his former colleagues to issue the Limehouse Declaration on 25 January 1981, the day after the Wembley conference of the Labour Party. The Declaration claimed that, 'A handful of trade union leaders can now dictate the choice of a future Prime Minister' and that the Labour Party had moved 'steadily away from its roots in the people of this country and its commitment to parliamentary government'. Its authors wanted 'to create an open, classless and more equal society, one which rejects ugly prejudices based upon sex, race or religion'. To this end they would set up a Council for Social Democracy to rally support for this aim. They wanted Britain to play a full part in the EEC, NATO, the UN and the Commonwealth. On the vital question of the economy they said,

Our economy needs a healthy public sector and a healthy private sector without frequent frontier changes. We want to eliminate poverty and promote greater equality without stifling enterprise or imposing bureaucracy from the centre. We need the innovating strength of a competitive economy with a fair distribution of rewards. We favour competitive public enterprise, co-operative ventures and profit sharing.

They also wanted decentralization and a system of practical democracy at work. They concluded by saying,

We recognize that for those people who have given much of their lives to the Labour Party, the choice that lies ahead will be deeply painful. But we believe that the need for a re-alignment of British politics must now be faced.[28]

It was a statement which could have been supported by the great majority in the previous Labour government and many Labour activists as well as the majority of Labour voters. On 5 February the Council published an advertisement in the *Guardian* appealing for support. The appeal carried 100 names in addition to the four. It included thirteen former Labour MPs, among them Lord George-Brown, Kenneth Robinson, Edmund Dell and Lord Diamond who had all served in recent Labour cabinets. Several distinguished academics were listed: Alan Bullock,

Sir Fred Dainton (Chancellor of Sheffield University), Professor James Meade (Nobel prize winner for economics), Sir Alec Cairncross (the economist who had advised the government, 1961–4), Lord Flowers (Rector of Imperial College), Professor Joan Mitchell (adviser to Shirley Williams and from Nottingham University), Lord Perry (Vice-Chancellor of the Open University), Sir Charles Carter (Vice-Chancellor of Lancaster University) and Professor David Marquand (Salford University). Among the many younger academics were John Frears, Stephen Haseler and Stuart Thompstone. The business world was represented by Lord Sainsbury and his son David. A touch of 'glamour' was added by Steve Race, the musician and broadcaster, and Janet Suzman, the actress. The only major trade union figure was Frank (later Lord) Chapple, leader of the electricians union (EEPTU). To what extent those on the list were 'workers by hand or by brain', as the Labour Party Constitution defines its members, is open to interpretation. Certainly they represented a great deal of brain power and a wide variety of practical experience. On 26 March 1981 the Social Democratic Party (SDP) was launched in the Connaught Rooms, London, in the presence of 500 journalists from TV, radio and the press.[24] Within days the SDP had 14 MPs – 13 former Labour and one former Conservative,' Christopher Brocklebank-Fowler. Within a matter of weeks it was claiming a membership of over 50,000.[25] As was only to be expected, the new party was attacked from both Right and Left. Mrs Thatcher saw them as socialists. Their erstwhile comrades in the Labour Solidarity Campaign, the group of MPs set up by Roy Hattersley to fight the Left in the Labour Party, believed, 'Their lack of firm policies and their determination to be all things to all people ensures them the backing not only of misguided but genuine protesters, but also a ragbag of political misfits and outcasts'.[26] The party seemed to be taking off so successfully that even some Liberals were worried and resentful. This was understandable as opinion polls, even before the SDP was formally set up gave it 23 and then 31 per cent support as against 13 and 13.5 for the Liberals. (In the second poll the Conservatives had 25.5 per cent and Labour 28.)[27]

The leaders of the SDP and the Liberal Party realized that they needed to co-operate with each other if they were to succeed and by the autumn of 1981 the conferences of the two parties agreed on an alliance. They then fought a series of remarkable by-elections at which they grabbed three seats from the Conservatives. At Croydon (22 October 1981) the little-known Liberal, William Pitt, won. At Crosby (26 November 1981) Shirley Williams overturned a Conservative majority of 19,272, and at Hillhead (Glasgow) on

23 March 1982 Roy Jenkins won against the odds. Yet within a matter of weeks Jenkins's victory was almost forgotten as the media focused their attention on a bleak, windswept group of islands in the South Atlantic.

However one views the SDP, it cannot be said that its founders chose an easy road or that their motives were crudely ambitious. Had Owen, Rodgers and Williams remained with Labour it is likely they would have been at least tolerated. Mrs Williams had lost her seat but was very popular and could surely have found another. She was regarded by many as a possible future Labour leader. Only Jenkins appeared to be debarred from possible re-election as a Labour candidate. As rational, experienced politicians, they must have known that they were likely to fail. As David Marquand, the biographer of Ramsay MacDonald, could remind his colleagues, those who had joined MacDonald's National Labour Party in 1931 had become clients of the Conservatives before being eliminated from the political scene. And Sir Oswald Mosley's attempt to launch the New Party had failed totally in the same period. The British two-party system punished severely those who were brave enough to challenge it. In Italy moderate socialists had broken with the Socialist Party in 1948 because of its pact with the Communists. They succeeded in establishing themselves as Social Democrats and gained a minor, but by no means insignificant, place in the political system. They could do so because the Italian system is based on proportional representation. The Alliance badly needed to change the British electoral system.

War in the Falklands

As the members of the British Cabinet (and most other people) slept at dawn on 2 April 1982 one of the last remnants of the British Empire was being invaded. It is safe to say that many Britons had no idea where the Falklands were or that they had long been the object of nationalistic fervour in Argentina where they are known as the 'Malvinas'. Argentina claimed the islands on the ground that it had succeeded to rights claimed by Spain in the eighteenth century. The British title to the islands 'is derived from early settlement reinforced by formal claims in the name of the Crown in the eighteenth century and completed by effective possession, occupation and administration for nearly 150 years.'[28] In 1982 virtually all the 1,800 inhabitants were of British ancestry and wanted to remain British. But as Britain's power declined and its purse got smaller it was prepared to consider 'decolonization'. From 1965 onwards it negotiated with Argentina to find a solution to the sovereignty dispute. It is beyond dispute that the long argument had been intensified by the military regime which had ruled Argentina since it had overthrown the country's elected President in 1976. It is also true that the small, but very noisy, Falklands lobby both inside and outside the Commons, worked hard to prevent any solution which diminished or abandoned British sovereignty. It appears that in 1980 Nicholas Ridley, the minister charged with dealing with the dispute, had come near to finding a solution. Hastings and Jenkins in their classic on the Falklands war claim:

It is hard to avoid the conclusion that, had the British cabinet had the courage of its own minister's convictions at this time, leaseback could have been negotiated between Port Stanley and Buenos Aires. The result would almost certainly have been no war and little disruption to the islanders' lifestyle.[29]

This would have meant recognizing Argentine sovereignty but with Argentina agreeing to continued British administration for a limited period. According to the two authors, strong vocal opposition in the Commons (2 December 1980) to the idea led to its abandonment by the Cabinet. This should have indicated to the Argentine rulers that any attempt to seize the islands would be at least risky. But perhaps other facts helped to mislead them. The British Antarctic Survey had announced it was closing its research station on South Georgia for lack of funds. The Ministry of Defence had made public its decision to withdraw the armed (Falklands patrol) ship *Endurance* from service. The decision, under the 1981 Nationality Act, not to grant a right to abode in Britain to about 800 Falklanders who did not have a grandparent born in the UK could have led the Argentine government to believe that Britain was not really serious about the fate of the islanders. The failure to implement the Shackleton Report (1977) which made proposals for the development of the islands' economy, seemed to indicate London's lack of commitment. Finally, perhaps Argentina misinterpreted Britain's action in giving up its last colony on the American mainland. Belize (formerly British Honduras) with its population of 147,000 became independent in September 1981. British troops did however remain because of fear of attack from neighbouring Guatemala which claimed the territory.

Relations between Britain and Argentina deteriorated even though talks continued. Facing rapidly growing opposition at home (due to deflationist economic policies and repression) the Argentine military rulers led by their President, General Galtieri, decided they needed to seize the islands to unite their nation. On 1 April 1982 their Foreign Minister, Nicanor Costa Mendez, informed the British Ambassador that the diplomatic channel as a means of settling the dispute was closed. The invasion took place the following day. Several Argentine soldiers were killed when the small detachments of British marines resisted. One British serviceman was severely wounded before the final, inevitable, surrender. The British troops, the governor, Rex Hunt, and any islanders who wished to go with them, were evacuated by the new rulers.

What could Britain do in these circumstances? Thatcher had already appealed to President Reagan who had phoned the Argentine President to no avail. Britain did manage to get the UN Security Council to adopt a resolution calling for the withdrawal of Argentine forces – even the Soviet Union did not vote against this! It got the support of the EEC, including an embargo on arms and military equipment to Argentina and a ban on imports from Argentina and the backing too of the Commonwealth and NATO. And even though most Latin American states supported Argentina's claim on sovereignty, few supported its use of force. The Bank of England took action to freeze Argentine assets in Britain. The Argentine regime, which already had a bad image because of its abuse of human rights, had put itself in the diplomatic doghouse and faced the possibility of crippling sanctions.

Had the Argentine junta not been so impatient (or desperate) and waited a few months longer, these measures might have been the limit of British retaliatory actions. The British Defence Minister, John Nott, backed strongly by his PM, was engaged in a cost-cutting exercise which meant, metaphorically speaking, the scuttling of what remained of the Royal Navy's big ships. It was planned, as the *Daily Telegraph* (18 May 1981) put it, 'To Gut The Navy'. Much of the surface fleet was to go, including the aircraft carriers *Invincible* and *Hermes*. The cuts were designed to save money and recognize that in future the RN's role was mainly the defence of the British Isles and its communications with Western Europe. It could best do this, so argued Sir Ronald Mason, Chief Scientific Adviser to the MoD, by abandoning surface vessels in favour of submarines. Opposition had come from the Navy Minister, Keith Speed, and the senior naval staff. Speed was forced out of office; the sailors remained to fight on from within. Unfortunately for General Galtieri these cuts had not been implemented by April 1982 and the First Sea Lord, Sir Henry Leach, saw the Falklands crisis as an opportunity to get the government to think again. In the absence abroad of the Chief of the Defence Staff, Sir Terence Lewin, Leach persuaded Mrs Thatcher (she needed little persuasion!) and through her the Cabinet, to send a task force to the South Atlantic. 'Certainly without his personal dynamism it is unlikely that the fleet would

311

have sailed so soon, and as a result more cautious counsels might have gained wider currency.'[30] Having got the task force accepted by the Cabinet, Thatcher decided that a small steering committee of appropriate ministers should take over the management of the crisis. This committee became known to the public as the War Cabinet. In addition to ministers and the Cabinet Secretary, Sir Robert Armstrong, the committee (officially, Overseas and Defence Committee South Atlantic or ODSA) included senior defence and FCO staff. Most members of the Cabinet were not on it.

On Monday 5 April bands played, flags were waved, women wept and men tried to look cheerful at Portsmouth as the task force glided out to sea. In London on the same day the Foreign Office was trying to keep its composure as its political bosses departed and new ones were installed. Out went Carrington, Atkins and Richard Luce, the junior minister whose duties included the Falklands. They took the responsibility for the incorrect interpretation of Argentina's intentions. Carrington also resented the anti-Foreign Office stance of a considerable number of Conservative backbenchers and Thatcher's appeasement of them. Francis Pym, not one of Thatcher's political friends, was appointed Foreign Secretary. However, with his conciliatory attitude he did not command much clout.

The task force eventually comprised over 100 ships and 27,000 personnel. It included the aircraft carriers *Hermes* and *Invincible*, older and larger destroyers, like the *Antrim* and *Glamorgan*, and the more modern Type 42 and Type 22. There were submarines and amphibious warfare vessels. Pressed into service were at least 70 civilian vessels, from the 67,000-ton *Queen Elizabeth 2*, used as a troop carrier, to a 690-ton seagoing tug, the *Yorkshireman*. The mission would have been impossible had not the armada been able to use US-leased facilities on the British-owned Ascension Island, about midway across the Atlantic. There the troops trained, the supplies were re-checked and re-loaded for combat, and the ancient Vulcan bombers and Nimrod reconnaissance planes found a base. Meanwhile the Argentine troops, many of them ill-trained conscripts, waited on the cold, bleak, desolate Islands in over-crowded, improvised quarters. As the diplomats went on talking, the military acted. On 25 April came the news that South Georgia had been recaptured. Remarkably, there were no British casualties. One Argentine sailor had been wounded and one was killed by accident the following day. However, Admiral 'Sandy' Woodward, commander of the task force, knew the retaking of South Georgia had been a near miracle. To take the main islands complete air and sea mastery would be needed. The British forces were operating

8,000 miles from home, the Argentines only 300 miles. For the first time since 1945 the Royal Navy was facing a modern fleet. Woodward knew that the weather would take its toll of his ships if they remained in those waters for long. The British needed swift action. It was these kinds of considerations which undoubtedly led to the order to sink the cruiser *General Belgrano* on 2 May. The cruiser went down after being hit by torpedoes from the submarine *Conqueror*. Critics of the action have argued that it was wrong to attack it as it was 35 miles outside the Total Exclusion Zone established by the RN around the Falklands, and that as an elderly ship it presented little threat to British ships. It is also argued that the action escalated the conflict and lost Britain international support. Finally, it has also been pointed out that the *Belgrano* appeared to be heading for its home base at the time of the action. Such reasoning ignores the fact that the vessel was providing aircraft direction for the Argentine air force and that it was equipped with modern missiles. Further, its removal was a major psychological blow to the Argentine navy which then kept out of the conflict. Two days later a Type 42 destroyer *Sheffield* sank after being hit by an Exocet missile. Do the critics of the *Belgrano* action believe this would not have happened had the Argentine cruiser not been sunk? Of the *Belgrano*'s crew 368 died; 21 men from the *Sheffield* met the same fate. Later the Type 42 *Coventry*, the Type 21 *Antelope* and *Ardent*, the landing ship *Sir Galahad* and the container ship *Atlantic Conveyor* joined the *Sheffield* at the bottom of the South Atlantic.

Operation Sutton, as the landings on the main islands were code-named, began on 21 May as Royal Marines and SAS troops stormed ashore and established a beachhead at San Carlos on the western end of East Falkland island. The mini-war effectively ended with the surrender of Port Stanley on 14 June to the British. In between these dates an assortment of crack British troops – paras, marines, Royal Artillery, Scots and Welsh Guards – had covered rough terrain in bad weather and forced the surrender of the numerically vastly superior Argentine forces. They had surprised the world, and very probably themselves, and the government which sent them. They could not know that their courage and daring would play its part in the re-election of the Prime Minister. Nor had they time to think that their actions speeded the fall of the Argentine junta, the members of which were subsequently put on trial.

The recovery of the Falklands cost Britain 255 killed and 777 wounded, 'three times the British casualties during the EOKA campaign in Cyprus, one-third the number of British killed in Korea, and a hundred fewer than those killed in Ulster since

1969'.[31] Argentine casualties were far heavier. It is almost a miracle that British casualties were so low: the dangers were enormous. This raises the whole question of whether the campaign was an appropriate response to the illegal Argentine occupation. Millions of people in Britain thought it was not; the great majority thought that it was. Many people felt a sense of excitement, pride and satisfaction at the exploits of 'our boys' on television every night. It was like old movies about the Second World War – only better! Such people forgot as one MP, a former soldier, put it that war is 'about picking up the remains of comrades in plastic bags'.[32] Anyway, it was a change from hearing about national decline, unemployment, cuts, the falling pound and more cuts. Some politicians, like Michael Foot and the Conservative MPs Sir Anthony Meyer and David Crouch, welcomed the sending of the task force, and then were appalled when the shooting started. Yet once the task force was under way it would have been irresponsible to leave it treading water in such an hostile environment. The Labour MP Andrew Faulds called the expedition 'absolute lunacy', and his opinion was not without foundation.[33] Firstly, there was the likelihood of appalling casualties, both military and civilian. No one could have known they would have been so light. There was a fear that Britain would lose its trade and influence in Latin America and a fear too that the conflict could have led to increased Soviet/Cuban influence in the area (especially as Britain was getting help from the U.S.A.). The expedition provided the Warsaw Pact with valuable information on how western weaponry stood the test of actual combat. Some were afraid that Britain's image among her friends would be dented, but any loss at the time of the *Belgrano* was probably made up later by the swift victory. Finally, there was, and remains, the massive financial cost of the undertaking, and the subsequent attempt to construct a 'Fortress Falklands' against any future aggression. Britain could have resettled the islanders on a lavish scale at a fraction of the cost. There was much talk of honour and dignity during the crisis but the same politicians who used such terms felt no problem in handing over millions of Hong Kong Chinese to the People's Republic of China (below, p. 331). One other aspect of the Falklands crisis which remains frightening is the ease with which Britain slipped into a shooting war, with a few ministers taking vital decisions 'in a fog of inaccurate, out-of-date and highly selected facts'.[34]

Notes

1 'The Medici of Madison Avenue', *Observer*, 24 March 1985.
2 David Butler and Dennis Kavanagh, *The British General Election of 1979* (London, 1980), 209.
3 Patrick Cosgrave, *Thatcher the First Term* (London, 1985), 63.
4 Butler and Kavanagh, op. cit., 419.
5 Ivor Crewe, 'The Labour Party and the Electorate' in Dennis Kavanagh, ed., *The Politics of the Labour Party* (London, 1982), 11.
6 Conversation with a working-class Conservative voter, Nottingham, 1985.
7 Cosgrave, op. cit., 67.
8 *Daily Mirror*, 7 May 1980.
9 Zig Layton-Henry, ed., *Conservative Party Politics* (London, 1980), 191.
10 Anthony Sampson, *The Changing Anatomy of Britain* (London, 1982), 52. 'I don't like her – either as a man, or as a woman.'
11 Richard Nixon, *The Memoirs of Richard Nixon* (London, 1979), 424–5.
12 Nixon, ibid., 424.
13 *Observer*, 17 February 1980.
14 Conservative Research Department, *The Campaign Guide 1983* (London, 1983), 54.
15 Michael Smith in *Guardian*, 4 December 1984.
16 *Personal Investor*, September 1985 and *Observer*, 14 July 1985.
17 Cosgrave, op. cit., 76.
18 Ian Bradley, *Breaking the Mould*? (London, 1981) 33–6.
19 Bradley, ibid., 63.
20 *The Campaign Guide 1983*, op. cit., 89.
21 Sampson, op. cit., 102.
22 *The Listener*, 29 November 1979.
23 *Guardian*, 5 February 1981.
24 *Daily Telegraph*, 27 March 1981.
25 *Guardian*, 22 May 1981.
26 *Daily Telegraph*, 27 March 1981.
27 Bradley, op. cit., 95.
28 *Britain and the Falklands Crisis: A Documentary Record*, Central Office of Information (London, 1982), 2.
29 Max Hastings and Simon Jenkins, *The Battle For The Falklands* (London, 1983), 56–7.
30 Hastings and Jenkins, ibid., 87.
31 Ibid., 357–8.
32 Ex-Guardsman and MP Don Concannon in conversation with the author.
33 Hansard (Commons), vol. 24 (20 May 1982), col. 497.
34 Ex-civil servant Clive Ponting in *Guardian*, 29 July 1985.

12   Thatcher's Second Term, 1983–7

Victory in June

When Britain went to the polls on 9 June 1983 the question was not who would win, but merely how big would be the Conservative majority. A secondary question was whether the alliance would replace Labour as the main opposition. For months before the election the Conservatives had been ahead in the opinion polls with Thatcher's popularity well ahead of that of her party. Not enough voters blamed the government for the nation's economic woes and, in any case, the Labour Party presented itself as a party at war with itself, led by an unworldly, ageing idealist. The Alliance, after its amazing popularity in 1981, had fallen back in support. The commanding Conservative lead was the result of a careful electoral strategy which had been unfolding for months. It appears to have been planned down to the last detail. No less than five different industrial psychiatrists and behavioural psychologists had been consulted about two sets of curtains – dark blue and light blue – for the newly-decorated press conference room at (Conservative) Central Office. Thatcher's ticket-only rallies were staged by Harvey Thomas, a veteran of the Billy Graham crusades. 'American influences were apparent at every turn of the campaign.'[1] Once again Saatchi and Saatchi were put to work for the Conservatives. The Falklands victory was a key factor together with Labour's incompetence and alleged extremism. The electorate actually gave the Conservatives 1 per cent fewer votes than in 1979 on a lower turnout (73 per cent as against 76). Yet their majority increased from 43 to 144. The 43 per cent gained by the Conservatives was 5 per cent lower than Labour had scored in 1966. Nevertheless, Labour had been severely mauled. With 28 per cent, its share of the vote was the lowest since 1918. The Alliance felt cheated because with only 2 per cent fewer votes than Labour it had won just 23 seats compared with Labour's 209. Of the 63 MPs who lost their seats, 30 were Labour and 24 were Alliance (4 Conservatives also went down). The casualties included Tony Benn, William Rodgers and Shirley Williams. Labour had lost support right across the board but its losses were heaviest among the skilled working class, trade unionists and owner-occupiers. It was estimated that only 39 per cent of trade unionists voted Labour. It also failed to capture young voters. Only 33 per cent voted Labour, compared with 42 per cent who gave their votes to the Conservatives. In geographical terms, the north–south divide had been strengthened with Labour gaining only two seats in the south of England outside London. It looked like becoming a ghetto party of the inner cities and areas of high, long-term, unemployment; a party of the unskilled, council-house tenants. The performance of the Alliance, facing its first major test, was monitored with interest. It had gained 26 per cent of the vote compared with the Liberal Party's 14 per cent in 1979. This must be regarded as a great achievement. In southern England it had replaced Labour as the opposition to the Conservatives. It had taken two votes from Labour for every one it took from the Conservatives. But although the Alliance had picked up votes everywhere, it had failed in the old Labour strongholds and it had not done so well in north-west Wales and parts of Scotland where the nationalist vote held. Having failed to make a major breakthrough, its problem was to consolidate the votes it had picked up.

Having won her second term Mrs Thatcher lost no time in reshuffling her government. Sir Geoffrey Howe moved to the Foreign Office and his place as Chancellor was taken by Nigel Lawson (b. 1932) who had served as Financial Secretary to the Treasury, 1979–81, and Secretary of State for Energy, 1981–3. The son of a tea merchant who had supported the Liberals, he was born and brought up in Hampstead. After Westminster School he read PPE at Oxford. On completion of national service in the navy he became a journalist on the *Financial Times*. Later he was City editor of the *Sunday Telegraph* and after that editor of the weekly *Spectator*. Leon Brittan (b. 1939) took over at the Home Office where he had previously served in a junior capacity 1979–81. Educated at Haberdashers' Aske's, Cambridge and Yale he had then built up a lucrative libel practice. He had served at the Treasury, 1981–3. Like Lawson he was of Jewish background and like him too he was regarded as a powerful addition to the Cabinet's intellectual capacity. Both men had entered the Commons in February 1974. Both were regarded as Thatcher's protégés. Michael Heseltine (b. 1933) moved from the Environment to Defence. Educated at Shrewsbury and Oxford and elected in 1966, Heseltine had been the darling of many a Conservative conference. He was seen as a rival and potential successor to Thatcher. Of her

317

critics, Pym was demoted to a powerful presence on the back benches and Prior was left brooding in Northern Ireland where he had been since 1981. As a whole, the new Cabinet was reckoned to be more subservient to the Prime Minister's whims and wishes than that of 1979.

In the Labour camp a dismayed Michael Foot took the responsibility for his party's overwhelming defeat and resigned. Denis Healey decided to give up the deputy leadership though he remained the shadow Foreign Secretary. Although four candidates stood in the leadership contest it soon became clear that the contest was between Neil Kinnock, on the Left, and Roy Hattersley on the Right. Kinnock was swept to victory on a majority of nearly 3–1 in Labour's newly established electoral college. Hattersley was then elected by a majority of 2–1 as his deputy. Most ordinary voters knew little about Kinnock and this was hardly surprising considering he had not held office and had only been on the NEC since 1978. From a Welsh mining family, Neil Kinnock had studied at the University of Wales (Cardiff) and had been elected to the Commons in 1970. He had climbed a long way up the party ladder as a 'soft', non-Marxist leftist supporting CND, opposing the EEC and calling for more public ownership. His personal charm and the backing of Michael Foot had taken him the rest of the way to the top. He had the advantage of youth (b. 1942) in his future contests with the 'Iron Lady'. In certain respects he resembled David Steel rather than David Owen who was now elected (unopposed) to the leadership of the SDP in place of Roy Jenkins. The two new leaders were soon having an impact. On 21 November 1983 the *Guardian* reported a Marplan poll indicating that both Kinnock and Owen were better liked than their respective predecessors though they still lagged behind Thatcher on the tests of competence and toughness. Even on competence Kinnock scored 42 per cent as against Foot's 24 per cent. But his rivals remained ahead: Thatcher 62, Steel 45, Owen 44. Kinnock was thought to be more in touch with the electorate than all his rivals, to be less extreme than Thatcher, to be behind only Steel on sincerity and to be behind only Thatcher on toughness. In the few weeks since he had been elected leader (1 October) his television performances had gained him a lot of support.

Mrs Thatcher was robbed of some of the rejoicing at the Conservative Party conference at Blackpool in October 1983 by one of those silly little scandals which afflict British politics from time to time. As the *Daily Telegraph* (15 October) put it, 'Mr Cecil Parkinson resigned in disgrace from the Cabinet yesterday after his fight to remain Trade and Industry Secretary was undermined overnight when his jilted mistress issued an unexpected statement to "put the record straight" about their affair.' Parkinson (b. 1931) was a married man; his secretary, Sara Keays, was expecting his child. A successful businessman and Cambridge graduate from a Lancashire working-class family, Parkinson's life had more than a touch of Joe Lampton about it. He had risen rapidly, becoming Party Chairman in 1981, and had served in the Falklands 'War Cabinet'. He was regarded as one of the key figures in the election victory of 1983 and was a close Thatcher associate. He had to go, not because of his complicated private life but because of his incompetent way of handling it. Parkinson's replacement as Chairman was John Selwyn Gummer (b. 1940), a parson's son and Cambridge graduate who was expected to give the party a more youthful image.

The second direct elections to the European Parliament, which took place in June 1984, indicated that Labour had made considerable headway under its new leader. A miserable turnout (32 per cent compared with 57 per cent in France and West Germany and 84 per cent in Italy) and the old, first-past-the-post system (the only country in the EEC using it) gave the Conservatives 46 seats (61 in 1979), Labour 33 (17) and the SNP 1 (1). The percentages of votes were: Conservatives 40.8, Labour 36.5 and Alliance 19.5. Conservative and Alliance support had weakened since the general election but the Alliance rightly felt it was the victim of a system which penalized third parties. It was all the more aggrieved because in the six by-elections held since the 1983 general election it had improved its vote by 10 per cent. On the same day as the Euro-elections, Mike Hancock, a well-known local Social Democrat, had taken Portsmouth South from the Conservatives on a 14 per cent by-election swing. Although the Euro-elections did represent a setback, Mrs Thatcher need not have mourned too much over them because she was already getting help from unexpected quarters.

The miners' strike

When Arthur Scargill (b. 1938) was elected president of the National Union of Mineworkers (NUM) in 1982 he was already a well-known figure. His militancy, oratory, which the *Observer* called 'a clever blend of northern clubland humour and populist Socialism', and organizational skills led to his election, in 1973, as Yorkshire area president of the union.[2] He was the youngest miner ever to reach that post. Unlike his predecessor, (Lord) Joe Gormley (president 1971–82), who had retired, Scargill looked at the world through Marxist spectacles. The man who was soon to become locked in battle with the flamboyant young Yorkshireman, was a soft-spoken, cunning old Scotsman, Ian MacGregor (b. 1912). A graduate in metallurgy from Glasgow University, he had become a wealthy industrialist and banker in the United States. He was called home by Sir Keith Joseph to run British Steel in 1980 and after drastically pruning that lossmaker – hit badly by the world recession and cheap foreign steel – he was almost begged by the government to put the National Coal Board (NCB) in order. He took over in 1983. 'Mac the hard man' had succeeded two 'softies': (Lord) Derek Ezra (1971–82) and Norman Siddall (1982–3). MacGregor's view of business was a rather simple and straightforward one: business was about making profits. If there were broader social considerations these were not really the concern of business.

Since 1979 many Conservatives (and many advocates of the supremacy of the market) had been appalled at Thatcher's readiness to continue subsidizing the NCB and other 'lame ducks'. The 1974 *Plan For Coal*, agreed by the NCB, NUM and the government and drawn up after the massive increase in oil prices, had foreseen a continued expansion of coal. This plan had been modified but it was overtaken by events, namely the world economic recession and the changing structure of the economy away from the 'smokestack' industries to service industries and those using much less fuel. For example, steel, which in 1980 had consumed 7 million tons of coal, used only 4 million in 1983. Since 1974 the mining industry had contracted from 250,000 men and 259 pits to 181,000 and 174 pits in March 1984.[3] The appointment of MacGregor was an indication that the government was looking for new, considerable savings. Unlike the government which had avoided confrontation with the miners in 1980–3, this was a Cabinet in which the 'free market' wing was much stronger than the social 'Wets'. Yet the Energy Secretary, Peter Walker, belonged to the 'Wets'. He could therefore be expected to favour conciliation with the NUM. The NCB was said to be looking for reductions in output which would mean the loss of 20,000 jobs within a year.[4] The Board could be more confident than on earlier occasions. Coal stocks were high both at the pit heads and at the power stations. The big users such as the chemical and steel industries also had large stocks and should there be a long, effective strike, there was plenty of relatively cheap coal quite near in Rotterdam. The NCB had evidence that the miners were not in a particularly militant mood. Alone in 1982, they had twice rejected, by secret ballots, their leadership's call for a mandate to order industrial action 'if necessary'.

The NUM imposed an overtime ban from 31 October 1983. The actual strike, Britain's longest and bitterest since 1926, erupted in the following spring. The immediate cause of the confrontation was the way the NCB went about the closure of Cortonwood pit in South Yorkshire and Polmaise pit in Scotland, although Polmaise was subsequently reprieved. The normal, and fairly lengthy, consultation procedures were cut short. The two area committees of the NUM retaliated with strike action. This move was then approved by the national executive of the NUM by 21 votes to 3. Any actions taken in other areas were given prior approval, thus encouraging strikes elsewhere. 'Flying pickets' were sent from the militant areas to persuade workers not yet on strike to join in. By 15 March 1984, 140 pits were idle. When the national executive met on 12 April the Leicester area called for a national ballot of the members to decide the issue of industrial action. Scargill ruled this out of order. His colleagues agreed with him by 13 to 8 with 3 abstentions.[5] This was one of the most important decisions made by any body in the trades union movement since 1945. The NUM leadership gave the NCB a powerful weapon which was to be used again and again. It split the NUM with potentially disastrous consequences for the Labour Party. Did Scargill, his close ally, Mike McGahey, and the other militants know that they lacked a majority? Writing in the *New Statesman* (22 March 1985) Peter Kellner recorded, 'contrary to all *published* polls conducted last spring, the private polls suggested that a national ballot would *not* have provided a majority for strike action.' The executive committee decision was backed by a special delegate conference – a conference of the active minority rather than the more balanced majority. Even so, the majority in favour of the strike was only 69 to 54. The conference also agreed that the rule requiring a 55 per cent vote in favour before a national strike could be called should be amended. In future only a simple majority would be required. In Nottinghamshire, elections to the NUM's area council returned a decisive majority of members who opposed strike action. The new council took office on 2 July. The Nottinghamshire miners had a tradition of independence and moderation; they also had the advantage of working more productive pits. Some felt it was the wrong strike at the wrong time forced on them by a leadership using less than democratic methods. It was the wrong time because coal stocks were high and because in spring and summer less coal was needed. It was, many felt, the wrong strike because the NCB's terms did not appear bad. On 28 March 1983 the House of Commons had voted improved redundancy terms which included alternative jobs where possible, early retirement for older men and, for those between twenty-one and fifty years old, who accepted redundancy, £1,000 for every year of service. On 4 September 1984 the NCB issued a statement confirming there would be no compulsory redundancies, with substantial allowances, transfer and resettlement for those moving to alternative pit jobs. Output would be held at 100 million tons and there would be continued high investment. Throughout this period both sides fought a 'hearts and minds' campaign through the media, with Scargill becoming one of the best-known figures in Britain. MacGregor appeared much less frequently, leaving much of the public relations work to his subordinates. The NCB also employed pollsters to monitor the feelings of the miners and their wives and moulded their propaganda accordingly. On 14 August 1984 the *Financial Times* reported that 73 per cent of the miners were still on strike. Out of 181,000 only 48,000 were at work, compared with 40,000 at the start of the strike. Over half those working were in Nottinghamshire. From the NUM's point of view this was an achievement, considering the increasing hardship suffered by the miners' families. Indeed, one of the features of the strike was the development of the wives' support groups in an industry which took a traditionist view of the place of women. A less desirable feature of the strike were the ugly clashes between pickets and police. As the *Economist* (26 January 1985) put it, 'the summer and winter battle lines of pickets and police made violence seem as British as brown ale'. Neither side was free from blame. Any mass movement like the NUM on strike excites a hooligan element, any organization like the police attracts to it a certain number of bullies. Desperate men seeing a threat to their jobs, communities and way of life are likely to seek desperate remedies. The more likely defeat becomes, the more likely they are to seek vengeance against 'traitors'. The number of such 'scabs' increased towards the end of the year. The NCB could still have been defeated as late as September had it not come to terms with NACODS (National Association of Colliery, Overmen, Deputies and Shotfirers), whose members – their work is directly concerned with safety – had voted to strike. After this the NUM's fate was sealed. The Christmas period marked an important turning point with the drift back to work picking up after the holidays. The strike finally came to an end in March 1985 when the strikers marched back to work with banners held high and bands playing – but without a settlement. Within a short time 20,000 men had decided to leave the pits.

The 'traitors' had not remained inactive during the strike, nor did they do so after it. A group of working miners took the NUM leadership to court claiming the strike was in breach of the union's rules. The NUM's response led to fines and the sequestration of union funds. In Nottinghamshire a campaign was opened for a new union of democratic miners, a campaign which resulted in a breakaway union in the autumn of 1985. Some strikers felt there were traitors other than the working miners. The question 'Where's Ramsay MacKinnock?'[6] had been posed on a banner at a rally of South Wales miners in Aberavon on 13 November 1984. Kinnock and many of his Labour colleagues were embarrassed by Scargill's refusal to call a membership ballot, by violence on the picket lines (which they condemned), by Scargill's uncompromising attitude – 'no pit closures' – and by some of his foreign contacts, one of which was with Libya. Both Kinnock and Norman Willis, the TUC General Secretary, condemned such contacts.

The costs of the strike were appalling. In his budget speech of 1985, the Chancellor of the Exchequer, Nigel Lawson, estimated the strike had reduced the level of national output by over 1.5 per cent and worsened the balance of payments by some £4 billion. It had increased public expenditure by £2.5 billion and public sector borrowing by £2.75 billion. Richard Bailey, writing in the *National Westminster Bank Quarterly Review* (August 1985) added:

The costs to the public in postponed tax cuts, and the loss of jobs in businesses dependent on the coal industry are impossible to quantify. The 115,000 miners who stayed out for the whole period each lost between £7,000 and £8,000 in wages, and their families piled up a grievous load of debt. The National Coal Board (NCB) lost between 40 to 50 valuable coal faces, as well as over £50 million worth of machinery and equipment. The miners' unions ended the strike with their funds run down.

There was also the bitterness, neighbour against neighbour, brother against brother, marital breakdown, violence. Was it worth it all? Mr Scargill thought so; so did Mr MacGregor; so did Nigel Lawson.

The rights and wrongs of the strike will be debated for a long time. Any final assessment will depend on what happens to the NUM and to the Labour Party and to the place of coal in Britain's economy. Imported coal is not so obviously cheap. Bailey summed it up as follows, 'When handling and inland transport costs are added in, British coal costs about the same as imported coal when sterling is relatively weak, except for the Thameside power stations which are farthest from the coal fields.' With the growth of the environmental lobby, opinion could move against the alternatives: oil and, especially, nuclear fuel. It is also costly to make men redundant and destroy communities. Scargill used the argument that the future of the sons of the present generation of miners were at risk. That is not untrue. But if pit work or the dole are all Britain can offer them then Britain is lost anyway. In a world of great uncertainties it would seem prudent *gradually* to take out of production the least economical pits and concentrate on the more profitable ones. Most politicians of all parties would agree with this. Scargill openly opposed this policy, offering his members instead a totally false picture of the possibilities. To say the least, the government showed no finesse in appointing MacGregor and MacGregor was no diplomat. It was Britain's tragedy that these two men occupied the posts they did.

Television battles

Roy Jenkins, then Home Secretary under Labour, appointed the Annan Committee on broadcasting in 1974 and it reported in 1977. Unlike the Pilkington Committee (above, pp. 74–5) it was strong in its criticism of the BBC and was also concerned about the 'diminishing number of independent sources of news, comment and opinion'. Annan led to the launch of Channel 4 in 1982. Responsible to the IBA and financed by the ITV companies through advertising revenue, it tries to give attention to minority interests – ethnic, social, political and intellectual. By 1985 it had broken new ground with a regular magazine programme about trade unions, *Union World*; an ethnic minorities slot, *Black On Black*; *Right To Reply*, which gives viewers the opportunity to make their criticisms of programme makers face-to-face on television; in-depth news coverage; intellectual seminars which universities could not afford to put on; marathon foreign television series such as Fassbinder's *Berlin Alexanderplatz* and many contributions made by independent production companies.

Another development was the extension of the number of hours of broadcasting with both BBC and ITV ('TV am') offering mainly news and chat from 6.50 and 6.15 respectively. In its first year 'Breakfast Television' had only limited impact.

The Independent Broadcasting Authority (IBA, to 1972 ITA) continued to appoint the programme companies, to supervise their programme arrangements, to control the advertising and to build, own and operate the transmitting stations for both ITV and independent local radio. From 1981 it was chaired by the ex-Labour politician Lord (George) Thomson. The IBA used its powers on occasion to promote regional and local interests by re-dividing the boundaries of the programme companies. These numbered 15 for television and 42 for local radio in 1985.

The BBC continued to invite criticism of its handling of controversial subjects. In 1981 the then Director-General (DG), Sir Ian Trethowan, ordered severe cuts of a *Panorama* programme on the security services. In 1985 his successor, Alasdair Milne, agreed to withdraw a programme on Northern Ireland at the request of the Home Secretary. The BBC also aroused controversy over the vetting of job applicants (below, p. 327). Dependent as it is on Parliament agreeing to increases in its licence fees, the BBC is more directly open to political pressure than are its ITV rivals. Its Board, like that of the IBA, is appointed by the Home Secretary. The Chairman from 1980–3 was a Conservative landowner, Lord Howard. He was replaced by Stuart Young, also Conservative, an accountant whose brother, Lord Young, was in the Cabinet.

Both BBC and ITV claimed to have financial worries and made staff redundant. The commercial TV companies suffered from increasing competition for advertising revenue from commercial radio and the growing number of free papers funded entirely by advertising.

Advertising expenditure percentage of total

	Press	TV	Poster/transport	Cinema	Radio
1970	72.1	22.6	4.0	1.1	0.2
1984	63.1	30.7	3.7	0.4	2.1

Source: Advertising Statistics Yearbook 1985, 30

Viewers' tastes were undoubtedly changing but old favourites could not be dislodged. In July 1985 Granada's working-class soap opera, Coronation Street, still attracted the greatest number of viewers (15 million). The BBC's Cockney rival, Eastenders, came seventh in the ratings. The single programme which attracted the most viewers in 1985 was the Live Aid pop show put out by the BBC in July. It was watched by a staggering 59 per cent of the population and collected £13.5 million from Britain alone for aid to starving Ethiopia. The Americanization of British TV continued with countless crime series such as Starsky and Hutch, Cagney and Lacey and Miami Vice and soap operas like Dallas and Dynasty being the most popular. All channels had doubts about the future. They feared the growth, in the next decade, of private receiving dishes capable of picking up TV signals over great distances and multi-national, all-entertainment commercial channels exploiting this growing market. The Hunt Report (1982) recommended expansion, with a minimum of restrictions, of cable TV but by 1985 it did not appear to be having much impact.

The cinema continued its decline over the 1970s and early 1980s despite the great success of particular films. Among the British films which made a great impact were: Gandhi, Chariots of Fire, 1984, A Passage To India and Dance With A Stranger. Perhaps film makers felt unable to cope with contemporary themes and felt audiences preferred to escape into the past. *Ploughman's Lunch*, a sceptical look at Thatcher's Britain, was almost alone in its contemporary setting.

Cinema admissions in millions

1971	1976	1983
176.0	103.9	63.1

Source: *Social Trends* 15 1985

Security, law and order

As Britain moved towards 1984 it was only natural that people should measure the reality of society against the nightmare world of Orwell's Airstrip One. Had we escaped Big Brother or had he grown smarter, making his surveillance and control less obvious? Few really believed our world was that of Winston Smith; most would admit we had been very naive in not realizing the extent of the state's control mechanisms.

In 1980 the Post Office Engineering Union claimed that the practice of phone tapping went well beyond the categories of terrorism and crime detection, embracing political organizations and trade unions. In 1982, the *New Statesman* (4 March) claimed that MI5, which is responsible for intelligence and security within Britain, had linked its Mayfair-based computer with a growing number of other government computer data banks, giving it access to information on 20 million people. Its own files had details of 500,000 'subversives'. It seems unlikely that the Data Protection Act (1984) will give the individual greater privacy from public data users. Under the Act data users will have to register with an official registrar and individuals will have access to information held about them. However, data involving national security, and certain aspects of criminal investigation, will be exempt, as will data held for domestic purposes, and that held by companies for payroll accounting. Cathy Massiter, who worked as an intelligence officer in MI5 for 14 years, claimed that during her years of service (1970–84), the organization's emphasis shifted from being essentially a counter-espionage service, aimed at hostile foreign powers, to being a domestic surveillance body. It infiltrated agents into organizations such as CND and broke the law to gain information. This had happened, she said, under both Labour and Conservative governments. One prominent person who said he was a victim of

MI5 was Lord Bethell, the writer and Conservative Euro-MP. He said that he had been the victim of a smear campaign by MI5 in 1970. He felt obliged to resign as a junior minister. MI5, he claimed, had not checked properly information it was given about him. He believed that there must be legislation, similar to that in the United States, to give the individual access to files held on him or her. Many people were shocked when the *Observer* (18 August 1985) published a report saying that 'MI5 secretly controls the hiring and firing of BBC staff'. The paper published a list of eight individuals whom it said had been blacklisted. The system had been in existence since 1937! The only dispute was whether MI5 had the final word in such cases. The only surprise here was that people were surprised by the revelations. It had been an open secret for many years.

Some people believed that the security service wasted so much energy on hunting the unorthodox that they missed their real targets. In 1979 Britain had been shocked to hear that Sir Anthony Blunt, a former intelligence officer and more recently the Queen's art adviser, had been a Soviet agent. Worse still, it was alleged that the former head of MI5 between 1956–65, the late Sir Roger Hollis, also worked for the Soviet Union. In 1985 the service was criticized for failing to detect the problems of one of its members, Michael Bettaney, who was convicted of attempting to pass information to the Russians. There was shock also at the apparent ease with which terrorists could strike. There was the IRA car bomb which killed six people and injured 100 others outside Harrods department store in London at Christmas 1983. There was the bomb which partly demolished the hotel in Brighton where Mrs Thatcher and other delegates to the 1984 Conservative Party conference were staying. The truth was that no West European state had proved capable of freeing itself from the curse of terrorism. As for the Bettaney case, West German and American experiences in 1985 indicated that Britain was not alone with such problems. This did not mean that there was not a need for better recruitment, training, management and control of the security service.

Complaints continued to be heard about Britain's police forces: that they suffered from corruption, harboured racial prejudice and sexism, bent the rules and used, on occasions, excessive force. Such accusations were made about the metropolitan police in a 1983 report drawn up for Sir David McNee, the head of the London police (1977–83) by the influential Policy Studies Institute. There were similar accusations about the Merseyside and Birmingham police forces. In November 1983, in one of a series of incidents, three Birmingham detectives who beat up a suspect in an attempt to get a confession were jailed.[7] There was increasing concern too about police involvement, through special branch activities, with politics and about the use of firearms by the police. The debate continued about whether crime was, with few exceptions, really more prevalent than in the past since crime statistics depend so much on how much crime the public reports and whether police chiefs are interested in particular types of crime such as traffic offences, drugs or pornography at particular times. There was a strong campaign after the Conservative victory of 1983 to re-introduce capital punishment. The Commons rejected this as it had in 1979 and 1982. As part of its contribution to the debate, the *Guardian* (4 July 1983) published the stories of six men, wrongly convicted of murder, who would have hanged had the death penalty been in force.

Tories in revolt

With rising unemployment and plunging support in the opinion polls it was only to be expected that there would be rumblings of discontent in the Conservative Party. In an attempt to improve her ratings, Thatcher decided on cosmetic surgery. At the beginning of September 1985 ministerial changes were announced. Lord Young of Graffham was appointed Secretary of State for Employment. The former Health Minister, Kenneth Clarke, was appointed his deputy and spokesman in the Commons. Both had Cabinet rank. There was criticism that the head of such an important ministry was not in the Commons. Leon Brittan was demoted slightly and moved from the Home Office to Trade and Industry. Norman Tebbit became Chancellor of the Duchy of Lancaster and Chairman of the Conservative Party. His predecessor as Chairman, John Selwyn Gummer, was demoted to Agriculture, Food and Fisheries. Douglas Hurd moved from Northern Ireland to the Home Office and his place was taken by Tom King (formerly Employment Secretary). Finally, among the major changes, Kenneth Baker took over from Patrick Jenkin at the Ministry of Environment. Jenkin had had a hard job pushing through the abolition of the GLC and the other metropolitan councils and forcing all the local authorities into cuts in services and now he was being thrown to the wolves.

By this time Thatcher faced more opposition from within her own party than any other Conservative Prime Minister since Chamberlain. If she glanced behind her towards the back benches in the new parliamentary session she would see virtually a government in exile: Carlisle, Gilmour, Heath, Jenkin, Prentice, Prior, Pym, Rippon, St John Stevas; while in the proper government worked the 'Wet' mole Peter Walker. They had all criticized certain aspects of government policy; some, like Heath, criticized almost everything. There was a great deal of criticism of Thatcher's alleged authoritarian style of government; the proposal to abolish the earnings-related pension (serps); the generous pay awards for top public servants in 1985; the privatization of the royal ordnance factories and naval dockyards; cuts in the diplomatic service and BBC external services; effective cuts in student grants and, above all, the failure to cut unemployment and 'rate capping', that is penalizing local authorities which did not fall in with the government's line on expenditure cuts. Pym denounced what he called 'government by slogan' and in May 1985 set up his Centre Forward ginger group.[8] There were rumours about a 'Walker faction' and Walker was seen by many as a potential successor to Thatcher.[9]

Confusion on defence

By June 1985 Labour's hopes were high as it climbed in the opinion polls. It faced dangers ahead however. Its official policies on defence, the EEC, public ownership and the unions were still the ones which had cost it the 1983 election. Kinnock, Hattersley and Healey had nudged the Party away from its earlier line but powerful voices and powerful votes within the party wanted no backsliding on 'socialism'. Since 1979 there had been a resurgence of CND. This was partly because it was easier to support such a movement when Labour was in opposition than when it was in government. There had also been the example of a similar powerful movement in West Germany and the intensification of the arms race after 1979 gave a boost to a movement which, although of the Left, united people from a wide variety of political backgrounds. CND wanted Britain to give up its own nuclear deterrent unilaterally and it opposed Cruise and Trident missiles. Basically, this was Labour's position too, as revealed in its policy document *Defence and Security of Britain* (August 1984). Labour would work within NATO to get it to agree on a policy of 'No first use' of nuclear weapons. It would also work to reduce defence spending towards the average level of our major European allies. Where did the Liberal–SDP Alliance stand on defence? Generally, the SDP supported NATO policies, including the aim of multilateral disarmament on the one hand and the deployment of Cruise missiles on the other. It wanted to retain Britain's nuclear force but rejected Trident which represented a new step in the arms race. The Liberal leader, David Steel, found no difficulty with this approach but the Liberal Assembly had adopted a more unilateralist stance on 20 September 1984.

Most polls showed that the majority of British people accepted that Britain needed to be in NATO. In a dangerous world it was too weak to defend itself alone. All the parties accepted this. Again the majority of the electorate felt some element of nuclear defence was necessary. Only CND seemed to want NATO to abandon its nuclear weapons unilaterally. There were great divisions and confusions on Britain's own nuclear forces. Most Labour and Liberal Party members were prepared to abandon the British bomb. The Conservatives and most of the SDP wanted to retain it. The question was, in what form? The last Labour government had started the Chevaline modernization programme which was designed to keep Britain's Polaris fleet effective until the mid 1990s. But what then? The Thatcher government had decided to acquire the Trident II submarine-launched missile system from the United States to replace Polaris. The government argued that its cost would be only 3 per cent of the total defence budget and 6 per cent of the equipment budget. The four submarines and their nuclear warheads would be designed and built in Britain, bringing employment to British workers. Trident would be a powerful weapon which would give Britain some say in the nuclear future. Its critics said it tied Britain even more to American nuclear strategy, especially since the Trident missiles would be serviced not in Britain but in the U.S.A. The government was on strong ground when it said that NATO's nuclear weapons had helped to prevent war – the invasion of Afghanistan and the Iran–Iraq war had happened because one side thought the other had no deterrent – but it was on much weaker ground in relation to Britain's own nuclear forces. Those who argued that Britain should have an independent nuclear capacity would have been more convincing had they looked to France rather than the United States for this element of our defence. France had built up and was maintaining an independent nuclear force. Perhaps this would become of critical importance for an independent European (EEC) defence strategy in the twenty-first century. There was confusion about the Cruise missiles. CND saw them as an intensification of the arms race, but if it was accepted that nuclear weapons were an essential part of defence, then they could be seen merely as a modernization of NATO's defensive armoury. Defence policy had never been decided on purely rational grounds but was a product of historical fears, electoral strategies, vested interests and the shape of the economy. No British party before or after 1945 had conceived a well thought out strategy based on a ruthlessly realistic appraisal of Britain's future. Britain continued to spend more than its allies (except the United States) and trade rivals on defence. Had this perhaps been a factor in her economic decline?

EEC, Gibraltar, Hong Kong

Like defence, Britain's continued membership of the EEC still excited passions in some quarters. The new leader of the Labour group in the European Parliament, Alf Lomas, elected by 18 votes to 14 in place of Barbara Castle in 1985, made it known that he would campaign for Britain's withdrawal from the EEC. Labour was isolated on this issue, though a minority in the Conservative Party grouped around Teddy Taylor had similar leanings. However, little was said about the various grants and loans made by the EEC for retraining, for the modernization of canals, roads and sewerages, for the development of tourist facilities and so on. But even those who supported the EEC found it difficult to support the CAP which was designed for countries with much larger agricultural sectors than Britain. Some progress towards reform was made in 1984 when, for the first time, the agriculture ministers of the Community agreed to reduce prices. In June 1984 the EEC heads of government agreed that net expenditure on agriculture would increase more slowly than the Community's income. Thatcher, like her predecessors, had agitated to get Britain's net contribution to the EEC budget reduced and from 1980 she negotiated refunds for Britain totalling £2,500 million, some two-thirds of the UK's net contribution. The agreement on the European Strategic Research Programme in Information Technology (ESPRIT) was designed to make EEC firms more competitive with their U.S. and Japanese counterparts in the 1990s. Agreement was also reached on the entry of Spain and Portugal into the EEC on 1 January 1986. Britain hoped to benefit in sales of industrial goods and cars to these markets. Britain and Spain agreed on terms for the opening of the frontier between Gibraltar and Spain and this was implemented on 10 April 1980. The government, however, remained committed to 'honour the fully and democratically expressed wishes of the people of Gibraltar' regarding their future.

No such guarantees were, or could, be given in the case of Hong Kong. After long negotiations with the People's Republic of China it was agreed that after the expiry of Britain's lease in 1997 the former colony would have a high degree of autonomy within the People's Republic. It would retain its own economic, legal and social system for fifty years. Those in Hong Kong who did not wish to register as Chinese could opt for a new form of nationality – British Nationals (Overseas) – which would not give them the right to settle in the UK. This may well lead to difficulties in the future.

Britain in 1985

What was Britain like in 1985, as Mrs Thatcher was roughly

halfway through her second term? Those of an optimistic disposition or those sympathetic to 'Thatcherism' could point out that for the 87 per cent of the workforce in employment, real disposable incomes, which reflect the buying power of incomes once taxes and rising prices are taken into account, were up considerably on 1979. More people possessed more consumer goods and more people were buying their own homes. The economy had recovered after the 1979–81 recession and Britain had enjoyed its longest (roughly five years) sustained upturn since 1945. It is true that there was more unemployment but this could be blamed on the increase in the population of working age (a product of the 'baby boom' of the 1960s), on the fact that more women were seeking employment outside the home and on the world-wide recession which had hit all the western economies. Abroad, the Conservative government had got Britain out of its embarrassing colonial legacies in Rhodesia and Hong Kong and showed the world that Britain was determined to resist aggression. It had maintained Britain's alliances, which, many believed, had been vital for the maintenance of a kind of peace since 1945. Sir Geoffrey Howe's efforts to get a better relationship with the Soviet bloc had earned him credit among the East European leadership, and his efforts on human rights had earned him respect from the peoples of those states.

The critics of Thatcherism had no difficulty in finding things to criticize. Unemployment had trebled since 1979, reaching record levels. The real situation was worse than the figures showed, considering that some young people and women were not registered and that some were involved in training or part-time employment which were not 'proper jobs'. At the end of July the Manpower Services Commission, in its annual report, presented a bleak picture of worsening unemployment rates among young people and lengthening periods on the dole for the 3.15 million jobless:

Numbers of unemployed in April 1985 by age (thousands)

Duration	Under 25	All ages
0–6 months	530	1,212
6–12 months	296	666
1–2 years	181	523
2–3 years	86	292
Over 3 years	73	458
All unemployed	1,166	3,151

The number of those out of work for over three years who were under 25 had increased by 37 per cent between April 1984 and April 1985. The total number of all those who had been unemployed for that period had increased by the same percentage.

In international terms Britain's unemployment was among the highest:

Unemployment percentage rate

	June/July 1984	*June/July 1985*
Australia	9.2	8.7
Belgium	13.2	12.3
Canada	11.1	10.5
France	9.3	9.6
Germany (FR)	9.2	9.4
Italy	11.8	12.6
Japan	2.8	2.6
Netherlands	17.1	15.7
Sweden	2.7	2.5
Switzerland	1.1	0.9
UK	12.6	13.1
U.S.A.	7.5	7.3

Source: The *Economist*, 10 August 1985

The oft-repeated Conservative argument that British workers were pricing themselves out of their jobs did not seem to have much substance. The *Economist* (10 August 1985) published figures indicating that British hourly labour costs (including social security and pension costs for employers) in manufacturing industry in 1984 were only higher than those of 3 states (Ireland, Spain, Greece) out of 18 (U.S.A., Canada, Australia, Norway, Switzerland, W. Germany, Sweden, Holland, Belgium, Denmark, Italy, Japan, France, Austria).

Egalitarian critics were concerned that under Thatcher Britain had become a more unequal society with the earnings of the higher paid having increased more rapidly than those of the lower paid, aided by the slashing of the top rates of income tax and by the abolition of the investment income surcharge. The pay of public sector employees had not risen as much as that of those employed in the private sector. The regional disparities had remained or widened, especially between the prosperous south-east and the north. The hardest hit areas were Yorkshire and Humberside, the West Midlands, Wales and, at the bottom, Northern Ireland.

Although the government had made great play about winning the fight against inflation, in the summer of 1985, at 7 per cent, Britain's rate of inflation was higher than that of such industrial states as Australia (4.4), Canada (3.9), France (6.4), West Germany (2.3), Japan (1.7), Switzerland and U.S.A. (3.7).

The advanced economies had all been hit by the recession and by the building up of manufacturing capacity in Asia and South

America. Britain was hit more than its neighbours. There was a rapid decline in various sectors with an increasing level of foreign penetration. In 1971 19 per cent of demand for chemical products was covered by imports; in 1982 it was 33 per cent. For electrical engineering products the percentages were 18 and 49 and for instrument engineering 37 and 62. The leap in vehicle imports was from 15 per cent to 45 per cent and in textiles from 17 to 40. Britain's imports had to be paid for and, increasingly, Britain was becoming dependent on its export of oil, the revenue from which was expected to shrink quite soon. This foreign penetration of the economy had not just happened under Thatcher (or Callaghan for that matter) but even among the government's friends, in boardrooms up and down the country, there was a feeling that the needs of industry came second to the needs of the City in Downing Street's calculations. Manufacturers were aggrieved by high interest rates, fluctuations in the pound (too weak then too strong), the high cost of fuel compared with what foreign competitors paid, high local authority rates and lack of help against what they considered unfair foreign competition (as from Japan).

The City of London itself which for so long had had a central place in Britain's economy and figured prominently in the minds of those who saw Britain's future more in providing services than manufactures, came in for sharp criticism. With the decline of sterling as an international currency and the decline of the British economy as a whole, the City had lost its former pre-eminent world position. It had been allowed to go its own way, that of a self-regulating monopoly, and had become staid, conservative, pursuing restrictive practices and out of date in some respects. A series of scandals and spectacular crashes led to the government commissioning Professor Jim Gower to investigate its workings. After two and a half years of research he concluded (January 1984) that much stronger safeguards were needed to protect investors. Some in the City felt there was a danger that too many of its activities would be taken over by foreign firms to the detriment of the British economy.

Britain's educational system – so important if the country is to meet the challenge of the computer age – was suffering from low morale due directly to government attacks. School teachers were striking and university teachers felt grossly undervalued.

All together, Britain had become a little meaner and a little shabbier under Thatcher. Owen was on target when he told the SDP conference of 'public squalor and private affluence', of public lavatories, schools and hospitals 'which stink, with paint peeling off the walls'. He could also have mentioned the slum mental institutions and prisons and the havoc caused in universities by senseless cuts.[10] Tourism had continued to grow (in part because of the weak pound earlier in the year) and had become an important industry. Yet foreign visitors found London streets among the most untidy in Europe, the hotels among the most expensive, the beaches among the dirtiest and standards of service generally low. It seemed in some way significant that Britain's youth became known, through the medium of TV, as rioters and brawlers. As the *Economist* (1 June 1985) commented:

What's wrong not just with British football but with Britain? The question needs asking after the mass manslaughter at the European football cup final in Brussels on Wednesday night, when Liverpool fans charged into an area occupied by supporters of the Italian club Juventus, and some 40 people were killed. . . . As a shamed Britain ponders the tragedy of Brussels, it would do well to examine the system of cultural values that made it possible.

The negative images of Brussels were to a degree replaced later by the marathon Live Aid pop concert and by a handful of British athletes such as Daley Thompson, Steve Ovett and Sebastian Coe by their sporting prowess. It seemed symbolic of Britain's position in 1985 that Harrods and the *Times* were foreign-owned. It seemed significant that Britain had attempted to regain the Blue Riband Atlantic crossing trophy, not with an ocean-going liner, but with a catamaran, the Virgin Atlantic Challenger, which sank! And was it not significant that the pound note had got smaller and then become a small coin (opposed by very many people)? The pound fell under Thatcher from £1 = $2.06 (May 1979) to £1 = $1.40 (September 1985), nearly reaching parity earlier in 1985. No one could seriously say that all these ills were the sole responsibility of the Thatcher government, but in 1979 the Conservatives had promised much and then delivered little.

The summer of 1985 was a bad one for Britain – it was the wettest for very many years – but a good one for Owen and Steel. For the first time since their honeymoon in 1981 the Alliance went ahead in the polls in late August. In July they had won a great by-election victory at Brecon and Radnor over the Conservatives. However, by the end of the summer it was Labour's turn to take the lead. At Labour's annual conference Kinnock gave a speech which the *Guardian* (2 October) called, 'the bravest, and most important speech by a Labour leader in over a generation'. He attacked the lack of realism of the Militant Tendency, other Left groups and Scargill – 'far-fetched resolutions. . .outdated, misplaced and irrelevant to the real needs of the people'. Of course, most of his speech was an attack on Thatcherism. The party of enterprise had presided over record bankruptcies; the party of tax cuts had arranged that the British people had the biggest tax burden ever; six years ago the high-tech industries had had a surplus with the rest of the world but now they ran a £2.3 billion deficit, etc. Ably supported by his deputy, Roy Hattersley, he had emerged as a leader but Kinnock still had a distance to go to unite his party behind a realistic reform platform, realistic both in domestic and foreign policy.

At a ceremony to mark the battle of Verdun, Mitterrand and Kohl stood hand in hand in a touching gesture which underlined the determination of France and Germany to put the past behind and work for a common future. No British leader (with the possible exception of Steel) fully understood that Britain's future too must be with them. The challenges of drugs, terrorism, the computer, mass unemployment, racism, space and the rise of new economic rivals can only be solved together. Europe must, as Attlee put it back in the 1940s, 'unite or perish'.

The Anglo-Irish Agreement

In yet another attempt to break the deadlock in Ireland Mrs Thatcher and the Irish Prime Minister, Dr Gareth Fitzgerald, signed the Anglo-Irish Agreement in November 1985. Both governments recognized Ulster as part of the United Kingdom so long as this was supported by the majority of those in the North. Under the Agreement an inter-governmental conference was established which would give the Irish government the right to comment on certain aspects of Northern Irish affairs. It also sought to improve cross-border co-operation especially in security matters.

What most people saw as a positive move was strongly contested by Ulster Unionist MPs and certain Conservatives. Ian Gow, a Treasury minister, resigned over the issue after only weeks in office. In Ulster all the Unionist MPs resigned their seats because they saw the Agreement as the first step towards Irish unity. All but one of them were re-elected at by-elections in January 1986. A one-day strike in Northern Ireland was organized as a show of force, without, however, deterring the government from its path.

The Westland Affair

The beginning of 1986 was dominated by the so-called Westland Affair which led to the resignation of Michael Heseltine, Secretary of State for Defence, and later of Leon Brittan, Secretary of State for Trade and Industry. Westland produced helicopters for both military and civil purposes. It was in difficulties. Heseltine wanted to see it kept safely in European hands, Brittan wanted to leave it to the shareholders. In practice this meant allowing the American firm Sikorsky to take the company over. The Prime Minister backed Leon Brittan. Just behind the scenes there were bitter personal rivalries and what looked like a growing split in the Conservative Party. Gallup's first poll published in 1986 showed the Conservatives in third place behind the Alliance and Labour. Another study revealed that it was believed Thatcher would be judged Britain's worst recent Prime Minister, with Winston Churchill being remembered as the best.[11] The government's popularity was also hit as a result of the use of British airbases by American planes to attack Libya. The American action on 15 April followed attacks on American planes over international waters in the Gulf of Sirte. Two in three people questioned by Gallup thought the government had been wrong to allow the Americans the use of airbases in Britain for this raid. Increased terrorist activity in Britain, it was feared, would result from the raids, as well as damage to long-term British interests.[12]

Moscow journey

The two by-elections which preceded the general election of 1987 gave the Alliance false hopes and depressed Labour. At Greenwich on 26 February Mrs Rosie Barnes, SDP/Alliance, captured the seat from Labour, and at Truro on 12 March Michael Taylor, Liberal/Alliance, retained the seat at the by-election caused by the death of David Penhaligon. By then the Conservatives were well on the way back to popularity from their low point in the summer of 1986. Saatchi and Saatchi had been hard at work, as had the Prime Minister's Press Secretary, Bernard Ingham. Among other exploits were the television commercials for the privatization of British Telecom, 'in effect, the most expensive party political broadcasts ever'.[13] By the end of November the Chancellor had found an extra £10 billion for spending on health, education and jobs, further helping to set the scene for the looming general election.

In yet another effort to boost her appeal, Mrs Thatcher went travelling. She followed in the footsteps of Harold Macmillan who nearly thirty years earlier had gone to Moscow to impress British voters. She made a highly successful visit to Gorbachev, and like Macmillan appeared on Soviet television. The first opinion polls after the Moscow trip showed the Conservatives at their highest level for three and a half years. By contrast, a slightly earlier visit by Neil Kinnock to see President Reagan proved to be a fiasco, largely due to the President's reluctance to endorse the Labour leader. One other electoral weapon used by the government was tax cuts, included in Chancellor Nigel Lawson's March Budget, which came through in the week before polling day.

Thatcher's hat trick

On 11 June 1987 Margaret Thatcher scored a historic victory by winning her third successive election. No other twentieth-century Prime Minister could claim such success. After 1945 the Conservatives had won in 1951, 1955 and 1959 but not under the same leader.

On closer inspection the Conservative victory of 1987 was not as impressive as it at first seemed. On a turnout of 75.5 per cent, the Conservatives gained 42.2 per cent of the UK vote, Labour gained 30.8 per cent of the vote and the Alliance 22.6 per cent. Labour's result was its worst since 1923 in terms of percentage poll. Yet everywhere there was a swing to Labour, reaching a mere 1.1 per cent in London and the South and a maximum of 7.5 per cent in Wales. Eveywhere there was a swing against the Alliance, held at 2 per cent in London and the South, but reaching a maximum of 5.3 per cent in both Wales and Scotland. There was a swing to the Conservatives in London and the South (1.2) and the Midlands (0.9), and swings against them in the North (-1.8), Wales (-1.5) and Scotland (-4.4). The Conservatives suffered a net loss of twenty-one seats and Labour a net gain of twenty, but the Conservatives actually gained seats from Labour in London and the Midlands. Their strength was being concentrated more and more in the south of England. The Alliance suffered a net loss of five seats. Its vote fell by 3 per cent, the Conservative vote declined slightly from 42.4 to 42.2 per cent, while Labour's rose by 3.2 per cent.

Only 10 of the 72 MPs elected in Scotland were Conservatives, and only 8 of the 38 in Wales. The Scottish National Party and Plaid Cymru each made a net gain of one seat giving them three seats each. The Afro-Caribbean and Asian communities saw four of their number elected, all as Labour MPs. Among them was Diane Abbott (Hackney North), the first ever black woman to be elected. The highest ever number of women were elected to the Commons: 21 Labour, 18 Conservative and 2 Alliance.

Northern Ireland produced a slight shift to moderation. The two rival Protestant-based parties, Official Unionist Party (OUP) and Democratic Unionist Party (DUP) of Ian Paisley entered an electoral pact which secured for them twelve of the seventeen seats. They lost one to the moderate, Catholic-based Social

Democratic and Labour Party (SDLP) which won three seats in all (one in 1983, one by-election win in 1986). The SDLP ended Enoch Powell's thirty-seven years in Parliament by taking Down South from him. The pro-IRA candidate Gerry Adams retained for Sinn Fein the seat he won in 1983 in Catholic West Belfast. One independent Unionist retained his seat in Down North. Both the Unionist (54 to 49.5) and Sinn Fein's (13.4 to 11.4) percentage of the vote fell, while those of the SDLP (17.9 to 21.1) and the non-sectarian Alliance Party (8 to 10) increased. Turnout was down from 72.8 to 67 per cent.

As David Butler pointed out,[14] the election results did not reveal a simple North/South divide, but rather a divide between 'haves and have-nots, the rich and poor. It was an election of social and political bifurcation, and the most polarized election in living memory.' By common consent, Labour had fought a good, professional, campaign but there were still doubts about its taxation and spending plans and its stance on defence. Many sections of society felt they had never had it so good and were prepared to thank Mrs Thatcher for that. The Alliance suffered from appearing less than united.

Notes

1 Michael Cockerell, Peter Hennessy and David Walker, *Sources Close to the Prime Minister* (London, 1984), 209.
2 Profile in *Observer*, 6 December 1981.
3 *Observer*, 18 March 1984.
4 *Keesing's Contemporary Archives*, November 1984, 33230.
5 *Keesing's Contemporary Archives*, November 1984, 33230.
6 Huw Beynon, *Digging Deeper* (London, 1985), 181.
7 *Guardian*, 14 November 1983.
8 *Guardian*, 15 May 1985 and *Guardian*, 20 May 1985. Francis Pym's ideas are developed in his book *The Politics of Consent* (London, 1984).
9 *Times*, 3 May 1985. Walker was profiled in *Observer*, 26 November 1984.
10 'Japan puts British robots in the shade', *New Society*, 18 October 1985. Professor Alan Pugh of Hull University, a robot pioneer, explains how government-imposed cuts have hit British research.
11 Robert J. Wybrow, *Britain Speaks Out, 1937–87. A Social History as Seen Through the Gallup Data* (London, 1989), 141.
12 Wybrow, op. cit., 142.
13 Michael Cockerell, *Live From Number 10* (London, 1988), 314.
14 David Butler, 'Election of haves and have-nots', in *The Times Guide to the House of Commons, June 1987* (London, 1987), 256.

13   The End of Thatcher: and Thatcherism?

The defeat of the opposition parties in the 1987 election forced them to look at themselves again. In the case of the Alliance it was a far more traumatic experience than for the Labour Party. Immediately after the election, Liberal leader David Steel called for the merger of the two Alliance parties. Months of, at times bitter, negotiations followed. Most Liberals favoured the move, though some did not like the idea of the loss of their traditional name. More SDP members had doubts about it. In the end, in January 1988, the SDP and the Liberals voted to merge. Their new party was named the Social and Liberal Democratic Party (SLD) and was launched in March 1988. It started out with David Steel and Robert Maclennan (formerly SDP) as joint leaders. David Owen refused to go with the majority of his colleagues into the new party and attempted to keep alive the old SDP. He was joined by two MPs, Rosie Barnes and John Cartwright. The other two SDP MPs, Charles Kennedy and Robert Maclennan, together with ex-MPs Shirley Williams and Roy Jenkins, did join. It was difficult for most Alliance supporters to understand the Owenite position. The differences between the two parties did not appear substantial. Personal rivalries did seem important. In his memoirs Owen described his earlier relations with Steel as 'edgy but civil',[1] and he was unable to give sound reasons of principle for not joining. His activities led to considerable disillusionment among former Alliance supporters. On 28 July 1988 Paddy Ashdown was elected leader of the SLD with 71.9 per cent of the vote, and Ian Wrigglesworth, formerly of the SDP, was elected President. The SDP finally called it a day on 3 June 1990 when its national committee voted by 17 to 5 to suspend the party constitution. In effect, this meant terminating the SDP's activities. The decision followed a number of extremely bad results for the SDP at by-elections in which it competed with the SLD. At the Bootle by-election in May 1990 the SDP was even beaten by the Monster Raving Loony Party of Screaming Lord Sutch!

The new leader of the Liberal Democrats, Paddy Ashdown

(b. 1941), had entered Parliament in 1983. Educated at Bedford School and Hong Kong University, he was a qualified Chinese interpreter. He had served as a captain in the Royal Marines, 1959–71 and then as a diplomat, 1971–6. Later he worked in management, including a time at Westland Helicopters, before devoting himself full-time to the Liberal cause. Handsome, he was a pleasant television personality.

Chastened and disappointed by the election of 1987, the Labour leadership had lost no time in bringing its policies more into line with what the electorate thought credible. Joe Rogaly in the *Financial Times* (26 May 1990) commented that Labour's policy document *Looking to the Future* 'has nothing to do with socialism'. Labour had abandoned its unilateral nuclear disarmament position, accepted the market economy, and sought to become the party of Europe. The first two changes were made easier by the collapse of Soviet-style Communism in East Europe, 1989–91. The Social Charter of the European Community – and Conservative opposition to it – helped Labour to see more clearly the potential of the EC for its working-class supporters.

'Black Monday', 1987

The Conservatives had enjoyed a great deal of good luck since 1979. The Thatcher era had coincided with the exploitation of North Sea oil and with low commodity prices which brought in turn low inflation. Technical innovations such as the auto bank and credit cards gave many a feeling of being better off as they often got deeper in debt. The period must also have seen the transfer of modest wealth, by inheritance from the first generation, who had experienced full employment for most of their working lives, to their children. Videos, microwave ovens, computers, radio cassette recorders and, to a lesser extent, mobile phones and satellite television all helped to create demand and give an air of excitement. Eight years of strongly rising share prices also helped. Without that rise very many would have been put off buying shares in the privatized undertakings. On 'Black Monday', 19 October 1987, things started to go wrong. Over £50 billion was wiped off the value of shares in London. By the end of the week values had fallen by nearly £102 billion.

The slump in share prices was worldwide and was prompted largely by the lack of confidence in the US economy with its large balance of trade and budget deficits. Prices had, in any case, risen unduly on a speculative wave based on the Reaganite mood of the 1980s. In the City of London sackings became commonplace. In December 1988 Morgan Grenfell announced 450 redundancies in the City. In January 1989 the Chase Manhattan Bank announced that 135 of its staff were to go. The financial services sector entered a lean period which lasted beyond the Thatcher era. Big names got into trouble because of the slump and major scandals helped to make small investors more wary about investing their savings in stocks, shares and unit trusts.

According to *Social Trends* (1991) fraud and forgery cases in England and Wales went up from 99,800 in 1971 to 134,500 in 1989. The clear-up rate fell from 83 per cent to 66 per cent. On 28 December 1985 the Johnson Mattey Bank fraud case was opened and on 15 June 1988 financier Peter Clowes was charged with perverting the course of justice over the collapse of the Barlow-Clowes investment empire. Many small savers suffered from this collapse. Clowes was sentenced in February 1992 to ten years' imprisonment for theft and fraud at the end of a 110-day trial. Passing sentence, Mr Justice Phillips said, 'I do not believe any judge in this country has been called upon to sentence a worse case of fraud.'

The investigation of the so-called Guinness scandal led to one of the longest trials in English criminal history. After 107 days three of the four defendants were given prison sentences following their conviction on twenty-eight charges relating to an illegal share support scheme involving more than £15 million of covert payments. Ernest Saunders, the former chairman of Guinness plc, was convicted on charges of fraud, false accounting and theft. His sentence of five years was subsequently halved on appeal. The well-known financier Sir Jack Lyons was convicted with him on conspiracy, false accounting and theft charges. The other two defendants were convicted on similar charges.

The strange death at sea of Robert Maxwell in November 1991 led to the break up of his debt-ridden multinational media and publishing empire. It was subsequently established that he had misused pension fund resources to finance his dealings. This was precisely the charge he had made against Arthur Scargill, the miners' leader, in his paper, the *Daily Mirror*. Scargill was found innocent. Later it was revealed that Maxwell had even bugged the offices of his executives, including his own son. Maxwell, a Jewish refugee from Czechoslovakia, had won the Military Cross for his bravery while serving in the British Army. He served one term as a Labour MP, reaching his first £1 million in 1964. Ten years later he was in deep trouble. In 1974 Department of Trade and Industry inspectors reported that Maxwell was not fitted for the stewardship of a public company. This did not stop his further rise in the business world. His case revealed the inadequacy of the law covering private pension funds.

The collapse of the Bank of Credit and Commerce International (BCCI) in 1991 seemed symbolic of the 1980s decade. Owned by Sheikh Zayed of Abu Dhabi it had offered easy credit for borrowers and high interest rates for lenders. *The Economist* (3–9 August 1991) described its customers as 'mostly corrupt but including a number of careless innocents. Sleazy drug traffickers share the sudden limelight with Arab terrorists, a deposed Panamanian dictator and Washington's most eminent lawyer . . . the Mafia and the Central Intelligence Agency.' Most of the victims in Britain were among the innocents – Asian small businessmen and a few local authorities.

Britain was by no means alone in having financial scandals. Japan, Germany, Italy, Switzerland and the United States all had their share.

Among the individuals who had initially done very well during the Thatcher era but were subsequently hit by the slump and/or their own mistakes were the Saatchi brothers. Their advertising firm had a market value of £30 million in 1987 but it had dropped to £1.6 million by 1990. Sophie Mirman's Sock Shop had a price tag of £51 million in 1988 but a year later went bust. East-Ender Alan Sugar's Amstrad fell in value from £590 million in 1984 to £159 million in 1990. Sir Terence Conran, founder of Habitat, saw his empire all but disappear, and Sir Bernard Ashley of the Laura Ashley chain was squeezed hard by high interest rates.[2] John Gunn's British and Commonwealth went rapidly downhill and the administrators had to be called in in 1990. It was estimated by the *Daily Telegraph* (5 June 1990) to be 'the biggest financial collapse the City has known'. Over 27,000 shareholders had their assets frozen.

Many more firms went bankrupt. In 1990, 28,935 had gone into receivership. In 1991, 47,777 did so. In the recession of 1981 there were 13,200 recorded business failures.[3]

Despite worries and scandals there were still many who were prepared to try to make a quick profit on the privatization offers. British Gas, British Airways and Rolls-Royce were privatized before the 1987 election; British Airports Authority, British Steel, and the electricity and water companies followed it.

Poll tax revolt

In April 1988 the government pushed through its legislation on what it called the community charge but what its critics called the poll tax. Officially the aim was to make everyone pay towards the costs of local government and not just, as under the rating system, householders. Under the old system the amount paid was fixed according to the size of dwelling. Under the community charge everyone in a given district would pay the same tax set by their local authority. The unemployed, students and certain other categories could claim exemption from most of the tax. Labour, the Liberals and the nationalist parties opposed the new system, as did some Conservatives including former Prime Minister, Edward Heath. There were various revolts in the Commons by Conservative MPs not happy with the new tax. Fearing defeat in the Lords the government called in its 'backwoodsmen' and, on 23 May, secured the second largest attendance in the twentieth century.

Many people in Scotland and a significant minority in England and Wales refused to pay the new tax. The Labour leaders condemned this type of opposition and disowned those of their followers who promoted it. In most cases such non-payment hit Labour-run councils, often already in bad shape financially, more than Conservative councils which were usually in more prosperous areas. Moreover, those seeking to avoid payment by not registering lost their right to vote, thus depriving the opposition parties of at least some votes.

On Saturday 30 March 1990 rioting broke out in London following a peaceful demonstration against the poll tax by around 40,000 people. A few hundred protesters went on the rampage in the Whitehall–Trafalgar Square–Leicester Square area of Central London. *The Times* (2 April 1990) reported, 'London's image as a safe and pleasant city was damaged by the riots which caught thousands of innocent tourists unawares.'

Prison riots

In 1989 Britain had a higher proportion of its population in prison than any other west European country except for Luxembourg.[4] By contrast, in West Germany an increasing number of prisons stood empty. There the prison population had fallen by 20 per cent since 1983. It was well known that British prison conditions had been below par for decades. Many of the 53,670 inmates (only 1,600 of them women), held in 160 prisons, lived in appalling conditions. Sooner or later serious trouble had been expected. Both prisoners and their guards were dissatisfied.

In one of a series of incidents, on 5 January 1987 prisoners took over Barlinnie Gaol, taking three prison officers hostage. Then, on 1 June, twenty-six prisoners staged a mass breakout from Haverigg Prison. All but three were soon recaptured. In Scotland at Longriggend Prison fifty-six prisoners staged a rooftop protest on 19 July 1988. Early in May 1989 there were three days of rioting at Risley Remand Centre. Its closure was announced in July after an inquiry. On 1 April 1990 prisoners took over part of Strangeways Prison, Manchester, and held it for three and a half weeks. This was the longest siege in British prison history. In August 1991 there were riots at the newly opened showpiece Moorlands Gaol, near Doncaster, and at Lindholme Prison in south Yorkshire. After the Strangeways siege Lord Justice Woolf was asked by Home Secretary Kenneth Baker to investigate conditions. He roundly condemned what he found. Baker promised better sanitary conditions and less overcrowding. He also introduced a new (serious) offence of prison mutiny and new security measures. There was also an unacceptably large number of suicides in Britain's prisons, mainly among younger inmates.

Even though it had more policemen and women than ever before – 87,900 in 1961, 139,900 in 1981, 148,200 in 1989 – Britain faced a tide of rising crime. Figures in *Social Trends* (1991) indicated that most classes of offences had been increasing. Burglaries in England and Wales were up from 451,500 in 1971 to 825,900 in 1989. Robberies were up from 7,500 to 33,200. The clear-up rate in these and other categories had fallen. Contrary to popular belief, the rise in sexual offences had been modest. Most crime was of a minor nature. A section of conservative opinion wanted tougher measures, including the re-introduction of capital punishment, to halt the rising levels of crime and violence. However, there was also increasing unease at the number of wrong or unsafe convictions. On 23 June 1988 the Commons again rejected capital punishment. On the same day it was reported that the West Midlands Serious Crimes Squad was to be disbanded after allegations of fabricated confessions. On 19 October 1989 the 'Guildford Four' were released from jail after their sentences for their alleged part in the Guildford pub bombings of 1974 were quashed. The convictions of the 'Maguire Seven' were also quashed. The 'Birmingham Six' had their convictions set aside after they had been in prison sixteen years and four months for their alleged part in the Birmingham pub bombing of 21 November 1974. The IRA had claimed responsibility for this crime which caused the death of twenty-one people. The Home Secretary, Kenneth Baker, immediately announced a Royal Commission to investigate the entire criminal justice system in England and Wales. The Birmingham Six had been convicted after investigations carried out by detectives of the West Midlands Serious Crimes Squad. In December 1991 the 'Broadwater Farm Three' had their convictions for the killings of a policeman in 1986 quashed. These were just four cases that were widely publicized. The importance given to confessions as evidence and the pressure on the police to get results were thought to be key elements in these, and similar, cases.

Peter Wright and official secrets

The security services continued to hit the headlines in the late 1980s as former agents leaked information about their work. Cathy Massiter (see p. 326) had made serious allegations about MI5 activities and she was followed by Peter Wright in his book *Spycatcher*. The government pursued his book across the world in an attempt to prevent its publication. These attempts failed in Australia and in the United States but they did turn a rather boring book into a bestseller. Wright claimed that he and his colleagues had 'bugged and burgled our way across London at the State's behest'.[5] He also claimed that MI5 had kept a file on former Prime Minister Harold Wilson. Allegations were made by others[6] that elements in MI5 actually sought to destabilize the Wilson government. The Security Service Act 1989 was an attempt to allay fears about the activities of MI5. The act established the post of Commissioner (an Appeal Court judge) – to oversee the issue of warrants for telephone tapping and other forms of surveillance – and a tribunal to investigate complaints. This act did not cover the work of MI6 or GCHQ. The government also introduced a new Official Secrets Act which became law in 1990. This reinforced the secrecy rule on civil servants. In future they would not be able to claim that they were leaking information in the public interest, as Clive Ponting had done during the Falklands campaign. At his trial a jury believed him. Former Prime Minister Edward Heath was one of a number of Conservatives who joined Labour and the Liberals in attacking the new legislation. Heath pointed out that, when a backbencher, Churchill had received leaked information about the inadequacy of Britain's defences. He had used this to warn the country.[7] The government, which had sought to prevent the *Sunday Times*, the *Guardian* and the *Observer* from publishing extracts from Peter Wright's book, was condemned by the European Court for breaching Article 10 of the European Convention on Human Rights. The court did not condemn the government's original attempt to prevent potentially sensitive material from being published, but it condemned the government's continued efforts after the book had become widely available abroad. The judgment pronounced on 26 November 1991 was the twenty-eighth against Britain since 1966 – almost double the highest number of violations by any of the other twenty-three signatories.

In another move, trade unions were banned in 1984 at the Government Communications Headquarters (GCHQ) in Cheltenham. GCHQ intercepts diplomatic, military, commercial and private communications obtained by spy satellites and listening posts around the world. Those who refused to give up their trade union membership were sacked. This was opposed by Labour and the Liberal Democrats.

Perhaps in an effort to improve the image of MI5, the government appointed a woman, Mrs Stella Rimington, to head M15 from 1992, and allowed publication of her name. Aged 56, and mother of two daughters, she was a graduate of Edinburgh University.

Disasters

Suddenly, Britain seemed to be prone to disasters. In March 1987, the *Herald of Free Enterprise*, a cross-channel ferry, capsized outside Zeebrugge harbour with the loss of 188 lives. Later, in June 1989, manslaughter charges were brought against P & O, the company owning the ferry, and seven of its employees. In March 1987 twelve people were killed in gales across Britain, and in October a hurricane killed nineteen in southern England, and 100 m.p.h. gales killed six in February 1988. The deaths and loss of property raised questions about warnings and safety measures against storms. On 6 July 1988 an explosion on the North Sea Piper Alfa oil rig claimed the lives of 170. It was later blamed on 'human error' but there was a massive payout to the relatives of the victims. The inquiry – which reported on 10 November 1988 – into the King's Cross underground disaster which had claimed the lives of thirty-one people (18 November 1987) criticized safety standards. On 12 December 1988, thirty-four were killed when two trains collided at Clapham, London.

Newer technology was beset with problems as grave as older technology. At Manchester Airport on 22 August 1985 a Boeing 737 burst into flames on the ground, 83 escaped but 54 perished. The crash of a Pan Am jumbo jet at Lockerbie, during darkness on 21 December, killed the 270 passengers and crew and eleven residents of the small Scottish town. Terrorists were responsible for the crash and recriminations followed about airport security at Frankfurt and Heathrow. The following month a Boeing 737 crashed on the bank of the M1 motorway near Kegworth, Leicestershire, just short of the East Midlands Airport. The death toll was 47, 82 were injured. Although 'human error' was blamed, crashes of other Boeing aircraft worldwide caused doubts to be raised about their safety.

Another 51 lives were lost when a Thames pleasure boat, the *Marchioness*, was sunk in a collision on 20 August 1989.

All these tragedies revealed the lack of training of the various staffs involved, poor maintenance of equipment, neglect of premises and, in some cases, more concern for profits than for safety. One consequence of the disasters was that Lloyd's of London, the insurers, went heavily into the red for the first time in 300 years, and many members, or 'names', were threatened with bankruptcy. Outmoded practices were thought to be a problem and there were allegations of fraud.

Football hooliganism

Football as an entertainment activity provoked much discussion in the 1980s. Tragedy and violence marred the game. A fire at Bradford City Football Club on 11 May 1985 resulted in fifty-five deaths and many more seriously injured. Serious criticisms were made of the state of the stadium. On the same day violence stopped the game in Birmingham. Later in the same month (on 29 May) thirty-eight Italian spectators were killed after a wall collapsed during violence at Heysel Stadium, Brussels, before the European Cup Final between Liverpool and Juventus. Subsequently, several English fans were convicted of manslaughter. The violence of English fans led to English teams being banned indefinitely from European competition. Shortly afterwards FIFA imposed a worldwide ban on English football teams. Thus was Britain's image as the home of gentlemanly sport badly shattered. On 12 June British fans were involved in a weekend of violence during the European soccer championships. Tragedy struck Liverpool again when on 15 April 1989 ninety-five Liverpool fans were crushed to death at Hillsborough football ground in Sheffield. Later, North Yorkshire police were blamed for the disaster due to lack of proper crowd control. Questions were again raised about conditions at football stadia. In November 1989 North Yorkshire police agreed to pay over £50 million to relatives of the victims. There was a partial lifting of the ban on English clubs in 1990/1 when two English clubs – Manchester United and Aston Villa – were re-admitted to Europe. Remarkably, Manchester United won the European Cup-Winners' Cup. The ban was finally lifted in the 1991/2 season. It is only fair to mention that Germany, among other states, also had problems with its football hooligans.

Continuing terrorism

Tragedies of another kind were caused by the continuing terrorism of the IRA. Twenty years after the arrival of British troops in Northern Ireland to defend the Catholics, the IRA stepped up its campaign against the British Army in 1989. It carried the war to Germany and England. The worst attack was at Deal, in Kent, on

22 September 1989, when forty musicians were killed at the Royal Marines School of Music. Of the many attacks in the late 1980s the most daring was the mortar attack on 10 Downing Street on 7 February 1991. Shortly before 10 a.m., when fifteen ministers and officials were discussing the Gulf War on the ground floor, a mortar bomb exploded in the garden. Windows were shattered but no one was hurt. The bomb, one of three, was fired from a disguised van 200 metres away. The assailants escaped on a motorbike. On 18 February one man was killed and more than forty were injured when a bomb exploded at Victoria Station in London. Paddington Station was also hit on the same day without any casualties. Earlier, terrorists had killed Ian Gow MP at his home with a car bomb.

Between 1969 and 1989 deaths due to civil disturbance in Northern Ireland reached a total of 2,772. By the end of 1991 the situation was as bad as ever with sectarian killings in Ulster and fire bombs in England.

Education reforms

The government pushed ahead with reforms in education and health. They were presented as extending the enterprise culture, giving more choice to consumers, making these services more attuned to modern needs, promoting excellence and, above all, making them more cost-effective. In fact, they were largely a strategy for reducing the cost of increasingly expensive services in a society with an ageing population and a declining economy.

Under the Educational Reform Act (1988) the schools were forced to introduce a National Curriculum which included certain core subjects such as maths and English. Few objected to this in principle since it was normal in other European countries and had been under discussion when Callaghan was Prime Minister. It was feared, however, that certain subjects could suffer under the scheme. There was to be far more testing of children to ensure that acceptable standards were being reached. The two separate exams, the GCE 'O' level and CSE, were merged into the new GCSE which was meant to cover a much wider range of achievement and be less narrowly academic. More controversial was legislation which allowed schools to opt out of locally authority control after a vote by parents. There was the fear that some of the best schools would do this leaving only poorer schools in poorer areas under local authority control. On 2 November 1988 Skegness Grammar School became the first school to vote to opt out of local authority control. In another controversial move local authorities were forced to produce 'league tables' of school exam results. Critics felt it would be unfair on schools, especially in inner city areas, which had special problems in employing and retaining good teachers, and where many children were not academically inclined. In a move which its supporters claimed was trying to help just such children, the creation of twenty city technology colleges was announced in October 1986. These were to be mixed-ability colleges with an emphasis on modern technological skills. They were to be a partnership between local industry and the government, taking pupils exclusively from the inner city in which each was located. Critics thought they would be merely taking resources away from the existing schools. The government also put money into providing funds for pupils to transfer from local authority schools to the private sector.

On 22 July 1986 the Commons voted by a majority of one to ban corporal punishment in schools. This brought Britain in line with other EC states.

The same trend towards introducing 'market principles' was present in the government's policy towards higher education. The government wanted universities to compete against each other to 'bid' for public money. Within universities, departments and even courses would compete with each other for resources. In future their budgets would be determined partly by the amount of research they conducted. They would be expected to get more money from student fees and the research councils, and less from the University Funding Committee (UFC), which replaced the University Grants Committee (UGC) in 1989. The emphasis was to be on educating more students, more cheaply, in more 'relevant' disciplines like business studies or engineering. Because there was a belief that the polytechnics did indeed do this, and there were more potential Conservatives there than had been previously recognized, more importance was given to them. They were released from local authority control and became free to call themselves universities if they wished. The UFC and the Polytechnics and Colleges Funding Council were to be merged from April 1993 into a single body. Altogether, some sensible (and some doubtful) reforms were being introduced but, as usual, without proper regard to finance.

The government gave university staff little encouragement. As the *Financial Times* (25 January 1990) commented, 'Since 1979, lecturers' pay has fallen more than 20 per cent relative to average earnings . . . Indeed, lecturers are one of the few groups whose pay actually buys less in terms of goods and services than it did in 1979.' The *Financial Times* urged the government to match its 'rhetoric about expansion with the resources needed for a realistic pay award for lecturers'. Two other changes which were the product of government policies were the abolition of tenure for the new generation of lecturers (or those existing lecturers who changed their jobs), and the growing number of those on temporary contracts.

The Education (Student Loans) Act 1990 provided for 'top-up' loans for students in higher education as an alternative to raising the grants students received in line with inflation. The grant element was to be frozen with students becoming increasingly dependent on loans, casual work, sponsorship and, perhaps above all, their parents. Most of those involved in higher education, including the students, opposed the scheme, as did the Labour Party. The greatest fear was that the scheme would put off potential students from poorer backgrounds. In the past Britain had prided itself on having a *relatively* large number of students from working-class and other non-academic families.

Great concern continued to be voiced about the relative ignorance of British youth compared with the young people of neighbouring countries. Too few young people in Britain had adequate education in maths, science or a foreign language. Too few continued their education after the age of 16. Too few received training once they entered employment. A report published by the Council for Industry and Higher Education in November 1991 revealed that the British workforce was significantly under-qualified compared with those of Germany and France. In a 'league table' of fifteen western industrial states, ranked in order of number of 18-year olds in full-time education, Britain came fourteenth. In terms of graduates per 1,000 in any one age group, Britain was behind France, West Germany, Japan and the USA in the number of engineering and technology graduates it produced, but ahead of both Germany and Japan in science, maths and computer graduates. Overall, Britain produced fewer graduates than each of these four states.[8]

In the winter of 1991–2 there were a number of student sit-ins at universities and polytechnics to protest against the under-funding of higher education.

NHS 'terminally ill'?

As in education, so in the National Health Service (NHS) the Conservatives were determined to introduce market principles. Prescription charges were greatly increased, as were dental charges and, a new departure, charges were introduced for eye tests. More fundamentally, general practitioners were allocated budgets to buy health care for patients, including non-emergency operations. Large hospitals, roughly 300 of them, were allowed to opt out of regional health authority control, becoming self-governing trusts within the NHS. They would sell their services to the NHS health authorities and to private hospitals and patients, and would be responsible for their own budgets. The regional health authorities would be free to buy the cheapest treatment for their patients wherever it was available, and where waiting lists were shortest. Attempts were made to cut down on the 'hotel side' of health care by sending patients home earlier. This was justified on the grounds of improvements in medical techniques and in housing. The government constantly reiterated the point that it was not planning to privatize the NHS, that it was wedded to a universal service, financed by taxation and free at the point of use. Many electors did not believe this. Nor did they believe the statistics that the government had increased spending on the NHS in real terms and that there were more doctors than ever before employed. The trouble was that developments in medical science were making the NHS more costly, and people were living longer and expecting more. The government was unable to deny, however, that hospitals were being forced to close wards in order to balance their books. John Chawner, Chairman of the Central Consultants Committee of the British Medical Association, believed in 1990, 'the NHS is chronically underfunded [and] is terminally ill from lack of cash'.[9]

The threat of AIDS, first identified in the early 1980s, still seemed very limited in Britain in the early 1990s. It appeared to be worst in central London and Edinburgh. The death of a few prominent figures – rock singer Freddie Mercury and film director Tony Richardson among them – helped to increase public awareness of AIDS, as did a government-sponsored publicity campaign.

The threat from cigarettes had not diminished. In its report *The Smoking Epidemic – Counting the Cost* (November 1991), the Health Education Council estimated that smoking was killing 110,000 people a year and costing the NHS £437 million. Figures in *Social Trends* (1991) indicated that fewer people admitted that they were smokers of cigarettes:

	1972	1982	1988
	%	%	%
Men	52	38	33
Women	42	33	30

Still, many young people appeared to be picking up the habit.

Rushdie and race relations

In 1989 the publishing world was involved in a bitter dispute about the novel *The Satanic Verses* by Salman Rushdie. Published in 1988 it was acclaimed by critics and won the Whitbread Prize for fiction. Some Muslims however thought it blasphemous and when it was brought to the attention of the Iranian leader Ayatollah Khomeini he sentenced Rushdie to death. At issue was a small part of the book which treated the Qur'ān and Islam in a satirical way. Rushdie later apologized to Muslims for causing offence but it did him little good and he was forced to go into hiding. Muslims in Britain called upon the government to ban the book or change the law to make possible its banning. Many writers and intellectuals rallied to Rushdie's support. The issue brought to the surface the sense of injustice felt by many, often younger Muslims, in Britain. The affair caused Britain to break off diplomatic relations with Iran. They were restored in 1990 after the death of Khomeini.[10]

Although Britain avoided the open racial confrontation which defaced the streets of France, Germany and Switzerland and other states in the late 1980s, many immigrant groups felt threatened. Allegations were made that the police did not investigate racist attacks quickly and thoroughly. Reports indicated that ethnic minorities were disadvantaged in many areas of national life. Although the Conservative Party, like the Labour Party and the Liberal Democrats, was adopting more parliamentary candidates from the immigrant communities, some Conservatives made remarks which did not endear them to British blacks and Asians. This was certainly true of Norman Tebbit who, in his memoirs,[11] wrote of illegal immigrants attracted by the prospects of easy living without work. Britain, like the other west European states, was faced with many applicants for political asylum. It was also faced with the new menace of gang warfare in south London and elsewhere among the 'crack' dealers in the West Indian community. There were signs too that the Chinese community was in danger of being infiltrated by the Mafia-like Triad gangs.

Labour win European elections

In the third direct elections to the European Parliament in June 1989 Labour were clear winners, gaining 45 seats (17 in 1984); the Conservatives were clear losers with 17 seats (45 in 1984); and the Scottish National Party gained one seat, as in 1984 and 1979. In Northern Ireland the two unionist parties – OUP and DUP – gained, as previously, one seat each, and the largely Catholic SDLP held its one seat. In Northern Ireland a system of

353

proportional representation was in operation. In the rest of the UK the old first-past-the-post system kept out the Liberal Democrats and the Greens who, to considerable surprise, won 15 per cent of the vote. The Conservatives had campaigned in a way that gave the impression that they were against the European Community. This followed a strongly anti-federalist speech by Thatcher at Bruges in September 1988. Labour, on the other hand, had become the party of Europe. Many Conservative MEPs and MPs started to feel that under Mrs Thatcher's leadership Britain was becoming dangerously isolated within the EC.

Resignations, sackings and reshuffles

In his book *Kill the Messenger*, Bernard Ingham, Mrs Thatcher's Press Secretary, wrote, 'I was beginning to dread trips abroad with the Prime Minister. I could never be sure who would resign next on our return.'[12] He was writing about the period 1989–90. After the election victory of 1987 Norman Tebbit decided to retire from the government but he remained Chairman of the Conservative Party, a post he had held since 1985, until the autumn. Tebbit, a former airline pilot and for seventeen years an official of the British Airline Pilots' Association, was noted for his abrasive style and loyalty to Thatcher. Nicholas Edwards (Wales) also resigned. John Biffen, who had criticized Thatcher's style, was sacked from his post of Leader of the House of Commons. He was replaced by John Wakeham. Also sacked were Lord Hailsham, Lord Chancellor since 1979, and Michael Jopling (Agriculture). Cecil Parkinson was brought back into the Cabinet as Energy Secretary. Two newcomers were John Major as Chief Secretary to the Treasury, and John Moore at Social Services. In October 1987 Lord Havers (Lord Chancellor) resigned, and Lord Whitelaw, who had served in all the Thatcher cabinets, went in December 1988. In July 1989 Moore, who had been talked of as a possible future leader, was sacked. Paul Channon was removed at the same time and George Younger (Defence) and Lord Young (Trade and Industry) resigned.

After the strong showing of the Greens in the Euro-elections of 1989, Nicholas Ridley was moved from Environment, where he had been since 1986, to Trade and Industry. His replacement was the 'wet' Chris Patten. Norman Fowler (Employment) and Peter Walker (Wales) left to 'spend more time with their families' in January and March 1990 respectively. After a row with the Prime Minister at the EC summit in Madrid in July 1989, Sir Geoffrey Howe was moved from the Foreign Office to become Leader of the House, and was replaced by Major. After Thatcher's return from the Commonwealth Conference in October 1989 she was faced with the resignation of Nigel Lawson as Chancellor. John Major replaced him. Douglas Hurd then replaced Major as Foreign Secretary. On her return from the Houston economic summit in July 1990 Thatcher had to find a replacement for her friend, Nicholas Ridley. He had provoked a storm when he described the EC as 'a German racket'. Ridley (b. 1929), educated at Eton and Balliol, was a civil engineer by training and a Thatcherite by conviction.

During her period in office Mrs Thatcher sacked fourteen Cabinet ministers and twenty-one decided to resign. The first Thatcher Cabinet had twenty-two members, the 1983 and 1987 Cabinets twenty-one members. Between June 1987 and November 1990 all but one of the Cabinet either resigned, were sacked, or were shuffled around. Kenneth Clarke QC went from Trade and Industry to Health and then to Education. His moves followed strong criticism of his policies at each ministry. Clarke (b. 1940) had joined the Cabinet in 1985 as Postmaster General and Minister for Employment. He was regarded as a 'Wet'. Educated at Nottingham High School and Cambridge, he had been tipped as a potential leader of the Conservative Party. John Major held the Foreign Office for a few weeks in the summer of 1990. It was difficult to believe that any of the ministers had a firm grip on their departments. By the summer of 1990 there had been fifteen major Cabinet reshuffles. This contrasted with the way things were run in Germany by Chancellor Kohl (and his predecessors). There, nine of Kohl's original seventeen ministers from 1983 were still serving in the same offices. By contrast, Thatcher had only three left of her 1983 Cabinet.

Thatcher's fall

On 3 December 1989 an almost unknown Conservative MP, Sir Anthony Meyer, decided to stand against Mrs Thatcher for the leadership of the Conservative Party. Mrs Thatcher was the first Conservative leader to be subject to annual re-election under rules established at the time of Edward Heath. This was the first time she had been challenged. Neither Sir Anthony nor anyone else expected him to win. He merely wished to test the unease in the party over various aspects of domestic policy, but above all over Europe. Remarkably, since he did not even campaign, he attracted 33 votes to his leader's 314. There were 24 spoilt papers and three did not vote. It was quite a decent vote for the Member for Clwyd North West. An old Etonian and former diplomat, Sir Anthony (b. 1920) was forfeiting his safe seat by standing. Apparently a number of MPs wrote to George Younger, Thatcher's campaign manager, expressing their reservations but indicating support. Thatcher did not read the signs and went on as before in her opposition to the EC. She did not seem to appreciate that there had been a major shift of power from the United States to the EC and Japan. The military might of the United States displayed in the lead-up to the Gulf War seemed to blind her to this fact. It was on the EC issue that Sir Geoffrey Howe resigned on 1 November 1990. He had been in all her Cabinets since 1979. Howe's departure robbed Thatcher of much of her remaining credibility with her own colleagues as well as with the electorate. On 14 November Michael Heseltine announced he would challenge her for the leadership of the party. His platform was an overall reform of the poll tax and a more positive stance on Europe. In the first round Thatcher polled 204 votes to 152 for Heseltine. There were 16 spoilt papers. Her friends stressed that her support was similar to that she had when first elected, and similar to that gained by Heath and Labour's Harold Wilson when they were first elected. They also pointed out that she was only four votes short, under Conservative Party rules, of winning on the first ballot. Her detractors stressed that 45 per cent had voted against her and that others had strong reservations. She was at an EC summit in Paris when the results were announced and emerged from the British embassy in fighting mood. Less than twenty-four hours later, after a night of consultations with Cabinet colleagues, she resigned. In the second round on 27 November, John Major gained 185 votes, Heseltine 131, and Douglas Hurd 56. Although just short of the 187 needed for victory, Major was declared elected when the other two candidates withdrew. Nicholas Ridley later wrote of the Conservative Party,

It is a very cruel animal . . . It is ruthless and cruel. Few that evening spared a moment to regret both the fact and the manner of her going, let alone permit themselves a tear. There was much unconcealed pleasure at the clever way they had got her out.[13]

John Major

When the victory of John Major was announced, Margaret Thatcher said she was 'thrilled'. Labour's John Cunningham called him a Thatcherite and Liberal Democrat Paddy Ashdown said he was 'a Thatcherite with a different face'. The Liberal MP Alan Beith commented, 'I like him and he is a very competent man, but I do not really understand what he believes.' His Cabinet colleague, Tony Newton, said he cared deeply about the plight of the under-privileged.

John Major (b. 1943) had reached the top job in British politics after just eleven years in Parliament and three years in the Cabinet.[14] He was the youngest Prime Minister for nearly a century. Born in Merton, Surrey, the son of a circus performer, he was educated at a grammar school in Wimbledon. He left school at 16, working as a labourer and as a clerk before joining the Standard Chartered Bank in 1965. During his banking career he was sent to Nigeria and later worked as personal assistant to the former Chancellor, Anthony Barber. In 1970 he married Norma Johnson and they had a son and a daughter.

Major's political commitment started at 16 when he joined the Young Conservatives. He served his time in local politics, rising to be chairman of the housing committee on Lambeth Borough Council. He was elected to the safe seat of Huntingdon in 1979. Between 1985 and 1987 he was at the Department of Social Security, first as Under-Secretary and then as Secretary of State. In 1987 he was appointed Chief Secretary to the Treasury. After a brief spell as Foreign Secretary he was appointed Chancellor in 1989. In ideological terms he was broadly acceptable to all sections of his party. He was liberal on such issues as immigration and in his opposition to capital punishment. He was reckoned to be for 'sound money' in the Conservative tradition but sympathetic to the less well-off. He called for a 'classless society'.[15] Finally, he was much more positive about the European Community than Margaret Thatcher had been.

'To many senior ministers, Cabinet government was no longer by confrontation but rather by discussion.'[16] Major sensibly retained the services of Douglas Hurd at the Foreign Office, and Kenneth Baker moved to the Home Office. He gave the Environment to Michael Heseltine and his friend Norman Lamont became Chancellor. Tom King stayed on at Defence. Kenneth Clarke and William Waldegrave retained their difficult portfolios, Education and the NHS respectively. Douglas Hurd (b. 1930) was a product of Eton and Cambridge. A former diplomat and author of political thrillers, he had been associated with Edward Heath. Kenneth Baker (b. 1934) had been educated at St Paul's and Oxford, and had served at Education since 1986 and before that at Environment (1985–6). Norman Lamont (b. 1942) had been a merchant banker with Rothschild and Sons after graduating from Cambridge. He had worked as Financial Secretary to the Treasury from 1986. Christopher Patten (b. 1944) was appointed Chairman of the Conservative Party with a seat in the Cabinet as Chancellor of the Duchy of Lancaster. He had been educated at St Benedict's School, Ealing, and Balliol College, Oxford. He was regarded as a 'Wet' and had served at Overseas Development. Major's government was one of lawyers and bankers and of Oxbridge. Its members lacked experience of manufacturing industry, science, and the educational background of most of the electorate. This was not new.

War in the Gulf

One of the first things John Major had to deal with was the continuing crisis in the Persian Gulf. On 2 August 1990 Iraq invaded Kuwait, the small Arab kingdom on the Persian Gulf. Having 13 per cent of the world's known supply of oil and a population of only 1.8 million (1986), it was rich, though most of its people were poor. The UN condemned the move, as did the Arab League and the United States and Soviet Union. The Iraqi dictator, Saddam Hussein, declared Kuwait annexed on 8 August, by which time a powerful coalition was building up against him. Months of diplomatic moves followed, until on 16 January 1991 Operation Desert Storm got under way. This was an offensive of the air and land forces of (mainly) the United States, Britain, France, Saudi Arabia, Egypt, Syria and Italy. Iraq was subjected to heavy aerial bombardment until on 24 February the land forces moved forward. By 27 February, Kuwait was in allied hands and Iraq had announced its readiness to accept unconditionally all UN resolutions. Military action by the US-led coalition ceased the following day.

Mrs Thatcher had announced her support for U.S. moves immediately after the invasion. She was backed up by the leaders of the opposition parties. This national unity continued under Major until the mini-war was over. The action cost the British armed forces 17 dead (9 killed by 'friendly fire' by the Americans), 43 wounded and 8 missing. The Americans lost something like 79 dead, 213 wounded and 50 missing. Iraq suffered heavy military and civilian casualties. The financial cost to Britain was around £3,000 million ($6,000 million), much of which it hoped to recover from Germany, Japan, Saudi Arabia and Kuwait.

Despite the national unity over the Gulf War, it raised many questions about the policy of Britain and the other western powers. They had aided Saddam in his eight-year war against Iran. Iraq had received sophisticated military and scientific equipment from the west as well as from the Soviet Union. Some asked why the coalition had allowed the Saddam Hussein regime to survive, especially when he started attacking, once again, the Kurdish minority in Iraq. The war allied the west with their former enemy Syria, a regime mixed up in international terrorism. The fall of Communism in the old Soviet Union meant that Syria had lost its chief backer and had to repair its bridges to the west. Iran came in from the cold, Britain restored relations with Tehran, and the Iranians remained neutral in the war. The war caused the spotlight to be turned on the Kuwaiti regime. It was revealed as an absolute monarchy with a poor record on human rights. Kuwait had been under British tutelage until 1961. Questions were also asked about the bombing of civilians by the United States and its allies. This contravened the 1949 Geneva Convention. Saddam was also guilty of this by firing rockets indiscriminately at Israel and Saudi Arabia. In London on 2 February 30,000 demonstrators gathered to oppose the war. Similar protests were held in Bonn and Los Angeles. Labour MPs Clare Short and Tony Banks were among those opposing military action. Edward Heath had his doubts and tried hard, in his personal capacity, to reason with Saddam.

Saddam attempted to link his occupation of Kuwait with the Israeli occupation of the West Bank and Gaza Strip. Although the United States, Britain and other western states claimed that this was a separate issue, it became clear that it was an issue which would not go away. All the British parties supported the Madrid peace conference at which, in October 1991, for the first time, the Israelis and Palestinians sat down together to discuss a settlement of their differences.

One happy side of the changing situation in the Middle East was the release of western hostages by Islamic fundamentalist groups allied to Iran. On 18 November 1991 Terry Waite, the Archbishop of Canterbury's special envoy, was released after 1,763 days in chains. He had been attempting to secure the release of others when he was abducted in Beirut. He was the last Briton to be set free in Lebanon.

The Gulf War helped Major's image for a short while, but the halo effect did not last long as the recession hit Conservative voters. Major also had to unite his party which was divided on Europe.

'Greed is everything'[17]

In the second half of the 1980s every Briton aged 4 and over spent, on average, over twenty-five hours each week watching television. Considering that most of their days were spent either at school or work, it meant that most of their evenings were occupied in front of the 'box'. Politicians as well as advertisers realized it was a very potent force of influence. Mrs Thatcher and her circle, just as Mr Wilson before them, were at odds with television. They regarded it, especially the BBC, as biased against them. One way or another they intended to reduce the power of the BBC and break the power of the unions in independent television. Their weapons were changes in the leadership of the BBC, a financial squeeze and deregulation of TV and radio. The appointment of James Marmaduke Hussey as Chairman of the Board of Governors of the BBC in 1986 was seen as a step in this direction. Other Board and personnel changes followed. Hussey demanded the resignation of the Director-General, Alasdair Milne, and an accountant, Michael Checkland, was appointed Director-General to steer the BBC in the direction of an even greater market orientation than in the past. The government restricted the BBC's revenue by not allowing its licence fee to keep pace with the rise in inflation. This was one of the policies spelt out in its White Paper, *Broadcasting in the '90s: Competition, Choice and Quality*. Other recommendations included in the new Broadcasting Act were the setting up of a new independent national TV service (Channel 5, 1993), three national commercial radio stations, and new local radio and TV channels. The Independent Broadcasting Authority was abolished and it was required to auction its broadcasting licences to the highest commercial bidders. It was replaced by two new bodies, the Independent Television Commission and the Radio Authority, which had fewer regulatory powers and whose decisions could be challenged in the courts. Under earlier legislation, the Broadcasting Complaints Commission and the Broadcasting Standards Council were established. The first examines complaints of unjust or unfair treatment on TV or radio, the second sets and monitors standards of taste and decency.

The existing TV networks were faced with increasing competition from satellite television, though this had progressed less than expected by 1992. The two satellite companies – Sky and British Satellite Broadcasting – set up in 1986, were forced to merge after sustaining massive losses. Employment for television technicians was deliberately casualized by requiring both the BBC and the ITV companies to commission a quarter of their programmes from independent programme-making companies.

Coronation Street retained high ratings as did the BBC's *EastEnders*. But they faced new soap challengers, *Neighbours* and *Home and Away*, from Australia, and *Brookside*, from Liverpool. Phil Redmond, who devised the Liverpool soap, explained in *Brookside: The Official Companion*: 'I wanted to tackle the relevant social issues. Things like long-term unemployment, women's position in society, the black economy, the micro-electronic technological revolution and its impact on both management and union structures within industry.' Later his programme explored many other issues which *Coronation Street* found too disturbing.

The press remained dominated by four or five key proprietors – Rupert Murdoch, Robert Maxwell, 'Tiny' Rowland, Conrad Black and Lord Stevens. Four out of five of them were not natives of the British Isles. The Murdoch and Maxwell empires were in deep financial trouble by the 1990s due to over-ambitious expansion worldwide. Although Maxwell gave conditional support to the Labour Party, most of the press remained firmly anti-Labour. An attempt to establish a new left-wing Sunday paper, the *Sunday Correspondent*, failed, though the more centrist new daily, *The Independent*, founded in 1986, rapidly established itself as a quality paper with a circulation of 400,000 by 1989, roughly equivalent to those of the *Guardian* and *The Times*. The 'quality' papers remained heavily dependent on advertising revenue.

Between 1984 and 1989 the number of cinema tickets sold rose annually. In 1955 on average there were 23.1 cinema visits per person in the UK annually. By 1984 this had dropped to under one visit. In 1989 it had risen to 1.5 per person per annum. As always, most of the films shown were American. In 1985 the Government withdrew all support for the film industry, including the Eady levy which had attracted inward investment for film production from Hollywood since 1951. Not surprisingly, by 1990 the production of feature films had fallen to its lowest level since the 1920s. It was only the puny privatized National Film Finance Corporation, renamed the British Screen Corporation, and the larger television companies, which financed new British productions, several of which received high critical acclaim both at home and abroad. A major contributor to this improvement was Channel Four Television, which had been set up in 1982. Film-makers had to consider the potential for exhibiting their products on television and as videos – an expanding market – as well as their traditional concern for the American market.

A few British films took a critical look at life in the 1950s. *Wish You Were Here* (1987), written and directed by David Leland, was a realistic portrayal of female teenage life in the 1950s. In *The Krays* Peter Medak dealt with organized crime in London in that era; *Scandal* retold the story of the Profumo affair (see p. 142). Ken Loach's *Hidden Agenda* was set in contemporary Ireland and was concerned with more recent political scandals. Loach also scored with *Riff-Raff*, a film about building workers, which was voted the European film of the year in 1991. *Personal Services* (1987), written by David Leland and directed by Terry Jones, was based on a real-life brothel in a London suburb which was patronized by highly respectable professional men many of whom seemed to have peculiar tastes. Janet Goddard's *A Letter To Brezhnev* (1985), written by Frank Clarke and directed by Chris

361

Bernard, was a clever Anglo-Russian romance, set against the background of the grim decay of Liverpool. *My Beautiful Laundrette* (1985), written by Hanif Kureshi and directed by Stephen Frears, had much to say about the experiences of the Asian immigrant community and about being gay in contemporary Britain. The films of David Puttnam achieved international recognition, and at least three of them – *Chariots of Fire* (1980), *Local Hero* (1982) and *Defence of the Realm* (1986) – were very relevant to the British experience. Support from Channel Four was crucial for the making of many of these and other films.

The film which best summed up the age of Reagan and Thatcher came from Hollywood, Oliver Stone's *Wall Street*. Loosely based on happenings in the United States – corporate raiding, insider trading and the troubles of the airline business – it was a cautionary tale of a would-be yuppie. The handsome, ruthless, entrepreneur (Michael Douglas) sums up the enterprise culture of the 1980s when he tells a shareholders' meeting:

'Greed, for want of a better word, is good. Greed is right. Greed works. Greed clarifies, cuts through the essence of the evolutionary spirit, greed in all its forms. Greed for life, for money, for love, knowledge has marked the upward surge of mankind . . .'

It would not only save their company but 'that other malfunctioning corporation called the USA'. The film delivers the answer from the lips of the trade union leader (Martin Sheen) who tells his yuppie son (Charlie Sheen), 'Stop going for the easy buck and produce something with your life. Create instead of living off the buying and selling of others.'

'What is the lady up to?'

As the first anniversary of Margaret Thatcher's resignation approached there was much looking back and many commentaries on Thatcher and Thatcherism. What had she achieved? Aided by the fact that she was the first woman Prime Minister in a major European democracy, she had exploited the interest to project her personality internationally. She was further helped by the presence of Ronald Reagan in the White House, 1981–9. At home her policies were buttressed by North Sea oil and privatization revenues. She had challenged the complacency and defeatism which had permeated Britain before 1980. She had gone some way to make people feel they had to be competitive. But she had in no way halted Britain's industrial decline. On the contrary, it had got worse. One indicator of this was that the number of people employed in manufacturing fell by more than 2 million between

1979 and early 1991, that is from 31 to 23 per cent of the total workforce.[18] There had been much talk of the 'enterprise society' but most people felt it went too far. It seemed that, in Britain, everything had a price tag on it. Abroad, Thatcher had lent Britain's weight to the developing movement towards democracy in the Soviet Union and East Europe. But she had expressed her hostility both to German unity and to Britain's ever closer ties to the EC. She had brought Britain close to isolation and helped to promote dangerous illusions about Britain's position in Europe and the world. At best her record was no better than that of other post-war Prime Ministers.

In the year since she had left office Margaret Thatcher had travelled extensively mostly to the United States, and had embarrassed her colleagues by her references to their policies. When EC policy was discussed in the Commons on 21–2 November 1991 she supported the government in the vote but lashed it verbally. She wanted a referendum on any moves towards closer EC ties. This was opposed by the government and most of the Labour Party. Outside the House she was even more vitriolic. Sir Norman Fowler remarked, 'It makes me very angry . . . if she goes on like this she is going to lose us the election.'[19] Her outpourings caused Sir Marcus Fox, MP, a man who had loyally supported her in government, to comment, 'What is the lady up to?'[20]

Which way for Europe?

In the years 1989–91 the world held its breath as the most dramatic, yet peaceful, events since 1945 unfolded. First the Soviet empire in East Europe collapsed like a house of cards, and then the Soviet Union itself broke up, renouncing the ideology it had proclaimed since 1917. Part and parcel of this movement were the developments in Germany commencing in the autumn of 1989 and ending with the restoration of German unity on 3 October 1990. Though Thatcher expressed doubts in public and private, the policy of Britain was to welcome this development. Like it or not, it meant that the new, united Germany was even more important in the EC than the old West Germany had been. With the uniting of Germany the EC got an additional 16 million citizens from the former Communist East Germany. The collapse of the Soviet Union also increased the stature of Germany as Europe's leading economy. These events took place at a time when the EC was on the road to closer ties through the coming of the single market in 1992.

Margaret Thatcher, whose government had fought the proposed Social Charter of the EC, opposed the introduction of a single currency for the EC, more power for the EC parliament, any moves towards a federal Europe, and a defence role for the EC. On all these issues most members welcomed progress. Only Britain opposed them all. Many Conservatives saw the EC merely as a free trade area rather than a community. The argument for a single currency was supported by many in business who felt it would reduce costs by eliminating currency transactions. It would also remove the dangers to businesses dealing in sterling, a relatively weak currency subject to fairly wide and damaging fluctuations. The need for a defence role for the EC was shown by the Gulf War and by the civil war in Yugoslavia in 1991. Britain wanted defence issues to be dealt with by the existing mechanisms of NATO. To complicate matters, Ireland is not a NATO member, and France withdrew her troops, but not her membership, in 1966. Unlike the other members, the British government of Mrs Thatcher did not want to be reminded that the first sentence of the 1957 Rome document, setting up the then European Economic Community, aimed at 'an ever closer union among the peoples of Europe'.

Britain had been forced by its own economic weakness to eventually join the Exchange Rate Mechanism (ERM) of the European Monetary System (EMS). Thatcher had opposed her Chancellor, Nigel Lawson, and her Foreign Minister, Geoffrey Howe, on this. However, Britain joined on 5 October 1990. Thatcher still opposed a single currency and an independent European central bank, expressing her views forcibly at the EC Rome summit in October 1990. This led to the resignation of Sir Geoffrey Howe. He felt his position was undermined by her approach.

Major had gone to the Maastricht summit of the leaders of the twelve EC states knowing that his negotiating position was severely limited both by the divisions within his own party and the determination of the other eleven to make progress towards a more integrated Community. After tough negotiations the twelve members of the EC struck a deal on 11 December 1991. This was a draft treaty under which the twelve states would establish a European Union which would eventually have its own defence and foreign policies, a single currency, a common policy on immigration, a Cohesion Fund designed to narrow the differences between the poor and the rich areas of the Union, and, not least, a strengthened European Parliament. Britain secured the right to opt out of the single currency. The Social Chapter was put aside but the other eleven members agreed they would implement it separately without Britain. On defence it was agreed that NATO would still underpin European defence. The single currency would only become a reality towards 2000.

Most Conservative MPs felt Major had secured a good compromise at Maastricht, most Labour and Liberal MPs felt he had isolated Britain further. Liberal leader Paddy Ashdown believed Major had condemned Britain to becoming 'semi-detached' in relation to the European Community. The Social Chapter, which Britain would not sign, prescribed minimum standards for employees on pay, holidays, sickness benefits, consultation and other matters. Major claimed that the cost of these would create more unemployment. But both unions and employers in other EC states felt British industry was being given an unfair advantage over them. Labour MPs believed British workers were being condemned to 'sweat shop' conditions relative to their neighbours. By the end of 1991, after just over a year in office, John Major had shown considerable skill in shifting his party from the Right to the Centre. He had also managed to establish himself abroad. However, with the election only months away, he faced severe economic problems and a Labour Party in better shape than it had been for over a decade.

Major's April victory

Confounding the pollsters, and despite the worst slump since the 1930s, the Conservatives won an unprecedented fourth term on 9 April 1992. On a UK turnout of 77.73 per cent they gained a 21-seat majority over all other parties.

	seats	net change	% vote (UK)	1987 %
Cons	336	−34	41.85	42.06
Lab	271	+39	34.16	30.58
Lib Dem	20	− 2	17.88	22.74
SNP	3	− 1	1.85	1.35
PC	4	+ 1	0.46	0.42
NI parties gained 17 seats.

The Conservative, Labour and Liberal Democrat parties had only gained the votes of 32.5, 26.5 and 13.9 percent respectively of those on the electoral register. Labour had been hit by its traditionally poor organization, boundary changes, loss of votes of poll tax opponents and the homeless who had failed to get on to the electoral register and the fact that Labour voters were less likely to vote than Conservatives. It was thought that Labour's tax proposals had frightened floating voters. Both Labour and Conservatives squeezed the Liberal vote. Most observers felt Labour leader Neil Kinnock bore a heavy responsibility for his party's defeat, and he and his deputy, Roy Hattersley, promptly announced their intention to resign.

Notes

1 David Owen, *Time to Declare* (London, 1991), 611.
2 See 'Thatcher's Winners and Losers', *Management Today*, March 1991. See also William Kay's *Tycoons* (London, 1985).
3 *Financial Times*, 30 December 1991.
4 *Guardian*, 8 October 1991.
5 Peter Wright, *Spycatcher* (New York, 1987), 54. On Wilson see pp. 362–71.
6 See David Leigh, *The Wilson Plot: The Intelligence Services and the Discrediting of a Prime Minister 1945–1976* (London, 1988).
7 *Financial Times*, 22 December 1988.
8 Alan Smithers and Pamela Robinson, *Beyond Compulsory Schooling: A Numerical Picture* (London, 1991).
9 *The Independent*, 9 November 1990, see his letter.
10 James Piscatori, 'The Rushdie Affair and the Politics of Ambiguity', *International Affairs*, October 1990, gives background.
11 Norman Tebbit, *Unfinished Business* (London, 1991), 129.
12 Bernard Ingham, *Kill the Messenger* (London, 1991), 386.
13 Nicholas Ridley, *My Style of Government* (London, 1991), 252. For an account of the moves to remove Thatcher see Alan Watkins, *A Conservative Coup: The Fall of Margaret Thatcher* (London, 1991).
14 For a biography of John Major see Nesta Wayne Ellis, *John Major* (London, 1991), Bruce Anderson, *John Major – the Making of the Prime Minister (London, 1991), and Edward Pearce. The Quiet Rise of John Major* (London, 1991).
15 *The Thatcher Legacy: The Guardian Collection, Number 3* (London, 1991), 65.
16 Peter Riddell, *The Thatcher Era and its Legacy* (London, 1991), 235. See also Hugo Young, *One Of Us* (London, 1991).
17 I wish to thank Professor Vincent Porter of the Polytechnic of Central London for his valuable suggestions regarding this section.
18 Riddell, op. cit., 233.
19 *The Independent on Sunday*, 24 November 1991.
20 Quoted on Radio Four on 23 November 1991.

List of Tables

1	Principal ministers 1945–92	368
2	Party strengths in House of Commons	369
3	Votes cast	370
4	Industrial stoppages: working days lost in selected industries	371
5	NATO: military expenditure (% gross domestic product)	372
6	UK Balance of payments	374
7	Balance of trade for selected countries (1977–84)	375
8	Coal: manpower and production	376
9	Crude oil production in 1983	376
10	Nuclear share of electricity (1984 %)	376
11	Trade union membership (% all employees)	377
12	Gross domestic product 1984	377
13	Annual growth rate	378
14	Taxes (% total output)	378
15	Housing facilities in 1980	379
16	Number of inhabitants per medical practitioner	380
17	Persons on NHS waiting list	380
18	Expectation of life in UK	380
19	Expectation of life at age 1 year	381
20	Infant mortality rate	381
21	Holidays taken by citizens/residents of Great Britain	382
22	World leaders after 1945	382

Table 1 Principal ministers 1945–92

	Prime Minister	Chancellor of the Exchequer	Foreign Secretary	Home Secretary	Other ministers of note
1945–51	C. Attlee	H. Dalton Sir S. Cripps H. Gaitskell	E. Bevin H. Morrison	C. Ede	H. Morrison A. Bevan
1951–55	Sir W. Churchill	R. Butler	Sir A. Eden	Sir. D. Maxwell-Fyfe G. Lloyd George	Lord Woolton H. Macmillan
1955–57	Sir A. Eden	R. Butler H. Macmillan	H. Macmillan S. Lloyd	G. Lloyd George	Marquess of Salisbury S. Lloyd
1957–63	H. Macmillan	P. Thorneycroft D. Heathcoat Amory S. Lloyd R. Maudling	S. Lloyd Earl of Home	R. Butler H. Brooke	I. Macleod Viscount Hailsham
1963–64	Sir A. Douglas-Home	R. Maudling	R. Butler	H. Brooke	
1964–70	H. Wilson	J. Callaghan R. Jenkins	P. Gordon Walker M. Stewart G. Brown M. Stewart	Sir F. Soskice R. Jenkins J. Callaghan	H. Bowden R. Crossman D. Healey
1970–74	E. Heath	I. Macleod A. Barber	Sir A. Douglas-Home	R. Maudling R. Carr	W. Whitelaw J. Prior
1974–76	H. Wilson	D. Healey	J. Callaghan	R. Jenkins	M. Foot
1976–79	J. Callaghan	D. Healey	A. Crosland D. Owen	R. Jenkins M. Rees	M. Foot H. Lever
1979	M. Thatcher	Sir G. Howe N. Lawson J. Major	Lord Carrington F. Pym Sir G. Howe J. Major D. Hurd	W. Whitelaw L. Brittan D. Hurd D. Waddington	Sir K. Joseph M. Heseltine N. Tebbit Lord Young
1990	J. Major	N. Lamont	D. Hurd	K. Baker K. Clarke	M. Heseltine

Table 2 Party strengths in House of Commons

	1945	1950	1951	1955	1959	1964	1966	1970	1974 Feb.	1974 Oct.	1979	1983	1987	1992
Conservative	213	298	321	345	365	303	253	330	296	276	339	397	375	336
Labour	393	315	295	277	258	317	363	287	301	319	268	209	229	271
Liberal**	12	9	6	6	9	9	12	6	14	13	11	23	22	20
Independent	14	–	–	–	–	1	–	–	–	–	1	–	–	–
Others	8	3	3	2	–	1*	2*	7*	24*†	27*†	16*†	21†	24	24†
Total	640	625	625	630	630	630	630	630	635	635	635	650	650	651

Notes: *Includes The Speaker
†Includes all Northern Ireland MPs
**Includes SDP MPs in 1983 and 1987

Table 3 Votes cast

	Con.	Lab.	Lib.**	Nat.	Comm.	Others*	Total votes cast	Total turnout
	%	%	%	%	%	%	%	%
1945	39.8	47.8	9.0	0.6	0.4	1.8	100	72.7
1950	43.5	46.1	9.1	0.6	0.3	0.4	100	84.0
1951	48.0	48.8	2.5	0.5	0.1	0.1	100	82.5
1955	49.7	46.4	2.7	0.9	0.1	0.2	100	76.7
1959	49.4	43.8	5.9	0.6	0.1	0.2	100	78.8
1964	43.4	44.1	11.2	0.9	0.2	0.2	100	77.1
1966	41.9	47.9	8.5	1.2	0.2	0.3	100	75.8
1970	46.4	42.9	7.5	1.7	0.1	1.4	100	72.0
Feb. 1974	38.2	37.2	19.3	2.6	0.1	2.6	100	78.7
Oct. 1974	35.8	39.2	18.3	3.5	0.1	3.1	100	72.8
1979	43.9	36.9	13.8	2.0	0.1	3.4	100	76.0
1983	42.4	27.6	25.4	1.5		3.1	100	72.7
1987	42.2	30.8	22.6	1.7	–	2.7	100	75.3

Notes: *Includes the Communist vote in 1983 and 1987
**Includes the SDP vote in 1983 and 1987

Table 4 Industrial stoppages: working days lost (per '000 employees) in selected industries (mining and quarrying, manufacturing, construction, transport, storage and communication)*

	1960–4	1965–9	1973–7	1978–82	1977	1978	1979	1980	1981	1982
United Kingdom	242	294	700	1,040	840	840	2,410	1,160	300	470
Australia[1]	350	456	1,430	1,150	590	870	1,390	1,190	1,500	790
Belgium	164	156	440	(390)	430	660	360	140	..	..
Canada	460	1,556	2,080	1,680	830	1,930	1,660	1,520	1,880	1,420
Denmark[2]	708	110	1,070	(260)	240	90	140	170	650	..
Finland	340	206	1,390	510	2,310	160	270	1,300	580	230
France	352	243	330	230	260	200	350	170	160	260
Germany (FR)	34	10	30	80	–	360	40	10	10	–
Italy[3]	1,220	1,574	1,970	1,580	1,560	880	2,560	1,590	950	1,920
Japan	302	198	250	40	70	60	40	50	20	20
Netherlands	62	12	100	60	150	–	190	40	20	70
New Zealand	154	242	630	(770)	910	890	860	800	520	..
Norway	212	4	120	130	40	90	110	40	40	390
Spain	..	..	1,370	..	3,420	1,850	3,290	..	..	..
Sweden	6	28	20	440	20	10	20	2,130	60	..
United States[4]	722	1,232	1,100	(880)	1,100	1,100	910	850	670	..

Source: *Employment Gazette* March 1984, 102

Notes: *The figures are restricted mainly to these four relatively strike-prone industry groups by the International Labour Office to reduce the effects of different industrial structures and improve the basis of comparison of strike rates between the countries only

Brackets indicate incomplete data

1 Australian figure includes electricity and gas, excludes communication

2 Figures up to 1974 relate to manufacturing

3 Includes gas, electricity and water, and political strikes from 1975 onwards

4 Includes gas, electricity and water

.. Not available

– Negligible/less than five

371

Table 5 NATO: military expenditure (% gross domestic product)

	1957	1958	1959	1960	1961	1962	1963	1964	1965	1966	1967	1968	1969	1970
North America														
Canada	5.6	5.2	4.6	4.3	4.3	4.2	3.7	3.6	3.0	2.8	2.9	2.6	2.4	2.4
USA	9.9	10.0	9.4	8.9	9.0	9.2	8.7	8.0	7.5	8.4	9.4	9.3	8.7	7.9
Europe														
Belgium	3.8	3.7	3.7	3.6	3.4	3.5	3.4	3.4	3.2	3.1	3.1	3.1	2.9	2.9
Denmark	3.1	2.9	2.6	2.7	2.6	3.0	3.0	2.8	2.8	2.7	2.7	2.8	2.5	2.4
France	7.3	6.8	6.6	6.4	6.2	6.0	5.6	5.3	5.2	5.0	5.0	4.8	4.2	4.2
Germany (FR)	4.1	3.0	4.4	4.0	4.0	4.8	5.2	4.6	4.3	4.1	4.3	3.6	3.6	3.3
Greece	5.1	4.8	4.9	4.9	4.2	4.0	3.9	3.6	3.5	3.6	4.3	4.7	4.8	4.8
Italy	3.5	3.4	3.3	3.3	3.1	3.2	3.3	3.3	3.3	3.4	3.1	3.0	2.7	2.7
Luxembourg	1.9	1.9	1.8	1.0	1.2	1.3	1.2	1.4	1.4	1.4	1.2	1.0	0.9	0.8
Netherlands	5.2	4.7	4.0	4.1	4.5	4.5	4.4	4.3	3.9	3.7	3.9	3.7	3.6	3.5
Norway	3.6	3.5	3.6	3.2	3.3	3.6	3.5	3.4	3.7	3.5	3.5	3.6	3.6	3.5
Portugal	4.0	4.0	4.3	4.2	6.4	7.0	6.5	6.7	6.2	6.3	7.3	7.4	6.8	7.0
Turkey	4.1	3.8	4.5	5.1	5.5	5.1	4.7	4.8	5.0	4.4	4.5	4.6	4.4	4.3
UK	7.2	7.0	6.7	6.5	6.3	6.4	6.2	6.0	5.9	5.7	5.7	5.4	5.0	4.8

Table 5 cont'd

	1971	1972	1973	1974	1975	1976	1977	1978	1979	1980	1981	1982	1983
North America													
Canada	2.2	2.1	1.9	1.9	1.9	1.8	1.9	2.0	1.8	1.8	1.8	2.1	2.1
USA	7.1	6.6	6.0	6.1	6.0	5.4	5.3	5.1	5.1	5.6	5.8	6.5	6.9
Europe													
Belgium	2.8	2.8	2.8	2.8	3.1	3.1	3.2	3.3	3.3	3.3	3.4	3.4	3.4
Denmark	2.5	2.3	2.1	2.4	2.6	2.3	2.3	2.3	2.3	2.4	2.5	2.5	...
France	4.0	3.9	3.8	3.7	3.9	3.8	3.9	4.0	3.9	4.0	4.2	4.2	4.2
Germany (FR)	3.3	3.4	3.4	3.6	3.6	3.5	3.4	3.3	3.3	3.3	3.4	3.4	3.4
Greece	4.7	4.6	4.1	4.2	6.5	6.9	7.0	6.7	6.3	5.7	7.0	7.0	7.1
Italy	2.9	3.1	2.9	2.9	2.8	2.3	2.4	2.4	2.4	2.4	2.5	2.6	2.8
Luxembourg	0.8	0.9	0.8	0.8	1.0	0.8	0.8	0.8	0.8	0.9	0.9	...	...
Netherlands	3.4	3.4	3.3	3.3	3.5	3.2	3.3	3.1	3.2	3.1	3.2	3.3	3.3
Norway	3.4	3.3	3.1	3.1	3.2	3.1	3.1	3.2	3.1	2.9	2.9	3.0	3.1
Portugal	7.4	6.9	6.0	7.4	5.3	4.0	3.5	3.5	3.5	3.5	3.5	3.4	3.4
Turkey	4.5	4.3	4.1	3.9	6.1	6.2	5.8	5.2	4.3	4.3	4.9	5.2	4.9
UK	5.0	5.2	4.9	5.1	5.0	4.9	4.7	4.6	4.7	5.1	4.9	5.1	5.6

Source: Stockholm International Peace Research Yearbook (1984)
Note: . . . Not available

Table 6 UK Balance of payments

	1946	1947	1948	1949	1950	1951	1952	1953	1954	1955
Visible trade	-103	-361	-151	-137	-51	-689	-279	-244	-204	-313
Invisibles	-127	-20	+177	+136	+358	+320	+442	+389	+321	+158
Current balance	-230	-381	+26	-1	+307	-369	+163	+145	+117	-155

	1956	1957	1958	1959	1960	1961	1962	1963	1964	1965
Visible trade	+53	-29	+29	-115	-401	-140	-100	-89	-510	-233
Invisibles	+155	+262	+317	+273	+157	+167	+230	+218	+152	+188
Current balance	+208	+233	+346	+158	-244	+27	+130	-129	-358	-45

	1966	1967	1968	1969	1970	1971	1972	1973	1974	1975
Visible trade	-77	-567	-682	-172	-42	+261	-722	-2383	-5235	-3236
Invisibles	+186	+273	+396	+635	+773	+829	+857	+1384	+1644	+1381
Current balance	+109	-294	-286	+463	+731	+1090	+135	-999	-3591	-1855

	1976	1977	1978	1979	1980	1981	1982
Visible trade	-3929	-2284	-1542	-3449	-1233	+2870	+2228
Invisibles	+3054	+2262	+2560	+2596	+1696	+3091	+1720
Current balance	-875	-22	+1018	-853	+2929	+5961	+3948

Sources: Central Statistical Office
United Kingdom Balance of Payments 1971 (HMSO 1971)
United Kingdom Balance of Payments 1967–77 (HMSO 1978)

Table 7 Balance of trade for selected countries (1977–84) (US $ million)

	Japan[1]	USA[2]	Germany (FR)	France	UK	Italy	Canada	Austra- lia	Brazil	Mexico	Korea Rep. of
1977	17,311	−31,091	19,640	−3,289	−3,937	−131	3,140	1,025	−100	−1,021	−477
1978	24,596	−33,966	24,730	101	−2,965	2,912	4,184	92	−1,158	−1,745	−1,780
1979	1,845	−27,555	16,850	−3,220	−7,207	−990	4,180	2,511	−2,717	−2,830	−4,395
1980	2,125	−25,512	8,990	−13,418	3,714	−16,417	8,001	1,378	−2,823	−2,830	−4,384
1981	19,967	−28,001	16,580	−9,970	7,756	−10,901	6,612	−2,323	1,185	−4,099	−3,628
1982	18,079	−36,469	25,260	−15,784	3,999	−8,130	14,959	−2,614	778	6,885	−2,594
1983	31,454	−61,055	21,870	−8,063	−812	. . .	14,877	241	. . .	. . .	−1,700

Source: IMF, *International Financial Statistics* August 1984
Notes: 1 Based on *Balance of Payments Monthly*
         2 Excludes military grants. Based on *Economic Indicators*
         . . . Not available

Table 8 Coal: manpower and production

	Employed in mines ('000)	Output (million tons)
1948	726.3	209.4
1960	582.9	193.6
1970	304.4	137.9
1974	256.7	100.2
1979	243.5	108.3
1980	242.6	113.0
1983	206.3	102.5

Source: Based on Coal Board figures

Table 9 Crude oil production in 1983 ('000 barrels per day)

China	2,107
Indonesia	1,385
Iran	2,467
Mexico	2,690
Saudi Arabia	5,053
UK	2,285
USA	8,649
USSR	12,326
Venezuela	1,790

Source: *Japan 1984 An International Comparison*, Keizai Koho Center Tokyo

Table 10 Nuclear share of electricity (1984 %)

Belgium	51
Finland	40
France	59
Germany (FR)	23
Japan	23
Sweden	40
Switzerland	37
UK	17
USA	14

Source: International Atomic Energy Agency quoted in *US News and World Report*, 12 August 1985

Table 11 Trade union membership
(% all employees)

	Men	Women	Total
1951	56	25	45
1961	53	24	43
1971	59	32	49
1981	59	38	50

Source: *Social Trends* 15 1985, 163

Table 12 Gross domestic product 1984
(US $ per capita)

Canada	13,284
France	9,094
Germany (FR)	10,070
Italy	6,183
Japan	10,278
Sweden	11,515
Switzerland	13,965
UK	7,556
USA	15,331

Source: Credit Suisse (Zurich, May 1985)

Table 13 Annual growth rate (%)

	1973–7	1978–82
Canada	4.1	1.6
France	3.4	2.1
Germany (FR)	2.3	1.6
Italy	3.0	1.7
Japan	4.1	4.5
Sweden	1.8	1.4
Switzerland	−0.4	1.5
UK	1.9	1.0
USA	2.9	1.6

Source: Bank of Japan, *Comparative International Statistics*, 1984

Table 14 Taxes (% total output)

	1975	1984		1975	1984
Australia	29.1	30.0	Japan	21.0	27.7
Belgium	41.1	45.4	Netherlands	43.6	45.4
Canada	32.9	34.8	Norway	44.8	46.3
Denmark	41.4	47.2	Spain	19.6	27.2
Finland	35.4	37.0	Sweden	43.9	50.6
France	37.4	45.4	Switzerland	29.6	32.2
Germany (FR)	36.0	37.3	UK	35.5	38.6
Italy	29.0	40.6	USA	29.6	29.0

Source: *US News and World Report*, 16 September 1985
Note: Taxes include levies by all levels of government

Table 15 Housing facilities in 1980 (% houses equipped)

	Austria	Belgium	France	Germany (FR)	Italy	Netherlands	Sweden	Switzerland	UK
Piped water	96	96	98	100	94	100	100	100	100
Flush toilet	94	100	86	98	..	100	100	99	..
Electric lighting	99	100	100	100	99	100	100	100	100
Central heating	33	46	48	58	33	41	100	93	57
Fixed bath or shower	72	74	76	98	63	100	100	95	98
Private garden	43	53	28	42	37	75	56	40	75
Communal garden	9	15	30	23	16	6	32	20	8

Note: . . . not available

Table 16 Number of inhabitants per medical practitioner

	1975	1979
Belgium	529	446
Denmark	512	469
France	653	513
Germany (FR)	488	452
Italy	430	346
Japan	847	. . .
Netherlands	603	541
Sweden	560	490
UK	660	633
USA	629	. . .

Source: Eurostat (EEC), *Review 1974–1983*, 112
Note: . . . Not available

Table 17 Persons on NHS waiting list ('000)

1966	1971	1976	1979	1980	1981	1982
604	596	722	809	767	745	894

Source: *Social Trends* 9 1979, 136 and *Social Trends* 15 1985, 114

Table 18 Expectation of life in UK (years)

	1951	1971	1981
Males	66.2	68.8	69.8
Females	71.2	75.0	76.2

Source: *Social Trends* 15 1985, 103

Table 19   Expectation of life (years) at age 1 year

	Year	Males	Females
Australia	1980	70.9	77.9
Bulgaria	1980	69.0	74.2
Canada	1978	70.7	78.4
France	1978	70.2	78.4
Germany (FR)	1980	69.9	76.7
Germany (GDR)	1978	68.8	74.6
Italy	1978	71.0	77.5
Japan	1980	73.2	78.7
Spain	1978	71.5	77.4
Sweden	1980	72.4	78.5
Switzerland	1980	72.1	78.7
England & Wales	1980	70.6	76.6
N Ireland	1978	68.5	74.8
Scotland	1980	68.7	75.0
USA	1979	69.2	74.6

Source: DHSS, *On the State of the Public Health for the Year 1982*, 30

Table 20   Infant mortality rate (per '000 live births)

	1976	1980
Belgium	16.2*	12.2
Bulgaria	23.2	20.2
Canada	14.3*	10.4
France	12.5	10.0
Germany (FR)	17.4	12.6
Germany (GDR)	14.1	12.1
Italy	19.1	14.3
Japan	9.3	7.5
Netherlands	10.5	8.6
Spain	18.7*	11.1
Sweden	8.3	6.9
England & Wales	14.3	12.0
N Ireland	18.3	13.4
Scotland	14.8	12.1
USA	15.1	12.5

Source: DHSS, *On the State of the Public Health for the Year 1977*, 23 and *On the State of the Public Health for the Year 1982*, 28
Note: *1975 figure

Table 21 Holidays taken by citizens/residents of Great Britain (millions)

	1951	1961	1971	1976	1982	1983
Taken in GB	25	30	34	38	33	34
Taken abroad	2	4	7	7	14	15

Source: *Social Trends* 9 1979, 187 and *Social Trends* 15 1985, 155

Table 22 World leaders after 1945

Presidents of the USA

Harry S. Truman	(D)	1945
Dwight D. Eisenhower	(R)	1953
John F. Kennedy	(D)	1961
Lyndon B. Johnson	(D)	1963
Richard M. Nixon	(R)	1969
Gerald R. Ford	(R)	1974
Jimmy Carter	(D)	1977
Ronald Reagan	(R)	1981
George Bush	(R)	1989

R = Republican D = Democrat

West German Chancellors

Konrad Adenauer	(CDU)	1949
Ludwig Erhard	(CDU)	1963
Kurt Georg Kiesinger	(CDU)	1966
Willy Brandt	(SPD)	1969
Helmut Schmidt	(SPD)	1974
Helmut Kohl	(CDU)	1982

CDU = Christian Democratic Union

SPD = Social Democratic Party of Germany

Presidents of the V French Republic

Charles de Gaulle	1958
Georges Pompidou	1969
Valéry Giscard d'Estaing	1974
François Mitterrand	1981

First/General Secretaries of the Soviet Communist Party

Joseph V. Stalin	1922
Georgi M. Malenkov	1953
Nikita Khrushchev	1953
Leonid Brezhnev	1964
Yuri Andropov	1982
Konstantin Chernenko	1984
Mikhail Gorbachev	1985

President of the Russian Federation

Boris Yeltsin	1991

Japanese Prime Ministers

Shigeru Yoshida	1946
Tetsu Katayama	1947
Hitoshi Ashida	1948
Shigeru Yoshida	1948
Ichiro Hatoyama	1954
Tanzan Ishibashi	1956
Nobusuke Kishi	1957
Hayato Ikeda	1960
Eisaku Sato	1964
Kakuei Tanaka	1972
Takeo Miki	1974
Takeo Fukuda	1976
Masayoshi Ohira	1978
Zenko Suzuki	1980
Yasuhiro Nakasone	1982
Noboru Takeshita	1987
Sousuke Uno (3 June)	1989
Toshiki Kaifu (9 August)	1989
Kiichy Miyazawa	1991

Index

Abbot, Diane, 338
Abdullah al-Asnag, 113, 114
Abel-Smith, Brian, 121
Aberavon, 323
Abortion Act, 214
Abrams, Dr Mark, 129, 153
Abse, Leo, 214
Adam Smith Institute, 296
Adams, Gerry, 339
Adamson, Campbell, 240
Aden, 112–14
Adenauer, Konrad, 78, 79, 126, 136, 137
Advertising statistics, 325
Advisory Conciliation and Arbitration Service (ACAS), 246
aerospace, 255
Afghanistan, 293
Agricultural Charter, 39
agriculture, 107
AIDS, 352
aircraft industry, 73, 255
Albania, 57
Aldermaston, 120, 131
Alexander, A. V., 3, 45
Alexander, Field Marshal, Sir H., 5
Algeria, 84, 237
Allaun, Frank, 120, 131
Alliance (Liberal-SDP) 316–17, 319, 338–9
Alliance Party, 228, 271
Alpass, J. H., 17
Amalgamated Engineering Union (AEU), 16, 34, 132
Amersham International, 300
Amery, Julian, 98
Amnesty International, 300
Anderson, Sir John, 7, 61

Anderson, Lindsay, 120
Andropov, Yuri, 296
Anglo-American Commission of Inquiry, 48, 49
Anglo-Iranian Oil Company, 64, 84
Anglo-Irish Agreement, 336
'Angry Brigade', 229–30
'Angry Young Men', 120–1
Anguilla, 189
Annan Committee, 324
Anne, Princess, 247
Antelope (HMS), 313
Anti-Apartheid movement, 265
Ardent (HMS), 313
Argentina, 295, 309–14
Armstrong, Sir Robert, 312
Armstrong, Sir William (later Lord), 212, 238
Army Bureau of Current Affairs, 13
Ashdown, Paddy, 340–1, 356
Ashfield by-election, 287, 307
Ashley, Sir Bernard, 343
Ashley, Jack, 7
Asquith, Anthony, 120
Association of Officers of Taxes, 264
Aston Villa, 348
Aswan Dam, 85
Atkins, Humphrey, 291, 312
Atlantic Conveyor, 313
Atlantic Nuclear Force, 170–1
Attlee, Clement R.: background and character, 19–21; defence and, 81; rivalry with Morrison, 8–9; view of socialism, 20; mentioned, 1, 2, 3, 4, 5, 18, 23, 25, 27, 31, 32, 33, 34, 35, 36, 45, 46, 48, 49, 52, 61, 62, 63, 65, 66, 78, 82, 115, 132, 160, 164, 211, 336

Attlee, Violet, 21
AUEW, 298
Australia, 103, 190, 272, 299, 333
Austria, 79, 266, 267, 268, 312, 333
Ayatollah Khomeini, 353

Bacon, Alice, 33
Bagehot, Walter, 211
Baghdad Pact, 84, 96, 112
Bailey, Richard, 323
Baker, Kenneth, 328, 345, 357
Balance of payments, 24, 90, 138, 154,
    164–5, 191, 192, 237, 254, 287–8
Baldwin, Stanley, 8, 19, 144, 264
Balfour Declaration, 46
Balogh, Thomas (later Lord), 163
Banana, the Revd Canaan, 300
Banda, Dr Hastings, 111
Bank of Credit and Commerce
    International, 343
Bank of England, 8, 26, 166
Bannister, Dr Roger, 72
Barbados, 112
Barber, Anthony (later Lord), 219,
    220, 221, 249
Bar Lev Line, 234
Barnes, Rosie, 337, 340
Bartlett, Vernon, 6
Beamish, Major Tufton, 33, 51
Beaton, James, 247
Beaver, Sir Hugh, 139
Beaverbrook, Lord, 1, 2, 76, 245
Beeching, Dr Richard (later Lord), 138
Begin, Menachem, 295
Beith, Alan, 356
Belgium, 5, 60, 61, 103, 254, 333
Belize, 310
Benn, Anthony Wedgwood, 119, 143,
    181, 234, 244, 252, 262, 290, 306, 317
Benn, William Wedgwood (Viscount
    Stansgate), 244
Berger, John, 120
Berkeley, Humphry, 145
Berlin Alexanderplatz, 324
Berlin blockade, 61
Berlin crisis, 136
Best, A. A., 7
Bethell, Lord, 327
Betjeman, John, 83
Bettaney, Michael, 327
Bernard, Chris, 361–2
Bevan, Aneurin: character, 22;
    nationalization and, 116; nuclear
    defence and 119; mentioned, 1, 8, 18,
    19, 22, 31, 33, 52, 61, 63, 64, 68, 81,

82, 86, 88, 116, 119, 131, 151, 245,
    263
'Beveridge, Sir William (later Lord), 8,
    10, 32, 73, 152
Beveridge Report, 31–2
Bevin, Ernest: early career, 21; foreign
    policy, 53; German nationalization
    plans, 59; mentioned, 1, 3, 8, 18, 21,
    24, 40, 43, 48, 56, 57, 59, 61, 63, 69,
    78
Bevins, Reginald, 80, 146, 211
Biafra, 188
Bidault, Georges, 78
Biffon, John, 354
Birmingham, 327, 348
Birmingham Handsworth, 305
'Birmingham Six', 345
Birmingham Stechford, 287
Black, Conrad, 361
'Black Monday', 341
Black on Black, 324
Blake, George, 142
Blakenham, Lord, 173
Blunt, Anthony, 327
Bolton, 282
Bolton Committee, 297
Bondfield, Margaret, 244
Booth, Albert, 262
Boothby, Sir Robert (later Lord), 1, 24,
    89
Bootle by-election, 340
Bottomley, Arthur, 6, 161, 167, 189
Bow Group, 151
Bowden, Herbert (later Lord), 192
Boyle, Sir Edward (later Lord), 89,
    141, 148, 150, 200
Boyson, Rhodes, 291
Bracken, Brendan, 7
Braddock, Bessie, 4
Bradford City Football Club, 348
Bradley, Tom, 306
Braine, John, 120
Brandt, Willy, 69, 134, 137, 155, 173,
    191, 247
Brayley, Lord, 249
'Breakcast Television', 324
Brecon and Radnor by-election, 325
Brenner, Otto, 104
Brezhnev, Leonid, 292, 352
Bristol, 303
British Aerospace, 297
British Airways, 27, 343
British and Commonwealth, 343
British Broadcasting Corporation, 3,
    27, 73, 75, 324–5, 327, 329, 359–60

British Gas, 343
British Guiana, 109
British Medical Association, 31, 352
British Nationality Act (1981), 304, 310
British National Oil Corporation, 268
British Overseas Airways Corporation, 72
British Petroleum, 237, 253, 255, 297
British Steel Corporation, 180, 320, 343
British Telecom, 337
British Transport Commission, 138
British Union of Fascists, 198
Brittan, Leon, 317, 328, 336–7
Brittan, Samuel, 102, 107, 139, 192
Brixton, 303, 304, 305
Broadcasting Committee (1949), Report of, 73–4
Broadcasting Complaints Commission, 360
Broadcasting in the '90s, 360
Broadcasting Standards Council, 360
'Broadwater Farm Three', 345
Brocklebank-Fowler, Christopher, 308
Brockway, Fenner (later Lord), 119
Bronowski, Dr Jacob, 148
Brook, Sir Norman, 211
Brookside, 360
Brown, Sir Fred, 146
Brown, George (Later Lord George-Brown): background, 159–60; becomes Foreign Secretary, 185; European vision, 191; resigns, 195; mentioned, 28, 83, 131, 151, 155, 162, 163, 164, 167, 176, 180, 181, 182, 232, 234, 288, 307
Brunner, John, 120
Brussels, Treaty of, 60
Building Societies, 256–7
Bulganin, Marshal, 78, 79
Bulgaria, 57, 280
Bullock Committee on Industrial Democracy, 267–8
Bullock, Sir Alan (later Lord). 267, 279, 307
Burgess, Guy, 36
Burma, 45
Burmah Oil Company, 268
Bush, President George, 364
Butler, David, 122, 174, 339
Butler, R. A. (later Lord): background, 94; part in Conservative reform, 39; view of Conservative Society, 145; mentioned, 1, 11, 13, 71, 72, 78, 81, 83, 85, 89, 96, 100, 126, 135, 143, 293

Butt, Ronald, 143
Byrnes, James F., 59

Cabinet Secretariat, 199
Cable and Wireless Ltd. 26–7, 296
Callaghan, James: background, 263–4; Chancellor of Exchequer, 164–7, 181, 183–4, 191–4; mentioned, 24, 132, 151, 160, 162, 169, 182, 190, 206, 209, 218, 278, 281, 287–90, 301, 306
Cambridge University, 105, 229
Cameron Commission, 206
Cameron, James, 120
Campaign for Democratic Socialism, 132–3, 153
Campaign for Labour Victory, 302
Campaign for Nuclear Disarmament, 119–20, 131–3, 318, 326, 329–30
Canada, 24, 90, 103, 207, 251, 266, 272, 275, 292, 333
Cannon, Les, 103
Canterbury, Archbishop of, 74, 111
capital punishment, 213–14, 328, 345
Carlisle, Mark, 291, 328
Carmarthen, 290
Carr, Robert (later Lord), 219, 226, 229
Carrington, John, 256
Carrington, Lord, 220, 261, 291, 299, 300, 312
Carron, William, 132, 139
Carter, Charles, 308
Carter, Jimmy, 292, 294
Cartwright, John, 340
Castle, Barbara, 24, 30, 31, 64, 161, 168, 171, 189, 190, 196, 208, 219, 223, 233, 244, 252, 262, 331
Catlin, Sir George, 244
Cavendish, Elizabeth, 98
Caves, Prof. R. E., 258
Central African Federation, 54–5, 111–12
Central Policy Review Staff, 220
Centre Forward Group, 329
Centre for Policy Studies, 296
Ceylon, 45
Chadwick, Edwin, 27
Chalfont, Lord, 172, 249, 389
Challe, Maurice, 87
Challenor, Det. Serg., 274
Chamberlain, Neville, 20, 80, 95, 144, 187, 232, 328
Chambers, Paul, 215
Chamoun, Camille, 112
Channel Four, 361, 362
Chapple, Lord (Frank), 103, 308

Chariots of Fire, 325, 362
Chataway, Christopher, 249
Chawner, John, 352
Checkland, Michael, 360
Chelmer, Lord, 174
Chelmsford, Lord, 44
Chernenko, Konstantin, 292
Chiang Kai-shek, 57
Chichester-Clark, James, 205, 228
Chile, 248, 295
China, 50, 62, 63, 89, 138, 171, 293, 314, 331
Christian Democracy, 61, 253
Church of Scotland, 111
Churchill, Randolph, 144
Churchill, Sir Winston, 27, 30, 38, 39, 44, 47, 50, 62, 64, 65, 71, 72, 73, 74, 77, 78, 80, 94, 95, 167, 184, 187, 337, 346
    election 1945, 1–13; 'Gestapo speech', 2, 3, 11
cinema admissions, 326
City of London, 334
Civil Service and Harold Wilson, 210–13
Clark, William, 89
Clarke, Joe, 292
Clarke, Kenneth, 328
Clerical and Admin, Workers' Union, 132
Clore, Charles, 141
Clowes, Peter, 342
coal industry, 26, 28–9, 104, 226, 237–9
Cockfield, F. A., 138
Coe, Sebastian, 335
Cold War, 35, 57–64, 83, 160
Cole, G. D. H., 20, 115, 116–17
Collins, Canon L. John, 119
Collins, Norman, 74, 215
Colonial Development and Welfare Act, 53–4
Colville, J. R., 212
Comet airliner, 72, 73
Commissioner for Admin. Act (1967), 213
Committee of 100, 133
Common Wealth Party, 3, 6, 16
Commonwealth, 72, 86, 89, 99, 111, 114, 135, 137, 185, 186, 189, 197, 198, 231–2, 278, 230, 307
Commonwealth Immigration Act, 135, 197, 198–9, 230
Communism (in Britain), 2, 3, 4, 6, 9, 24, 32, 35–7, 103, 121, 182–3, 197, 238, 253

Communism (in western Europe), 60, 253
Communist information bureau, 60
Community Charge, 343–4
Compton, Sir Edmund, 229
Computers and Privacy, 275
Concorde, 172, 180, 246
Confederation of British Industries, 222
Conqueror (HMS), 313
Conran, Sir Terrance, 343
Conservative Party: Reginald Bevins on, 146; Chelmer reforms, 173–4; MPs (1970s), 251; post-war reforms in, 37–9; mentioned, 3, 4, 6, 10, 11, 13, 36, 66, 82, 96, 97, 99, 115, 122–3, 127, 140, 143–6, 154–6, 176, 179, 181, 200, 207, 216, 221, 222, 230, 239–40, 243, 248, 257, 259–61, 265, 278, 287–91, 293–6, 316–17, 319, 328–9, 331, 338–9, 351, 353, 356, 365
Constantinople Convention, 86
Contracts of Employment Act (1963), 208
Conway, Jim, 132
Cooper, Lady Diana Duff, 95
Co-operative Party, 36
Coronation Street, 325, 360
Corrigan, Mairead, 271
Cotton, Jack, 141
Council of Europe, 61
Council house sales, 296
Council of Ireland, 228
Cousins, Frank, 122, 131–2, 139, 161, 165, 171, 181, 192
Coventry (HMS), 313
Craig, William, 204
Creech Jones, Arthur, 52, 55, 68
Crewe, Ivor, 290
crime, 142, 273–6, 327–8
Criminal Justice Act (1972), 277
Cripps, Sir Stafford, 3, 8, 18, 19, 22, 25, 44, 45, 63
Cromer, Lord, 165, 166
Crookshank, Harry, 78
Crosby by-election, 308
Crosland, Anthony, 117, 127, 132, 233, 243, 262, 263
Crossman, Richard, 68, 116, 152, 160, 161, 164, 168, 169, 175, 182, 184, 185, 191, 194, 199, 205, 209, 216, 226
Crouch, David, 314
Crowther-Hunt, Lord, 212
Crowther Report, 148
Croydon by-election, 308
Cruise missiles, 329–30
Cuba, 50, 299

Cunningham, Andrew, 225–6, 249
Cunningham, John, 356
Cyprus, 86, 88, 89, 109, 114, 154, 248, 263, 313
Czechoslovakia, 36, 60, 61, 85, 197

Daily Express, 3, 288
Daily Herald, 3, 76
Daily Mail, 3, 175, 288
Daily Mirror, 3, 135, 289, 342
Daily Sketch, 3, 76
Daily Telegraph, 3, 289, 311, 318, 343
Daily Worker, 9
Dainton, Sir Fred (later Lord), 308
Dallas, 325
Dalton, Hugh, 20, 21, 24, 45, 47, 50, 52, 53, 68, 82, 83, 96, 132, 243, 263
Dance With A Stranger, 325
Data Protection Act (1984), 326
Davenport, Nicholas, 21
Davies, Clement, 26
Davies, Howard, 120
Davies, John, 220, 221, 229, 260
D'Avigdor-Goldsmid, Sir Henry, 236
D'Avigdor-Goldsmid, Jack, 236
Davis, John, 296
Deakin, Arthur, 37
Debord, Guy, 229
Decimal Currency Board, 181
Defence, 61, 63, 66, 73, 99, 101, 106, 107–8, 169–72, 184, 187, 195, 329–30
Defence Committee South Atlantic, 312
Defence of the Realm, 362
de Freitas, Sir Geoffrey, 362
de Gaulle, Charles, 126, 136, 137, 191, 196, 232
Delfont, Bernard (later Lord), 262
Dell, Edmund, 307
Democratic Unionists, 302, 338, 353
Denmark, 101, 232, 270, 272, 275, 333
Denning, Lord, 142
Department of Economic Affairs, 159, 175, 185
Der Spiegel, 303
Detroit, 283
Deutscher Gewerkschaftsbund, 102–3
De Valera, President, 5
devaluation, 25, 164, 169, 183, 193–4
Devlin, Bernadette, 203
Devlin, Lord, 111
devolution (Scotland and Wales), 269–70
Diamond, Lord, 307
Diana, Lady, 303
Dien Bien Phu, 78

Dilhorne, Lord, 98
disasters, 347–8
Disraeli, Benjamin, 27
divorce, 214, 277
docks and dockers, 104
Domestic Violence Act, 277
Domicile and Matrimonial Proceedings Act (1973), 277
Donnelly, Desmond, 207
Donovan Commission, 207
Douglas, Michael, 362
Douglas-Home, Sir Alec, 143, 145, 146, 153, 154–5, 159, 162, 171, 172–3, 219, 220, 232, 235, 249, 261
Dreadnought submarine, 109
drug-taking, 215, 304
Du Cann, Edward, 172, 173
Dulles, John Foster, 79, 84, 85–6, 89
Dynasty, 325

East Enders, 360
Eccles, Sir David, 81, 97, 140, 148
Ecology Party, 288, 289
economic growth: under Macmillan, 100–2; under Thatcher, 332
Economist, 2, 322, 333, 335, 343
Edelman, Maurice, 17, 24, 52
Eden, Sir Anthony: background, 71, 77, 78, 80, 83, 85–91, 94, 95, 97, 99
Eden, Douglas, 302
education, 34, 66, 121, 147–51, 246, 304, 334, 349–51
Education Act (1944), 149
Education For All, 305
Education Reform Act (1988), 349
Education (Student Loans) Act, 351
Edwardes, Michael, 297
Edwards, Bob, 114
Edwards, Nicholas, 291, 354
EEC referendum, 250, 252–3, 302
EETPU, 298
Egremont, Lord, 98
Egypt, 64, 84–8, 113, 234–6, 293
Eire, 5; *see also* Ireland
Eisenhower, Dwight D., 78, 79, 85, 86, 89, 96, 109, 126
Eisenhower, doctrine, 112
Electrical Trades Union, 16, 35, 37, 103
Elizabeth II, 73, 94, 144, 164
Eliot, T. S., 72
Ellesmere Port, 303
Elliot, Captain W. S., 17, 89
Employment Acts (1980 and 1982), 298
Endurance (HMS), 310
engineers, 257–8

Ennals, David, 263
Enterprise Allowance Scheme, 297
EOKA campaign, 313
Essex University, 197, 229
Ethiopia, 248, 325
Europe: as post-war third force, 61; *see also* European
Europe, eastern, *see under* individual countries
European Coal and Steel Community, 61
European Economic Community, 96, 109, 133–6, 172, 190–2, 232–4, 245, 252–5, 237, 301, 305, 307, 318, 329, 330, 331, 341, 354, 356, 363–5
European elections: 1979, 302; 1984, 319; 1989; 354–5
European Free Trade Area, 133, 134, 135, 190
European movement, 253
European Strategic Research Programme, 331
Evans, Harold, 98
Evans, S. N., 17, 51, 88
EXCO, 297
Ezra, Lord (Derek), 320

Fabian Colonial Bureau, 128
Fabian Society, 132, 244
Fair Deal at Work, 207–8
Fairlie, Henry, 139
Falkender, Lady (Marcia Williams), 162–3, 249
Falklands War, 309–14, 318
family planning, 214
Farouk, King, 84
Faulds, Andrew, 236, 314
Faulkner, Brian, 228
Faulkner, William, 72
Fawzi, Mahmoud, 87
Feather, Victor (Lord), 208, 224, 253
Federation of Malaya, 55
Feisal, King, 237
Ferranti, 255
Fidler, Michael, 236
FIFA, 348
Field, Anthony, 249
film industry, 76, 325–6, 361–2
Financial Times, 141, 143, 154, 244, 289, 316, 322, 341, 351
Finland, 79, 251, 270
Finsberg, Geoffrey, 236
Fire Brigades Union, 35
Fisher, Anthony, 295
Fiske, Sir William, 181

Fitt, Gerard, 205, 218, 240
Fitzgerald, Gareth, 336
Flowers, Lord, 308
Follick, Mont, 17
Foot, Michael, 21, 49, 119, 131, 192, 210, 234, 244, 245, 252, 253, 262, 305, 314, 318
Foot, Paul, 291
Football hooliganism, 348
Forbes, Bryan, 76
Ford, Gerald, 248
Ford Motor Co., 229
Foreign Ministers' conferences: Moscow, 60; London, 60
Foreign Office, Labour view of, 56
foreign trade, 61, 63, 100–1
Forrestal, James, 68
Forte, Lord, 297
Forward, 127
Fowler, Henry, 166
Fowler, Norman, 354, 363
Fox, Sir Marcus, 363
France, 5, 57, 60, 61, 73, 84, 87, 88, 89, 90, 101, 102, 103, 104, 138, 139, 171, 189, 196, 207, 247, 256, 266, 275, 292, 294, 304, 319, 330, 333, 336, 351, 353, 358
Fraser, Hugh, 236, 259
Fraser, Malcolm, 299
Frears, John, 308
Frears, Stephen, 362
Freeman, John, 63
French planning, 139
Friedman, Milton, 295
Fuchs, Klaus, 36
Fulton Report, 211–12
Future of Socialism, 117, 127
Fyfe, Sir David Maxwell-, *see* Kilmuir

Gagarin, Yuri, 108
Gaitskell, Hugh, 63, 81, 82, 85, 94, 117–18, 127–8, 130–4, 136, 141, 151, 152, 153, 155, 159, 198, 220, 263, 293
Galtieri, General, 310, 311
gas industry, 26
Galt, William, 27
Gandhi, Indira, 293
Gandhi, Mahatma, 44, 45, 325
Gardiner, Lord, 167
Gazier, Albert, 87
GCHQ, 346
general elections: 1892, 10; 1935, 16; 1945, 1–13; 1950, 39–40; 1951, 65–6; 1955, 81–2; 1959, 122–3; 1964, 153–6; 1966, 176, 179; 1970, 215–16;

1974 (Feb.), 239–40; 1974 (Oct.),
249–51; 1979, 287–90; 1983, 316–18;
1987, 338–9
Geneva conferences, 79, 81
Gent, Sir Edward, 55
George VI, 19, 20, 72
German Christian Democrats, 59
German Democratic Republic, 61, 79,
136, 280, 363
German Federal Republic, 61, 73, 79,
100, 101, 102–3, 104, 105, 136, 171,
184, 207, 247, 254, 256, 237, 258, 266,
275, 280, 283, 287, 292, 294, 297, 298,
304, 319, 329, 333, 336, 343, 344, 348,
351, 353, 355, 358, 363
German rearmament, 81
German Social Democrats, 59, 69, 266
Germany: British policy in, 58–61, 66,
69, 79, 284
Ghana, 54, 99
Gibraltar, 101, 331
Gilmour, Sir Ian, 291, 328
Giscard d'Estaing, Valéry, 247, 292
Gladwyn, Lord, 264
Glamorgan (HMS), 312
Glasgow, 283
Glubb, General Sir John Bagot, 85
Godwin, Anne, 132
Gold Coast, 54
Goldsmith, James, 262
Goldwater, Barry, 294
Goddhart, Philip, 236
Gorbachev, Mikhail, 292, 337
Gormley, Joe (Lord), 238, 319
Gorst, John, 236
Gould, Mrs Ayrton, 49
Government of India Acts: 1919, 44;
1935, 44
Government of Ireland Act 1920, 203
Gow, Ian, 336
Gower, Jim, 334
Grade, Lew (Lord), 262
Granada Television, 75
Granick, David, 105
Greece, 5, 50, 53, 58, 69, 79, 87, 99,
248, 333
Greene, Sid, 139
Green Party, 354
Greenwood, Anthony, 119, 161, 171,
185
Greenwood, Arthur, 18, 161
Grey, C. F., 28
Griffiths, James, 3, 26, 31, 82, 88, 131,
161, 180, 189
Grimond, Jo, 264

Grosvenor, Gerald (Earl Grosvenor),
282
Guardian (Manchester), 3, 298, 318,
328, 335, 346, 361
Guardianship of Children Act (1973),
277
Guatemala, 310
'Guildford Four', 345
Gulf War, 349, 356, 358–9
Gummer, John Selwyn, 319, 328
Gunn, John, 297, 343
Gunter, Ray, 160, 195, 208
Gurion, David Ben, 84

Habershon, Roy, 229
Haekkerup, Per, 134
Hagana, 48, 49, 68
Haile Selassie, 248
Hailsham, Lord (Quintin Hogg), 7, 97,
126, 143, 144, 155, 219, 261, 290, 291,
354
Hain, Peter, 264
Halifax, Earl of, 41
Hall, Stewart, 121
Halsey, A. H., 282
Hammarskjöld, Dag, 87
Hancock, Mike, 319
Harris, John, 153
Harrison, Tom, 12, 282
Hart, Judith, 189, 254
Haseler, Stephen, 302, 308
Hastings, Max, 310
Hattersley, Roy, 302, 308, 318, 329, 336
Hawkins, Jim, 29
von Hayek, Friedrich August, 295
Healey, Denis, 114, 132, 160, 171, 205,
233, 243, 246, 247, 262, 266, 306, 318,
329
health, *see* National Health Service
Heath, Edward, 38, 75, 97, 126, 137,
143, 146, 173–4, 201–3, 215–16,
219–21, 223, 226, 228, 230–1, 232,
233–4, 237–40, 248, 249, 259–61,
288, 291, 328, 344, 346, 356
Heathcoat Amory, Derek (Viscount
Amory), 126, 138
Hemingway, Ernest, 72
Herald of Free Enterprise, 347
Herbert, A. P., 18
Hermes (HMS) 311
Heseltine, Michael, 336, 356, 357
Heysel Stadium, 348
Hill, Lord (Charles), 22, 38, 98, 140
Hillary, Edmund, 72
Hillhead by-election, 308

Index

Hillsborough, 348
Hinden, Rita, 128
Hoffman, Prof. J. D., 39
Hogg, Quintin, *see* Hailsham
Hollis, Christopher, 97, 146
Hollis, Sir Roger, 327
Homicide Act, 100
Hong Kong, 101, 304, 314, 331, 332
Hooson, Emlyn, 232
Hopkinson, Henry, 99
Horsbrugh, Florence, 97
housing, 33, 73, 106, 222, 269, 283
Housing Finance Act (1972), 222
Howard, Lord, 325
Howe, Sir Geoffrey, 260, 261, 291, 317, 332, 354, 356, 364
Hughes, Cledwyn, 167
Hull, 303
Hull, Cordell, 80
Hungary, 57, 86, 90, 93, 121
Hunt Report, 325
Hunt, Rex, 311
Hurd, Douglas, 328, 356, 357
Hussein, King of Jordan, 112
Hussey, James Marmaduke, 360
Hyams, Harry, 141
Hyde, Douglas, 9

Illford North by-election, 237
immigration, 135, 156, 176, 197–201, 203, 278, 304
Imperial Airways, 27
income redistribution, 281–3
incomes policies, 35, 138, 182, 222, 237, 238–9, 246, 281–2
Independent, 361
Independent Broadcasting Authority, 324, 360
Independent Television Commission, 360
Independent Labour Party, 6, 11, 16
India, 43–6, 50, 55, 87, 135, 171, 189, 293
Indian National Congress, 47
indicative planning, 139
Indo-China, 45, 78
Industrial Charter, 39, 96
industrial democracy, 117, 267–8
industrial growth: under Macmillan, 98–102
Industrial Injuries Act, 29
industrial management, 104–5, 148–9, 257–9
industrial relations, 37, 82, 102–4, 182–3, 207–9, 223, 238–9, 266–8, 298

Industrial Relations Act, 223, 246
Industrial Reorganization Corporation, 180–221
Industrial Training Boards, 304
industry, manufacturing, 334
Industry and Society, 118
Infant Mortality Rates, 227
inflation, 266, 333
In My Way, 191
In Place of Fear, 116, 208
In Place of Strife, 207–9
Ingham, Bernard, 337, 354
Institute of Economic Affairs, 295
International Computers Ltd, 180
International Federation of Free Trade Unions, 111
International Monetary Fund, 90, 138
investment in industry, 256
Invincible (HMS), 311
Iran, 64–5, 84, 237, 292, 293, 330, 353, 358–9
Iraq, 84, 85, 112, 237, 292, 330, 358–9
Ireland, Northern, 203–6, 218, 227–9, 232, 239–40, 247, 270–2, 333, 338–9, 348–9
Ireland, Republic of, 5, 56, 203–6, 207, 228, 23, 266, 270, 333
Iremonger, Tom, 236
Irish Republican Army, 204, 227–30, 247, 270–2, 273, 345, 348–9
Irgun Zvi Leumi, 49
iron and steel industry, 26
Isaacs, George A., 37
Israel, 79, 84, 88–90, 171, 234–6, 247, 259, 270, 359; *see also* Palestine
Italy, 5, 61, 101, 103, 207, 266, 294, 319, 333, 343, 358
Ivanov, Eugene, 142

Jagan, Dr Cheddi, 109
Jaguar, 296
Jamaica, 53, 91, 112, 270
James, Lord, 279
Janner, Barnett, 49, 52
Japan, 5, 62, 73, 99, 100, 101, 103, 105, 190, 207, 256–8, 266, 280, 294, 297, 331, 333, 343, 351, 358, 364
Jay, Douglas, 88, 127, 132, 134, 164, 190, 192
Jay, Peter, 263
Jenkin, Patrick, 291, 328
Jenkins, Arthur, 243
Jenkins, Clive, 121
Jenkins, Roy, 132, 194, 209, 233, 243, 262, 263, 265, 278, 306, 308, 324, 340

Jenkins, Simon, 310
Jewish Agency, 48, 68
Jewish Brigade of British Army, 48
Jinnah, Mahomed Ali, 44
John Paul, Pope, 293
Johnson, Donald, 157
Johnson, Paul, 121
Johnson, President Lyndon B., 169–70, 183, 184, 195
Johnston, Thomas, 3
Jones, Aubrey, 166
Jones, Dr Frank, 256
Jones, Thomas, 8
Jones, Trevor, 264
Jopling, Michael, 354
Jordan, 112
Joseph, Sir Keith, 89, 219, 226–7, 261, 291, 296, 320
Joyce, William, 5
Juliana, Queen of the Netherlands, 5

Kagan, Sir Joseph (later Lord), 262
Kaldor, Nicholas (later Lord), 163
Kassim, General Abdel Karim, 113
Kaufman, Gerald, 163
Kaunda, Kenneth, 111, 300
Kearton, Sir Frank, 180
Keays, Sara, 319
Keeler, Christine, 142
Kegworth, 347
Kellner, Peter, 321
Kennedy, Charles, 340
Kennedy, President John F., 135, 136–7, 154, 155, 156, 158, 169
Kennedy, Kathleen, 137
Kenya, 110, 114, 115, 199
Kenyatta, Jomo, 110
Keynes, J. M. (later Lord), 23
Khomeini, Ayatollah, 292
Khrushchev, Nikita, 78, 79, 86, 126, 159
Kilbrandon Report, 270
Kill the Messenger, 354
Kilmuir, Earl of, 12, 39, 71, 81, 94, 96
King, Prof. Anthony, 174
King, Cecil, 173, 182, 215
King David Hotel, 49, 51
King, Martin Luther, 201
King, Tom, 328
King's Cross disaster, 347
Kinley, Alderman John, 17
Kinnock, Neil, 318, 323, 329, 335, 336, 337
Kirk, Peter, 89
Kirkpatrick, Sir Ivone, 69

Kohl, Helmut, 292, 336, 355
Korea, 313
Korean War, 37, 62–3, 70, 72, 77, 78
The Krays, 361
Kureshi, Hanif, 362
Kuwait, 112, 358–9

Labour Committee for Europe, 244
Labour Party, 4, 6, 10, 11, 13, 32, 36, 39, 53–4, 66, 74, 82, 85, 88, 89, 103, 111, 115–19, 121–2, 127–34, 140, 154–6, 176, 179, 189, 215, 239–40, 261–4, 278, 287–90, 298, 301–2, 305–7, 316–17, 318, 319, 329–30, 331, 338–9, 341, 347, 353, 365
Labour Party conferences: 1940, 47; 1945, 2; 1946, 43; 1954, 81; 1957, 119; 1960, 132; 1961, 133; 1962, 134; 1967, 193; 1975 (EEC), 253; 1979, 301; 1980, 305
Laker, Sir Freddie, 297
Lambton, Lord, 145
Lamont, Norman, 357
Lancaster University, 308
Lansbury, George, 20
Laski, Harold J., 1, 3, 8, 43, 263, 264
'Laski controversy', 3–4
Lawson, Nigel, 317, 323, 338, 364
Leach, Sir Henry, 311
League of Nations, 46
Lebanon, 270, 358
Lee, Fred, 196
Lee, Jennie, 118
Leland, David, 361
Lend-Lease, 23
Lennox-Boyd, Alan, 81, 96
Lessing, Doris, 121
Letter to Brezhnev, A, 361–2
Let us face the future, 2
Lever, Harold, 51, 52, 233
Levy, Benn, 52
Lewin, Sir Terence, 311
Lewis, John, 17
Leyland (later British Leyland Motor corporation), 180, 255
Liberal Party, 3, 4, 6, 32, 66, 111, 123, 127, 140, 156, 162, 179, 232, 236, 240, 246, 264–5, 287, 288, 289, 306, 318, 319, 329, 347, 353, 365
Libya, 237, 293, 323
Limehouse Declaration, 307
Lindop, Sir Norman, 276
Live Aid, 335
Liverpool, 303
Liverpool Edge Hill by-election, 287

Index

Lloyd, Selwyn (later Lord Selwyn-Lloyd), 74, 80, 81, 87, 96, 138, 139, 140, 183
Lloyd George, David, 5
Lloyd George, Gwilym, 81
Lloyd's, 348
local government, 224–5, 226–7
Lockerbie, 347
Lofthouse College, 238
Logan, David, 17
Lomas, Alf, 331
Lomé Convention, 254
London, 304, 335
London Belongs to Me, 74
London Passenger Transport Board, 25
London School of Economics, 197
Loneliness of the Long Distance Runner, 76
Longford, Lord, 132, 134, 160, 194
Look Back in Anger, 76, 120
Lords, House of, 34, 209, 227
Lovett, Robert A., 68
Lowndes, Marie Belloc, 7
Luce, Richard, 312
Lutyens, Sir Edwin, 44
Luxembourg, 61, 270
Lynch, Jack, 228
Lyons, Sir Jack, 342
Lyttelton, Oliver (later Lord Chandos), 1, 71

Maastricht Treaty, 364–5
MacArthur, General Douglas, 3, 62, 63
MacDonald, J. Ramsay, 8, 18, 19, 20, 21, 22, 23, 44, 162, 244, 287, 301, 309
MacDonald, Malcolm, 47, 199
Mackenzie, Sir Compton, 120
Mckenzie, Norman, 121
Mackintosh, John P., 210
Maclean, Donald, 36
Maclennan, Robert, 340
Macleod, Ian, 38, 110, 126, 143, 144, 145, 173, 174, 200
Macmillan, Harold: background, 94–6; Cabinets, 96–8, 140–1; Kennedy and 137; Suez and, 90; test ban treaty achievement, 138; 'Wind of change' speech, 111; mentioned 5, 20, 22, 23, 38, 64, 73, 97, 98, 99, 100, 102, 106, 107–8, 122, 126, 130, 135, 143, 144, 145, 154, 175, 220, 261, 291, 293, 337
Macpherson, Thomas, 17
McCluskey, Con and Pat, 204
McGahey, Mick, 238, 321
McKeown, Ciaran, 271

McMahon Act, 109
McMeeking Committee, 148
McNee, Sir David, 327
'Maguire Seven', 345
Major, John: 354–5; background, 356–7, 358
Makarios, Archbishop, 99, 248
Malawi, 3, 4, 111
Malaya, Malaysia, 55–6, 68–9, 100, 109, 114
Malayan people's Anti-Japanese Army, 53
Malenkov, Georgi, 78
Malta, 88, 101, 111
Management Today, 256, 259
Manchester, 303
Manchester Airport, 347
Manchester United, 348
Manifesto Group, 302
Mansfield, 29
Mao Tse Tung, 293
Marchioness, 347
Margach, James, 98, 103, 143, 220
Mark, Sir Robert, 274–5
Marquand, David, 307, 308
Marris, Peter, 121
Marsh, (Sir) Richard, 180, 182, 289
Marshall Aid, 25, 58, 63
Marshall, General George, 60
Marten, Neil, 234
Martin, Kingsley, 20, 120
Marwick, Arthur, 33
Mason, Roy, 132
Massiter, Cathy, 326, 346
Mau Mau, 110
Mauding, Reginald, 97, 110, 141, 143, 144, 172–3, 211, 219, 226, 228
Mauriac, François, 72
Mawby, Ray, 149
Maxton, James, 11
Maxwell, Robert, 342, 361
Maxwell-Fyfe Report, 39
Mayhew, Christopher, 132, 192, 249
Meade, James, 308
Médak, Peter, 361
Meir, Golda, 247
Mellish, Bob, 132
Members of Parliament: backgrounds, 16–17, 146, 174, 251
Mendez, Nicanor Costa, 310
Menzies, Sir Robert, 87
Mercury, Freddie, 352
Messina conference, 96
Meyer, Sir Anthony, 314, 355
Mexico, 50, 268

MI5, 326–7, 346–7
Middle East, *see under* separate
  countries
Middle Way, 139, 293
Mikardo, Ian, 52, 131, 233
Miliband, Ralph, 121
Militant Tendency, 302, 306, 335
Mill, John Stuart, 43
Milligan, Spike, 120
Mills, Lord, 140
Milne, Alasdair, 360
Milne, Eddie, 239
Mittbestimmung, 117, 267–8
Mitchell, Colin, 236
Mitchell, Joan, 308
Mitterrand, President, 292, 336
Monckton, Sir Walter (later Lord), 81,
  89
Montgomery, Field Marshal Lord, 5
Moore, Henry, 120
Moore, John, 354
Morgan, Dr H. B., 31
Morley, Eric, 282
Morrison, Herbert (later Lord), 1, 3, 8,
  18, 19, 21–2, 25, 27, 47, 52, 63, 82,
  95, 118
Mort, David, 28
Mortimer, Jim, 246
Mosley, Sir Oswald, 198, 309
Motherwell by-election, 1
motor-vehicle industry, 104, 107, 246,
  255
Mountbatten, Lord, 45, 89, 198, 293
Moyne, Lord, 48
Mozambique, 169, 299
Mugabe, Robert, 299, 300
Mulley, Fred, 132
Murdoch, Iris, 120
Murdoch, Rupert, 33, 77, 361
Murray, Len, 238
Mussadiq, Dr Muhammed, 65
Muzorewa, Bishop, 299, 300
My Beautiful Laundrette, 262

NACODS, 322
Nassau (Polaris) agreement, 136, 137–8
Nasser, President Gamal Abdel, 84,
  85–8, 96
National Assistance Board, 29
National Board for Prices and Incomes,
  166, 175, 222, 239
National Coal Board, 22, 226, 237, 268,
  320–4
National Council for Academic
  Rewards, 147

National Curriculum, 349
National Economic Development
  Council, 138–9
National Enterprise Board, 255
National Film Finance Corporation, 76,
  361
National Front, 197, 239, 250, 288, 289
National Health Service, 29–32, 64,
  226–7, 241, 246, 351–2
National Health Service Acts, 29, 31,
  226
National Incomes Commission (NIC),
  139
National Industrial Relations Court,
  223–4
National Insurance Acts (1946), 29, 30
National Labour Party, 309
National Plan (1965), 167
National Union of Agricultural
  Workers, 16
National Union of General and
  Municipal Workers, 16
National Union of Miners, 16, 237–9,
  319–24
National Union of Railwaymen, 16
nationalization: 1945–51, 25–9, 34; pre-
  1945, 27; 1974, 255
nationalization debate in Labour Party,
  127–30
Neave, Airey, 261, 271, 293
Neguib, General, 84
Nehru, Jawaharlal, 85, 89, 93, 99
Netherlands, 60, 284, 333
Neville, John, 120
New Left, 120–2
New Left Review, 121
New Reasoner, 121
New Statesman, 103, 119, 120, 309, 321,
  326
New Zealand, 190, 252, 253
Newcastle upon Tyne: corruption in,
  225–6, 303
News Chronicle, 3, 76, 120
Newsom Report (1963), 148
Newton, Tony, 356
Nibmar, 185
Nicolson, Nigel, 89
Niemöller, Martin, 120
Nigeria, 112, 188
Nixon, Richard M., 234, 247, 294, 295
Nkomo, Joshua, 299, 300
Mkrumah, Kwame, 54, 100
Nobel Prize-winners: British, 284
Noel-Baker, Philip, 3
Norman, Montagu, 8

North Atlantic Treaty Organization, 58, 61, 79, 99, 101, 107, 132, 133, 170–1, 272, 305, 307, 311, 329–30
North Sea gas and oil, 221, 266, 268, 288
Northedge, F. S., 108
Northern Ireland Labour Party, 271
Norway, 88, 232, 272, 275
Nott, John, 291, 311
Nottingham, 303
Nottingham University, 297, 308
nuclear development, 79–80, 99, 119, 138, 170–2
Nuclear Test Ban Treaty, 138
nuclear weapons (British), 61–2, 72, 79–80, 81, 99, 107–8, 109, 119–20, 131–2, 136, 329–30
Nuri es-Said, 112
Nutting, Anthony, 85, 87–8, 89
Nyasaland, 111

Observer, 77, 142, 145, 296, 319, 327, 346
Official Unionists, 302, 338, 353
Oil Crisis (1973), 234–7
Oil Petroleum Exporting Countries, 237
Ojukwu, Odumegwu, 188, 189
O'Neill, Terence, 204–5, 218, 227–8
Open University, 280, 308
Operation 'Musketeer', 88
Operation Sutton, 313
opinion polls, 12, 91, 122, 127, 129–30, 140, 153, 154, 172, 189, 194, 233, 255 318, 321, 329–30
Oppenheim, Sally, 261, 291
Organization for European Economic Co-operation (OEEC), 61
Organization of African Unity, 299
Organization of Arab Petroleum Exporting Countries, 236–7
Ormsby-Gore, David (later Lord Harlech), 98
Orpington by-election, 140
Orwell, George, 118, 282, 326
Osborne, John, 76, 120
Overseas Development, Ministry of, 189–90
Overseas Food Corporation, 53
Ovett, Steve, 335
Owen, David, 263, 302, 306, 309, 318, 334

Paget, Reginald, 132
Paisley, Rev. Ian, 204–5, 338

Pakistan, 45, 55, 84, 135, 189, 304
Palestine, 46–53, 56, 57, 359
Palestine Arab Workers' Society, 47
Papworth, Bert, 35
Parkinson, Cecil, 318, 354
Parliament: Commons reform, 210–11; Lords Reform, 209–10
Patten, Chris, 354, 357
Pearce, Lord, 231
Peart, Fred, 160, 190, 243
Peckham, 305
Peerage Act, 143
Penhaligon, David, 337
Perry, Lord, 308
Personal Services, 361
Pétain, Marshal, 5
Pethick-Lawrence, Lord, 45
Petroleum and Submarine Pipe-lines Act (1975), 268
Peyton, John, 260
Philadelphia, 283
Philby, Kim, 142
Philips-Price, Morgan, 49
Phillips, Morgan, 26
Pierrepoint, Albert, 214
Pilkington Committee on Broadcasting, 74–5, 324
Pineau, Christian, 87
Piper Alfa, 347
Piratin, Phil, 9, 35, 52
Pitt, William, 308
Plaid Cymru, 239–40, 250, 253, 269–70, 290, 338
Plan For Coal, 320
Platts-Mills, John, 52
Poland, 58, 86, 293, 294
police, 273, 276, 327–8, 345
Police Act (1976), 275
Police Complaints Board, 275
Police National Computer, 275–6
Policy Studies Institute, 327
Poll tax, 343–4
Polmaise pit, 321
polytechnics, 280
Pompidou, President Georges, 232, 247
Ponting, Clive, 346
Poole, Lord, 144, 145
Portland Spy Scandal, 142
Portsmouth South by-election, 319
Portugal, 248, 299, 331
Post Office Engineering Union, 326
Post Office Workers' Union, 132
Postponement of Polling Day Act 1945, 4
Potsdam conference (1945), 3, 21, 58

Poulson, John, 225–6
poverty, 283
Powell, Enoch, 38, 97, 145, 173, 201–3, 210, 219, 239, 240, 250, 252, 253, 338
premium bonds, 96
Prentice, Reg, 132, 189, 246, 289, 292, 302, 328
Press Council, 77
Press, Royal Commissions on, 76–7
Preston, 303
Prevention of Terrorism Act, 247, 272
Priestley, J. B., 119
Prince of Wales, 295, 297
Prior, James, 219, 261, 298, 328
prisons, 344–5
privatization, 296, 329, 343
Profumo, John, 97, 142, 161
Provisional IRA, 270–2, 293, 327
public schools, 34, 105, 121, 150, 259
public schools, Report of Committee on, 259
Pugh, Alan, 336
Puttnam, David, 362
Putting Britain Right Ahead, 174–5
Pym, Francis, 291, 312, 318, 328

Queen Elizabeth II, 180, 312

race relations legislation, 200–1, 278
Race, Steve, 308
Rachman, Peter, 141
Radice, Giles, 268
railways, 27
Rank and File Mobilizing Committee, 306
rate increases, 225
Rayne, Sir Max, 262
Reagan, President, 292, 293, 294, 295, 311, 338, 362
Red Lion Square riot, 274
Real Domestic Product, 284
Redcliffe-Maud Committee, 224, 225
Redgrave, Vanessa, 120
Reece, Gordon, 288
Rees, Merlyn, 247, 271, 278
Regional Payroll Subsidy, 191
Reid, Thomas, 17, 52
Reith, Lord, 7
Renwick, Lord, 74, 215
Representation of the People Act: 1948, 34; 1969, 213
Resale Price Maintenance, 146
Reza Shah, 64
Rhodesia, 53, 54–5, 110–11, 154, 167–9, 175, 185–7, 189, 209, 231, 288, 293, 299–301, 312
Rhodesia Front, 300
Richardson, Jo, 277
Richardson, Tony, 76, 352
Ridley, Nicholas, 310, 354–5
Right To Reply, 324
riots: 1981, 303–4; 1985, 305
Rimington, Stella, 347
Rippon, Geoffrey, 220, 328
Ritchie-Calder, Lord, 5, 119–20
Robbins, Lionel (later Lord), 147
Robens, Lord, 138
Robinson, Kenneth, 226, 307
Rodgers, William, 132, 302, 306, 317
Rogaly, Joe, 341
Rolls Royce, 221, 255, 343
Room at the Top, 120
Roosevelt, President Franklin D., 64
Rose, Jack, 141
Rose, Philip, 141
Rose, Richard, 129
Ross, William, 252
Rothschild, Lord, 220
Royal College of Physicians, 7
Royal Commission on Population, 197
Royal Institute of British Architects, 141
Rumania, 57
Rushdie, Salman, 353
Russell, Bertrand, 72, 119, 133
Russia, 57; *see also* Soviet Union

Saatchi brothers, 288, 316, 343
Sadat, President, 293
Sainsbury, David, 308
Sainsbury, Lord, 308
St-John Stevas, Norman, 261, 291, 328
Salford University, 308
Salisbury, Lord, 81, 94, 98, 99
Samuel, Ralph, 121
Samuels, Sir Harold, 141
Sandelson, Neville, 302
Sandys, Duncan (later Lord Duncan-Sandys), 7, 96, 110
Satanic Verses, 353
Saturday Night and Sunday Morning, 76
Saudi Arabia, 65, 237, 358
Saunders, Ernest, 342
Scargill, Arthur, 319–24, 335
Scarman, Lord, 304
Schmidt, Helmut, 247, 292
Schumacher, Karl, 69
Schumacher, E. F., 256
Schuman, Robert, 78

Index

Schweitzer, Dr Albert, 99
Science and Technology, Select Committee on, 257
Scotland, 224, 269–70, 288
Scotsman, 77
Scott, Norman, 265
Scottish Labour Party, 288
Scottish National Party (SNP), 1, 6, 194, 239, 250, 253, 269–70, 288, 289, 302, 319, 338
Screaming Lord Sutch, 340
Seafield colliery, 238
Security Service Act (1989), 346
Selective Employment Tax, 181
Selsdon Park conference, 293
Sex Discrimination Act (1975), 277
Sexual Offences Act, 214
Seychelles, 99
Shackleton Report (1977), 310
Shah of Iran, 237, 263
Shankhill, 271
Sharett, Moshe, 84
Shawcross, Lord, 215
Sheffield University, 313
Sheldon, Robert, 193
Sherman, Sir Alfred, 296
Shinwell, Emanuel (later Lord), 1, 8, 19, 26, 29, 52, 64, 88, 119
shipbuilding, 104, 255
Shonfield, Andrew, 101
Shore, Peter, 163, 192, 233, 245, 252, 262
Short, Edward, 243, 249
Siddall, Norman, 320
Sierra Leone, 114
Signposts for the Sixties, 133, 151
Sillars, Jim, 288
Sillitoe, Alan, 32, 76, 120
Silkin, John, 252
Silverman, Sydney, 30, 49, 52, 89, 213
Simon, Sir John, 19
Simon of Wythenshawe, Lord, 120
Simonstown agreements, 187, 231–2
Simpson, Margaret, 6
Sinclair, Sir Clive, 297
Singapore, 55, 114, 195, 231, 270
Sinn Fein, 339
Small is Beautiful, 256
Smith, Cyril, 264
Smith, Ian, 167–9, 185–6, 299
Smith, Norman, 24
Smith, Ron, 132, 139
Smith, T. Dan, 225–6, 249
Smoking Epidemic, 352
Soames, Sir Christopher (later Lord),

97, 145, 291, 299, 300
Social and Liberal Democratic Party, 340; *see also* Liberals
Social Democratic Alliance, 302
Social Democratic and Labour Party, 228, 240, 271, 302, 339, 353
Social Democratic Party, 308–9, 318, 329–30, 334, 340
Social Democratic Party (Italy), 309
Socialism and the New Despotism, 116
Socialist Commentary, 116, 128
Socialist Union, 117
Soper, Dr Donald (later Lord), 120
Soskice, Sir Frank (Lord Stow Hill), 160, 180
Sound Broadcasting Act, 75
South Africa, 9, 54, 56, 111, 187–8, 190, 231–2, 248, 263, 299, 305
South Arabia, Federation of, 112
South Wales: corruption in, 226
Soviet Union, 33, 50, 57, 58, 59, 62, 64, 69, 70, 78–9, 86, 90, 107–8, 119, 132, 136, 137, 138, 188, 189, 231, 248, 288, 289, 358, 363
Spain, 101, 266, 294, 331
Special Air Services, 271
Special Branch, 273
Spectator, 317
Speed, Keith, 311
Spence, Sir Basil, 141
Spycatcher, 346
Stalin, Joseph, 57, 63, 64, 77, 78, 79
standard of living, 105–7
Stanley, Oliver, 71, 74
Stansgate, Viscount (William Wedgwood Benn), 244
Steel, David, 165, 214, 265, 288, 306, 318, 335, 336, 340
steel industry, 27–8, 34, 180
sterling, 23–5, 102, 165–6, 181, 183, 192–4, 266, 335
Stewart, Michael, 161, 185, 190, 192, 195
Stone, Oliver, 362
Stonehouse, John, 265
'Stop-go' economic policies, 139
Storey, David, 120
Strachey, John, 52, 54, 68, 69
Strangeways Prison, 345
Strauss, George, 52, 214
Street, Professor Henry, 208
strikes, *see* industrial relations
students' revolt, 197
Suez operation, 83–8
Suez canal, 85, 86

Sugay, Alan, 343
Sun, 77, 288, 289
Sunday Correspondent, 361
Sunday Express, 155
Sunday Telegraph, 317
Sunday Times, 77, 289, 346
supply and training of teachers in
    technical colleges, 148
Suzman, Janet, 308
·Sweden, 101, 103, 207, 251, 259, 266,
    275, 280, 333
Swingler, Stephen, 131
Switzerland, 266, 297, 299, 333, 343,
    353
Syria, 112, 358

Taiwan, 294
Tanganyika, 114, 115
Tanzania, 114, 189, 199, 299
Tate and Lyle, 53
Taverne, Dic, 239
taxation, 72, 83, 106, 122, 155, 165–6,
    181, 183, 196, 245–6
Taylor, A. J. P., 23, 120
Taylor, Teddy, 303, 331
Tebbit, Norman, 328, 353, 354
technical colleges, 148
Technical Education, White Paper on
    104–5
Technology, Colleges of, 147
Technology, Minister of, 161
Tehran Declaration, 64
Television Act, 74
television development, 74–6, 324–5
television licences, 74
Tenzing, Sherpa, 72
Tereshkova, Valentina, 108
terms of trade, 106–7
Thatcher, Margaret, 161, 219, 260–1,
    276, 288, 289, 292, 295, 296, 298, 300,
    308, 311, 317, 318, 328, 331, 334,
    335, 337, 338, 354, 358, 359; defeated
    as leader, 356, 362–3
Thatcherism, 293–8, 332
Theatres Act (1968), 214
The Entertainer, 76
The Road to Serfdom, 295
This Sporting Life, 120
Thomas Cook, 221
Thomas Harvey, 316
Thomas, Hugh (later Lord), 68, 54, 90,
    121, 296
Thompson, Daley, 335
Thompstone, Stuart, 308
Thomson, George (later Lord), 114,

190, 233, 253, 324
Thomson, Roy (later Lord), 76
Thorneycroft, Peter (later Lord), 96
Thorpe, Jeremy, 236, 240, 264–5
Time, 303
Times, 3, 77, 142–3, 249, 262, 289, 335,
    344, 361
Tito, President, 79, 85
Tomlinson, George, 3
Tory Reform Committee, 32
Town and Country Planning Acts, 33,
    141
Trade Union Act, 207; 1984, 298
Trade Unions in 1940s, 16, 34–7; in
    1980s, 298
Trades Disputes Acts: (1900), 207;
    (1972), 34, 207
Trades Union Congress, 35, 36, 74,
    102, 139, 166, 167, 184, 208, 223, 238,
    246, 267–8, 298
Transport and General Workers'
    Union, 16, 37, 131, 224
Trent, Lord, 183
Triad gangs, 353
Tribune, 119, 133
Trident missiles, 329–30
Trinidad, 112
Triple Alliance Party, 56
Trudeau, Pierre, 155, 292
Truman, President Harry S., 21, 48, 58,
    63, 68
Truman Doctrine, 58
Tudeh Party, 65
Tunku Abdul Rahman, 56
Turkey, 57, 79, 84
Turner, Graham, 258

U-2 incident, 126
Uganda, 114, 115, 199
Underhill, Lord (Reg), 331, 333
unemployment, 232, 237, 266, 237,
    332–3
Union of Democratic Miners, 322
Union of Post Office Workers, 16
Union World, 324
United Africa Company, 53, 54
United African National Council, 300
United Nations, 50, 51, 52, 62, 79, 86,
    87, 88, 89, 90, 112, 167, 235, 236,
    299, 317, 331
United Nations Association, 120
United States of America, 9, 50, 53, 57,
    58, 59, 60, 62, 65, 69, 70, 79, 84, 85,
    89, 90, 100, 101, 103, 105, 107, 108,
    109, 112, 119, 132, 135, 169, 186, 197,

Index

United States of America (*cont.*):
207, 234, 235, 251, 266, 275, 283, 284,
292, 294, 295, 298, 327, 330, 343, 351,
358–9, 363
United States of America, loan to
Britain, 23–4
Universities and New Left Review, 121
University Funding Committee, 350
UGC, 350

V-Bombers, 109, 131, 171, 312
Vaneigem, Raoul, 229
Varley, Eric, 252
Vassall, John, 142
Victory for Socialism, 131, 133, 153
Vietnam, 154, 183, 197, 215, 229
Vietnamese refugees, 305
Virgin Atlantic Challenger, 335

wage comparisons, 282–3
Waite, Terry, 359
Wales, 269–70
Walker, Patrick Gordon, 127, 132, 159,
165, 195
Walker, Peter, 164, 219, 291, 320–4,
328, 329, 354
Wall St, 362
Walsall North by-election, 287
war: impact of Second World War on
Britain, 23–4
Warbey, William, 52, 56, 57
Warsaw Pact, 314
Water Act (1973), 226
Watergate scandal, 247
Watson, Samuel, 132
Webber, W. J. P., 132
Wedgwood, J. C., 19
Weinstock, Lord, 297
Weizmann, Chaim, 48
Welsh Nationalist Party, 239–40, 250,
269–70
Wesker, Arnold, 120
West Midlands Serious Crimes Squad,
345
West Indies, 112, 135, 197–8
Westminster Bank Review, 323
Whitelaw, William (later Lord), 219,
228, 238, 239, 260, 290, 354
Whiteley, Willie, 14
Wigan, 282
Wigg, George (later Lord), 26, 65, 161,
163, 169
Wilkinson, Ellen, 3, 8, 22
Williams, Betty, 271
Williams, Francis (later Lord Francis-

Williams), 20
Williams, Sir Robin, 150
Williams, Shirley, 233, 244, 246, 261,
302, 306, 308, 317, 340
Williams, Tom, 1, 52
Williamson, W., 29
Willis, Norman, 323
Wilson, Gladys (Mary), 153
Wilson, Harold, (later Lord):
background and early career, 151–4;
first Cabinet, 159–69; 'Kitchen
Cabinet', 162–3; Seamen's strike,
182–3; meets Smith, 186; South
Africa, 187, 231; EEC, 190;
devaluation, 193, 194, 195, 209,
215–16; Israel, 235–6; Cabinet
(1974), 243; resigns, 261–2;
mentioned, 63, 73, 76, 82, 131, 158,
172, 175–6, 177, 183, 192, 203, 232,
234, 245, 253, 260, 263, 270, 290, 301,
346, 356, 359
Wish You Were Here, 362
women: employment, 279; in
professions, 276; 'lib', 276–7
Woodcock, George, 139
Woodward, Admiral 'Sandy', 312
Woolton, Lord, 38, 71, 74
Woolf, Lord, 345
Woolwich West by-election, 287
Workington by-election, 287
World Bank, 85
Wrigglesworth, Ian, 340
Wright, Basil, 120
Wright, Peter, 346
Wyatt, Woodrow, 13, 103, 192

Yemen, 113
Yom Kippur War, 234–6
York, Archbishop of, 74
Yorshireman, 312
Young Conservatives, 38, 174
Young Lady, 292
Young, Lord, 325, 328, 354
Young, Stuart, 325
Younger, George, 291, 354, 355
Youth Training Scheme, 304
Yugoslavia, 57, 79, 364

Zambia, 54, 111, 299, 300
Zanu, 299–300
Zanzibar, 114
Zapu, 299–300
Zilliacus, Konni, 17, 49, 52, 57
Zimbabwe, *see* Rhodesia
Zionism, Zionists, 10, 41, 46–53, 67, 68